Preface

This book is designed as an introduction to computer programming. It is written for any-one who wants to learn to program in C++, but who has little or no previous programming background or mathematics beyond high school algebra. Its simplified approach stresses top-down logic design and modular structured programming for business applications.

The philosophy of this text is to present the C++ language at a level that the new student or programmer can understand. This text may be used as a one-semester or two-quarter introduction to computer programming for freshman or sophomore computer science, business, social science, or physical science majors. Instructors currently using Basic, QuickBasic, C, or Pascal to teach programming may want to consider using C++.

Special Features

Teaching by Example

The text takes a "teach by example" approach that both simplifies and reinforces the learning process by showing examples of how the programming elements work. In addition, each chapter introduces one or more complete sample programs that illustrate how the textbook material can be applied to actual programming applications.

Furthermore, each sample program illustrates the program development process from start to finish. This process includes defining the format of the input and output, identifying the processing requirements, developing the logic, and coding the program. The output of each sample program is shown after the program code.

Incorporation of the Program Development Process

The program development process is emphasized throughout the textbook, not in just one chapter. More than 40 complete sample programs are illustrated. The reader is introduced early to the importance of using top-down logic design and modular structured programming to construct high-quality, easy-to-read programs. For each sample program, the complete logic design is shown—hierarchy charts, pseudocode, and program flowcharts—as well as the other steps in the program development process.

Menu-Driven Programming

Menu-driven programs are introduced in Chapter 6. This chapter includes topics on data validation, guidelines for creating effective menus, and techniques for menu selection processing. This topic, which is often excluded from some C++ textbooks, is presented in an easy-to-follow manner.

Comprehensive Coverage of Files

Comprehensive coverage of sequential files, updating sequential files, random access files, and indexed files are presented. These important topics are presented from top to bottom in a nontechnical manner that the reader can understand.

Program Dissections

Each sample program is dissected, taking the reader through the code step-by-step and explaining how the program statements work together to produce the output.

Conversational Tone

The text's conversational tone makes it easy for the new programmer to read. Many C++ programming textbooks are written at a technical level, but care has been taken here to simplify complex topics and present them at a level that the student can understand.

Checkpoint Exercises

Checkpoint exercises that appear throughout the textbook reinforce the main topics covered in the chapters. The exercises include "self-directed" questions and activities that provide feedback to the students on how well they understand the material covered since the last checkpoint. Answers to the checkpoint exercises appear in Appendix E.

Chapter Summaries

The chapter summaries highlight important concepts, define key terms, and describe major programming elements. The summaries provide a comprehensive review that helps reinforce the chapter material.

Programming Projects

Every chapter contains a set of programming projects that gives the student the opportunity to apply the material to a programming application. Different projects may be assigned or the same project may be expanded, using a spiral approach, as new material is covered.

Introduction to C++ Programming: A Modular Approach

DAVID M. COLLOPY
Ohio University

Prentice Hall
Upper Saddle River, New Jersey   Columbus, Ohio

Dedicated to the memory of my father Eugene R. Collopy, who taught me the value of hard work, *to my mother* Mickey, *and to my family* Cindy, Ryan, and Susie Q *for their support.*

Library of Congress Cataloging-in-Publication Data

Collopy, David M.
Introduction to C++ programming: a modular approach / David M. Collopy.
 p. cm.
 Includes index.
 ISBN 0-13-888801-9
 1. C++ (Computer program language) I. Title.
QA76.73.C153C655 1999
005.13'3—dc21

98-4594
CIP

Cover photo: © SuperStock
Editor: Charles E. Stewart, Jr.
Production Editor: Alexandrina Benedicto Wolf
Design Coordinator: Karrie M. Converse
Cover Designer: Janoski Advertising
Editorial/Production Supervision: Custom Editorial Productions, Inc.
Production Manager: Deidra M. Schwartz
Marketing Manager: Ben Leonard

This book was set in Times Roman by Custom Editorial Productions, Inc., and was printed and bound by R.R. Donnelley & Sons Company. The cover was printed by Phoenix Color Corp.

 © 1999 by Prentice-Hall, Inc.
Simon & Schuster/A Viacom Company
Upper Saddle River, New Jersey 07458

Printed in the United States of America

10 9 8 7 6 5 4 3 2 1

ISBN: 0-13-888801-9

Prentice-Hall International (UK) Limited, *London*
Prentice-Hall of Australia Pty. Limited, *Sydney*
Prentice-Hall of Canada, Inc., *Toronto*
Prentice-Hall Hispanoamericana, S. A., *Mexico*
Prentice-Hall of India Private Limited, *New Delhi*
Prentice-Hall of Japan, Inc., *Tokyo*
Simon & Schuster Asia Pte. Ltd., *Singapore*
Editora Prentice-Hall do Brasil, Ltda., *Rio de Janeiro*

Teaching Strategy

This book takes a unique approach to presenting pointers and local/global variables. Pointers are introduced in the text as needed; the use of local/global variables is presented from a business programming perspective.

Pointers

Students normally have difficulty grasping the concept of pointers. Instead of presenting pointers all at once in one chapter, when a situation calls for a pointer, it is explained and illustrated. This approach makes it easier for the reader to understand when and why pointers are necessary as well as how to use them.

Global and Local Variables

This text departs from "traditional" C++ in its approach to global and local variables. Although it is reasonable to argue that local variables protect the variables in one function from errors made in another, this isn't necessarily the best way to develop a program to meet the needs of the business enterprise. Corporate applications differ from retail applications and require a different design strategy.

Essentially, local variables are used to build applications that require a series of features commonly found in software packages developed for retail sales. Global variables, on the other hand, are often used to construct corporate applications that are developed and maintained by in-house programmers.

What Is Not Covered

This book uses a procedural or non-object-oriented approach to learning how to program in C++. It does not dwell upon the more complex features of the language. Instead, the book focuses on providing a solid background in the basic essentials of C++ . It presents the language in an easy-to-read style that emphasizes business applications and modular structured design.

Topics excluded are object-oriented programming, classes, inheritance, unions, function and operator overloading, virtual functions, polymorphism, and related items. These topics are reserved for the more advanced texts that use the object-oriented approach to programming.

Instructor's Manual

The Instructor's Manual provides both planning guidelines and teaching tips. It includes the following materials for each chapter:

- Learning objectives
- Study guides
- Lecture outlines
- Test bank
- Answers to test bank

Acknowledgments

First and foremost, I would like to express my sincere gratitude and thanks to all the people who contributed helpful comments and suggestions for improving this text, including the following: H.E. Drensmore, Purdue University; Michael A. Miller, DeVry Institute of Technology; Zhizhang Shen, Plymouth State University; Terry Simkin, New Hampshire Technical Institute; and R.J. Wolfe, DePaul University.

A special thanks goes to my family, Cindy and Ryan, for giving me the quiet time that I needed to make this book a success.

I would also like to thank the editorial staff at Prentice Hall for their dedication, leadership, and effort in turning this project into a unique introduction to C++ programming.

David M. Collopy

Contents

8 PAGE AND CONTROL BREAKS 229

9 MULTILEVEL CONTROL BREAKS 261

10 ARRAYS AND SORTING 301

11 MULTIDIMENSION ARRAYS 349

12 SEQUENTIAL FILES 387

1   Basic Concepts

Overview

Learning Objectives

After you have read this chapter and completed the exercises, you should be able to:

- define the term "computer" and discuss the hardware and software components associated with computers
- discuss the hierarchical organization of data

- understand the program development process
- distinguish between syntax and logical errors
- describe the process that C++ goes through to convert source statements into an executable program
- design and write simple programming applications in C++

What Is a Computer?

A **computer** is an electronic device that accepts input, processes it according to a given set of instructions, and provides the results of the processing. This process is shown schematically in Figure 1.1. **Input** is a term used to define the **data** or unprocessed facts manipulated by the computer. **Output** refers to the processed information or results produced by the computer. Output takes many forms. Some examples of output are a list of names or values, a payroll check, a ticket to a baseball game, a printed report, and an updated file.

Essentially, a computer converts data into meaningful information. It is an electronic data processing device with internal storage for holding data and program instructions. Although a computer can perform complex computations with extraordinary speed and accuracy, it cannot do anything on its own. It must be told what to do every step of the way. The instructions that the computer follows are called a **program**, and the individual responsible for writing computer programs is called a **programmer**.

A **computer system** consists of software (the instructions for processing the data) and hardware (the physical equipment used to process the data). **Software** includes application programs and the operating system. **Hardware** consists of input/output devices and the central processing or system unit. We will discuss these components in the sections that follow.

The Computer System

Software Concepts

Software tells the computer what to do. It issues commands and directs the hardware in performing its work. There are two major types of software: applications and systems.

Written for end users, **applications software** is designed to perform a specific task, such as billing customers, administering payroll, taking inventory, or collecting accounts receivable. An **end user** is anyone who uses a computer system to perform a task related to data processing. Applications software may be acquired by purchasing off-the-shelf packages or by designing and creating them for one's own purpose (custom made).

Packaged or **off-the-shelf** programs are prewritten and ready to use. They are available from many retail outlets and software firms. There are thousands of packaged programs on the market today, designed for many different applications.

FIGURE 1.1   Basic Functions Performed by the Computer

Custom-made programs are usually written by in-house, trained professionals employed as programmers or by outside consulting firms specializing in custom programming.

In business, applications software has one main objective—to provide management with accurate, up-to-date, and timely information about the operations of the company.

Systems software is normally supplied by the manufacturer of the computer system and consists of utility programs and operating aids that facilitate the use and performance of the computer. It includes the computer's operating system and related software that manages the system's resources and controls the operations of the hardware.

The **operating system** acts as an interface between the applications software and the computer itself. It allows the user to enter and run applications software. Other functions performed by the operating system include managing internal resources, controlling input/output operations, interpreting system commands, loading and executing programs, scheduling and running jobs, and organizing and manipulating files.

Hardware Concepts

Hardware is the physical components of the computer system. It includes input/output devices, the central processing unit, and secondary storage devices. The term hardware refers to the actual equipment used to process the input data.

Input devices, such as the keyboard and mouse, are used to enter data and programs into the computer. They translate input that people understand into electronic signals that the computer understands.

Output devices, such as printers and monitors, on the other hand, are used to display the results processed by the computer. They translate the electronic signals that the computer understands into a form that people understand.

The **central processing unit** (CPU) is considered to be the heart of the computer. It is responsible for processing the data and producing the output. The CPU is composed of the control unit, the arithmetic/logic unit, and the storage unit, as shown in Figure 1.2.

The **control unit** supervises and monitors the activities performed by the computer system. It does not process the data itself, but directs the processing operations and coordinates the flow of data to the arithmetic/logic and storage units.

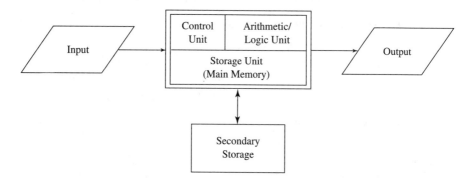

FIGURE 1.2   The Computer System

After the control unit instructs the input device to load the program and data, it interprets the program statements one at a time and tells the arithmetic/logic unit to carry out the instructions. It also tells the input device when to read more data and the output device when to write the results.

As the name implies, the **arithmetic/logic unit** (ALU) performs the arithmetic and logical operations required by the program. Arithmetic computations include addition, subtraction, multiplication, and division. Logical operations involve comparing the values of two data items to determine if one value is equal to, less than, or greater than the other. Hence, the major function of the ALU is to do the work, that is, to carry out the processing activities specified by the program.

The **primary storage unit**, or main memory, accepts input data, program instructions, intermediate results and values, and processed information and temporarily stores them for subsequent processing. Before the computer can execute a program, the instructions and data must reside within the computer's memory.

There are two important facts to know about the storage unit. First, the amount of storage space is limited; only a finite number of characters can be held at any one time. Second, the contents of storage are nonpermanent and are only temporarily maintained while the computer's power is on. Once the computer is turned off, the contents of main memory are lost and cannot be recovered unless they were previously saved to a secondary storage device.

Secondary storage media, such as magnetic tape or disks, permanently store data, programs, and processed information so that they are available to the computer on a per-need basis. That is, programs and data may be accessed by and transferred to the computer when they are called by the CPU. The contents of secondary storage remain intact until they are physically removed or deleted by the programmer.

Data Organization

Data is organized in a special way to facilitate processing by the computer. Individual characters entered at the keyboard can be organized into hierarchical structures ranging from simple data fields to complex networks of integrated databases.

As shown in Figure 1.3, fields can be grouped to form a record, and records can be grouped to form a file. Note also that a field is simply a collection of characters.

The following list contains data organization terms and their definitions:

Character: A letter, numeric digit, punctuation mark, or special symbol such as %, @, and &.

Field: A set of characters grouped together to form a single unit of data. For example, in Figure 1.3, five characters have been grouped together to form the customer's account number and 11 characters have been assigned to hold the customer's name.

Record: A set of logically related fields. In Figure 1.3, a record consists of the following fields: account number, customer name, credit limit, and balance due.

File: A set of logically related records. When records for a specific application are grouped together, they are called a file. For example, if an accounts receivable application services 2,453 customers, then the customer file would consist of 2,453 records.

	(field 1)	(field 2)	(field 3)	(field 4)
	Account Number	Customer Name	Credit Limit	Balance Due
(record 1)	12345	Brad Anders	5000.00	2500.00
(record 2)	16789	Tara Atkins	7000.00	5748.00
(record 3)	20161	Karen Baker	5000.00	0000.00
⋮	⋮	⋮	⋮	⋮
⋮	⋮	⋮	⋮	⋮
⋮	⋮	⋮	⋮	⋮
(record n)	97865	Dave Zetler	3000.00	0125.00

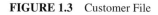

(character)

FIGURE 1.3   Customer File

Database: A set of integrated records or files. A database consists of a pool of centrally located files that may be accessed and processed by multiple applications. For example, a customer database could be set up to store the customer accounts file for the home office as well as the customer accounts files for all the branch offices.

Checkpoint 1A

1. Define the term *computer*.
2. Distinguish between applications software and systems software.
3. Explain the purpose of the input/output devices. Give examples of each.
4. Define the term *central processing unit* (CPU). Identify and explain the three components of the CPU.
5. Explain the difference between primary storage and secondary storage.
6. Explain how data is organized.

Planning the Program

Programs should be planned. Trial-and-error guesswork has no place in the programming profession. Designing a program can be compared to building an expressway. The engineer lays out detailed plans before going through the time, trouble, and expense of building a complex network of highways. Construction does not begin until the completed plan has been carefully laid out in writing. Similarly, the programmer should plan carefully and write out the design for a program before sitting down at the computer. A good plan can save hours of frustration at the keyboard and produce successful results within a shorter period of time.

Structured program development not only saves time, it also increases programmer productivity. Programming can be a complex process involving a multitude of interrelated operations and computations. However, when the processing activities are planned carefully, even the most difficult application can be effectively and efficiently managed. When used properly, the seven-step program development process presented below will help to produce a more reliable program in less time and one that can be maintained more easily throughout its use.

The Program Development Process

Step 1: Define the problem

- Determine the objectives of the program. Write a brief statement or paragraph describing the purpose of the program.

Step 2: Analyze the problem

- Determine what the output should look like. Sketch a rough draft of the output. Use paper and pencil to lay out the fields, records, and files. Design and erase as you go.
- Determine the input. Use the output to determine the input data. Focus on identifying the input required by the program to produce the output.
- Define the processing tasks required by the program. Identify the steps, activities, or calculations required to manipulate the input data and produce the output.
- List the processing tasks on paper. Don't pay attention to their order; simply write them down as they are identified. Once all of the tasks have been listed, arrange them in processing order. If possible, group related tasks together, but only when it is obvious they belong together.

Step 3: Design the logic

- Use the ordered list of tasks identified in Step 2 to design the program logic. There are three basic design tools that we may use to develop the program logic—hierarchy charts, pseudocode, and program flowcharts. Pseudocode and flowcharting will be illustrated later in this chapter. Hierarchy charts will be introduced in Chapter 3.
- Check the program logic and make corrections as needed. When the logic is complete, the programmer checks it over manually by tracing the flow of data through the logic. This process of verifying the logic is called **desk checking**. Of course, corrections are made until the logic produces the desired output.

Step 4: Code the program

- The hierarchy chart, pseudocode, or flowchart is used to translate the program logic into C++ statements, that is, the program is coded from the logic design. For the student programmer, this can be accomplished by writing out the program code on paper.
- Desk check the C++ statements and make corrections as needed.

Step 5: Key in the program

- Using the editor, enter the program code into the computer by keying in the statements.

Step 6: Test and debug the program

- Test the code by running the program. If errors are found during the run, it is the programmer's responsibility to fix those parts of the program that did not work. In programming, an error is called a **bug**, and **debugging** refers to the process of eliminating errors. In short, a bug is any code that prevents a program from producing the correct output.

Step 7: Gather the program documentation

- Gather the documentation that you have created throughout the programming process. Documentation provides information about the program and is used as a reference when updating or maintaining the program. Documentation includes a statement of the problem, input/output definitions, a list of the processing functions, the logic design, a program listing, and samples of the output.

Designing Reports

For the most part, business application programs are written to provide management with meaningful information. Management uses this information to monitor the operations of the company and to assist its employees in making profitable decisions about the business.

But before any information can be produced by the computer, it must first be carefully planned. The data processing results should be organized so that they provide the information that management needs. The output should provide meaningful, relevant, and timely information about the business enterprise.

Take a look at the computer-generated report shown in Figure 1.4. As simple as it may seem, it provides management with relevant information about the company's customers. It consists of column headings that form a four-column report with information about each customer's name, balance due, monthly payment made, and new balance.

The body of the report is made up of **detail lines**. The first detail line of the report gives information about the account belonging to a customer named Ayers. At the time the report was generated, Ayers had a previous balance of $500, made a $200 payment, and currently owes $300. The customer named Walker, on the other hand, has paid in full.

CUSTOMER NAME	BALANCE DUE	MONTHLY PAYMENT	NEW BALANCE
Ayers	500.00	200.00	300.00
Fontaine	750.00	600.00	150.00
Howard	400.00	300.00	100.00
Ryan	300.00	175.00	125.00
Walker	563.00	563.00	000.00
TOTALS	2513.00	1838.00	675.00

FIGURE 1.4   Accounts Receivable Report

TABLE 1.1   Printer Specifications

	Horizontal	Vertical
Micro	80-character line with 10 CPI	6 LPI
Mainframe	132-character line with 10–12 CPI	6–8 LPI

This particular report shows the current status of the accounts receivable system. When customers call to ask their current balance due, the customer service department can retrieve this information readily. Similarly, management can use the information in the report to monitor overdue accounts.

The last line in Figure 1.4 shows report totals for balances due, monthly payments, and new balances.

Reports may vary significantly in design, size, and layout. Usually, clients have a rough idea of what they want the report to look like, as well as the information it should contain. However, it may be necessary for the programmer to sit down and work with a client to design the layout of the report.

Forms and reports are designed to fit the horizontal and vertical spacing given for the printer being used. Common printer specifications for the micro- and mainframe computers are shown in Table 1.1. Spacing across the page is measured in **characters per inch** (CPI); spacing down the page is given as **lines per inch** (LPI). From the table, we see that the 80-character line printer for the microcomputer has a horizontal spacing of 10 CPI and a vertical spacing of 6 LPI.

The report shown in Figure 1.5, for Tamarack Automotive Services, was designed with the help of a **printer spacing chart** (Figure 1.6). The printer spacing chart in Figure 1.6 is

```
              TAMARACK AUTOMOTIVE SERVICES
                   Accounts Receivable
                        mm/dd/yy

        CUSTOMER     BALANCE      MONTHLY        NEW
          NAME         DUE        PAYMENT      BALANCE

        Ayers        500.00       200.00       300.00
        Fontaine     750.00       600.00       150.00
        Howard       400.00       300.00       100.00
        Ryan         300.00       175.00       125.00
        Walker       563.00       563.00       000.00

        TOTALS:     2513.00      1838.00       675.00

        LARGEST NEW BALANCE    $ 300.00
        LARGEST PAYMENT MADE   $ 600.00
```

FIGURE 1.5   Output Report

```
                1           2          3          4          5
        1234567890123456789012345678901234567890123456789 0123...


PT1                     TAMARACK AUTOMOTIVE SERVICES
PT2                         Accounts Receivable
PT3                              mm/dd/yy


HL1         CUSTOMER       BALANCE      MONTHLY        NEW
HL2           NAME          DUE         PAYMENT      BALANCE

DL          X-------X     999.99       999.99       999.99
  .             |            |            |            |
  .             ▼            ▼            ▼            ▼
  .          X-------X     999.99       999.99       999.99

TL1         TOTALS:      9999.99      9999.99      9999.99


SL1         LARGEST NEW BALANCE    $ 999.99
SL2         LARGEST PAYMENT MADE   $ 999.99
```

FIGURE 1.6   Printer Spacing Chart

made up of rows and columns corresponding to the horizontal and vertical print positions of the printer. A programmer uses the print chart to design and lay out reports. Once the design is complete, the programmer codes C++ statements to set up page titles, column headings, detail lines, and so on. The abbreviations PT, HL, DL, TL, and SL shown on the left side of the printer spacing chart stand for Page Title, Heading Line, Detail Line, Total Line, and Summary Line, respectively. They are notations that remind the programmer to define and assign names to the appropriate print lines at coding time. We will discuss this topic further in the section that follows, titled *Report Planning Guidelines*. Also note the use of the Xs and the 9s. They specify the maximum field size (print positions) reserved for printing character (X) and numeric (9) data.

Report Planning Guidelines

There are guidelines the programmer should follow when designing printer output for the user. The purpose of the guidelines is to provide a set of standards or procedures that help produce reports that are easier to read and understand. It can be extremely frustrating for the user to thumb through a stack of computer reports that are difficult to read or understand.

The following guidelines were used to design the report shown in Figure 1.6.

Step 1: Start on a new page

Start the report at the top of the page. Skip five or six lines before printing the page titles.

Step 2: Page titles

Center the page title (*PT*) by subtracting the number of characters in the line from 80. Then compute the starting position of the left margin by dividing the difference by 2. Code the line on the printer spacing chart, beginning at the left margin. Single-space multiple page titles and use *PT1, PT2, PT3,* and so on to identify them.

Step 3: Heading lines

Skip two lines and center the heading line (*HL*). Unless instructed otherwise by the user, leave two blank lines between the last page title and the first heading line. Column headings are normally centered above the data to which they refer. Single-space multiple headings and use *HL1, HL2, HL3*, and so on to identify them.

Note: Print the page titles, column headings, and page number at the top of each page.

Step 4: Detail lines

Skip a line and print the first detail line (*DL*). Detail lines represent the body of the report and are normally single spaced. They should be centered on the printer spacing chart before coding the column headings. Use the following method to center the detail lines. First, print one detail line on a piece of scrap paper. Second, decide how many spaces you want between the data items; usually three to five blank spaces will do. Third, use the method described in Step 2 to center the line. Center each column heading above the data to which it refers.

Step 5: Total lines

Use one or two blank lines to separate the last detail line from the first total line (*TL*). Single-space multiple total lines and use *TL1, TL2, TL3*, and so on to identify them.

Step 6: Summary lines

Skip two lines and print the summary line (*SL*). Single-space multiple summary lines and use *SL1, SL2, SL3*, and so on to identify them.

Errors and Debugging

During program execution, one of three things may occur:

1. Errors are detected by the computer.
2. The computer detects no errors, but the output is incorrect.
3. The computer detects no errors, and the output is correct.

Case 1: Syntax Errors

If an error was detected during the run, then the program contains one or more syntax errors. A **syntax error** is an error that violates the rules of the programming language. In other words, a statement was incorrectly coded and has been rejected as erroneous. Often syntax errors are the result of misspelling or miskeying. Whatever the cause, syntax errors must be corrected and the program reexecuted before the program will run successfully.

Case 2: Logic Errors

A **logic error** is an error either in the design of the program or in the implementation of the design. At times, logic errors can be extremely difficult to locate. Unlike syntax errors, the computer has no way of detecting logic errors. Logic errors are usually the result of poor program planning or faulty reasoning. Even though the statements coded are syntactically correct, the program produces incorrect output.

For example, if the programmer assigns the numeric value 4 to hours worked when 40 should have been assigned, the program will run but produce output different from what was expected. Also, if pay rate and hours worked were added instead of multiplied, the program would run but produce incorrect results.

Case 3: Clean Run

A **clean run** occurs when the program produces the correct output. It is often a surprise to the student programmer to discover that programs normally do not run cleanly on the first try. Programming involves managing a multitude of details and complex logic. Once this is understood, it is no longer a surprise to the student to see errors during a run. The major purpose of the program development process is to reduce the number and complexity of errors by applying a structured approach to managing the programming application.

Compiling a Program

The compilation process that follows has been simplified to provide a basic understanding of how programs are executed by the computer. The exact details of this process are involved and complex and, therefore, are beyond the scope of this text.

Programmers write instructions in a programming language for the computer to follow. These English-like commands, called the **source program**, are read by the computer and stored in memory for subsequent processing. Since the computer cannot execute the source program in this form, each statement must undergo a series of transformations before it can be processed by the computer.

As Figure 1.7 shows, the source program is created by entering the C++ statements into the **text editor**. Next, the **compiler** translates the source program into an intermediate form called the object program. The **object program** represents the machine code equivalent of the source program. Each statement in the source program is read and scanned by the compiler. During the scanning process, the compiler translates the source statements into **machine code** (binary code that the computer understands) and checks for syntax errors.

If errors are detected, the compiler flags the erroneous statements and prints a list of **diagnostic error messages** that briefly describe any syntax errors. At this point, it is up to the programmer to fix the errors and recompile the program. This process of locating and fixing errors, called debugging, continues until the compiler indicates that no errors were found during the compilation.

Even though the object module (program) exists in machine code form, it cannot be executed directly by the computer. It must first undergo further transformation by the linker before the program is ready for execution. C++ programs normally contain references to precoded functions that are stored in library files. The primary objective of the **linker** is to include the precompiled library code into the object program and to create an **executable program**.

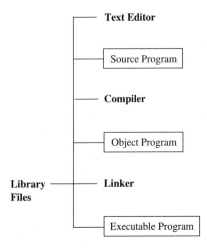

FIGURE 1.7   Compiler and Linker

The final step results in execution of the program. It is during the final step that the program produces the output.

Checkpoint 1B

1. What is the purpose of the program development process?
2. Identify and explain the seven steps in the program development process.
3. What is the purpose of the report planning guidelines?
4. Explain the difference between a syntax error and a logic error.
5. Differentiate between a source program and an object program.

Developing Our First Program

This section introduces our first C++ program. The program logic and code were developed using the program development process. Although the program is a relatively simple one, it is important to realize that the planning process can be applied to any application, simple or complex. Once you are familiar with the steps, you will be able to design the program logic and construct the code in less time.

Walk through the steps. Try to get a feel for how the planning process works.

Sample Program CHAP1A

Write a program to compute the course grade for Terry Miller. Assume that Terry earned 45 out of 50 points on the midterm and 42 out of 50 points on the final exam. Compute the course grade by adding the points for midterm and final exam.

Step 1: Define the problem

Write a program to compute the course grade for Terry Miller.

Step 2: Analyze the problem

Input: Midterm and final scores
Processing: Course grade = midterm + final
Output: Print the course grade

Step 3: Design the logic

Pseudocode: Pseudocode uses English-like statements to outline or describe the processing tasks performed by the program. The pseudocode for sample program CHAP1A is shown below.

```
START
Initialize midterm to 45
Initialize final to 42
Compute course grade
Print course grade
END
```

Program Flowchart: A flowchart is a pictorial diagram that shows detailed processing steps and the order they are performed by the computer. Figure 1.8 shows the flowchart version of the program logic.

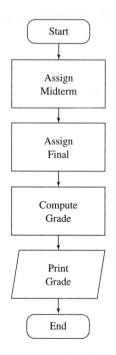

FIGURE 1.8   Program Flowchart for CHAP1A

Figure 1.9 shows the standard flowchart symbols. The shape of each symbol indicates a particular type of activity. For example, a rectangle specifies a processing activity, and a parallelogram specifies an input/output operation.

Step 4: Code the program

Use the logic design (hierarchy chart, pseudocode, or flowchart) to code the program on paper. Afterwards, walk through the code and make corrections as needed.

Step 5: Key in the program

Use the program editor to enter the statements developed in Step 4. The program code and output are shown in Figures 1.10 and 1.11, respectively.

Step 6: Test and debug the program

Test the code by executing the program. If errors are detected by the compiler, correct them and rerun the program.

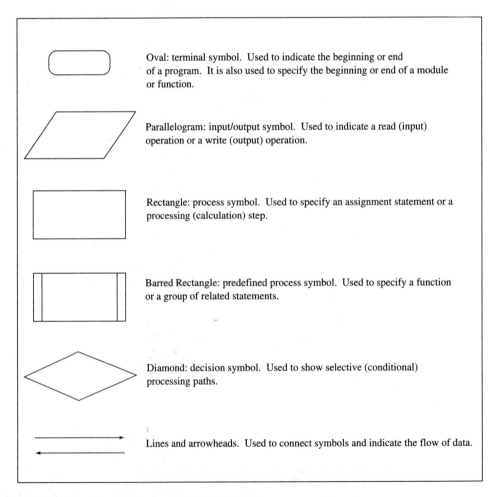

FIGURE 1.9   Standard Program Flowchart Symbols

```
//    Compute the course grade for Terry Miller

#include <iostream.h>

int midterm;                    // midterm score
int final;                      // final score
int grade;                      // course grade

main()
{
    midterm = 45;
    final = 42;
    grade = midterm + final;
    cout << "Course grade is: " << grade;
}
```

FIGURE 1.10   Program Code for CHAP1A

```
Course grade is: 87
```

FIGURE 1.11   Program Output for CHAP1A

Dissection of Sample Program CHAP1A

This is where we dissect and analyze the program. Our purpose is to look at one statement or one block of code at a time and explain what is does. As we go through the code, focus on how the different parts of the program work.

```
//    Compute the course grade for Terry Miller
```

A **comment** begins with //. Comments are used by the programmer to document the program and are ignored by the compiler. The above comment tells us what the program does.

```
#include <iostream.h>
```

This directive tells the compiler to include the *iostream.h* header file in the program. In brief, this file contains definitions that enable the program to display the output on the screen. Since we intend to print Terry Miller's course grade on the screen, the *#include* statement is required. This statement is covered in detail in Chapter 2.

```
int midterm;                    // midterm score
int final;                      // final score
int grade;                      // course grade
```

The above statements define the program variables. By definition, a **statement** is a command that tells the computer to do something, and a **variable** is a data item that may assume different values. The variables *midterm, final,* and *grade* are declared as integers (*int*). **Integer variables** hold whole numbers—numbers without decimal points—59, 71, 655, 1458, and so on.

Note that above statements end with a semicolon. A **semicolon** marks the end of each statement. Also note the statement comments. Although optional, we will normally use statement comments to document the purpose of the variables.

```
main()
{
```

All C++ programs begin with the main() function. It signals the start of the program. The left brace { marks the beginning of the body of the main() function. A C++ program normally consists of one or more functions. In general, a **function** represents a series of statements that perform a specifc task.

```
    midterm = 45;
    final = 42;
```

The above statements mean: Initialize *midterm* to 45 and *final* to 42. Both statements assign the value shown on the right side of the equal sign to the variable shown on the left side.

```
    grade = midterm + final;
```

This statement means: Add the value stored at *final* to the contents of *midterm* and assign the sum to *grade*. Addition, subtraction, multiplication, and division are specified by using the **arithmetic operators** +, -, *, and /, respectively. The arithmetic operators tell the compiler what actions to perform on the variables.

```
    cout << "Course grade is: " << grade;
```

The above statement means: Print the output on the screen. The *cout* statement, along with the **insertion operator** <<, tells the compiler to print the message (string of characters) enclosed within double quotation marks and the *grade* on the screen.

Since *grade* equals 87, the *cout* statement displays Course grade is: 87 on the screen.

```
}
```

The right brace marks the end of the main() and the end of the program.

Sample Program CHAP1B

Sample program CHAP1B (Figure 1.13, p.18) computes the total pay earned by an employee who is paid $25.10 per hour and has worked 38.5 hours during the week. The output is shown in Figure 1.14, p.18.

The following specifications apply:

Input (internal):

Define and initialize the program variables. Use the variable names and values shown below.

    pay rate = 25.10
        hours = 38.5

Output (screen):

Use the variable name *totalPay* for the output and print the following information on the screen.

```
Author        Payroll Program
Total pay is $ 999.99
```

Note: 9s are used to specify the maximum field size reserved for printing numeric data.

Processing Requirements:

- Define and initialize the program variables.
- Compute the total pay:
  totalPay = payrate × hours
- Print the output on the screen.

Pseudocode:

START
Initialize pay rate
Initialize hours worked
Compute total pay
Print total pay
END

Program Flowchart: See Figure 1.12.

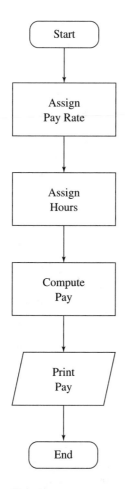

FIGURE 1.12   Program Flowchart for CHAP1B

```
//    Compute total pay given the pay rate and
//    hours worked

#include <iostream.h>
#include <iomanip.h>

float payrate;                      // hourly pay rate
float hours;                        // hours worked
float totalPay;                     // total pay

main()
{
    payrate = 25.10;
    hours = 38.5;
    totalPay = payrate * hours;
    cout << "DCollopy    Payroll Program\n\n";
    cout << setiosflags(ios::fixed);
    cout << setiosflags(ios::showpoint);
    cout << setprecision(2);
    cout << "Total pay is $" << totalPay;
}
```

FIGURE 1.13   Program Code for CHAP1B

```
DCollopy      Payroll Program

Total pay is $ 966.35
```

FIGURE 1.14   Program Output for CHAP1B

Dissection of Sample Program CHAP1B

```
//    Compute total pay given the pay rate and
//    hours worked
```

The above statements are line comments that document the purpose of the program.

```
#include <iostream.h>
```

The above statement enables the program to display output on the screen.

```
#include <iomanip.h>
```

This directive tells the compiler to include the *iomanip.h* header file in the program. In brief, this file contains definitions that enable the program to alter or manipulate the format of the output. Since we intend to show the output as a floating-point value with two decimal positions, the *#include* statement is required.

```
float payrate;
float hours;
float totalPay;
```

The above statements declare the program variables. Each data item (*payrate, hours*, and *totalPay*) is defined as a float or floating-point variable. **Floating-point** variables hold floating-point values—numbers with decimal points—8.5, 53.14, 237.85, 490.619, and so on.

```
main()
{
```

The above statement means: Define the main() function. The left brace ({) marks the beginning of the body of the main() function.

```
payrate = 25.10;
hours = 38.5;
```

The above statements assign the value on the right side of the equal sign to the variable on the left. Hence, *payrate* equals 25.10 and *hours* equal 38.5.

```
totalPay = payrate * hours;
```

This statement means: Multiply the value stored at *payrate* times the contents of *hours* and assign the product to *totalPay*.

```
cout << "DCollopy    Payroll Program\n\n";
```

The above statement prints the string of characters enclosed within double quotation marks on the screen. When executed, this statement displays the programmer's name and the program title on the screen. The \n is called a **newline character**. One \n represents a single space; two mean a double space. Hence, the *cout* statement executes a double space after printing the line. The \n\n is not part of the actual printed output. It is, however, used to control the line spacing of the output.

```
cout << setiosflags(ios::fixed);
cout << setiosflags(ios::showpoint);
cout << setprecision(2);
```

The above statements tell the compiler how to format the output. The first *cout* statement says to format the output as a fixed-decimal number. The second says to show the decimal point. The third says to format the output to two decimal places. Hence, the output variable that follows (*totalPay*) will display as a floating-point number with two digits to the right of the decimal point.

The *setiosflags()* and *setprecision()* format specifiers are called **output manipulators**. They are used by the program to specify the format of the output. But more on this when we get to Chapter 2.

```
cout << "Total pay is $" << totalPay;
```

The above statement prints the string of characters enclosed wihin double quotation marks and the content of *totalPay* on the screen. Since *totalPay* equals 966.35, the *cout* statement displays Total pay is $966.35 on the screen.

```
}
```

The right brace marks the end of the main() function as well as the end of the program.

Rules for Forming Identifier Names

C++ has a set of rules for creating identifier names. **Identifiers** are programmer-defined names. Identifiers are used to describe variables, constants, modules, and functions, as well as other elements in the program. The rules for creating identifiers are as follows:

1. A name may contain up to 32 characters.
2. A name may consist of letters (uppercase and lowercase), numeric digits, and the underscore.
3. A name may not begin with a numeric digit.
4. A name may not include blanks or special characters.
5. A name may not be a **keyword** (words reserved by C++ that have special meaning).

Each name should be meaningful and self-documenting. Examples of valid identifiers are *InputData, quantity, date_of_birth, payrate, _netPay,* and *item_cost_*. Examples of invalid identifiers are *1st_name, total count, $VALUE, ID-NUMBER, *TaxTotal,* and *%increase*.

Case Sensitivity

C++ is case sensitive. For example, C++ interprets *taxrate, TaxRate,* and *TAXRATE* as three different identifier names. It is important to keep case sensitivity in mind when coding statements in C++.

Although identifiers may be written in upper- and/or lowercase letters, there are situations that stipulate that certain elements be coded in upper- or lowercase. We will discuss these cases as they occur.

Keywords

An identifier is a programmer-defined name that describes various elements in the program, whereas a keyword is a predefined name that indicates a specific action or operation. Essentially, a keyword is a reserved word that has special meaning to the compiler. As such, keywords may not be redefined or used in the program as identifiers. Although they may vary from one system to another, the standard keywords include the following:

asm	double	new	switch
auto	else	operator	template
break	enum	private	this
case	extern	protected	throw
catch	float	public	try
char	for	register	typedef
class	friend	return	union
const	goto	short	unsigned
continue	if	signed	virtual
default	inline	sizeof	void
delete	int	static	volatile
do	long	struct	while

Checkpoint 1C

1. Identify two methods used to design program logic.
2. For the identifier names given below, indicate whether they are valid or invalid.
   a. *_answer_*
   b. *2nd_chance*
   c. *street number*
   d. *balanceDue*
   e. *total_expense$*
   f. *discount%*
   g. *sum.total*
   h. *xYz*
   i. *payment-code*
   j. *_result*
3. Distinguish between identifiers and keywords.
4. Explain what is meant by the statement, "C++ is case sensitive."

Summary

1. A computer is an electronic device that accepts input, processes it according to a given set of instructions, and provides the results in the form of output.

2. Instructions written for the computer to follow are called a program, and the individual responsible for writing computer programs is called a programmer.

3. Applications software is designed to perform a specific task, such as billing customers, administering payroll, taking inventory, or collecting accounts receivable.

4. Systems software is normally supplied by the manufacturer of the computer system and consists of utility programs and operating aids that facilitate the use and performance of the computer.

5. Hardware is the physical components of the computer and includes input/output devices, the central processing unit, and secondary storage devices.

6. Data is organized into fields, records, files, and databases to facilitate processing by the computer.

7. The program development process represents a structured approach to constructing programs that are more reliable and easier to understand and maintain. The seven-step procedure includes defining the problem, analyzing the problem, designing the logic, coding the program, keying in the program, testing and debugging the program, and gathering the program documentation.

8. Programmers use hierarchy charts, pseudocode, and program flowcharts to design program logic.

9. A printer spacing chart is used to plan printer-generated output. It consists of a grid of rows and columns that is used to design the format of the report.

10. Errors can be made in either syntax or logic. A syntax error occurs when the rules for constructing a valid statement are violated. A logic error occurs when the program produces incorrect results.

11. A program is compiled and translated into machine code before it can be executed by the computer. Since the computer cannot execute the source program in its current form, each statement must undergo a series of transformations before it can be processed by the computer.

12. In general, identifiers are programmer-defined names that describe the variables, constants, modules, and functions required by the program.

13. An identifier name may include letters, digits, and the underscore. An identifier may not include a blank space, be the same as a keyword, or begin with a digit.

14. C++ is case sensitive and treats the identifiers *miles* and *Miles* as two completely different variable names.

15. A keyword is a reserved word that has special meaning to the compiler. Keywords may not be used as programmer-defined identifiers.

Programming Projects

For each project, design the logic and write the program to produce the output. Code your name as the author and include the current date on the output. Model your program after the sample programs presented in the chapter. Verify your output.

Project 1–1   Charge Account

Write a program to compute and print the monthly finance charge. Assume a monthly finance rate of 1.5% on the unpaid balance.

Input (internal):

Define and initialize the input. Use the variable names and values shown below.

    balance = 3400.00
    payments = 400.00
    charges = 100.00

Output (screen):

Use the variable names shown below to describe the output.

    newBalance
    finCharge

Print the following information on the screen:

```
Author     CHARGE ACCOUNT     mm/dd/yy
Monthly finance charge $ 99.99
```

Processing Requirements:

- Define and initialize the program variables.
- Compute the new balance:
  balance – payments + charges

- Compute the monthly finance charge:
  balance × rate
- Print the output on the screen.

Project 1–2   Payroll

Write a program to compute and print the net pay. Assume deductions amount to 9% of the gross pay.

Input (internal):

Define and initialize the input. Use the variable names and values shown below.

    payrate = 7.76
    hours = 40

Output (screen):

Use the variable names shown below to describe the output.

    grossPay
    deductions
    netPay

Print the following information on the screen:

```
Author      PAYROLL REPORT      mm/dd/yy
Net pay: $ 999.99
```

Processing Requirements:

- Define and initialize the program variables.
- Compute the gross pay:
  payrate × hours
- Compute the deductions:
  grossPay × 0.09
- Compute the net pay:
  grossPay – deductions
- Print the output on the screen.

Project 1–3   Sales

Write a program to calculate and print the net profit.

Input (internal):

Define and initialize the input. Use the variable names and values shown below.

    totalSales = 12710.14
    salesCost = 6235.38

Output (screen):

Use the variable name *netProfit* for the output and print the following information on the screen:

```
Author     SALES PROFIT     mm/dd/yy
Net profit is $ 999.99
```

Processing Requirements:

- Define and initialize the program variables.
- Compute the net profit:
  totalSales – salesCost
- Print the output on the screen.

Project 1-4   Inventory

Write a program to compute and print the potential profit.

Input (internal):

Define and initialize the input. Use the variable names and values shown below.

    quantity = 48
    unitCost = 4.49
    unitPrice = 9.95

Output (screen):

Use the variable names shown below to describe the output.

    unitProfit
    itemProfit

Print the following information on the screen:

```
Author     INVENTORY PROFIT     mm/dd/yy
Item profit is $ 999.99
```

Processing Requirements:

- Define and initialize the program variables.
- Compute the unit profit:
  unitPrice – unitCost
- Compute the potential profit:
  quantity × unitProfit
- Print the output on the screen.

Project 1-5   Personnel

Write a program to calculate and print the annual salary. Assume the employee receives a 6% increase in pay.

Input (internal):

Define and initialize the input. Use the variable names and values shown below.

    oldSalary = 40126.00
    percent = 0.06

Output (screen):

Use the variable names shown below to describe the output.

    raise
    newSalary

Print the following information on the screen:

```
Author     PERSONNEL REPORT     mm/dd/yy
New salary: $ 999.99
```

Processing Requirements:
- Define and initialize the program variables.
- Compute the raise:
  oldSalary × percent
- Compute the annual salary:
  oldSalary + raise
- Print the output on the screen.

Project 1–6   Accounts Payable

Write a program to compute and print the amount due.

Input (internal):

Define and initialize the input. Use the variable names and values shown below.

invoiceBill = 4563.78
discountRate = 0.06

Output (screen):

Use the variable names shown below to describe the output.

discount
amountDue

Print the following information on the screen:

```
Author     ACCOUNTS PAYABLE     mm/dd/yy
Amount due: $ 9999.99
```

Processing Requirements:
- Define and initialize the program variables.
- Compute the discount amount:
  invoiceBill × discountRate
- Compute the amount due:
  invoiceBill − discount
- Print the output on the screen.

Project 1–7   Production Output

Write a program to compute and print the production cost.

Input (internal):

Define and initialize the input. Use the variable names and values shown below.

unitsMade = 72
unitCost = 4.25

Output (screen):

Use the variable name *itemCost* for the output and print the following information on the screen:

```
Author    PRODUCTION OUTPUT     mm/dd/yy
Item cost: $ 9999.99
```

Processing Requirements:

- Define and initialize the program variables.
- Compute the production cost:
  unitsMade × unitCost
- Print the output on the screen.

2   Taking a Closer Look

Overview

Learning Objectives

After you have read this chapter and completed the exercises, you should be able to:

- discuss the basic structure of a C++ program and the purpose of the main() function
- define constants and variables
- declare and assign data to integer and floating-point data types
- declare and assign data to character and string data types
- code standard input and output operations using *cin* and *cout*
- write programs to accept input from the keyboard

Functions: The Basic Structure

C++ uses functions as its basic building block. Essentially, a C++ program consists of a series of functions that interact with one another to perform the processing task. In this text, we shall distinguish between functions that represent modules and functions that perform an operation.

A **module** is a self-contained, logical unit of a program that performs a major processing task. Consider, for instance, a program that reads data, performs calculations, and prints output. Since each of these activities represents a major processing task, they are coded as separate modules—one for reading the input, one for performing the calculations, and one for printing the output.

A module may include calls to other modules or functions. When one module calls another, processing control is transferred to that module. A module that calls another is referred to as the **calling module**, and the module that is called is referred to as the **called module**. After all the modules have been developed, they are assembled to form the completed program.

A **function** is a routine that accepts data and returns a value. Examples of routines are converting miles to kilometers, generating a random number, finding the square root of a number, determining a maximum and a minimum value, and so forth.

Although arguments are passed to functions, normally they are not passed to modules. When arguments are passed, data is transferred to a function. **Arguments** represent variables or values. Upon executing the function, a computed result is returned to the calling environment. When a result is returned, data is transferred to the calling environment. Functions may be either precoded or defined by the programmer.

C++ comes with a library of precoded functions and/or objects that are used to assist the program in performing its processing activities. An **object** may be either a variable or a routine. The library includes functions that perform standard input/output, mathematical, and character string operations, to mention a few. Later in the chapter, we will learn how to include the standard library in our programs.

Comments

Comments, introduced in the sample programs in Chapter 1, are text statements that document and describe the program. Comments are optional, nonexecutable statements that are placed in the program to explain what the program does and how the code works. (Nonexecutable statements are not processed by the computer.) A comment begins with //.

Examples:

```
1. //  A comment may be coded like this

2. //  A comment
   //  may be coded
   //  like this

3. //  First Comment     //******  Second Comment   ******

4. //*******************************************
   //*                                         *
   //*          Comments may be boxed           *
   //*                                         *
   //*******************************************

5. float  payrate;   // hourly pay rate
   float  hours;      // hours worked this week
```

Examples 1 through 5 demonstrate how to code a comment. Look at the last example. It shows how to use comments to document the program variables.

The #include Directive

Format:

```
#include <filename>
```

Purpose: To merge a file with the source program. The *#include* preprocessing directive tells the preprocessor to replace the directive with a copy of the file specified by the *filename* argument enclosed within angle brackets <>.

The **preprocessor** is a utility program that performs various modifications to the source program. A **preprocessing directive** instructs the preprocessor to modify the source code before the compiler executes the program. The # symbol indicates that the *include* represents an instruction to the preprocessor. Directives do not end with a semicolon.

Unlike other programming languages, C++ does not have the input/output functions built in. For applications that do not require these functions, they are not included with the program. This, of course, streamlines the compilation process and provides a more efficient programming environment.

Example:

```
#include <iostream.h>
```

According to the example, a copy of the **input/output stream header file** replaces the directive in the source code. The *iostream.h* header file enables the program to perform basic input and output operations. That is, the *iostream.h* header file contains information about the commands that allows the program to accept input from the keyboard and display output on the screen.

The main() Function

Format:

```
main()
{
    statements;
}
```

Purpose: To define the main() function. All C++ programs begin with the main() function. It signals the start of the program. The opening and closing parentheses () indicate that the identifier is a function. The opening and closing braces { } define the body of the function.

Normally, the body consists of a sequence of statements that end with a semicolon. Statements tell the computer what to do—what operations to perform. A semicolon specifies the end of each statement. The statement body may include calls to other functions and modules.

Perhaps we should pause here to mention that C++ is a "freeform" language. This means that we may code a statement on the line anywhere we wish. However, for the sake of clarity, we will adopt the practice of indenting the body of a function or module four spaces to the right. We will also code one statement per line. This makes the code easier to read and understand.

Data Types

Data type stipulates how and in what format the data is stored in memory. The most basic or common data types are integer, long, float, double, void, and character. Although C++ allows for other data types, these are the ones that we will normally use to design and implement our program.

Integer: An integer is a whole number. Examples of integer values are 5, 16, and 8724. An integer variable is declared by specifying *int* as the data type. Typically, integer variables hold data in the range –32768 to 32767. The actual range of values may vary from one compiler to another.

If larger integers are required, then specify *long* as the data type. A long integer holds data well beyond the range –32768 to 32767. Long integers are declared by specifying *long*.

Float: Real or floating-point numbers have decimal points. Examples of floating-point values are 2.651, 74.8, and 653.49. A floating-point variable is declared by specifying *float* as the data type.

If larger floating-point values are required, then specify *double* as the data type. A double-precision variable holds extremely small or large data values. Double-precision variables are declared by specifying *double*.

Void: The *void* data type is normally used by a called module to indicate that arguments are neither passed to or returned from the module. We will discuss the *void* data type when we get to Chapter 3.

Character: A character is any single letter, numeric digit, punctuation mark, or special symbol. A character is declared by specifying *char* for the data type.

If we need more than one character, then we may define a string. A **string** is a group of two or more characters. A string variable is declared by specifying *char* for the data type.

Numeric Constants

A **numeric constant** is the actual value assigned to a numeric variable. Numeric constants include integer and floating-point values. In either case, the data type of the constant must be compatible with the type specified for the variable.

Integer Constants: An integer constant is a whole number. Integer constants consist of digits and a unary sign (+ or −). The sign is written in front of the number and may be omitted for positive values. Examples of integer constants are:

        0   −34   245
        14   900   +48
        78   1234   73503

Floating-Point Constants: A floating-point constant is a real number; a numeric value with a decimal point. Floating-point constants consist of digits, a decimal point, and a unary sign. Positive values may have their signs omitted. Examples of floating-point constants are:

        9.1   10.0   45.127
       −0.75   0.1234   123.987
       87.004   5672.3   +8734.0071

Dollar signs, percent signs, commas, and other special symbols are not permitted. Any illegal character coded in the constant will cause an error.

Numeric Variables

A **numeric variable** reserves a location in memory for storing numeric data. Numeric variables define integer and floating-point data. All variable declarations end with a semicolon.

Integer Variables: An integer variable allocates storage space in memory for integer data. Examples of integer variables are:

```
int  lineCount;
long bigNum;
int  item_num, quantity, reorder_point;
int  employee_num, grossPay, deductions, netPay;
```

We may define one variable at a time, or several may be declared on the same line. Note that multiple variable declarations are separated by commas. Here, the commas serve as **delimiters**; they indicate where one variable name begins and another ends.

Floating-Point Variables: A floating-point variable reserves storage space in memory for floating-point data. Examples of floating-point variables are:

```
float amount_due;
float score, variance;
double distance;
double dividend, divisor, quotient;
```

Note: It is important to understand that the contents of a variable may change several times before a program completes its processing task.

Assigning Data to Numeric Variables

Numeric assignment statements assign either integer or floating-point data to the storage areas reserved for the variables. The value assigned to a variable may be in the form of a constant, a variable, or an arithmetic expression. For each assignment statement, the constant, variable, or expression on the right side of the equal operator (=) is assigned to the variable specified on the left side of the operator. Data previously stored at a variable is overwritten by the assignment statement. Assignment statements end with a semicolon.

Examples of assignment statements are:

```
//---- Variable Declarations -----------------

    int    factor, count, product, onOrder = 2;
    float  cost = 14.58, amount_due;
    double total;

//---- Numeric Assignment Statements ---------

    factor = 76;
    amount_due = 5.98;

    count = onOrder;
    total = cost;

    product = factor * count;
```

The first pair assigns the integer constant 76 to *factor* and the floating-point constant 5.98 to *amount_due*. The second pair assigns the contents of *onOrder* to *count* and the value stored at *cost* to *total*.

Note that *total* is a double. This means that the floating-point value stored at cost is **promoted** (converted) to a double and then assigned to *total*. The declaration of *cost* not only defines the variable, it also initializes it to 14.58. Similarly, *onOrder* is initialized to 2.

The last statement assigns the integer expression, *factor * count*, to *product*.

Since C++ is data type sensitive, we must be careful to assign integer constants to integer variables, float constants to float variables, and so on. Otherwise errors may occur. We can, however, promote compatible types as we did when 14.58 was promoted to a double.

Global and Local Variables

A variable may be declared either inside or outside a function or module. A **global variable** is declared outside main() and is available to the entire program. As a rule, we will declare all global variables above the main() function. This means that any variable declared inside main() is local to main() and is not available to any function called by main().

A **local variable**, on the other hand, is declared inside a specific program function and is not available to any other function. A local variable is declared only after the function is actually called by the program and is released upon a return to the calling environment. As a rule, we will declare local variables after the function name.

Strange as it may seem, local variables do not have to be unique across functions. The same identifier name can be used in one or more functions. C++ treats each occurrence of the identifier as a separate variable. This means that we may declare a variable called *total* in function1 to accumulate daily sales and another variable also called *total* in function2 to track the number of employees. As far as C++ is concerned, the two variables are altogether different.

Symbolic Constants: The #define Directive

Format:

```
#define IDENTIFIER constant
```

Purpose: To define symbolic constants. The *#define* directive tells the preprocessor to substitute all occurrences of the *IDENTIFIER* with the *constant*. A defined constant retains its value during the program run. To make them stand out, symbolic constants are coded in uppercase letters. Normally, the *#define* directives are placed at the beginning of the program. Notice that the *#define* directive does not end with a semicolon.

Example:

```
#define RATE 0.08
    .....

interest = deposit * RATE;
```

According to the example, the *#define* directive instructs the preprocessor to substitute all occurrences of *RATE* with the constant 0.08 before the program is executed.

Output Manipulators

Output manipulators are used to display an output stream. Some manipulators take arguments, while others do not. Those that take arguments require the *iomanip.h* header file. Essentially, the manipulators are used to change the default format settings, output newline characters, and define the field width and decimal precision for output data items. Some common manipulators are shown in Table 2.1. For example, the *setw* manipulator sets the minimum field width for output data items and *setprecision( )* sets the number of decimal places for floating-point values.

Examples of data manipulators are:

```
1. cout << setw(2) << 245 << setw(4) << 63 << endl;
```

   OUTPUT: 245   63

TABLE 2.1   Common Manipulators

Manipulators	Meaning
endl	output newline character
setiosflags()	turn on stream flags
resetiosflags()	turn off stream flags
setw()	set field width
setprecision()	set decimal precision

Notice that the first integer (245) is shown with three digits, not two. In this case, the *cout* statement inserted the actual number of digits required to show the constant. The second integer (63) is right justified in a four-position field. **Right justification** shifts the data to the right end of the field. Hence, the output is right aligned in a four-position field and is shown with two leading spaces. The *endl* manipulator advances to a new line after printing the output.

```
2. cout << setw(8) << setprecision(2) << 12.34
        << setw(8) << setprecision(2) << 56.7759 << endl;
```

OUTPUT: 12.34   56.78

The first output item (12.34) is right justified and is shown with three leading spaces and two decimal places to the right of the decimal point. The second item (56.78) is also right justified with three leading spaces and two decimal places. Since the decimal precision is set to 2, the computer rounds the output to the nearest hundredth and drops the right most digits 5 and 9.

```
3. cout << setw(3) << setprecision(1) << 7.6
        << setw(7) << setprecision(2) << 7.6 << endl;
```

OUTPUT: 7.6   7.60

The first two manipulators force the output to print as a floating-point 7.6, whereas the second two force the output to print with two decimal places. Notice the spacing between the output values; the second value is right justified in a seven-position field.

Note: The *setprecision* manipulator stays in effect until it is changed by the program. However, the *setw* manipulator only applies to the next output item.

Format Flags

The **input/output stream (ios) flags** are member functions of the *iostream.h* header file. Like the manipulators, the flags are used to format a stream of data. The flags are often used as arguments in the *setiosflags* and *resetiosflags* manipulators. Some common ios format flags are shown in Table 2.2. For example, the *showpoint* flag forces a decimal point to print for all floating-point items shown in the *cout* statement.

Examples of ios flags are:

```
1. cout << setiosflag(ios::fixed|ios::showpoint) << 614.00;
```

OUTPUT: 614.00

TABLE 2.2 Common Input/Output Stream Flags

ios Flags	Meaning
left	left justify output
right	right justify output
fixed	show as fixed decimal
dec	show output in base 10
oct	show output in base 8
hex	show output in base 16
showpoint	show decimal point
uppercase	show hex in uppercase

The *setiosflags* manipulator consists of two arguments separated by the I symbol. The :: symbol indicates that the flag is a member function of the *iostream.h* header file. The *ios::fixed* flag specifies that floating-point values will be displayed in normal fixed decimal notation and the *ios::showpoint* flag forces the decimal point to print for all floating-point values. Notice that output shows a decimal point and two zeros.

```
2. cout << setiosflags(ios::fixed)
        << setiosflags(ios::showpoint)
        << setprecision(4) << setw(10) << 244.2;
```

OUTPUT: 244.2000

The output has four decimal places and is right justified in a 10-position field. Hence, two leading spaces occupy the leftmost positions in the output field.

```
3. cout << setiosflags(ios::left) << setw(5) << "Age"
        << resetiosflags(ios::left) << setw(6) << 21;
```

OUTPUT: Age   21

The output, *Age* and *21*, are left justified and right justified, respectively. Observe the spacing between the output items. Two spaces follow the string *Age* and four spaces precede the numeric value *21*.

Notice that the (*ios::left*) format flag was used twice, once to change the default justification from right to left (to print the string *Age*), and once to reset the justification back to right. This was done to get around a compiler error. Most compilers would use the *setiosflags(ios::right)* manipulator to set the default justification back to right.

Note: The ios format flags stay in effect until they are changed by the program.

Screen Output Using cout

Format:

```
cout << variable/s;
```

Header File: *iostream.h (iomanip.h)*

Purpose: To print an output stream on the screen. Actually, the *cout* statement may include messages (strings of characters) and data manipulators as well as variable arguments. When present, messages are enclosed within double quotation marks and are used either to prompt the user to enter data at the keyboard or to describe the output displayed on the screen. When present, the **output manipulators** are used to format the data stored at the variables. The *cout* statement ends with a semicolon.

The *variable* argument refers to the data that is printed on the screen. Multiple variables are separated by the insertion operator <<. At run time, the data is "inserted" in the output stream and displayed on the screen. A semicolon marks the end of the *cout* statement. Be sure to include the *iostream.h* header file in the program. If the output requires special formatting, also include the *iomanip.h* header file. The header files contain the declarations for the *cout* statement and the output manipulators.

Examples:

For each example, assume the variables contain the following data: *grade* = 87, *hours* = 3, *minutes* = 45, *num1* = 5.0, and *num2* = 34.5678.

```
cout << "This is my first course in C++.";
```

   OUTPUT: This is my first course in C++.

The *cout* statement inserts the message enclosed within double quotation marks in the output stream. In other words, the output message is displayed on the screen. Observe that there are no manipulators or variable arguments in the statement.

```
cout << grade;
```

   OUTPUT: 87

The *cout* statement displays the value of the variable *grade* in decimal form. Since the value stored at the variable represents an integer, the output shows *grade* as a decimal integer.

```
cout << "\nCourse grade is: " << grade;
```

   OUTPUT: Course grade is: 87
   [advance to new line]

The *cout* statement advances to a new line, prints *grade* as a decimal integer and displays the output on the screen. The \n (backslash *n*), the newline character, advances the cursor to the beginning of a new line. When coded at the beginning of the message string, the cursor advances to a new line before the statement prints the output. The newline character is not displayed as part of the actual output.

```
cout << "Course grade is:" << grade << endl;
```

   OUTPUT: Course grade is: 87
   [advance to new line]

The *cout* statement prints *grade* as a decimal integer, displays the output on the screen, and advances to a new line. When the newline character or end line (*endl*) is coded at the end of the control string, the cursor advances to a new line after the program prints the output.

```
cout << "Time spent on project: " << hours
    << " hours and " << minutes << " minutes\n";
```

   OUTPUT: Time spent on project: 3 hours and 45 minutes
   [advance to new line]

The *cout* statement displays the output on the screen and the program advances to a new line. Notice how the data has been inserted between the messages.

```
cout << setiosflags(ios::fixed)
     << setiosflags(ios::showpoint)
     << setw(3) << setprecision(1) << num1
     << setw(5) << setprecision(2) << num1
     << setw(7) << setprecision(3) << num1
     << setw(9) << setprecision(4) << num1;
```

OUTPUT: 5.0 5.00 5.000   5.0000

The data manipulators print the output in fixed decimal form with decimal points (*showpoint*). For example, the *setw(3)* manipulator specifies that the output is three positions wide and the *setprecision(1)* manipulator indicates that the output is rounded to the nearest tenth. Observe the spacing between the values. The output corresponds to the spacing specified by the width manipulator. Notice that numeric output is right justified.

```
cout << setiosflags(ios::fixed)
     << setiosflags(ios::showpoint)
     << setw(4) << setprecision(1) << num2
     << setw(6) << setprecision(2) << num2
     << setw(7) << setprecision(3) << num2;
```

OUTPUT: 34.6 34.57 34.568

The *setw(4)* and *setprecision(1)* manipulators tell the compiler that the output is four positions wide, with one position to the right of the decimal point. The decimal point is included in the width. Similarly, *setw(6)* and *setprecision(2)* specify a field width of six with two decimal places and *setw(7)* and *setprecision(3)* specify a field width of seven with three decimal places.

Escape Sequences

An **escape sequence** is a sequence of characters that begins with a backslash \; the compiler treats the sequence as a single character. We have already been using the newline \n escape sequence to advance to a new line. Some common escape sequences are shown in Table 2.3. For example, the \f escape sequence tells the compiler to "escape" the normal meaning of the character *f* and to advance to the top of the next page.

Examples of escape sequences are:

1. cout "Saved by the bell!\a";

    OUTPUT: Saved by the bell! <sound the bell>

2. cout "My name is Shawn O\'Brien.";

    OUTPUT: My name is Shawn O'Brien.

3. cout "The coach said, \"Practice two hours a day.\"";

    OUTPUT: The coach said, "Practice two hours a day."

4. cout "Student Name:\tExam1\tExam2\tExam3";

    OUTPUT: Student Name: Exam1   Exam2   Exam3

TABLE 2.3 Escape Sequences

Escape Sequence	Meaning
\a	alert—sound the bell
\f	form feed—advance to top of next page
\r	carriage return—return to beginning of line
\n	newline—advance to next line
\b	backspace—move back one space
\t	tab—move to next tab setting
\\	backslash—print a backslash
\'	single quotation mark—print a single quotation mark
\"	double quotation mark—print a double quotation mark
\0	zero—null character

Note: The single and double quotation marks have special meaning to the compiler. We may, however, use them for other purposes by coding them as escape sequences (see examples 2 and 3 in the list at the bottom of the previous page).

In example 4, the actual number of spaces inserted by the tab \t escape sequence depends on the compiler you are using.

Keyboard Input Using cin

Format:

```
cin >> variable/s;
```

Header File: *iostream.h*

Purpose: To read an input stream from the keyboard. The *cin* statement waits for the user to input data and then press the Enter key. Once a data item is entered, it is converted to the type declared for the variable and the result is stored at the variable. The *cin* statement ends with a semicolon.

The *variable* argument referes to the data that is entered at the keyboard. Multiple variables are separated by the **extraction operator** >>. At run time, the data is "extracted" from the input stream and assigned to the variables. A semicolon marks the end of the *cin* statement.

It is important to understand that C++ treats the input (letters, digits, and special characters) as a continuous stream of characters. In other words, *cin* reads the input stream and converts the data items to the types specified by the variables.

Examples:

For each example, assume the variables are declared as: *int grade, int hours, int minutes, int num1, int num2, int iNum, long lNum, float num3, float num4, float fNum,* and *double dNum.*

```
INPUT:  87
cin >> grade;
STORAGE:  grade = 87
```

The stream item 87 is entered at the keyboard. After the Enter key is pressed, the *cin* statement converts the 87 to a decimal integer and assigns the result to *grade*.

INPUT: 3 45
cin >> hours >> minutes;
STORAGE: hours = 3
              minutes = 45

The data is entered at the keyboard. After the Enter key is pressed, the *cin* statement converts the 3 and the 45 to decimal integers and assigns the results to *hours* and *minutes*, respectively. The space (**white space**) shown between the numbers 3 and 45 serves as a delimiter. It tells *cin* that the input stream consists of two substrings.

INPUT: 19 245   38.6   4.812
cin >> num1 >> num2 >> num3 >> num4;
STORAGE: num1 = 19
              num2 = 245
              num3 = 38.6
              num4 = 4.812

Four substrings are entered at the keyboard. After the Enter key is pressed, the *cin* statement converts the first two substrings to decimal integers and the last two to floating-point numbers. The results are assigned to the variables. Notice that the white space separating the data may vary.

INPUT: 27 453935 899.95 3.141593
cin >> iNum >> lNum >> fNum >> dNum;
STORAGE: iNum = 27
              lNum = 453935
              fNum = 899.95
              dNum = 3.141593

The *cin* statement reads the input stream and identifies the substrings. According to the control string, the first substring is converted to an *integer*, the second to *long*, the third to *float*, and the fourth to *double*.

Arithmetic Operations

Arithmetic operations represent the standard mathematical operations of addition, subtraction, multiplication, division, and modulus (remainder). The symbols used to express the arithmetic operations are shown in Table 2.4.

Modulus, which uses the % operator, is the only arithmetic operation that requires integer variables. When executed, **modulus** computes the remainder by dividing the first integer by the value of the second. For example, the expression $a = b$ % c, where $b = 11$ and $c = 3$, results in a modulus of 2. In other words, the remainder 2 is assigned to a.

This section also introduces three frequently used math functions that manipulate numeric data—fabs(), pow(), and sqrt(). Since these functions require the *math.h* header file, we must include it with the other header files. The argument types and return types are doubles.

TABLE 2.4   Arithmetic Operators

Operator	Operation	Example
+	addition	b + c
−	subtraction	b − c
*	multiplication	b * c
/	division	b / c
%	modulus	b % c

Absolute Value: The fabs() function returns the absolute value of a number. The absolute value of a positive or negative number is the number itself, without reference to its sign. Examples of absolute values are:

```
fabs(1.5)   returns 1.5          fabs(-1.5) returns 1.5
fabs(27.0) returns 27.0          fabs(-0.9) returns 0.9
```

Exponentiation: The pow() function returns the power of a number. Exponentiation raises a number to a given power. Examples of exponentiations are:

```
pow(5.0, 2.0) returns   25.0     pow(2.0, 7.0)  returns   128.0
pow(4.0, 4.0) returns 256.0      pow(10.0, 3.0) returns 1000.0
```

Square Root: The sqrt() function returns the square root of a positive number. Negative arguments produce errors. The square root of a number represents a factor that when multiplied by itself gives the number. Examples of square roots are:

```
sqrt(25.0) returns 5.0           sqrt(9.0)    returns  3.0
sqrt(81.0) returns 9.0           sqrt(100.0) returns 10.0
```

Note: See Appendix D for a summary reference of math and related functions.

Arithmetic Expressions

An **arithmetic expression** is a statement that combines numeric constants and/or variables with one or more arithmetic operators. For example, the following arithmetic expression computes take-home pay:

```
pay = hours * payrate + bonus;
```

The statement consists of three variables (*hours, payrate,* and *bonus*) and two operators (* and +). The expression is evaluated according to the **order of precedence**. The result, determined by the expression on the right side of the equal sign, is assigned to the variable (*pay*) shown on the left. An arithmetic expression ends with a semicolon.

The order of precedence is also known as the **hierarchy of operations**. When an expression contains two or more arithmetic operators, the computer determines the order in which to perform the operations. The hierarchy of operations is shown in Table 2.5.

For example, let *hours* = 20.0, *payrate* = 8.00, and *bonus* = 15.00. Then, by substitution,

```
pay = 20.0 * 8.00 + 15.00;
```

TABLE 2.5 Hierarchy of Operations

Order	Hierarchy of Operations
1	exponentiation
2	multiplication, division, modulus
3	addition, subtraction

According to the hierarchy of operations, multiplication is performed first (20.0 * 8.00 = 160.00), then the addition (160.00 + 15.00 = 175.00).

By using parentheses, we can change the order in which the computer performs the operations. For example, if we insert parentheses in the statement as shown, we can change the resulting value of the expression:

```
pay = 20.0 * (8.00 + 15.00);
```

In this particular case, the expression will produce an incorrect result (20.0 * 23.00 = 460.00). However, there will be situations when parentheses are required in order to produce the correct result.

Checkpoint 2A

1. Describe the basic structure of a C++ program and define the terms *module* and *function*.
2. Explain the purpose of the *#define* preprocessing directive.
3. Explain the purpose of the input/output stream header file.
4. Explain the purpose of the main() function. Is it necessary for each program to contain this function?
5. For the following statements, locate and correct any syntax errors:

   a. `/  Account Receivable System   /`
   b. `#include <iostream.h>`
   c. ```
      main();
        {
            // This is a C program
        }
      ```
   d. `int total_amount            //  total amount due`
   e. `int age;                    //  age in months`
   f. `int dept, emplNum, wages:   //  data fields`
   g. `cin >> GPA;`
   h. `cout << &result;`
   i. `cout << "*** " << totalCount;`
   j. `cin >> num1, num2, num3;`

6. The sample program below computes the product of two integers by multiplying the value of the first integer by the value of the second. Locate and correct any logic errors. Desk check the code by tracing the flow of data through the program, line by line.
      ```

```
#include <iostream.h>

main()
{
    int num1, num2, result;

    num1 = 30;
    num2 = 40;
    cout "\nThe product is: " << result;
    result = num1 * num2;
}
```

7. Evaluate the following statements:
   a. `fabs(-2.7);`
   b. `pow(4.0, 2.0);`
   c. `sqrt(81);`
   d. `fabs(16.8);`
   e. `sqrt(-4.0);`
   f. `pow(5.0, 3.0);`

8. Differentiate between global and local variables.

Sample Program CHAP2A

Sample program CHAP2A (Figure 2.2, p. 45) is an interactive program that accepts data from the keyboard, computes earned pay, and prints the output on the screen. An interactive program involves a dialog between the user and the computer. For example, the payroll program tells (prompts) the user when to enter pay rate and hours worked. Figure 2.3 (p. 45) shows the input and output.

The following specifications apply:

Input (keyboard):

Prompt for and enter the following data:

Pay Rate	Hours Worked
25.10	38.5

Output (screen):

Print the following information on the screen:

`Total pay is $999.99`

Processing Requirements:

- Define the program variables.
- Compute the total pay:
  pay rate × hours worked
- Print the output on the screen.

Pseudocode:

START
Prompt and enter the pay rate
Prompt and enter the hours worked

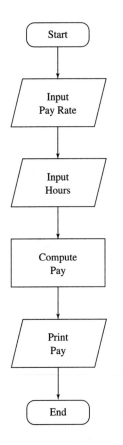

FIGURE 2.1   Program Flowchart for CHAP2A

Compute total pay
Print total pay
END

Program Flowchart: See Figure 2.1.

Dissection of Sample Program CHAP2A

The first nine lines are comments. Comments, of course, are not processed by the computer. From now on, we will use this method to document the purpose of the program and to identify the program name, author, and run date.

```
#include <iostream.h>
#include <iomanip.h>
```

The above statements mean: Include the header files in the program. The *iostream.h* header file contains the declarations for the *cin* and *cout* instructions, and the *iomanip.h* header file contains the declarations for the data manipulators. Since we intend to input data from the keyboard and display (and format) output on the screen, we must include these declarations in the source program.

```
float payrate;
float hours;
float totalPay;
```

The above statements mean: Declare the program variables. Notice that *payrate, hours,* and *totalPay* represent global variables.

```
main()
{
    cout << "Enter pay rate: $";
```

The above statement means: Print the message enclosed within double quotation marks on the screen. The message serves as a prompt that tells the user to enter the pay rate.

```
    cin >> payrate;
```

The above statement means: Read the input, convert the data to a floating-point number, and assign the result to *payrate*.

```
    cout << "Enter hours worked: ";
    cin  >> hours;
```

The above statements mean: Prompt for and enter hours worked. Convert the input to float and assign the result to *hours*.

```
    totalPay = payrate * hours;
```

The previous statement means: Multiply the *payrate* by the number of hours worked and store the result in *totalPay*.

```
    cout << setiosflags(ios::fixed)
         << setiosflags(ios::showpoint)
         << setprecision(2)
         << "\nTotal pay is $" << totalPay << endl;
}
```

The above statements mean: Format *totalPay* as a fixed decimal value, show result with two decimal places, and display the output on the screen. The **endl** is equivalent to the newline character (\n). Hence, the *cout* statement executes a single space after printing the line.

Nonnumeric Constants

There are two types of **nonnumeric constants**, character and string. A character constant is a single character assigned to a character variable; a string constant is a group of characters assigned to a string variable. Be sure to match the data types of the constants to those of the variables. A type mismatch can cause problems that may be difficult to find.

Character Constants: A **character constant** is any single letter (uppercase or lowercase), decimal digit, punctuation mark, or special symbol. Character constants are enclosed within single quotation marks. Examples of character constants are:

```
'R'    'y'    'n'    '$'    '-'    '5'    '1'    ' '    '0'
```

```
//---------- SIMPLE PAYROLL -------------------------------
//    This program accepts data from the keyboard and computes
//    total pay.
//
//              PROGRAM-ID: CHAP2A
//              PROGRAMMER: David M. Collopy
//              RUN DATE:   mm/dd/yy
//
//**********************************************************
#include <iostream.h>
#include <iomanip.h>

float payrate;                  //  hourly pay rate
float hours;                    //  hours worked
float totalPay;                 //  total pay

main()
{
    cout << "Enter pay rate: $";
    cin >> payrate;
    cout << "Enter hours worked: ";
    cin >> hours;
    totalPay = payrate * hours;
    cout << setiosflags(ios::fixed);
         << setiosflags(ios::showpoint);
         << setprecision(2);
         << "\nTotal pay is $" << totalPay << endl;
}
```

FIGURE 2.2   Program Code for CHAP2A

String Constants: A **string constant** represents a group of two or more characters. String constants are enclosed within double quotation marks and are also called character arrays. An **array** is a collection of related items, and a character array is a collection of characters that make up the string. Examples of string constants are:

```
"MAJESTIC MUSIC DISCOUNT"      "Accounts Receivable Report"
        "Ohio University"      "February 14th"
                "Tuesday"      "C++ Programming I"
```

```
Enter pay rate: $ 25.10
Enter hours worked: 38.5

Total pay is $ 966.35
```

FIGURE 2.3   Screen Input and Output for CHAP2A

Nonnumeric Variables

Character and string variables are used to reserve storage space for nonnumeric data. A character variable reserves storage for exactly one character, whereas a string variable or character array allocates enough space to hold the entire string.

Character Variables: A **character variable** reserves storage space in memory for one character of data. Examples of character variables are:

```
char sign;
char flag, no, yes;
char setup, middle_initial;
char symbol, dollar;
```

String Variables: A **string variable** (also called a **character array**) reserves storage space in memory for string data. A string variable is defined by specifying type *char* and a length. The length is enclosed within brackets [ ] and must be long enough to hold the entire string and the string terminator. The **string terminator** or **null character** \0 marks the end of the string.

When defined, a character array represents an address to a location in memory where string data is stored. Examples of string variables are:

```
char day[10];
char letter_head[24];
char university[28];
char reportLine[27];
char course[16];
char celebrate[14];
```

The lengths shown for the string variables include the null character. For example, the variable called *day* allocates storage space for 10 characters. If the string Tuesday is stored at *day*, then the contents of *day* will look like this:

	0	1	2	3	4	5	6	7	8	9
day:	T	u	e	s	d	a	y	\0		

According to the example, Tuesday occupies storage positions 0–6 (storage positions are numbered from left to right starting with 0) and the null character \0 marks the end of the data. Hence, the variable *day* may hold a maximum of nine characters of data; the last position is reserved for the null character.

Assigning Data to Nonnumeric Variables

Nonnumeric assignment statements assign either character or string data to the storage areas reserved for the variables. Data assigned to a character or string variable can be in the form of either a constant or a variable. An assignment statement ends with a semicolon.

Examples of character assignment statements are:

```
//---- Character Declarations -----

    char sign;
    char flag, no = 'n', yes = 'y';
```

```
    char middle_initial;
    char symbol, dollar = '$';

//---- Character Assignment Statements ----

    sign = '-';
    middle_initial = 'M';
    flag = yes;
    symbol = dollar;
```

The first pair assigns the character '-' to *sign* and the letter 'M' to *middle_initial*. The second pair assigns the contents of the *yes* to *flag* and the character stored at *dollar* to *symbol*. The declarations of *no*, *yes*, and *dollar* not only define the variables, they also initialize them.

Examples of string assignment statements are:

```
//---- String Declarations --------------------------

    char letter_head[24] = "MAJESTIC MUSIC DISCOUNT";
    char mySchool[] = "Ohio University";
    char day[10];
    char celebrate[20], birthday[] = "November 18th";

//---- String Assignment Statements -------------------------

    strcpy(day, "Thursday");      // day = "Thursday"
    strcpy(celebrate, birthday);  // celebrate = "November 18th"
```

Look at *letter_head, mySchool,* and *birthday*. Notice that constants were assigned to them when they were declared. The length of *letter_head* is explicitly defined by the declaration, whereas the lengths of *mySchool* and *birthday* are implicitly determined by the lengths of the strings assigned to the variables.

As odd as it may seem, we can only use the equal sign to assign data to a string variable when the variable is declared. For example, the following assignment statement will cause an error:

```
day = "Thursday";
```

We can, however, assign a string of characters to a string variable by using the **string copy function**—strcpy(). Before we can use strcpy(), we must include the **string header file** in our program by coding:

```
#include<string.h>
```

Now look at the string copy functions. Thursday is assigned to *day* and the contents of *birthday* are assigned to *celebrate*. We will discuss the details of strcpy() in Chapter 4.

Printing Nonnumeric Output

Until now, we have been using the *cout* statement to display numeric values on the screen. In this section, we will learn how to use the *cout* statement to format the output stream and print character and string data on the screen.

Examples:

For each example, assume the variables contain the following data: *char1* = `'N'`, *char2* = `'F'`, *char3* = `'L'`, and *message[]* = `"Total points:"`.

```
cout << char1 << char2 << char3;
OUTPUT:  NFL
```

The *cout* statement indicates that three characters are printed side by side.

```
cout << char1 << " " << char2 << "   " << char3;
OUTPUT:  N F   L
```

The blank spaces enclosed within the double quotation marks separate the characters in the output. One space separates the N from the F and three spaces separate the F from the L.

```
cout << message << 8.5;
OUTPUT:  Total points: 8.5
```

The *cout* statement displays a brief message and a floating-point constant on the screen. Notice that the string stored at the variable *message* is displayed on the screen.

```
cout << "C++ is fun" << '!';
OUTPUT:  C++ is fun!
```

The *cout* statement shows the output "C++ is fun" and '!' as a continuous string of characters.

```
cout << setw(14) << "C++ is fun" << '!';
OUTPUT:      C++ is fun!
```

The output appears on the right. C++ uses shift right as the default justification. Hence, the program tells the compiler to right justify (shift right) the string in a 14-position field. Since the 10 character message is shorter than the 14-position field, the compiler pads the first four positions with spaces.

```
cout << setiosflags(ios::left)
     << setw(14) << "C++ is fun" << '!';
OUTPUT:  C++ is fun    !
```

The output appears on the left. The *setiosflags(ios::left)* manipulator tells the compiler to left justify (shift left) the string. Since the message is shorter than the output field, the compiler pads the last four positions with spaces. Notice that the exclamation point is printed at the end of the field. **Left justification** occurs when the data shifts left or is left aligned in the field.

Reading Nonnumeric Data

Thus far, we have been using *cin* statement to read numeric data from the keyboard. In this section, we will learn how to use the *cin* statement to input character and string data.

Examples:

For each example, assume the variables are defined as follows: *char name[16], char grade, int studentNum, char firstName[10],* and *char lastName[15]*.

```
INPUT:  Maxwell B
cin >> name >> grade;
STORAGE:  name = Maxwell
grade = B
```

The space separating the data items tells *cin* that the input stream consists of two substrings. According to the variable declarations, the first substring, `Maxwell`, is converted to a string and assigned to *name* and the second substring, `B`, is converted to a character and assigned to *grade*.

> **INPUT:** `1118 Ryan Adams`
> `cin >> studentNum >> firstName >> lastName;`
> **STORAGE:** `studentNum = 1118`
> `firstName = Ryan`
> `clastName = Adams`

According to the input statement, the first substring, `1118`, is converted to a decimal integer and assigned to *studentNum*, the second substring, `Ryan`, is converted to a string and assigned to *firstName*, and the third substring, `Adams`, is converted to a string and assigned to *lastName*.

The return Statement

Format:

```
return value;
```

Purpose: To transfer control. The *return* statement sends control back to the calling environment (function, module, operating system, etc.). We will use this statement to exit a lower-level module and to return to the calling module. The *return* statement ends with a semicolon.

The value argument is optional. If present, the value is returned to the calling environment. Return values can be in the form of a constant, variable, or arithmetic expression.

Examples:

1. `return;`
2. `return 0;`
3. `return (result);`
4. `return (x + y);`

Example 1 causes a return to the calling environment. Examples 2–4 not only send control back to their respective calling environments, they also return a value—a 0, the value stored at result, and the sum (x + y), respectively. Parentheses may be used to enclose the *return* expression.

Checkpoint 2B

1. What is a character array?
2. Explain the purpose of the *return* statement.
3. Determine if the following assignment statements are valid or invalid:
   a. `int     number1 = 521;`
   b. `float   number2 = 35.02;`
   c. `double number3 = 250000;`
   d. `char    last_name[7] = 'Wilson';`
   e. `char    firstName[7] = "Annette";`
   f. `int     number4 = 326.89;`
   g. `long    number5 = 64000`

```
    h. char    middle_initial = "I";
    i. char    response[2] = 'Y';
    j. float   number6 = 2402;
```

4. Determine if the following *#define* directives are valid or invalid:

```
    a. #define   TAX_RATE = 0.18
    b. #define   payrate 10.50
    c. define    COST 19.95
    d. #define   INTEREST .08
    e. define    ZERO 0;
```

5. Evaluate the following arithmetic expressions:

```
    a. cost = 25 + 18 * 2;
    b. amountDue = 3 * 4 / 6;
    c. outcome = 3.00 * 40 + 1.5 * 6.00 + 10;
    d. result = (3.00 * (40 + 1.5) * 6.00) + 10;
```

6. Code the *#define* directive to assign 7.85 to *DISCOUNT*.

7. Code the variable declaration for a string variable called *title* that will hold 20 characters.

8. Code the *cout* statement to print the value of *average* (type float). The output has a field width of five with two decimal places.

9. Code the *cin* statement to read the following input stream: 35 394 847628 325.90 4.268975. Use the following variable names: *iNum1, iNum2, lNum, fNum*, and *dNum*.

Sample Program CHAP2B

Sample program CHAP2B (Figure 2.5, p. 52) accepts the input from the keyboard and computes the volume of a storage carton. Figure 2.6 (p. 53) shows the input and output.
    The following specifications apply:

Input (keyboard):

Prompt for and enter the following data in feet:

Length	Width	Height
4.3	5.2	7.1

Output (screen):

Print the following information on the screen:

```
Volume = 999.99
```

Processing Requirements:

- Define the program variables.
- Compute the volume:
    length × width × height
- Print the output on the screen.

Pseudocode:

```
    START
    Prompt and enter the length
    Prompt and enter the width
```

Prompt and enter the height
Compute the volume
Print the volume
END

Program Flowchart: See Figure 2.4.

Dissection of Sample Program CHAP2B

```
#include <iostream.h>
#include <iomanip.h>
```

The above statements mean: Include the input/output stream and manipulator header files in the source program.

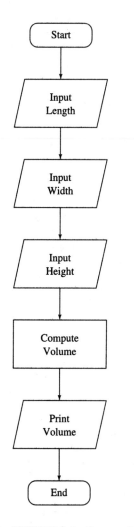

FIGURE 2.4   Program Flowchart for CHAP2B

```
float length,
      width,
      height,
      volume;
```

The above statements define the program variables. The *length, width*, and *height* are input variables, whereas *volume* is computed by the program.

```
main()
{
    cout << "Enter the length: ";
    cin >> length;
    cout << " Enter the width: ";
    cin >> width;

//---------- VOLUME ---------------------------------------
//    Compute the volume of a storage carton given the length,
//    width, and height.
//
//              PROGRAM-ID: CHAP2B
//              PROGRAMMER: David M. Collopy
//              RUN DATE:   mm/dd/yy
//
//*******************************************************************

#include <iostream.h>
#include <iosmanip.h>

float length,                   // length of the carton
      width,                    // width of the carton
      height,                   // height of the carton
      volume;                   // volume of the carton

main()
{
    cout << "Enter the length: ";
    cin >> length;
    cout << " Enter the width: ";
    cin >> width;
    cout << "Enter the height: ";
    cin >> height;
    volume = length * width * height;
    cout << setiosflags(ios::fixed)
         << setiosflags(ios::showpoint)
         << setprecision(2)
         << "\nVolume = " << volume << endl;
    return 0;
}
```

FIGURE 2.5 Sample Program CHAP2B: Compute the Volume of a Storage Carton

```
Enter the length:  4.3
Enter the width:   5.2
Enter the height:  7.1

Volume = 158.76
```

FIGURE 2.6   Screen Input and Output for CHAP2B

```
cout << "Enter the height: ";
cin >> height;
```

The above statements mean: Prompt for and enter the data. The input data is converted to *float* and assigned to *length, width*, and *height*, respectively.

```
volume = length * width * height;
```

The previous statement means: Compute the product and assign the result to *volume*.

```
cout << setiosflags(ios::fixed)
     << setiosflags(ios::showpoint)
     << setprecision(2)
     << "\nVolume = " << volume << endl;
```

The above statements mean: Format the *volume* in fixed-point decimal form, display the output on the screen, and advance to the next line.

```
    return 0;
}
```

The above statement returns a 0 to the operating system. Zero indicates a successful run. The closing brace marks the end of the main() function.

Summary

1. A C++ program consists of functions. There are two types of functions—those that define modules and those that define an operation.

2. A module is a logical unit that performs a specific task. A function is a routine that performs a specific operation and returns a value.

3. Comments are nonexecutable statements that are used to document the program.

4. The *#include* directive tells the compiler to insert a series of precoded functions in the source program.

5. All C++ programs have a main() function that signals the start of the program.

6. Data type stipulates how (in what format) the data is stored in memory. Numeric data types define integer and floating-point data. Nonnumeric data types define character and string data.

7. A numeric constant represents the value assigned to a numeric variable. The constant may be either an integer or a floating-point number.

8. A numeric variable reserves a location in memory for integer or floating-point data. A variable may assume different values during the program run.

9. The value assigned to a numeric variable may be in the form of a constant, a variable, or an arithmetic expression.

10. A global variable is declared outside main() and is available to the entire program. A local variable is declared inside a specific function and is only available to that function.

11. The *#define* directive equates a constant to an identifier. Symbolic constants are written in uppercase and retain their values during the program run.

12. Output manipulators are used to display a stream of data. They are primarily used to change the default format settings, output newline characters, and to define field widths and decimal precision for the output data items.

13. Format flags are often used as arguments in the *setiosflags* and *resetiosflags* data manipulators. Some common format flags are: left, right, fixed, showpoint, and uppercase.

14. An arithmetic expression is a statement that may include numeric constants and variables connected by one or more arithmetic operators.

15. According to the hierarchy of operations, the computer performs exponentiation first, multiplication, division, and modulus second, and addition and subtraction last.

16. The *cout* statement formats the data stored at the program variables and displays the output on the screen.

17. An escape sequence represents a sequence of characters that begin with a backslash \; the compiler treats the sequence as a single character.

18. The *cin* statement reads data from the keyboard and assigns the input to the program variables.

19. A character constant is any single letter, digit, punctuation mark, or special symbol enclosed within single quotation marks.

20. A string constant consists of two or more characters enclosed within double quotation marks.

21. A nonnumeric variable reserves a location in memory for storing character data. There are two types of nonnumeric variables—character and string.

22. The return statement is used to exit either a module or a function.

Programming Projects

For each project, design the logic and write the program to produce the output. Model your program after the samples presented in the chapter. Verify your output.

Note: Xs are used to specify the maximum field size reserved for printing string data.

Project 2–1   Charge Account

Write a program to compute and print the month-end balance. Assume an annual finance rate of 18% on the unpaid balance.

Input (keyboard):

For each customer, prompt for and enter the following data:

Last Name	Previous Balance	Payments	Charges
Allen	5000.00	0.00	200.00
Davis	2150.00	150.00	0.00
Fisher	3400.00	400.00	100.00
Navarez	625.00	125.00	74.00
Stiers	820.00	0.00	0.00
Wyatt	1070.00	200.00	45.00

Output (screen):

For each customer, print the following billing information:

```
Author       CHARGE ACCOUNT       mm/dd/yy


Customer:             X--------X
Finance charge:    $  99.99
Month-end balance: $9999.99
```

Processing Requirements:

- Compute the new balance:
  previous balance – payments + charges
- Compute the finance charge:
  new balance × (annual rate / 12)
- Compute the month-end balance:
  new balance + finance charge

Project 2–2   Payroll

Write a program to calculate and print the net pay. Assume the current federal income tax (FIT) rate is 15%.

Input (keyboard):

For each employee, prompt for and enter the following data:

Employee	Hours Worked	Hourly Pay Rate
Bauer	40	7.50
Erickson	38	12.00
Howard	40	9.75
Miller	40	10.25
Rossi	35	8.00
York	36	11.00

Output (screen):

For each employee, print the following payroll information:

```
Author       PAYROLL REPORT    mm/dd/yy
```

```
Employee:  X--------X
Gross pay: $999.99
FIT:       $ 99.99
Net Pay:   $999.99
```

Processing Requirements:

- Compute the gross pay:
  hours × pay rate
- Compute the federal income tax:
  gross pay × FIT rate
- Compute the net pay:
  gross pay – FIT

Project 2–3   Sales

Write a program to calculate and print the net profit.

Input (keyboard):

For each salesperson, prompt for and enter the following data:

Salesperson Name	Total Sales	Cost of Sales
Conrad	8120.52	6450.71
Hickle	2245.78	1072.49
Perkins	12710.14	9735.38
Tian	4567.51	3119.22
Zimmerman	5793.59	4204.45

Output (screen):

For each salesperson, print the following sales information:

```
Author      SALES REPORT      mm/dd/yy


Salesperson:   X--------X
Total Sales:   $99999.99
Cost of Sales: $99999.99
Net Profit:    $99999.99
```

Processing Requirements:

- Compute the net profit:
  total sales – cost of sales

Project 2–4   Inventory

Write a program to calculate and print the potential profit.

Input (keyboard):

For each item, prompt for and enter the following data:

Item Number	Description	Quantity on Hand	Unit Cost	Selling Price
1000	Hammers	24	4.75	9.49
2000	Saws	14	7.50	14.99

3000	Drills	10	7.83	15.95
4000	Screwdrivers	36	2.27	4.98
5000	Pliers	12	2.65	5.49

Output (screen):

For each item, print the following inventory information:

```
Author                 INVENTORY REPORT              mm/dd/yy

Item Number: 9999      Description: X--------X
Quantity:    999
Item Profit: $999.99
```

Processing Requirements:

- Compute the total cost:
  quantity × unit cost
- Compute the total income:
  quantity × selling price
- Compute the potential profit:
  total income – total cost

Project 2–5   Personnel

Write a program to compute and print the annual salary.

Input (keyboard):

For each employee, prompt for and enter the following data:

Employee Number	Employee Name	Dept Number	Annual Salary	Percent Increase
1926	Andrews	10	29000.00	0.10
2071	Cooper	14	30250.00	0.12
3550	Feldman	22	24175.00	0.07
4298	Palmer	35	33400.00	0.11
5409	Shields	47	27500.00	0.08
6552	Wolfe	31	31773.00	0.10

Output (screen):

For each employee, print the following personnel information:

```
Author               PERSONNEL REPORT            mm/dd/yy

Employee Number:    9999    Name: X--------X
Department Number: 99
Percent Increase:  0.99
New Salary:         $99999.99
```

Processing Requirements:

- Compute the raise:
  annual salary × percent increase
- Compute the annual salary:
  annual salary + raise

Project 2–6   Accounts Payable

Write a program to compute and print the amount due.

Input (keyboard):

For each vendor, prompt for and enter the following data:

Vendor Number	Vendor Name	Invoice Number	Invoice Amount	Discount Rate
217	Metacraft	A1239	2309.12	0.10
349	IntraTell	T9823	670.00	0.09
712	Reylock	F0176	4563.78	0.12
501	Universal	W0105	1200.00	0.09
196	Northland	X2781	3429.34	0.10

Output (screen):

For each vendor, print the following information:

```
Author            ACCOUNTS PAYABLE        mm/dd/yy

Invoice Number:     XXXX
Vendor Number:      999
Vendor Name:        X--------X
Invoice Amount:     $99999.99
Discount Amount:    $   999.99
Amount Due:         $99999.99
```

Processing Requirements:

- Compute the discount amount:
  invoice amount × discount rate
- Compute the amount due:
  invoice amount – discount amount

Project 2–7   Production Output

Write a program to compute and print the production cost.

Input (keyboard):

For each item, prompt for and enter the following data:

Employee Name	Product Number	Units Produced	Unit Cost
Baum	A1234	24	5.50
Fitch	C4510	36	7.94
Hildebrand	R0934	18	6.75
Mullins	E3371	36	3.79
Renner	H9733	24	4.25
Tate	Z0182	27	8.10
West	A3235	30	2.95

Output (screen):

For each item, print the following production information:

```
Author              PRODUCTION OUTPUT           mm/dd/yy

Product Number:   XXXXX    Employee: X--------X
Units Produced:   999
Cost Per Unit:    $  99.99
Total Unit Cost: $9999.99
```

Processing Requirements:

- Compute the production cost:
  units produced × unit cost

3 Modular Programming

Overview

Learning Objectives

After you have read this chapter and completed the exercises, you should be able to:

- discuss the concepts and benefits of modular structured programming
- divide a program into a series of self-contained modules
- explain the purpose of the logic structures—sequence, selection, and iteration
- explain why programming guidelines are necessary
- write C++ programs using top-down design and modular structured programming techniques

Modular Structured Programming

Modular structured programming is a design strategy that is used to manage, organize, and develop computer programs. It consists of a "divide and conquer" approach that breaks up the program into a series of logical units called modules.

Managing the Project

Real-world applications often involve pages upon pages of program logic and code. Even now, at our level, it is becoming clear that we need a better way to organize and manage the program logic.

The purpose of **modular structured programming** is to provide a methodology for managing the programming task. This method allows us to divide a large application into a finite number of self-contained modules. In this way, a large program becomes a series of smaller, logically related tasks that can be developed and tested independently. It is much easier to program one module at a time than to undertake an entire project all at once.

From Chapter 2, we know that a module is a self-contained, logical unit of a program that performs a major processing task. Once the modules have been coded and tested, they are assembled to form the completed program.

Once again, consider a program that reads input, performs calculations, and prints output. These activities represent three different processing tasks. For logical purposes, it would be better to create three modules—one for reading the input, one for performing the calculations, and one for printing the results—than to combine the tasks into a single block of code.

Modular programming facilitates program management and error control. For example, if a payroll program produces an incorrect result for net pay, we can examine the calculations module directly and correct any errors. Similarly, we examine the output module to fix errors related to printing paychecks.

Modular programming simplifies the debugging process and saves time, since errors can be traced more readily. Modular programs are also easier to design, read, and maintain.

Logic Structures

Any programming application, no matter how simple or complex, can be constructed using a combination of three basic logic structures: sequence, selection, and iteration.

Sequence: Sequence refers to the process of executing one statement after another in the order that they appear in the program. For example, input length, input width, input height, compute the volume, and print the output.

Selection: Selection refers to the process of choosing one of two processing options. Consider a payroll application. Compute regular pay. If hours worked exceed 40, compute overtime pay. Otherwise, skip the overtime routine.

A selection process that requires more than two options is called a **case** structure. For example, a bookstore may offer a 10% discount to customers purchasing two to nine books, a 20% discount for 10–24 books, and a 30% discount for 25 or more books.

Iteration: Iteration refers to the process of repeating a series of statements a given number of times. Iteration is also called **looping**. Suppose we want to compute the paychecks for a department that has 20 employees. We would instruct the computer to compute gross pay, subtract deductions, and print the check, and to repeat these steps 20 times—once for each employee.

Creating a Program Module

Format:

```
void module(void)
{
    statements;
    return;
}
```

Purpose: To define a program module. According to the format, module refers to the name given to the block of code enclosed within braces. Type void indicates that arguments are neither passed to the module nor returned to the calling environment. The statement body performs the processing task. It may include calls to other modules and/or functions. The *return* statement signals the end of the module and sends control back to the calling environment.

Example:

```
//----------------------------------------------------------
//              INPUT DATA
//----------------------------------------------------------
void InputData(void)
{
    cout << "Enter the length: ";
    cin >> length;
    cout << "Enter the width: ";
    cin >> width;
    cout << "Enter the height: ";
    cin >> height;
    return;
}
```

In the example, *InputData* prompts the user to enter the data for the *length, width,* and *height.* Assume that the variables have been declared as floats. Furthermore, assume that the user enters the following data at the prompts—4.3, 5.2, and 7.1.

Hence, the input is converted to float and stored in the variables specified by the *cin* statements; that is, *length* = 4.3, *width* = 5.2, and *height* = 7.1. After accepting the data, the *return* statement sends control back to the calling environment. Since types are void, the module neither receives arguments nor returns a value. Notice how the boxed comment is used to identify the module.

Programmer-Defined Functions

Format:

```
type function(argument/s)
{
    declarations;
     . . . . .
    statements;
    return identifier;
}
```

Purpose: To create a programmer-defined function. According to the format, type refers to the data type of the identifier returned by the function to the calling environment, and function refers to the name of the procedure. The arguments, enclosed within parentheses, give the types and the names of the data items passed to the function.

The body of the function is enclosed within braces. Each data item required by the procedure is declared by the function. The *return* statement marks the end of the function and sends the processed result, shown as the identifier, to the calling environment.

Example:

```
float average;
float num1;
float num2;

     . . . . .

average = averagefn(num1, num2);            // function call statement
     . . . . .

//---------- fn: compute average ---------------------
float averagefn(float x, float y)
{
    float result;

    result = (x + y) / 2;
    return result;
}
```

When the function is called, the floating-point arguments, *num1* and *num2*, are passed to averagefn(). Once called, the function declares the local variables required and then computes the average. The last statement returns the *result* to the calling statement. The value returned replaces the calling statement.

For example, assume that *num1* = 15.2 and *num2* = 27.6. When the program executes the calling statement, the arguments 15.2 and 27.6 are passed to the function and assigned to the local variables *x* and *y*, respectively. Next the variable *result* is declared as a float and the function computes the result, 21.4. The last statement then returns the result to the calling statement. The return value (21.4) replaces the calling statement and is assigned to the variable *average*.

As a standard, we will postfix *fn* (short for function) to the end of the function name. This is how the name averagefn() was derived. Notice that a comment line is used to identify the function.

Function Prototypes

Format:

```
type function(type list);
```

Purpose: To describe a function. A **function prototype** describes the parameters of the function to the compiler. It gives information about the name, the number and types of arguments passed, and type of the value returned. It allows the compiler to check for errors—to ensure that the arguments specified by the calling statement match the arguments defined by the function. All prototypes should be coded at the beginning of the program before main(); see Sample Program CHAP3A for placement of the prototypes. Each function prototype ends with a semicolon.

Since modules are functions, they, too, should be prototyped. Make it a habit to prototype all programmer-defined functions. Beginning with this chapter, we will code the function prototypes right after the preprocessing directives.

Examples:

1. `void GetInput(void);`
2. `float averagefn(int, int);`
3. `float milesfn(float);`

The first prototype tells us that the module neither receives arguments nor returns a value. Look at the second example. It describes a function that receives two integer arguments and returns a floating-point value. The last example receives a floating-point argument and returns a floating-point value.

Checkpoint 3A

1. Explain the purpose of modular structured programming.
2. Identify and explain the three basic logic structures.
3. Code the prototype to describe a programmer-defined function that receives an integer value and returns a floating-point value. Give it the name *function1*.
4. Code the prototype to describe a programmer-defined function that receives a character and returns no value. Give it the name *function2*.
5. Code the prototype to describe a module that receives no arguments and returns no arguments. Give it the name *Output*.

Sample Program CHAP3A

The one function program shown in Figure 3.1 was introduced in Chapter 2. Although the code is shown in its original form, the program will be modified to demonstrate the technique of modular structured programming.

The program computes the volume of a storage carton given the length, width, and height in feet. The input and output are shown in Figure 3.2 (p. 68); the specifications were given in Chapter 2.

Sample program CHAP3A (Figure 3.5, p. 68) illustrates the modular version of the volume program. Since the pseudocode remains the same, it will not be repeated here. Note that in Figure 3.4 (p. 67) a *MAINLINE* has been added to the flowchart. We will discuss this further in the program dissection.

Hierarchy Chart: A **hierarchy chart** or block diagram divides the program into levels of tasks (modules) and shows the relationship between them. Figure 3.3 shows the hierarchy chart for the sample program. The first level specifies the purpose of the program, whereas the second level shows the processing tasks performed by the program. In general, as we move down the chart, higher level tasks requiring more detail are further subdivided into subordinate tasks.

Program Flowchart: See Figure 3.4.

Dissection of Sample Program CHAP3A

The top-down modular version of the volume program consists of four modules: *MAINLINE CONTROL, INPUT DATA, CALCULATE VOLUME*, and *PRINT OUTPUT*. Here, the *MAINLINE* controls the sequence of calls to the other three modules in the program. Notice that the lower-level modules carry out the detail processing tasks required by the program.

```
//---------- VOLUME----------------------------------------
//  Compute the volume of a storage carton given the length,
//  width, and height.
//
//              PROGRAM-ID: CHAP2B from Chapter 2
//              PROGRAMMER: David M. Collopy
//              RUN-TIME:   mm/dd/yy
//
//*************************************************************
#include<iostream.h>
#include<iomanip.h>

float length,                        // length of carton
      width,                         // width of carton
      height,                        // height of carton
      volume;                        // volume of carton

main()
{
    cout << "Enter the length ";
    cin >> length;
    cout << "Enter the width ";
    cin >> width;
    cout << "Enter the height ";
    cin >> height;
    volume = length * width * height;
    cout << setiosflags(ios::fixed)
         << setiosflags(ios::showpoint)
         << setprecision(2)
         << "\nVolume = " << volume << endl;
}
```

FIGURE 3.1   Program Code to Compute the Volume of a Storage Carton

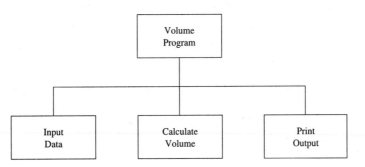

```
Enter the length: 4.3
Enter the width:  5.2
Enter the height: 7.1

Volume = 158.76
```

FIGURE 3.2   Screen Input and Output

This arrangement of modules, from high-level control logic to low-level detail, is called top-down programming. **Top-down** refers to the strategy of developing the program control logic first and the detailed processing steps last.

FIGURE 3.3   Hierarchy Chart for CHAP3A

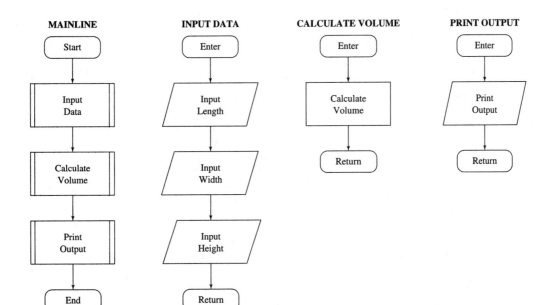

FIGURE 3.4   Program Flowchart for CHAP3A

Notice how the line comments are used to identify the different parts of the program and to highlight the processing modules. This makes the program code easier to read and understand.

```
//------ PREPROCESSING DIRECTIVES ------------------------------

#include <iostream.h>
#include <iomanip.h>
```

The line comment tells us that this is where the preprocessing directives are written in the program. The *#include* directives instruct the compiler to insert the input/output stream and manipulator header files in the source program.

```
//----------- VOLUME----------------------------------------
//    Compute the volume of a storage carton. This program
//    demonstrates top-down structured programming.
//
//             PROGRAM-ID: CHAP3A
//             PROGRAMMER: David M. Collopy
//             RUN-TIME:   mm/dd/yy
//
//**********************************************************

//----------- PREPROCESSING DIRECTIVES ---------------------
#include<iostream.h>
#include<iomanip.h>

//----------- FUNCTION PROTOTYPES ---------------------------

void InputData(void);           // input data
void CalcVolume(void);          // calculate volume
void PrnOutput(void);           // print output

//----------- PROGRAM VARIABLES -----------------------------

float length,                   // length of carton
      width,                    // width of carton
      height,                   // height of carton
      volume;                   // volume of carton

//-----------------------------------------------------------
//                MAINLINE CONTROL
//-----------------------------------------------------------
main()
{
    InputData();                // input data
    CalcVolume();               // calculate volume
```

FIGURE 3.5   Sample Program CHAP3A: Modular Version of the Volume Program

```
        PrnOutput();                    // print output
        return 0;
    }


    //-----------------------------------------------------------
    //              INPUT DATA
    //-----------------------------------------------------------
    void InputData(void)
    {
        cout << "Enter the length ";
        cin >> length;
        cout << "Enter the width ";
        cin >> width;
        cout << "Enter the height ";
        cin >> height;
        return;
    }


    //-----------------------------------------------------------
    //              CALCULATE VOLUME
    //-----------------------------------------------------------
    void CalcVolume(void)
    {
        volume = length * width * height;
        return;
    }


    //-----------------------------------------------------------
    //              PRINT OUTPUT
    //-----------------------------------------------------------
    void PrnOutput(void)
    {
        cout << setiosflags(ios::fixed)
             << setiosflags(ios::showpoint)
             << setprecision(2)
             << "\nVolume = " << volume << endl;
        return;
    }
```

FIGURE 3.5 *Continued*

```
//-------- FUNCTION PROTOTYPES ------------------------------

void InputData(void);
void CalcVolume(void);
void PrnOutput(void);
```

The above statements describe the program modules to the compiler. According to the prototypes, type void indicates that the modules do not receive arguments or return values.

```
//-------- PROGRAM VARIABLES --------------------------------

float length,
      width,
      height,
      volume;
```

The above statement defines the variables required by the program.

```
//------------------------------------------------------------
//              MAINLINE CONTROL
//------------------------------------------------------------
main()
{
```

The comment tells us that this is the *MAINLINE CONTROL* module. The MAINLINE includes calls to the other modules in the program. We use a box comment to identify the program modules.

```
      InputData();
```

The above statement means: Transfer control to the *InputData* module. The empty parentheses () tell the compiler that arguments are not passed to the module.

```
      CalcVolume();
      PrnOutput();
```

The above statements mean: Transfer control to the modules in the order listed—*CalcVolume* and *PrnOutput*—and perform the processing given there.

```
      return 0;
}
```

The above statements mean: For a successful run, return a 0 to the operating system.

```
//------------------------------------------------------------
//              INPUT DATA
//------------------------------------------------------------
void InputData(void)
{
```

The above comments identify the *InputData* module. The opening brace marks the beginning of the statement body of the module.

```
      cout << "Enter the length: ";
      cin >> length;
      cout << "Enter the width: ";
      cin >> width;
      cout << "Enter the height: ";
      cin >> height;
      return;
}
```

The above statements mean: Prompt the user to input the length, width, and height of the storage carton. The *return* statement sends control back to main(), and the closing brace marks the end of the module.

```
//-------------------------------------------------------------
//              CALCULATE VOLUME
//-------------------------------------------------------------
void CalcVolume(void)
{
    volume = length * width * height;
    return;
}
```

The above statements mean: Compute the volume of the storage carton and return to main().

```
/*-----------------------------------------------------------------*/
/*              PRINT OUTPUT                                        */
/*-----------------------------------------------------------------*/
void PrnOutput(void)
{
    cout << setiosflags(ios::fixed)
         << setiosflags(ios::showpoint)
         << setprecision(2)
         << "\nVolume = " << volume << endl;
    return;
}
```

The above statements mean: Format *volume* as a fixed decimal value, show the result with two decimal places, display the output on the screen, and advance to the next line. Afterwards, return to main().

To further illustrate the concepts of top-down design and modular structured programming, let us look at a second example. Sample program CHAP3B (Figure 3.7, p. 73) shows the code without modules and sample program CHAP3C (Figure 3.11, p. 75) shows the code with modules. The input and output are shown in Figure 3.8 (p. 73).

Sample Program CHAP3B

Sample program CHAP3B (Figure 3.7) computes and prints the raise and percent increase in salary for Mr. Wilson.

The following specifications apply:

Input (keyboard):

Prompt for and enter the following data:

Employee Name	Old Salary	New Salary
Wilson	25000.00	26450.00

Output (screen):

Print the following output on the screen:

```
Wilson received a 9.9% raise and
now earns $9999.99 more a year.
```

Processing Requirements:

- Define the program variables.
- Compute the raise:
  new salary – old salary

- Compute the percent increase:
  (raise / old salary) × 100
- Print the output on the screen.

Pseudocode:

START
Prompt and enter the employee name
Prompt and enter the old salary
Prompt and enter the new salary
Compute the raise
Compute the percent increase
Print the percent increase and raise
END

Program Flowchart: See Figure 3.6.

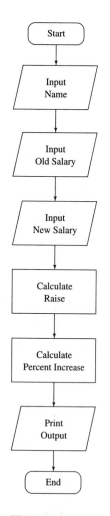

FIGURE 3.6   Program Flowchart for CHAP3B

```
//----------- RAISE ----------------------------------------
//     Compute the raise and percent increase in salary for
//     Mr. Wilson.
//
//              PROGRAM-ID: CHAP3B
//              PROGRAMMER: David M. Collopy
//              RUN-TIME:   mm/dd/yy
//
//**********************************************************
#include<iostream.h>
#include<iomanip.h>

char  name[21];                 // employee name
float oldSalary,                // old salary
      newSalary,                // new salary
      raise,                    // dollar increase in salary
      percent;                  // percent increase salary

main()
{
    cout << "Enter employee name: ";
    cin >> name;
    cout << "Enter old salary: ";
    cin >> oldSalary;
    cout << "Enter new salary: ";
    cin >> newSalary;
    raise = newSalary - oldSalary;
    percent = (raise / oldSalary) * 100;
    cout << endl << name << " received a "
         << setiosflags(ios::fixed)
         << setiosflags(ios::showpoint)
         << setprecision(1) << percent
         << "% raise and " << "\nnow earns $"
         << setprecision(2) << raise << " more a year.";
    return 0;
}
```

FIGURE 3.7 Sample Program CHAP3B: Compute Raise and Percent Increase in Salary for
Mr. Wilson

```
Enter employee name: Wilson
   Enter old salary: 25000.00
   Enter new salary: 26450.00

Wilson received a 5.8% raise and
now earns $1450.00 more a year.
```

FIGURE 3.8 Screen Input and Output for CHAP3B

Sample Program CHAP3C

Sample program CHAP3C (Figure 3.11, p. 75) shows the modular version of the raise program. From top down, the MAINLINE controls the order that the modules are called by the program. One by one, the modules perform the detailed processing tasks required to produce the desired output.

The following specifications apply:

Hierarchy Chart: See Figure 3.9.

Program Flowchart: See Figure 3.10.

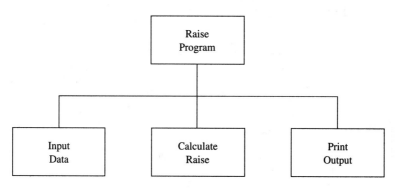

FIGURE 3.9   Hierarchy Chart for CHAP3C

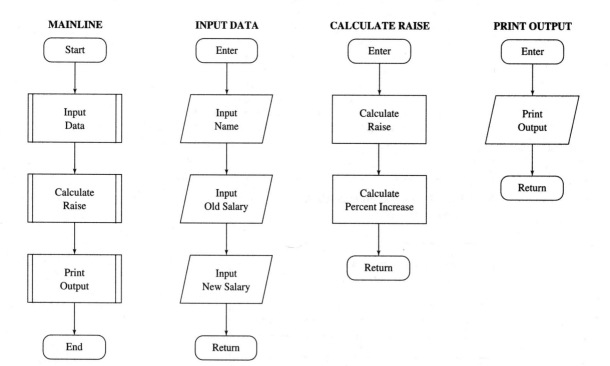

FIGURE 3.10   Program Flowchart for CHAP3C

```
//---------- RAISE----------------------------------------
//   Compute the raise and percent increase in salary. This
//   program demonstrates modular structured programming.
//
//           PROGRAM-ID: CHAP3C
//           PROGRAMMER: David M. Collopy
//           RUN-TIME:   mm/dd/yy
//
//***********************************************************

//---------- PREPROCESSING DIRECTIVES ----------------------
#include<iostream.h>
#include<iomanip.h>

//---------- FUNCTION PROTOTYPES ---------------------------

void InputData(void);          // input data
void CalcRaise(void);          // calculate volume
void PrnOutput(void);          // print output
void percentfn(float, float);  // convert to percent

//---------- PROGRAM VARIABLES -----------------------------

char  name[21];                // employee name
float oldSalary,               // old salary
      newSalary,               // new salary
      raise,                   // dollar increase in salary
      percent;                 // percent increase in salary

//---------------------------------------------------------
//            MAINLINE CONTROL
//---------------------------------------------------------
main()
{
    InputData();               // input data
    CalcRaise();               // calculate raise
    PrnOutput();               // print output
    return 0;
}


//---------------------------------------------------------
//            INPUT DATA
//---------------------------------------------------------
void InputData(void)
{
    cout << "Enter employee name: ";
    cin >> name;
    cout << "Enter old salary: ";
```

(continued on next page)

FIGURE 3.11   Sample Program CHAP3C: Modular Version of the Raise Program

```
        cin >> oldSalary;
        cout << "Enter new salary: ";
        cin >> newSalary;
        return;
    }


//------------------------------------------------------------
//                  CALCULATE RAISE
//------------------------------------------------------------
void CalcRaise(void)
{
    raise = newSalary - oldSalary;
    percent = percentfn(raise, oldSalary);
    return;
}


//------------------------------------------------------------
//                  PRINT OUTPUT
//------------------------------------------------------------
void PrnOutput(void)
{
    cout << endl << name << " received a "
         << setiosflags(ios::fixed)
         << setiosflags(ios::showpoint)
         << setprecision(1) << percent
         << "% raise and " << "\nnow earns $"
         << setprecision << raise << " more a year."
    return;
}

//-----------fn: percent increase ------------------------
void percentfn(float amount, float salary)
{
    float result;

    result + (amount / salary) * 100;
    return result;
}
```

FIGURE 3.11 *Continued*

Dissection of Sample Program CHAP3C

```
PROGRAM VARIABLES:

char   name[21];
```

The above statement means: Define the string variable *name* and reserve enough storage space in memory for 20 characters of data; the last position is reserved for the null character.

```
float oldSalary,
      newSalary,
      raise,
      percent;
```

The above statement means: Define the variables required by the program.

```
MAINLINE CONTROL:

main()
{
    InputData();
    CalcRaise();
    PrnOutput();
    return 0;
}
```

The above statements mean: Branch to and execute the modules in the order listed. The last statement returns 0 to the calling environment.

```
INPUT DATA:

void InputData(void)
{
    cout << "Enter employee name: ";
    cin >> name;
```

The above statements mean: Prompt the user to enter the employee's name. The *cin* statement reads the input stream, converts it to a string, and assigns the result to *name*.

```
    cout << "   Enter old salary: ";
    cin >> oldSalary;
    cout << "   Enter new salary: ";
    cin >> newSalary;
    return;
}
```

The above statements mean: Prompt the user to enter the old and the new salaries. The *cin* statements read and assign the input to the variables *oldSalary* and *newSalary*, respectively.

```
CALCULATE RAISE:

void CalcRaise(void)
{
    raise = newSalary - oldSalary;
```

The above statement means: Compute the dollar amount of the raise and assign the result to *raise*.

```
    percent = percentfn(raise, oldSalary);
```

The above function call passes the value of the arguments *raise* and *oldSalary* to percentfn(). After the function computes the percent increase in salary, the return value replaces the function call and the *result* is assigned to the variable *percent*.

```
        return;
}
```

The above statement means: Return to the *MAINLINE CONTROL* module.

```
PRINT OUTPUT:
```

```
void PrnOutput(void)
{
    cout << endl << name << " received a "
        << setiosflags(ios::fixed)
        << setiosflags(ios::showpoint)
        << setprecision(1) << percent
```

The above statements mean: Format *percent* as as fixed decimal value, show the result with one decimal place, and display the output on the screen.

```
        << "% raise and " << "\nnow earns $"
        << setprecision(2) << raise << " more a year."
    return;
}
```

The above statements mean: Print the percent symbol and the message enclosed within double quotation marks. Single space, print *raise* as a fixed-point decimal number, and display the output on the screen.

```
fn: percent increase:
```

```
float percentfn(float amount, float salary)
{
    float result;

    result = (amount / salary) * 100;
    return result;
}
```

The above function defines the variables (*amount, salary,* and *result*) required by the procedure and computes the percent increase in salary. During the call, *raise* is assigned to *amount*, and *oldSalary* is assigned to *salary*. To show the result as a percentage, the expression enclosed within parentheses is multiplied by 100. The function returns the *result* to the calling statement.

Structured Programming

Structured programming represents the technique of writing programs that emphasizes top-down design and modular programming. This approach aids in the design and construction of high-quality programs that are easy to read, test, and debug.

Modular programming refers to the process of dividing up a program into smaller self-contained modules or functions. The basic idea is to group logically related statements that perform a single task.

Programming Guidelines

The purpose of **programming guidelines** is to provide standards that help design and construct programs that are reliable and easier to maintain over the life of the system.

The following guidelines apply to structured programming:

1. A module should have one entry point and one exit point. In sample program CHAP3C, control enters each module at the top and exits with the return at the bottom.

2. A module should perform one task. For example, reading data and computing totals represent two tasks. Therefore, they should be separate. Avoid putting unrelated tasks in the same module. Group only those statements that belong together.

3. A program should:
   - be self-documenting (use identifier names that describe the variables, modules, and functions)
   - use comments to document the code and explain any unusual or complex processing
   - use simple coding structures
   - use comments to identify the modules and functions
   - consist of no more than 24 statements per module

It pays to develop good habits early. If we use the guidelines regularly, we should be able to write quality programs in less time. But not only that, we should be able to enjoy the benefits derived from structured programming as well.

1. Programs are easier to maintain—to update and modify.

2. Programs are easier to design and code—fewer errors are encountered during the development stages.

3. Programs are more reliable—fewer errors are encountered during production runs.

4. Programs are easier to read and understand, even by someone who is unfamiliar with them.

5. Programs are easier to test and debug.

6. Documentation is easier to write and maintain.

Checkpoint 3B

1. Describe top-down design and modular programming.

2. What three guidelines apply to structured programming? Why are they important?

3. Identify the six benefits associated with structured programming.

Summary

1. Modular structured programming is a design strategy that breaks up a program into a series of self-contained modules that are designed, programmed, and tested independently.

2. Logic structures—sequence, selection, and iteration—are used to construct a program.

3. Sequence refers to the process of executing one statement after another in the order that they appear in the program.

4. Selection refers to the process of choosing between two processing options. A selection process that requires more than two options is called a case structure.

5. Iteration refers to the process of repeating a series of statements a given number of times.

6. A module is a logical segment of the program that performs a single processing task. Modules neither receive nor return values.

7. A programmer-defined function is a routine that performs an operation and returns a value to the calling environment. The arguments passed to the function are manipulated by the routine to produce the return value.

8. A function prototype describes the parameters of the function to the compiler—function name, number and types of arguments, and the return type. Function prototypes are coded at the beginning of the program.

9. A hierarchy chart divides the program into levels of tasks and shows the relationship among them. As we move down the chart, higher level tasks requiring more detail are further subdivided into subordinate tasks.

10. Top-down refers to the design strategy that focuses on coding the high-level control logic first and the detailed processing steps last.

11. The mainline, coded at the beginning of a program, controls the calls to the modules and the order in which they are processed.

12. Structured programming represents the technique of writing programs that emphasizes top-down design and modular programming.

13. The purpose of the programming guidelines is to provide standards that help design and construct quality programs that are easier to code, test, and debug.

Programming Projects

For each project, design the logic and write the modular structured program to produce the output. Model your program after the sample programs presented in the chapter. Verify your output.

Project 3–1 Charge Account

Write a program to compute and print the month-end balance. Assume an annual finance rate of 18% on the unpaid balance.

Input (keyboard):

For each customer, prompt for and enter the following data:

Last Name	Previous Balance	Payments	Charges
Allen	5000.00	0.00	200.00
Davis	2150.00	150.00	0.00
Fisher	3400.00	400.00	100.00
Navarez	625.00	125.00	74.00
Stiers	820.00	0.00	0.00
Wyatt	1070.00	200.00	45.00

Output (screen):

For each customer, print the following report:

```
Author      CHARGE ACCOUNT      mm/dd/yy

Customer:               X--------X
Finance charge:     $   99.99
Month-end balance: $9999.99
```

Processing Requirements:

- Compute the new balance:
  previous balance – payments + charges
- Compute the finance charge:
  new balance × (annual rate / 12)
- Compute the month-end balance:
  new balance + finance charge

Project 3–2   Payroll

Write a program to calculate and print the net pay. Assume the current federal income tax (FIT) rate is 15%.

Input (keyboard):

For each employee, prompt for and enter the following data:

Employee	Hours Worked	Hourly Pay Rate
Bauer	40	7.50
Erickson	38	12.00
Howard	40	9.75
Miller	40	10.25
Rossi	35	8.00
York	36	11.00

Output (screen):

For each employee, print the following report:

```
Author      PAYROLL REPORT      mm/dd/yy

Employee:  X--------X
Gross Pay: $999.99
FIT:       $ 99.99
Net Pay:   $999.99
```

Processing Requirements:

- Compute the gross pay:
  hours × pay rate
- Compute the federal income tax:
  gross pay × FIT rate
- Compute the net pay:
  gross pay – FIT

Project 3–3   Sales

Write a program to calculate and print the net profit.

Input (keyboard):

For each salesperson, prompt for and enter the following data:

Salesperson Name	Total Sales	Cost of Sales
Conrad	8120.52	6450.71
Hickle	2245.78	1072.49
Perkins	12710.14	9735.38
Tian	4567.51	3119.22
Zimmerman	5793.59	4204.45

Output (screen):

For each salesperson, print the following report:

```
Author       SALES REPORT      mm/dd/yy

Salesperson:    X----------X
Total Sales:    $99999.99
Cost of Sales:  $99999.99
Net Profit:     $99999.99
```

Processing Requirements:

- Compute the net profit:
  total sales – cost of sales

Project 3–4   Inventory

Write a program to calculate and print the potential profit.

Input (keyboard):

For each item, prompt for and enter the following data:

Item Number	Description	Quantity on Hand	Unit Cost	Selling Price
1000	Hammers	24	4.75	9.49
2000	Saws	14	7.50	14.99
3000	Drills	10	7.83	15.95
4000	Screwdrivers	36	2.27	4.98
5000	Pliers	12	2.65	5.49

Output (screen):

For each item, print the following report:

```
Author            INVENTORY REPORT          mm/dd/yy

Item Number: 9999      Description: X--------X
```

```
Quantity:    999
Item Profit: $999.99
```

Processing Requirements:

- Compute the total cost:
  quantity × unit cost
- Compute the total income:
  quantity × selling price
- Compute the potential profit:
  total income – total cost

Project 3–5 Personnel

Write a program to compute and print the annual salary.

Input (keyboard):

For each employee, prompt for and enter the following data:

Employee Number	Employee Name	Department Number	Annual Salary	Percent Increase
1926	Andrews	10	29000.00	0.10
2071	Cooper	14	30250.00	0.12
3550	Feldman	22	24175.00	0.07
4298	Palmer	35	33400.00	0.11
5409	Shields	47	27500.00	0.08
6552	Wolfe	31	31773.00	0.10

Output (screen):

For each employee, print the following report:

```
Author           PERSONNEL REPORT            mm/dd/yy

Employee Number:    9999    Name: X--------X
Department Number: 99
Percent Increase:  0.99
New Salary:        $99999.99
```

Processing Requirements:

- Compute the raise:
  annual salary × percent increase
- Compute the annual salary:
  annual salary + raise

Project 3–6 Accounts Payable

Write a program to compute and print the amount due.

Input (keyboard):

For each vendor, prompt for and enter the following data:

Vendor Number	Vendor Name	Invoice Number	Invoice Amount	Discount Rate
217	Metacraft	A1239	2309.12	0.10
349	IntraTell	T9823	670.00	0.09

Vendor Number	Vendor Name	Invoice Number	Invoice Amount	Discount Rate
712	Reylock	F0176	4563.78	0.12
501	Universal	W0105	1200.00	0.09
196	Northland	X2781	3429.34	0.10

Output (screen):

For each vendor, print the following report:

```
Author            ACCOUNTS PAYABLE         mm/dd/yy

Invoice Number:   XXXX
Vendor Number:    999
Vendor Name:      X---------X
Invoice Amount:   $99999.99
Discount Amount:  $   999.99
Amount Due:       $99999.99
```

Processing Requirements:

- Compute the discount amount:
  invoice amount × discount rate
- Compute the amount due:
  invoice amount – discount amount

Project 3–7   Production Output

Write a program to compute and print the production cost.

Input (keyboard):

For each item, prompt for and enter the following data:

Employee Name	Product Number	Units Produced	Unit Cost
Baum	A1234	24	5.50
Fitch	C4510	36	7.94
Hildebrand	R0934	18	6.75
Mullins	E3371	36	3.79
Renner	H9733	24	4.25
Tate	Z0182	27	8.10
West	A3235	30	2.95

Output (screen):

For each item, print the following report:

```
Author            PRODUCTION OUTPUT        mm/dd/yy

Product Number:   XXXXX    Employee: X--------X
Units Produced:   999
Cost Per Unit:    $   99.99
Total Unit Cost:  $9999.99
```

Processing Requirements:

- Compute the production cost:
  units produced × unit cost

4 String Functions and Loops

Overview

Learning Objectives

After you have read this chapter and completed the exercises, you should be able to:

- manipulate string data using the strcat(), strcpy(), strcmp(), and strlen() functions
- use the cin.get() function to clear the keyboard buffer
- understand the concepts of iteration and loop processing
- use relational and logical operators to write conditional statements
- set up loops using the *while, do/while,* and *for* statements
- format printer output and accumulate report totals
- code nested loops

String Functions

Business-related programs are often required to input and process string data as well as numeric data. Items such as company names, customer telephone numbers, shipping addresses, job titles, item descriptions, and so on represent strings.

Strings, like numbers, can be processed by the computer. For example, strings may be compared or concatenated (joined), one string may be assigned to another, or the number of characters in a string may be counted. In the sections that follow, we will learn how to manipulate strings, as well as how to set up a processing loop.

The strcat() Function

Format:

```
strcat(string1, string2);
```

Header File: *string.h*

Purpose: To concatenate strings. This function joins the second string to the first. Both arguments must be strings. The first string must be large enough to hold the combined string. The resulting string is placed in *string1*, while the contents of *string2* remain unchanged. The strcat() function ends with a semicolon.

Example:

```
char fullName[40] = "Tera ";
char lastName[20] = "Kennedy";
   : :
   : :
strcat(fullName, lastName);
```

When processed, strcat() joins the contents of *fullName* and *lastName* into a single string and stores the result at *fullName*. After execution, *fullName* contains the string Tera Kennedy; *lastName* still holds the string Kennedy.

Look at the space between the first name and last name. It is actually part of the string value assigned to *fullName*. The strcat() function does not add spaces between strings.

The strcpy() Function

Format:

```
strcpy(string1, string2);
```

Header File: *string.h*

Purpose: To copy a string. This function copies the contents of the second string to the first. Both arguments must be strings. The first string must be large enough to hold the second. The original contents of *string1* are replaced by the contents of *string2*; the contents of *string2* remain unchanged. The strcpy() function ends with a semicolon.

Example:

```
char prevDept[20] = "Accounting";
char currDept[20] = "Marketing";
   : :
   : :
strcpy(prevDept, currDept);
```

At run time, the string stored at *currDept* is copied to *prevDept*. The prior contents of *prevDept* are replaced, while the contents of *currDept* remain unchanged. After performing the copy, both variables contain the string `Marketing`.

The strcmp() Function

Format:

```
strcmp(string1, string2);
```

Header File: *string.h*

Purpose: To compare strings. This function compares the contents of *string1* and *string2*, and returns a 0 if they are equal. A return code less than 0 indicates that *string1* is less than *string2*, whereas a return code greater than 0 indicates that *string1* is greater than or equal to *string2*. The first argument specifies a string variable, whereas the second argument may be either a string variable or a literal. (A **literal** is a string enclosed within double quotation marks.) The strcmp() function ends with a semicolon.

Examples:

```
1. char name[21] = "Dan Barry";
      : :
      : :
   strcmp(name, "stop run");
2. char salesRep[21] = "Stacy Adams";
   char prevSalesRep[21] = "Stacy Adams";
         : :
         : :
   strcmp(salesRep, prevSalesRep);
```

In Example 1, since stop run is greater than (appears later in the alphabet—see Appendix A) Dan Barry (the string stored at *name*), the compare function returns a value other than 0, indicating that the strings are not equal. In Example 2, the comparison returns a 0 since the contents of the string variables are equal—both contain the string `Stacy Adams`.

The strlen() Function

Format:

```
strlen(string);
```

Header File: *string.h*

Purpose: To determine the number of characters in a string. The strlen() function returns the number of characters found in the string argument. It does not include the null character in the count. The strlen() function ends with a semicolon.

Example:

```
int   count;
char lastName[20] = "Huffman";
     : :

     : :
count = strlen(lastName);
```

During execution of the strlen() function, the total number of characters found in *lastName* is assigned to the variable *count*. Hence, *count* is 7.

Checkpoint 4A

Use the following variable declarations to answer Questions 1–4. For each question, assume the initial values given below.

```
char firstName[20] = "Molly";      char product1[7] = "Pliers";
char lastName[10] = "McPherson";   char product2[10] = "Saw";
char message[20] = "My name is ";  int count;
```

1. Code the strcat() statement that will produce the desired results shown for a through c.
    a. Molly McPherson
    b. McPherson Molly
    c. My name is Molly
2. Code the strcpy() statement to copy the contents of *lastName* to *message*.
3. Evaluate the following strcmp() statements:
    a. strcmp(firstName, "John");
    b. strcmp(firstName, "Molly");
    c. strcmp(product1, product2);
4. Determine the value of *count* for the following strlen() statements.
    a. count = strlen(message);
    b. count = strlen(product1);
    c. count = strlen(product2);
    d. count = strlen("How long is this string?");

5. Using the variable declarations given below, indicate whether the following statements are valid or invalid:

```
char brandName[20] = "Easton Electric";
char company[10] = "Dunn ";
char extension[20] = "Tire Company";
```

  a. `strcat(company, brandName);`
  b. `strcpy(company, extension);`
  c. `strcpy(extension, brandName);`
  d. `strcat(company, extension);`

String Input: The cin.get() Function

In Chapter 2, we learned how to use the *cin* statement to read (input) string data from the keyboard. Recall that the white space separating the data items tells *cin* that the input stream consists of substrings. The white space acts as a delimiter that separates the input stream into substrings. Because of the white space, we cannot directly assign the string `Karen L. Moore` to the string variable *fullName*. In this section, we will see how to use the cin.get () function to solve this problem. The dot (.) indicates that *get* is a member function of the *cin* statement or object. The cin.get () function ends with a semicolon.

Example:

```
char fullName[21];
  . . . . .
cin.get(fullName, 20);
```

According to the example, cin.get() reads the input stream up to the Enter key code (*n*) and places the result in *fullName*. The statement stores everything except the Enter key code. At most, 20 characters are stored at *fullName*; the last position is reserved for the null character \\0.

    For example, assume the input stream `Karen L. Moore\n`. Upon executing the cin.get(), *fullName* will contain the string `Karen L. Moore\0`.

    Note: Appendix C shows a summary reference of input functions that read data.

Clearing the Input Buffer

The cin.get() can be used to remove any data left in the keyboard (input file) buffer. A **file buffer** is a temporary storage area reserved for file streams. So far, we have used the standard file buffers to input data from the keyboard and to write output to the screen. Since problems sometimes occur when reading data from the keyboard, we will show how to use the cin.get() to clear the standard input buffer.

Example:

```
  . . . . .
cout << "\nEnter the part number: ";
cin >> partNum;
cin.get();
cout << "\nEnter the color code: ";
cin >> colorCode;
  . . . . .
```

This example clears the standard input buffer, after the part number is keyed in. But why is it necessary to clear the keyboard buffer in the first place? The problem is that the user must press the Enter key after typing in the data. Although the input is assigned to *partNum*, the Enter key code remains in the buffer. Hence, the next *cin* statement picks up the Enter key code and assigns it to *colorCode*. In other words, if the buffer is not cleared before the next *cin* statement, the program will not allow the user to enter the color code, and bad data will be assigned to it.

In general, if the next *cin* statement reads a single character or a string, then clear the buffer first. Or simply clear the buffer after each *cin* statement rather than worry about when to do it.

Iteration and Loop Processing

Iteration is an important part of programming. A program can be set up to repeat a series of statements to process a group of related records. As an example, consider a program that computes the gross pay for Marie Osborne, given her pay rate and hours worked. But suppose we want to compute the gross pay for 10 employees. Can we do this without running the program 10 times?

We could prompt for pay rate and hours for 10 employees (payrate1, payrate2, … payrate10, and hours1, hours2, … hours10), and code 10 independent segments to compute and print the gross pay for each employee. Although this method would work, it isn't very efficient. What if there are 50 employees? We would have to recode the program 50 times. Fortunately, there is a better way.

What we want the computer to do is to execute the program once, but repeat, or loop through, the instructions until all the data has been processed.

By definition, a **loop** is a logic structure that allows the program to process a set of statements until a given condition has been met. In other words, the condition tells the computer how many times to repeat the statements in the loop. In our example, the condition would tell the computer to repeat the payroll calculations until the program has computed gross pay for all 10 employees.

Additionally, the **body of a loop** represents the set of instructions that is executed a specified number of times by the computer. The term **iteration** refers to the process of repeating a series of instructions a specific number of times.

Every loop has an entrance point and an exit point that encloses the body of the loop and controls the iteration process. In this chapter, we will see how to test for the occurrence of a specific condition to determine whether to repeat or exit the loop.

There are two types of loop structures: leading decision and trailing decision. A **leading decision** (*while* and *for*) performs the condition test at the beginning of the loop; a **trailing decision** (*do/while*) performs the decision test at the end of the loop.

Relational Operators

Relational operators are used to set up relational tests. A **relational test**, also called a **condition test**, compares the value of two data items. The outcome of the test is either true or false. If the test is true, the condition statement evaluates to 1; otherwise, it evaluates to 0.

TABLE 4.1 Relational Operators

Relational Operator	Description	Condition Test
==	equal to	(A == B)
!=	not equal to	(A != B)
<	less than	(A < B)
<=	less than or equal to	(A <= B)
>	greater than	(A > B)
>=	greater than or equal to	(A >= B)

Be sure to compare data items of like types. That is, compare integers to integers, floats to floats, and so on.

A list of relational operators is shown in Table 4.1. The constant, variable, or expression on the right of the relational operator is compared to the constant, variable, or expression on the left.

Caution: Use the equal sign (=) to assign a value to a variable and the double equal sign (= =) to compare two values.

Examples:

For each example, assume the variables contain the following data: *quantity* = 90, *price* = 7.25, *lineCount* = 46, *maxLines* = 45, *payrate* = 12.65, *profit* = 78.99, *cost* = 41.00, and *sales* = 3600.

Condition Test	Evaluates
(quantity == 144)	(0) false
(price != 9.95)	(1) true
(lineCount < maxLines)	(0) false
(payrate <= 15.50)	(1) true
(profit > 2 * cost)	(0) false
(sales >= 4500)	(0) false

Logical Operators

Logical operators are used to set up compound conditions or relational tests. A **compound condition** consists of two or more simple relational tests that are connected by logical operators. There are three logical operators, *and* (&&), *or* (||), and *not* (!).

Logical And Operator: The outcome of an *and* (&&) expression evaluates true when all conditions are true; otherwise, it is false.

Condition1	and	Condition2	Evaluates
true	&&	true	true
true	&&	false	false
false	&&	true	false
false	&&	false	false

Logical Or Operator: The outcome of an *or* (||) expression evaluates true when one or more of the conditions are true; otherwise, it is false.

Condition1	or	Condition2	Evaluates
true	||	true	true
true	||	false	true
false	||	true	true
false	||	false	false

Logical Not Operator: The outcome of a *not* (!) expression is reversed. A true condition becomes false and a false condition becomes true.

Not	Condition	Evaluates
!	true	false
!	false	true

Examples:

For each example, assume the variables contain the following data: *exam* = 75, *choice* = 8, *response* = 0, *size* = 4, and *color* = 3.

Compound Conditions	Evaluates
(exam >= 80 && exam < 90)	false
(choice <= 1 || choice > 5)	true
(response != 0 && exam > 70)	false
(response < choice || exam > 80)	true
(color == 2 || size > 0 && size < 5)	true

Order of Precedence: For compound conditions, the order of precedence is always *and* before *or*. Look at the last example; the *and* condition is evaluated first. We may, however, use parentheses to change the order of precedence. For example, we may insert the parentheses as shown to indicate that the *or* is performed before the *and*.

```
((color == 2 || size > 0) && size < 5)
```

Then according to the order of precedence, the *or* condition is evaluated first and the *and* condition is evaluated second.

Checkpoint 4B

1. Briefly explain the concept of iteration and loop processing.
2. Evaluate (true or false) the following simple conditions using these variable values: *grossPay* = 1125.95, *amount* = 75, *totalBill* = 312.10, *pageCount* = 3, *taxableAmount* = 1500.00.
   a. `(grossPay <= 1200.00)`
   b. `(amount != 80)`
   c. `(totalBill > 400.00)`
   d. `(pageCount == 4)`
   e. `(grossPay > taxableAmount)`

3. Evaluate (true or false) the following compound conditions using these variable values: *qtyOnHand* = 25, *qtyOnOrder* = 30, *average* = 79, *score1* = 90, *score2* = 85, *score3* = 70.

   a. `(qtyOnOrder < 25 && qtyOnHand <= 30)`

   b. `(qtyOnHand <= 30 || average >= 50)`

   c. `(score1 == 90 && score2 < score1)`

   d. `(score2 > average && score3 < average)`

   e. `(score1 < average || score2 < average || score3 < average)`

   f. `(qtyOnHand < 20 || qtyOnOrder > 35)`

Increment and Decrement Operators

Formats:

Increment	Decrement
variable++;	variable − −;
++variable;	− − variable;

Purpose: To modify the value of a counting variable. The increment operator ++ adds 1 to the value of the variable, whereas the decrement operator − − subtracts one. According to the format, the increment/decrement operators may be placed either before or after the variable name.

Examples:

1. ++count;

2. count++;

3. − −quantity;

4. quantity− −;

Although the expressions ++*count* and *count*++ both increment the value of the variable (add 1 to *count*), they may have different effects. In Example 1, the expression ++*count* increments the current value of *count* and then assigns the new value to the expression. However, in the second example, *count*++ assigns the current value of *count* to the expression and then increments *count*.

In the last two examples, the expressions − −*quantity* and *quantity*− − both decrement the value of the variable (subtract 1 from *quantity*), yet they may have different effects. In Example 3, the expression − −*quantity* decrements the current value of *quantity* and then assigns the new value to the expression. In the fourth example, *quantity*− − assigns the current value of *quantity* to the expression and then decrements *quantity*.

The while Loop

Format:

```
while (condition)  {
    statements;
}
```

Purpose: To set up a conditional loop. The *while* statement performs the statements inside the loop as long as the condition is true. Since the condition test is made at the beginning of the loop, there may be situations where the statement body is not executed at all.

Each time the *while* statement is encountered, the condition is evaluated to determine whether to continue or to exit the loop. As long as the condition is true, the program executes the statements inside the braces. At the end of the loop, control passes back to the *while* statement; the right brace marks the end of the loop. We may omit the braces when the body of the loop contains only one statement.

To terminate the loop, a statement or an operation inside the loop is used to modify the condition. Once the condition is false, control exits and continues with the first statement after the loop.

The *while* loop performs the following tasks:

- initializes the control variable (used to set up the condition test)
- evaluates the condition
- performs the statement body of the loop
- modifies the control variable

Examples:

1. Print the integers 1–8:

```
count = 1;
while (count < 9)   {
    cout << count << "    ";
    count++;
}
```

OUTPUT: 1   2   3   4   5   6   7   8

The control variable is initialized to 1 and compared to the ending value. As long as *count* is less than 9, the current value of the control variable is printed on the screen. On each pass through the loop, *count* is incremented by 1.

2. Clear the screen:

```
line = 1;
while (line < 25)   {
    cout << "\n";
    line++;
}
```

OUTPUT: a blank screen

As long as the control variable is less than 25, the cursor advances to a new line. This clears the screen by forcing 24 lines to scroll off the screen.

Note: You may be able to clear the screen with either the **system** call system ("cls"); or the function call clrscr();. The system call exits to the operating system and executes a *cls* command to clear the screen. Check your C++ reference manual for your clear screen function.

3. Example of an infinite (endless) loop:

```
count = 1;
while (count < 9)   {
cout << count << "    ";
}
```

OUTPUT: 1   1   1   1   1   1   1   1 . . .

An endless string of ones will fill the screen. Since *count* is never incremented, the value of *count* is always less than 9.

4. Example of dead code—code that does not execute:

```
count = 1;
while (count > 10)   {
       :   :
    count++;
}
```

OUTPUT: none

Each time this segment is executed, *count* is initialized to 1. Since *count* equals 1 when the *while* condition is evaluated, control never enters the loop.

Checkpoint 4C

1. What is the equivalent assignment statement for each of the following?
   a. sold--
   b. --amount
   c. ++addOne
   d. page++

2. What is the equivalent increment/decrement operator for each of the following?
   a. numberStudents = numberStudents + 1;
   b. employees = employees - 1;
   c. row = row + 1;
   d. qtyOnHand = qtyOnHand - 1;

3. List the processes involved in a *while* loop.

4. What will print when the following statements are executed?
   ```
   a. count = 1;
      while (count <= 5)   {
          cout << count * 10 << "    ";
          count++;
      }
   b. count = 1;
      while (count < 10)   {
          cout << count - 1 << "    ";
          count++;
      }
   ```

```
c. count = 10;
   while (count > 0)  {
        cout << count << "    ";
        count--;
   }
d. count = 1;
   while (count > 10)  {
        cout << count + 3 << "    ";
        count++;
   }
```

Sample Program CHAP4A

Sample program CHAP4A (Figure 4.3, p. 99) computes and prints the game points and field goal average earned by each player during a recent basketball game. Figure 4.4 (p. 101) shows the program's input and output for one player.

The following specifications apply:

Input (keyboard):

Prompt for and enter the following record (enter "stop run" to quit):

Player's Name	Field Goals Attempted	Field Goals Completed
Dan Barry	23	15

Output (screen):

Print the following game statistics (see Figure 4.4):

```
Basketball Field Goal Statistics
           Player:  X--------X
    Points scored:  99
Field goal average:  99.9
```

Processing Requirements:

- Compute the points scored:
  shots completed × 2
- Compute the field goal average:
  (shots completed / shots attempted) × 100

Pseudocode:

    START
    Prompt and enter player's name
    LOOP until name = "stop run"
        Prompt and enter field goals attempted
        Prompt and enter field goals completed
        Compute points scored

Compute field goal average
Print points scored and field goal average
Prompt and enter player's name
    End LOOP
    END

Hierarchy Chart: See Figure 4.1.

Program Flowchart: See Figure 4.2.

Dissection of Sample Program CHAP4A

```
MAINLINE CONTROL:
main()
{
    ProcessingLoop();
    return 0;
}
```

The above statements mean: Transfer control to the *ProcessingLoop* and execute the statements given there. When control returns to the *MAINLINE*, return 0 to the operating system.

```
PROCESSING LOOP:
Void ProcessingLoop(void)
{
    InputPlayer();
```

These statements mean: Transfer control to *InputPlayer* and perform the processing specified there. When placed here, this call is commonly referred to as the **priming input** call. It inputs the first "record" and gets the loop processing started; it allows the program to enter the loop.

```
    while (strcmp(name, "stop run") != 0)  {
```

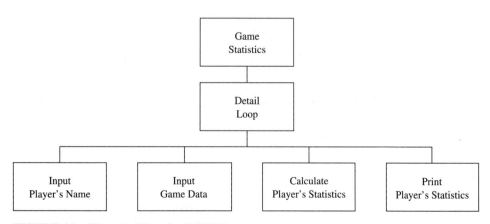

FIGURE 4.1 Hierarchy Chart for CHAP4A

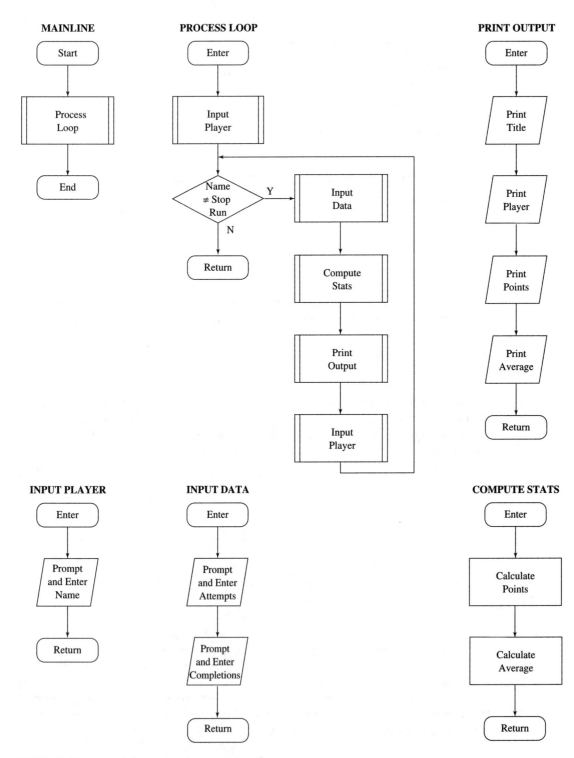

FIGURE 4.2   Program Flowchart for CHAP4A

```
//---------- GAME STATISTICS ------------------------------
// Use a while loop to compute the game points and field goal
// average earned by each player during a basketball game.
//
//          PROGRAM-ID: CHAP4A
//          PROGRAMMER: David M. Collopy
//          RUN-TIME:  mm/dd/yy
//
//***********************************************************

//---------- PREPROCESSING DIRECTIVES ----------------------

#include <iostream.h>
#include <iomanip.h>
#include <string.h>

//---------- FUNCTION PROTOTYPES ---------------------------

void ProcessLoop(void);       // processing loop
void InputPlayer(void);       // input player's name
void InputData(void);         // input data
void ComputeStats(void);      // compute player's stats
void PrnOutput(void);         // print the output

//---------- PROGRAM VARIABLES -----------------------------

char  name[21];               // player's name
float attempts,               // field goals attempted
      completes,              // field goals completed
      average;                // field goal average
int   points;                 // total game points

//----------------------------------------------------------
//              MAINLINE CONTROL
//----------------------------------------------------------
main()
{
    ProcessingLoop();         // processing loop
    return 0;
}

//----------------------------------------------------------
//              PROCESSING LOOP
//----------------------------------------------------------
void ProcessingLoop(void)
{
    InputPlayer();
    while (strcmp(name, "stop run") != 0)  {
```

(continued on next page)

FIGURE 4.3 Sample Program CHAP4A: Compute Game Points and Field Goal Average per Player

```
            InputData();
            ComputeStats();
            PrnOutput();
            InputPlayer();
        }
        return;
}


//-------------------------------------------------------------
//              INPUT PLAYER'S NAME
//-------------------------------------------------------------
void InputPlayer(void)
{
        clrscr();
        cout << "Enter player or 'stop run' to quit: ";
        cin.get(name, 20);
        return;
}


//-------------------------------------------------------------
//              INPUT DATA
//-------------------------------------------------------------
void InputData(void)
{
        cout << "        Enter field goals attempted: ";
        cin >> attempts;
        cout << "        Enter field goals completed: ";
        cin >> completes;
        cin.get();                    // clear keyboard buffer
        return;
}


//-------------------------------------------------------------
//              COMPUTE PLAYER'S STATS
//-------------------------------------------------------------
void ComputeStats(void)
{
        points = completes * 2;
        average = (completes / attempts) * 100;
        return;
}


//-------------------------------------------------------------
//              PRINT OUTPUT
//-------------------------------------------------------------
void PrnOutput(void)
{
        cout << "\nBasketball Field Goal Statistics\n";
```

FIGURE 4.3 *Continued*

```
        cout << "\n                  Player: " << name << endl;
        cout << "         Points scored: " << points << endl;
        cout << setiosflags(ios::fixed)
             << setiosflags(ios::showpoint)
             << setprecision(1)
             << " Field goal average: " << average << endl;
        return;
}
```

FIGURE 4.3 *Continued*

```
Enter player or 'stop run' to quit: Dan Barry
      Enter field goals attempted: 23
      Enter field goals completed: 15

Basketball Field Goal Statistics

           Player: Dan Barry
     Points scored: 30
Field goal average: 65.2
```

FIGURE 4.4 Screen Input and Output for CHAP4A

This statement (p. 97) means: Compare *name* to the string literal `"stop run"` and, based on the outcome, set the function return code. In other words, as long as *name* is not equal to "*stop run*", enter the loop. Otherwise, exit and continue with the first statement after the loop.

Here is how it works. The statement `strcmp(name, "stop run")` sets the function return code to a nonzero value as long as *name* is not equal to "*stop run*". The *while* condition is then evaluated as *while (nonzero != 0),* which is true; therefore the statements in the loop are executed.

When the contents of *name* equal "*stop run*", the function returns a 0 and the *while* condition evaluates to false. Execution then continues with the first statement after the loop.

```
    InputData();
    ComputeStats();
    PrnOutput();
```

The above statements mean: Execute the modules in the order listed—*InputData, ComputeStats*, and *PrnOutput*.

```
    InputPlayer();
```

The above statement means: Transfer control to the *InputPlayer* module. Since this call is inside the loop, it is referred to as the **looping input** call. The priming input call gets the first record, and the looping input call gets the other records.

```
    }
    return;
}
```

The above statement means: Return control to the calling module, the *MAINLINE*.

```
INPUT PLAYER'S NAME:
void InputPlayer(void)
{
    clrscr();
    cout << "Enter player or 'stop run' to quit: ";
    cin.get(name, 20);
    return;
}
```

The above statements mean: Clear the screen and prompt for the player's name. According to the *cin* statement, the input stream is read up to (but not including) the press Enter key code and stored at the string variable called *name*. Control then returns to the *ProcessingLoop*.

```
INPUT DATA:
void InputData(void)
{
    cout << "      Enter field goals attempted: ";
    cin >> attempts;
    cout << "      Enter field goals completed: ";
    cin >> completes;
    cin.get();
    return;
}
```

The above statements mean: Prompt the user to input the field goals attempted and the field goals completed. Assign the data to the variables as shown. The cin.get() clears the keyboard buffer before the program reads the name of the next player.

```
COMPUTE PLAYER'S STATS:
void ComputeStats(void)
{
    points = completes * 2;
```

The above statement means: Multiply the field goals completed by 2 and assign the results to *points*.

```
    average = (completes / attempts) * 100;
    return;
}
```

The above statements mean: Divide the number of field goals completed by the number attempted. Convert the outcome to a percentage by multiplying the result by 100 and assign the product to *average*.

```
PRINT THE OUTPUT:
void PrnOutput(void)
{
    cout << "\nBasketball Field Goal Statistics\n";
```

```
cout << "\n                Player: " << name << endl;
cout << "        Points scored: " << points << endl;
cout << setiosflags(ios::fixed)
     << setiosflags(ios::showpoint)
     << setprecision(1)
     << " Field goal average: " << average << endl;
return;
{
```

These statements mean: Print the report title, format and print the player's name, points scored, and the field goal average, and advance to the next line.

The do/while Loop

Format:

```
do   {
    statements;
} while (condition);
```

Purpose: To set up a conditional loop. The *do/while* statement performs the statements inside the loop before testing the condition. Hence, the body of the loop will always be executed at least once. Note that the *do/while* loop ends with a semicolon.

Each time the ending *while* decision is encountered, the condition is evaluated to determine whether to continue or to exit the loop. As long as the condition is true, control passes back to the *do* statement to repeat the loop. The braces are required when the loop contains more than one statement.

To terminate the loop, a statement or an operation inside the loop is used to modify the condition. Once the condition is false, control exits and continues with the first statement after the loop.

The *do/while* loop performs the following tasks:

• initializes the control variable
• performs the statements body of the loop
• modifies the control variable
• evaluates the condition

Examples:

1. Print the integers 1–8:

```
count = 1;
do   {
    cout << "    " << count;
    count++;
} while (count < 9);
```

OUTPUT: 1 2 3 4 5 6 7 8

Processing begins by setting *count* to 1. Look at the output. The test at the end of the loop compares the current value of count to the ending condition. While *count* is less than 9, control branches back to repeat the loop.

2. Set up a detail processing loop:

```
InputPlayer();
do    {
        InputData();
        ComputeStats();
        PrnOutput();
        InputPlayer();
} while (strcmp(name, "stop run") != 0);
```

OUTPUT: none directly from this module

We could substitute this section of code for the *while* loop shown in sample program CHAP4A; the output would be exactly the same.

Note that the test at the end of the loop compares the player's name to the ending condition. While *name* is not equal to "*stop run*", control branches back and repeats the loop.

The for Loop

Format:

```
for (initialize; test; modify)   {
    statements;
}
```

Purpose: To set up a counter-controlled loop. The *for* statement repeats the statements in the loop a given number of times; the statement body executes as long as the condition test is true. According to the format, the *for* loop consists of three arguments that initialize, test, and modify the control variable.

On the first pass, the control variable is initialized and tested. If the outcome of the test is true, then the program performs the statements in the loop. On subsequent passes, the control variable is modified and tested. As long as the outcome is true, the loop continues. Control exits the *for* loop when the condition test is false.

We may omit the braces when the body of the loop contains only one statement.

The *for* loop performs the following tasks:

• initializes the control variable
• evaluates the condition
• performs the statement body of the loop
• modifies the control variable

Examples:

1. Print the integers 1–10:

```
for (count = 1; count <= 10; count++)   {
    cout << "    " << count;
}
```

OUTPUT: 1   2   3   4   5   6   7   8   9   10

The loop continues until *count* is greater than 10.

2. Print the odd numbers between 1 and 10:

```
for (num = 1; num < 10; num = num + 2)   {
    cout << "    " << num;
}
```

OUTPUT: 1   3   5   7   9

Only the odd numbers are printed. This is accomplished by setting the control variable to 1 and incrementing it thereafter in multiples of 2.

3. Compute and print the sum and square for the integers 1–5:

```
cout << "num   sum   square\n";
cout << "----------------\n";
for (num = 1; num <= 5; num++)   {
    square = num * num;
    sum = sum + num;
    cout << setw(2) << num
                    << setw(5) << sum
                    << setw(7) << square << endl;
}
```

OUTPUT:

num	sum	square
1	1	1
2	3	4
3	6	9
4	10	16
5	15	25

The output continues to print until the control variable, *num*, exceeds 5.

Nested Loops

A **nested loop** is a loop within a loop. Nested loops may go two, three, four, or more levels deep. The actual number of levels depends mostly on the application at hand. Rarely will you find it necessary to go beyond three levels.

It is important to realize that each **inner loop** must be completely enclosed within the preceding **outer loop**. For a two-level nested loop, the inner loop must be enclosed within the outer loop.

Examples:

1. A two-level nested *while* loop:

```
outer = 1;
while (outer <= 3)   {
    cout << "\n Outside " << outer;
    inner = 1;
    while (inner <= 2)   {
        cout << "\n    Inside " << inner;
        inner++;
    }
    outer++;
}
```

2. A two-level nested *do/while* loop:

```
outer = 1;
do   {
    cout << "\n Outside " << outer;
```

```
          inner = 1;
          do  {
              cout << "\n     Inside " << inner;
              inner++;
          } while (inner <= 2);
          outer++;
      } while (outer <= 3);
```

3. Two-level nested *for* loop:

```
for (outer = 1; outer <= 3; outer++)  {
    cout << "\n Outside " << outer;
    for (inner = 1; inner <= 2; inner++)  {
        cout << "\n     Inside " << inner;
    }
}
```

OUTPUT: Outside 1
                  Inside 1
                  Inside 2
              Outside 2
                  Inside 1
                  Inside 2
              Outside 3
                  Inside 1
                  Inside 2

Examples 1–3 produce the same output. Walk through the code. Pay close attention to the processing performed by inner loops and outer loops.

Checkpoint 4D

1. Differentiate between a *while* loop and a *do/while* loop.

2. Code a *for* loop to print the even numbers between 1 and 11; that is, 2, 4, 6, 8, and 10.

3. What will the following nested *for* loop print?

```
for (x = 1; x <= 2; x++)  {
    for (y = 1; y <= 3; y++)  {
        cout << "    " << x * y;
    }
}
```

Sample Program CHAP4B

Sample program CHAP4B (Figure 4.7, p. 110) produces a multiplication table for the integers 1 through 8. Figure 4.8 (p. 111) shows the multiplication table.

The following specifications apply:

Input (internal):

Generate the integers 1–8 internally using a nested *for* loop.

Output (screen):

Print the multiplication table for the integers 1–8 (see Figure 4.8).

Processing Requirements:

- Use nested *for* loops to generate the row and column values.
- Compute the product:
  row × *column*

Pseudocode:

```
START
Clear screen
Print title and headings
Initialize row to 1
LOOP for row <= 8
   Initialize column to 1
   LOOP for column <= 8
     Product = row × column
     Print product
     Column = column + 1
   End LOOP
   Row = row + 1
End LOOP
END
```

Hierarchy Chart: See Figure 4.5.

Program Flowchart: See Figure 4.6 (p. 109).

Dissection of Sample Program CHAP4B

Take a look at the program code (Figure 4.7) and the screen output (Figure 4.8). Once again, notice how the *MAINLINE* controls the order of calls to the other modules in the program.

The following statements mean: Print the title and column headings on the screen, and return to the *MAINLINE*.

```
PRINT HEADINGS:
void PrnHeadings(void)
{
    cout << "  M U L T I P L I C A T I O N    T A B L E \n";
    cout << "\n";
    cout << "    |   1    2    3    4    5    6    7    8\n";
    cout << "    |                                      \n";
    cout << "=============================================\n";
    return;
}
```

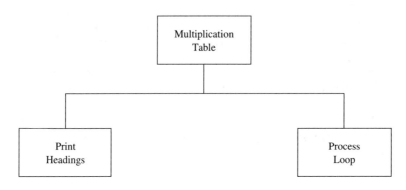

FIGURE 4.5   Hierarchy Chart for CHAP4B

```
PROCESSING LOOP:

void ProcessLoop(void)
{
     for (row = 1; row <= 8; row++)   {
         cout << row << "   |";
```

The above statements mean: Initialize *row* and test for the ending condition. As long as *row* is less than or equal to 8, enter the loop. Format and print the current value of *row*.

```
for (column = 1; column <= 8; column++) {
    product = row * column;
    cout << " " << setw(2) << product << "   ";
}
```

The above statements mean: Initialize *column* and test for the ending condition. As long as *column* is less than or equal to 8, enter the loop and compute the *product*: *row * column*; format and print the *product*. The output prints across the screen.

The closing brace marks the end of the inner loop. Control exits the loop and continues with the next statement.

```
    cout << "\n     |   \n";
}
```

The above statement means: Advance a line, print the vertical bar, and advance to the next line. The closing brace marks the end of the outer loop. Control exits the loop and passes back to the outer *for* statement.

```
    return;
}
```

The above statement means: Branch back to the *MAINLINE*. The closing brace marks the end of the processing loop.

Printer Output

Until now, we have been writing the program output on the screen. However, there may be times when we want the output to go to the printer. Setting up the printer for output involves

MAINLINE

PRINT HEADINGS

PROCESS LOOP

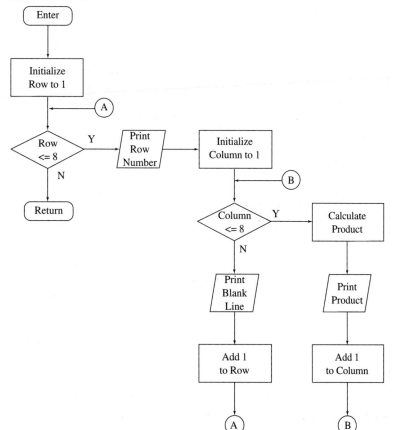

FIGURE 4.6   Program Flowchart for CHAP4B

```
//---------- MULTIPLICATION TABLE---------------------------
//       Use a nested for loop to compute and print a
//       multiplication table for the integers 1-8.
//
//              PROGRAM-ID: CHAP4B
//              PROGRAMMER: David M. Collopy
//              RUN DATE:   mm/dd/yy
//
//**************************************************************

//---------- PREPROCESSING DIRECTIVES----------------------

#include <iostream.h>
#include <iomanip.h>

//---------- FUNCTION PROTOTYPES---------------------------

void PrnHeadings(void);        // print headings
void ProcessLoop(void);        // processing loop

//---------- PROGRAM VARIABLES ----------------------------

int row,                       // row counter
    column,                    // column counter
    product;                   // row-column product
//-----------------------------------------------------------
//              MAINLINE CONTROL
//-----------------------------------------------------------
main()
{
    clrscr();                  // clear screen
    PrnHeadings();             // print headings
    ProcessLoop();             // processing loop
    return 0;
}
//-----------------------------------------------------------
//              PRINT HEADINGS
//-----------------------------------------------------------
void PrnHeadings(void)
{
    cout << " M U L T I P L I C A T I O N   T A B L E \n";
    cout << "\n";
    cout << "     | 1    2    3    4    5    6    7    8\n";
```

FIGURE 4.7 Sample Program CHAP4B: Compute and Print the Multiplication Table for the Integers 1–8

```
        cout << "       |                                          \n";
        cout << "==========================================\n";
        return;
}
//------------------------------------------------------------
//                  PROCESSING LOOP
//------------------------------------------------------------
void ProcessLoop(void)
{
        for (row = 1; row <= 8; row++)  {
            cout << row << "   |";
            for (column = 1; column <= 8; column++) {
                product = row * column;
                cout << " " << setw(2) << product << "   ";
            }
            cout << "\n     |  \n";
        }
        return;
}
```

FIGURE 4.7 *Continued*

```
    M U L T I P L I C A T I O N   T A B L E

        |  1    2    3    4    5    6    7    8
        |
========================================
    1   |  1    2    3    4    5    6    7    8
        |
    2   |  2    3    6    8   10   12   14   16
        |
    3   |  3    6    9   12   15   18   21   24
        |
    4   |  4    8   12   16   20   24   28   32
        |
    5   |  5   10   15   20   25   30   35   40
        |
    6   |  6   12   18   24   30   36   42   48
        |
    7   |  7   14   21   28   35   42   49   56
        |
    8   |  8   16   24   32   40   48   56   64
```

FIGURE 4.8 Screen Output for CHAP4B

including the *fstream.h* header file in the program, assigning a name to the printer, and declaring the name as the output file stream. The name assigned to the file stream is used to direct the program output to the printer. Once the output has been printed, the printer file should be closed. The data manipulators may also be used to format the output written to the printer.

The process of setting up the printer for output is illustrated below:

1. `#include<fstream.h>`

2. `ofstream lineout("PRN");`

3. ```
lineout << setiosflags(ios::fixed)
        << setiosflags(ios::showpoint)
        << setprecision(2)
        << "\nVolume = " << volume;
```

4. `lineout.close();`

First, include the *fstream.h* header file in your program. The header file defines the characteristics of output file stream (*ofstream*) to the compiler. Second, the identifier name *lineout* is assigned to the *ofstream*. The device name *PRN* associates *lineout* with the printer. This step normally takes place before the *MAINLINE* routine. Third, notice that the data manipulators are applied to the output. The insertion operators << indicate that *volume* is edited and written to the printer. Last, the printer file is closed.

## Checkpoint 4E

1. Differentiate between *cout* and printer output.

2. What will the following statement do?

   `lineout << "Welcome to C++.";`

3. Determine whether the following statements are valid or invalid:
   a. `cout << "This is a valid printer statement.";`
   b. `printer >> "This is a valid printer statement.";`
   c. `dataOut >> "This is a valid printer statement.";`

## Sample Program CHAP4C

Sample program CHAP4C (Figure 4.11, p. 116) computes and prints the daily billing log for Action Advertising. Figure 4.12 (p. 119) shows the output for CHAP4C. The program specifications are shown below.

**Input (keyboard):**

Prompt for and enter the following data (enter "stop run" to quit):

| Client's Name | Time Spent on Account | Hourly Charge |
|---|---|---|
| Carson Pontiac | 3.0 | 50.00 |
| Bright Cleaners | 5.1 | 75.00 |
| Davis Delivery | 1.6 | 35.00 |
| Terrace TV | 2.4 | 45.00 |
| Zenkido Karate | 2.9 | 35.00 |
```

Output (printer):

Print the daily billing log (see Figure 4.12)

Processing Requirements:

- Compute the bill:
  time × charge
- Accumulate a total for the daily bill.
- Compute the average daily bill:
  total bill / number of clients

Pseudocode:

```
START
Clear the screen
Print report titles and headings
Prompt and enter client's name
LOOP until name = "stop run"
    Prompt and enter time spent on account
    Prompt and enter hourly charge
    Add 1 to client count
    Compute client's bill
    Accumulate total bill
    Print client's bill
Prompt and enter client's name
End LOOP
Compute average bill
Print total and average bill
END
```

Hierarchy Chart: See Figure 4.9.

Program Flowchart: See Figure 4.10.

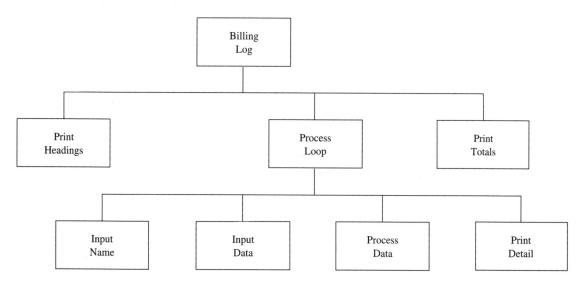

FIGURE 4.9   Hierarchy Chart for CHAP4C

MAINLINE

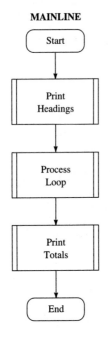

PROCESS LOOP

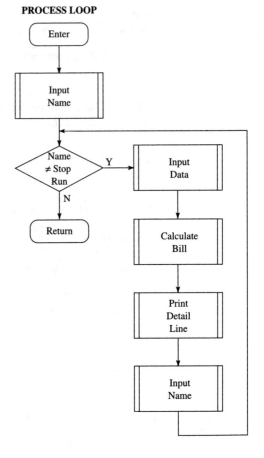

PRINT HEADINGS

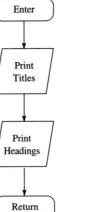

INPUT NAME

FIGURE 4.10   Program Flowchart for CHAP4C

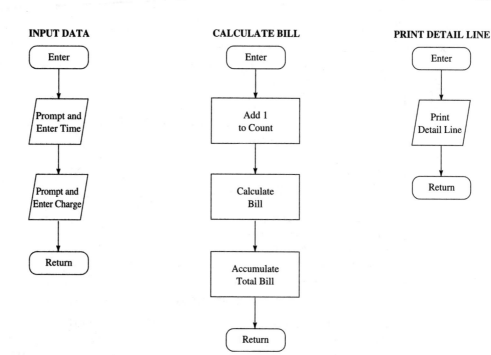

INPUT DATA

Enter

Prompt and
Enter Time

Prompt and
Enter Charge

Return

CALCULATE BILL

Enter

Add 1
to Count

Calculate
Bill

Accumulate
Total Bill

Return

PRINT DETAIL LINE

Enter

Print
Detail Line

Return

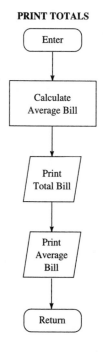

PRINT TOTALS

Enter

Calculate
Average Bill

Print
Total Bill

Print
Average
Bill

Return

FIGURE 4.10 *Continued*

```
//---------- BILLING LOG ---------------------------------
//        Compute and print the daily billing log for Action
//        Advertising.
//
//              PROGRAM-ID: CHAP4C
//              PROGRAMMER: David M. Collopy
//              RUN DATE:   mm/dd/yy
//
//*********************************************************

//---------- PREPROCESSING DIRECTIVES----------------------

#include <iostream.h>
#include <fstream.h>
#include <iomanip.h>
#include <conio.h>
#include <string.h>

//---------- FUNCTION PROTOTYPES--------------------------

void PrnHeadings(void);          // print headings
void ProcessLoop(void);          // processing loop
void InputName(void);            // input client's name
void InputData(void);            // input billing data
void CalcBill(void);             // calculate bill
void PrnDetail(void);            // print detail line
void PrnTotals(void);            // print total line

//---------- PROGRAM SETUP -------------------------------
char PT1[] = "     A C T I O N   A D V E R T I S I N G";
char PT2[] = "               Daily Billing Log";
char HL1[] = "               Time Spent    Hourly     Daily";
char HL2[] = "   Account     on Account    Charge      Bill";
char TL1[] = "Total Daily Billing:              $";
char TL2[] = "Average Daily Billing:            $";

char  name[16];                  // client's full name
int   count;                     // number of clients
float time,                      // time spent on account
      charge,                    // hourly charge for work
      bill,                      // client's daily bill
      totalBill,                 // report total billing
      avrBill;                   // report average billing
ofstream printer("PRN");         // open printer file

//-------------------------------------------------------
//              MAINLINE CONTROL
//-------------------------------------------------------
```

FIGURE 4.11   Sample Program CHAP4C: Compute and Print the Daily Billing Log for Action Advertising

```
main()
{
    PrnHeadings();                  // print headings
    ProcessLoop();                  // processing loop
    PrnTotals();                    // print total lines
    printer.close();                // close printer file
    return 0;
}
//------------------------------------------------------------
//              PRINT HEADINGS
//------------------------------------------------------------
void PrnHeadings(void)
{
    printer << "\f";                // reset to top of page
    printer << PT1 << endl;         // print page title-1
    printer << PT2 << endl;         // print page title-2
    printer << "\n\n";              // double space
    printer << HL1 << endl;         // print heading line-1
    printer << HL2 << endl;         // print heading line-2
    printer << endl;                // single space
    return;
}
//------------------------------------------------------------
//              PROCESSING LOOP
//------------------------------------------------------------
void ProcessLoop(void)
{
    InputName();                    // input client's name
    while (strcmp(name, "stop run") != 0)  {
        InputData();                // input billing data
        CalcBill();                 // calculate bill
        PrnDetail();                // print detail line
        InputName();                // input client's name
    }
    return;
}
//------------------------------------------------------------
//              INPUT CLIENT'S NAME
//------------------------------------------------------------
void InputName(void)
{
    clrscr();
    cout << "Enter client or 'stop' to quit: ";
    cin.get(name, 15);              // get name only
    return;
}
//------------------------------------------------------------
//              INPUT BILLING DATA
```

(continued on next page)

FIGURE 4.11 *Continued*

```
//-----------------------------------------------------------
void InputData(void)
{
    cout << "Enter time spent on account: ";
    cin >> time;
    cout << "        Enter hourly charge: ";
    cin >> charge;
    cin.get();                     // clear keyboard buffer
    return;
}
//-----------------------------------------------------------
//              CALCULATE BILL
//-----------------------------------------------------------
void CalcBill(void)
{
    count++;
    bill = time * charge;
    totalBill = totalBill + bill;
    return;
}
//-----------------------------------------------------------
//              PRINT DETAIL LINE
//-----------------------------------------------------------
void PrnDetail(void)
{
    printer << setiosflags(ios::left)      // left justify
            << setw(15) << name
            << resetiosflags(ios::left)    // right justify
            << setiosflags(ios::fixed)
            << setiosflags(ios::showpoint)
            << setw(6) << setprecision(1) << time
            << setw(13) << setprecision(2) << charge
            << setw(11) << bill << endl;
    return;
}
//-----------------------------------------------------------
//              PRINT TOTAL LINES
//-----------------------------------------------------------
void PrnTotals(void)
{
    avrBill = totalBill / count;
    printer << endl;
    printer << TL1 << setw(6) << totalBill << endl;
    printer << TL2 << setw(6) << avrBill << endl;
    return;
}
```

FIGURE 4.11 *Continued*

```
            A C T I O N   A D V E R T I S I N G
                 Daily Billing Log

                   Time Spent      Hourly      Daily
        Account     on Account     Charge       Bill

    Carson Pontiac      3.0         50.00      150.00
    Bright Cleaners     5.1         75.00      382.50
    Davis Delivery      1.6         35.00       56.00
    Terrace TV          2.4         45.00      108.00
    Zenkido Karate      2.9         35.00      101.50

    Total Daily Billing:                    $ 798.00
    Average Daily Billing:                  $ 159.60
```

FIGURE 4.12   Program Output for CHAP4C

Dissection of Sample Program CHAP4C

Since we have seen most of the code before, we will focus on how the titles and column headings were defined and printed on the report.

PROGRAM SETUP:

```
char PT1[] = "        A C T I O N   A D V E R T I S I N G";
char PT2[] = "                Daily Billing Log";
```

The above statements mean: Assign the literal strings to the page titles, *PT1* and *PT2*. The lengths of the variables are implicitly determined by the number of characters in the strings.

```
char HL1[] = "                Time Spent      Hourly      Daily";
char HL2[] = "      Account    on Account     Charge       Bill";
```

The previous statements mean: Assign the literal strings to the heading line variables, *HL1* and *HL2*.

```
char TL1[] = "Total Daily Billing:                    $";
char TL2[] = "Average Daily Billing:                  $";
```

The above statements mean: Assign the literal strings to the total line variables, *TL1* and *TL2*.

```
char   name[16];
int    count;
float  time,
       charge,
       bill,
       totalBill,
       avrBill;
```

The above statements define the variables required by the program to process the input and to produce the output.

PRINT HEADINGS:

```
void PrnHeadings(void)
{
    printer << "\f";
    printer << PT1 << endl;
    printer << PT2 << endl;
    printer << "\n\n";
    printer << HL1 << endl;
    printer << HL2 << endl;
    printer << endl;
    return;
}
```

The above statements print the report titles and column headings on the printer. Look at the first statement. The \f escape character causes the printer to advance to the top of the next page. Hence, the titles and column headings will be printed on the top of the page.

Notice that we may use either the \n (newline character) or the *endl* (end line) symbol to advance to the next line.

PRINT DETAIL LINE:

```
void PrnDetail(void)
{
    printer << setiosflags(ios::left)
            << setw(15) << name
            << resetiosflags(ios::left)
            << setiosflags(ios::fixed)
            << setiosflags(ios::showpoint)
            << setw(6) << setprecision(1) << time
            << setw(13) << setprecision(2) << charge
            << setw(11) << bill << endl;
    return;
}
```

The above statements format and print the detail lines. The *(ios::left)* format flag was used twice, once to set justification to left (to print the client's name) and once to reset justification back to the default value of right. Again, this was done to get around a compiler error. Other compilers may react differently and require the *setiosflags(ios::right)* manipulator to set justification back to right. Your instructor or supervisor will let you know which manipulator to use.

Summary

1. The strcat() function joins two strings—concatenates one string to another.

2. The strcpy() function copies one string to another.

3. The strcmp() function compares two strings. If they are equal, the function returns a zero. If the first string is less than the second, the function returns a negative value. If the first string is greater than the second, the function returns a positive value.

4. The strlen() function returns the number of characters found in the string argument, excluding the null character.

5. The function cin.get(name, 15) reads up to 15 characters from the keyboard buffer and assigns the input to the identifier *name*. This form of the function is primarily used to read a series of words from the keyboard.

6. The cin.get() function may also be used to clear the keyboard buffer. This form of the function is often used to prevent bad data from entering the program.

7. Iteration is the process of repeating a series of statements a specific number of times.

8. A loop represents a logic structure that processes a set of instructions repetitively until a condition is met. The body of a loop represents the section of code that is repeated during the iteration process.

9. Relational operators are used to set up conditions or relational tests that compare two values.

10. The logical operators, &&, ||, and !, are used to implement compound conditions. A compound condition consists of two or more simple relational tests that are connected by the logical operators.

11. Each time a *while* statement is encountered, the condition is tested. As long as the test is true, the statements inside the loop are executed. The looping process continues until the ending condition is satisfied.

12. On the first pass, the *do/while* loop performs the statements inside the loop before testing the condition. Here, the condition is evaluated at the end of the loop to determine whether to continue or to exit the loop.

13. The *for* statement represents a counter-controlled loop that automatically initializes, tests, and modifies the control variable. A *for* loop should be used when the number of iterations is known.

14. A nested loop is a loop within a loop. Nested loops may be constructed with the *while, do/while*, or *for* statements. They may be mixed or matched.

15. Setting up the printer for output involves including the *fstream.h* header file in the program, assigning a name to the printer, and declaring the name as the output file stream.

16. The *fstream.h* header file, together with the *ofstream* member function, allows the program to direct the output to the printer. The device name *PRN* associates the output object with the printer.

Programming Projects

For each project, design the logic and write the modular structured program to produce the output. Model your program after the samples presented in the chapter. Verify your output.

Project 4–1   Charge Account

Write a program to compute and print a report showing the month-end balance for each customer. Assume an annual finance rate of 18% on the unpaid balance.

Input (keyboard):

For each customer, prompt for and enter the following data:

Customer Name	Previous Balance	Payments & Credits	Purchases & Charges
Allen	5000.00	0.00	200.00
Davis	2150.00	150.00	0.00
Fisher	3400.00	400.00	100.00
Navarez	625.00	125.00	74.00
Stiers	820.00	0.00	0.00
Wyatt	1070.00	200.00	45.00

Output (printer):

Print the following customer accounts report:

```
Author                    CUSTOMER ACCOUNTS              Page 01
                              mm/dd/yy


Customer   Previous    Payments    Purchases    Finance    Month-end
Name       Balance     & Credits   & Charges    Charge     Balance

X-------X  9999.99     9999.99     9999.99      999.99     9999.99
   :          :           :           :           :           :
   :          :           :           :           :           :
X-------X  9999.99     9999.99     9999.99      999.99     9999.99

Totals:    99999.99    99999.99    99999.99     9999.99    99999.99
```

Processing Requirements:

- Compute the new balance:
  previous balance – payments + purchases
- Compute the finance charge:
  new balance × (annual rate / 12)
- Compute the month-end balance:
  new balance + finance charge
- Accumulate totals for previous balance, payments, purchases, finance charge, and month-end balance.

Project 4–2   Payroll

Write a program to calculate and print a weekly payroll roster. Assume the current federal income tax (FIT) rate is 15%.

Input (keyboard):

For each employee, prompt for and enter the following payroll data:

Employee Name	Hours Worked	Hourly Pay Rate
T. Bauer	40	7.50
S. Erickson	38	12.00
S. Howard	40	9.75

D. Miller	40	10.25
B. Rossi	35	8.00
T. York	36	11.00

Output (printer):

Print the following payroll report:

```
Author                  WEEKLY PAYROLL REPORT              Page 01
                             mm/dd/yy


Employee    Hours    Hourly
Name        Worked   Pay Rate   Gross Pay    FIT     Net Pay

X-------X     99       99.99       999.99    99.99    999.99
    :         :          :           :         :        :
    :         :          :           :         :        :
X-------X     99       99.99       999.99    99.99    999.99

              Totals:            9999.99   999.99   9999.99

              Average Net Pay:                       9999.99
```

Processing Requirements:

- Compute the gross pay:
  hours × pay rate
- Compute the federal income tax:
  gross pay × FIT rate
- Compute the net pay:
  gross pay – FIT
- Accumulate totals for gross pay, FIT, and net pay.
- Compute the average net pay:
  total net pay / number of employees

Project 4–3   Sales

Write a program to calculate and print a sales report.

Input (keyboard):

For each salesperson, prompt for and enter the following sales data:

Salesperson	Total Sales	Cost of Sales
Lisa Conrad	8120.52	6450.71
Roy Hickle	2245.78	1072.49
Tara Perkins	12710.14	9735.38
Dennis Tian	4567.51	3119.22
Ann Zimmerman	5793.59	4204.45

Output (printer):

Print the following sales report:

```
Author                  SALES REPORT                      Page 01
                             mm/dd/yy
```

```
Salesperson    Total Sales    Cost of Sales    Net Profit
-----------------------------------------------------------
X---------X      99999.99        99999.99        99999.99
    :               :               :               :
    :               :               :               :
X---------X      99999.99        99999.99        99999.99
                                 Total:          999999.99

                                 Average:         99999.99
```

Processing Requirements:

- Compute the net profit:
  total sales – cost of sales
- Accumulate a total for net profit.
- Compute average net profit:
  total net profit / number of salespeople

Project 4–4   Inventory

Write a program to compute and print an inventory profit report.

Input (keyboard):

For each item, prompt for and enter the following inventory data:

Item Number	Description	Quantity on Hand	Unit Cost	Selling Price
1000	Hammers	24	4.75	9.49
2000	Saws	14	7.50	14.99
3000	Drills	10	7.83	15.95
4000	Screwdrivers	36	2.27	4.98
5000	Pliers	12	2.65	5.49

Output (printer):

Print the following inventory profit report:

```
Author           INVENTORY PROFIT REPORT        Page 01
                       mm/dd/yy

Item Number    Description        Quantity    Item Profit
   9999        X----------X          99         999.99
    :              :                  :            :
    :              :                  :            :
   9999        X----------X          99         999.99

                          Total Profit:        9999.99
```

Processing Requirements:

- Compute the total cost:
  quantity × unit cost
- Compute the total income:
  quantity × selling price

- Compute the item profit:
  total income − total cost
- Accumulate a total for item profit.

Project 4–5   Personnel

Write a program to compute and print the annual salary report for the personnel department.

Input (keyboard):

For each employee, prompt for and enter the following personnel data:

Employee Number	Employee Name	Department Number	Annual Salary	Percent Increase
1926	Dana Andrews	10	29000	0.10
2071	Scott Cooper	14	30250	0.12
3550	Todd Feldman	22	24175	0.07
4298	Lori Palmer	35	33400	0.11
5409	Bob Shields	47	27500	0.08
6552	Pam Wolfe	31	31773	0.10

Output (printer):

Print the following personnel report:

```
Author                 PERSONNEL ANNUAL SALARY REPORT          Page 01
                              mm/dd/yy


---- Employee ----      Dept.    Old       Dollar
Number    Last Name     Number   Salary    Increase    New Salary

 9999   X----------X      99    99999.99   9999.99      99999.99
   :         :             :        :         :            :
   :         :             :        :         :            :
 9999   X----------X      99    99999.99   9999.99      99999.99

                               Total:   99999.99     999999.99

             Average Dollar Increase:   9999.99
```

Processing Requirements:

- Compute the dollar increase:
  old salary × % increase
- Compute the new salary:
  old salary + dollar increase
- Accumulate totals for dollar increase and new salary.
- Compute the average dollar increase:
  total dollar increase / number of employees

Project 4–6   Accounts Payable

Write a program to compute and print an accounts payable report.

Input (keyboard):

For each vendor, prompt for and enter the following data:

Vendor Number	Vendor Name	Invoice Number	Invoice Amount	Discount Rate
217	Metacraft	A1239	2309.12	0.10
349	IntraTell	T9823	670.00	0.09
712	Reylock	F0176	4563.78	0.12
501	Universal	W0105	1200.00	0.09
196	Northland	X2781	3429.34	0.10

Output (printer):

Print the following accounts payable report:

```
Author                  ACCOUNTS PAYABLE              Page 01
                            mm/dd/yy


Vendor              Invoice    Invoice    Discount   Amount
Number  Vendor Name Number     Amount     Amount     Due

 999    X--------X   XXXX      9999.99    999.99     9999.99
  :        :          :          :          :          :
  :        :          :          :          :          :
 999    X--------X   XXXX      9999.99    999.99     9999.99

            Totals:           99999.99   9999.99    99999.99
```

Processing Requirements:

- Compute the discount amount:
  invoice amount × discount rate
- Compute the amount due:
  invoice amount – discount amount
- Accumulate totals for invoice amount, discount amount, and amount due.

Project 4–7   Production Output

Write a program to compute and print a production cost report.

Input (keyboard):

For each item, prompt for and enter the following production data:

Employee Name	Product Number	Units Produced	Unit Cost
Alan Baum	A1234	24	5.50
Marie Fitch	C4510	36	7.94
Lee Hildebrand	R0934	18	6.75
David Mullins	E3371	36	3.79
Nicole Renner	H9733	24	4.25
Erica Tate	Z0182	27	8.10
Terry West	A3235	30	2.95

Output (printer):

Print the following production report:

```
Author          PRODUCTION COST REPORT       Page 01
                      mm/dd/yy

        Product      Units         Unit       Production
        Number       Produced      Cost       Cost

        XXXXX          99          99.99        999.99
          :            :            :             :
          :            :            :             :
        XXXXX          99          99.99        999.99

        Totals:       999         999.99       9999.99
```

Processing Requirements:

- Compute the production cost:
  units produced × unit cost
- Accumulate totals for units produced, unit cost, and production cost.

5   Branching

Learning Objectives

After you have read this chapter and completed the exercises, you should be able to:

- distinguish between conditional and unconditional branching
- use *if* and *if/else* decision statements to select alternate processing paths
- code nested decisions using the *if* and *if/else* statements
- use the *switch* and *break* statements to code multipath decisions
- understand why programmers avoid the *goto* statement

Selecting Alternate Processing Paths

Decision processing is common to most programming applications. Computers can be programmed to do much more than repeat a series of statements over and over again. In this chapter, we will learn how to code decision tests that will be used to select and perform alternate processing tasks.

In programming, decisions can be made by comparing two values to see if one is equal to, greater than, or less than the other. Based on the outcome, control branches to the appropriate statement or module and performs the processing given there. In other words, the computer can be programmed to select and follow a particular course of action depending on the comparative values of two data items.

Consider for example, the following segment that determines the sales commission rate:

```
if (salesIncome < 5000)
   commRate = .05;
else
   commRate = .07;
```

According to the code, if *salesIncome* is less than $5,000, the commission rate is set to 5%. Else, the rate is set to 7%.

Unconditional and Conditional Branching

In programming, there are two types of branch statements: unconditional and conditional. An **unconditional branch** sends control directly to a specific location in the program. In English, for example, the statement "Go to work" tells us unconditionally *what to do—go to work*. Unconditional branches are implemented with the *goto* statement.

On the other hand, a **conditional branch** is taken only if a certain condition is met. Once again, in English, the statement "If it is snowing, wear your boots" tells us conditionally when to wear our boots. Conditional branches are implemented with the *if, if/else*, and *switch* statements.

The if Statement

Format:
```
if (condition)  {
    statements;
}
```

Purpose: To set up a conditional branch. The commands in the body of the *if* statement are executed only if the condition or relation test is true. Otherwise, control skips the statement body and continues with the first command after the *if*. The braces may be omitted when the body contains only one statement.

Examples:
```
1. if (credits < 45)  {
      cout << "Welcome freshman";
  }
```

If credit hours are less than 45, then print the welcome message.

```
2. if (payment > balance)   {
      cout << "Customer overpaid";
      cout << "Credit the account";
   }
```

If *payment* is greater than *balance*, then print the overpaid message.

Nested if Statements

Format:

```
if (condition1)   {
    if (condition2)   {
        statements;
        . . . . .
    }
}
```

Purpose: To set up a multiconditional branch. A **nested** *if* statement consists of at least one *if* inside the branch of another. According to the format, the statement body is executed only if all the conditions are true. Any time a condition is false, control exits and continues with the first command after the nested *if* statement.

Example:

Two-level nested *if* statement

```
if (credits < 45)   {
    if (female == 1)   {
        femaleFresh++;
        cout << "Welcome lady freshman";
    {
{
```

If credit hours are less than 45 and the student is a female, then add 1 to the female freshmen counter and print the welcome message.

The if/else Statement

Format:

```
if (condition)   {
    true path;
}
else   {
    false path;
}
```

Purpose: To set up a two-way conditional branch. This command performs the statement body of the true path only if the condition is true. Otherwise, control performs the statement body of the false path.

After executing either the true or false path, control skips to the first command after the *if/else* statement. We may omit the braces when the body contains only one statement.

Examples:

```
1. if (credits < 45)   {
       cout << "Welcome freshman";
   }
   else   {
       cout << "Welcome upperclassman";
   }
```

If credit hours are less than 45, then print `Welcome freshman`. Else, print `Welcome upperclassman`.

```
2. if (payment > balance)   {
       cout << "Customer overpaid";
       cout << "Credit the account";
   }
   else   {
       cout << "Thank you for your payment";
   }
```

If *payment* is greater than *balance*, then print the overpaid message. Else, print the thank you notice.

Nested if/else Statements

Format:

```
if (condition1)   {
    statements;
}
else if (condition2)   {
    statements;
    .....
}
```

Purpose: To set up a multipath conditional branch. A **nested** *if/else* consists of at least one *if/else* inside the false path of another. If a given condition is true, the program executes the statement body of the true path and then skips to the first command after the nested *if/else* statement. For nested *if/else* statements, each *else* is paired with the nearest *if*.

Example:

```
if (credits < 45)   {
    cout << "Welcome freshman";
}
else if (credits < 90)   {
    cout << "Welcome sophomore";
}
else if (credits < 135)   {
    cout << "Welcome junior";
}
else   {
    cout << "Welcome senior";
}
```

If a condition is true, the program prints the corresponding welcome message, control exits the nested *if/else* statement, and processing continues with the first executable statement after the closing brace. For example, if credit hours equal 120, the program prints the message `Welcome junior` and control skips to the first statement after the closing brace.

Note that credit hours exceeding 134 will automatically produce the message `Welcome senior`. Also note that each *else* is paired with the nearest *if*—the third *else* is paired to the third *if*, the second *else* is paired to the second *if*, and so forth.

Checkpoint 5A

1. Distinguish between *unconditional* and *conditional* branching.
2. Identify the type of branching (conditional or unconditional) that occurs with the following statements:
   a. *if*
   b. *goto*
   c. *if/else*
3. What will print when the following statements are executed?

   a.
```
purchase = 450;
if (purchase > 500)   {
    cout << "Thank you for your purchase.";
}
else   {
    cout << "Thank you.";
}
```

   b.
```
purchase = 20.00;
taxBracket = 1;
if (taxBracket < 2)   {
    tax = purchase * 0.03;
    cout << "Tax = " << tax;
}
```

   c.
```
purchase = 50.00;
taxBracket = 3;
if (taxBracket < 2)   {
    tax = purchase * 0.03;
}
else   {
    tax = purchase * 0.05;
}
cout << "Tax = " << tax;
```

   d.
```
color = 4;
if (color < 10)   {
    if (color == 4)   {
        cout << "Color is Red.";
}
```

   e.
```
color = 7;
if (color < 10)   {
    if (color == 4)   {
        cout << "Color is Red.";
    }
}
```

Sample Program CHAP5A

Beale-Ross Corporation pays its sales staff on commission as follows:

	Commission Formula
0 < sales <= 10,000	.10 (sales)
10,000 < sales <= 20,000	1,000 + .07 (sales − 10,000)
20,000 < sales <= 35,000	1,700 + .05 (sales − 20,000)
35,000 < sales	2,450 + .02 (sales − 35,000)

Write a program to compute the earned commission for the sales staff, print the monthly sales report, and show the top salesperson for the month. Sample program CHAP5A is shown in Figure 5.3 (p. 138); the program's output is shown in Figure 5.4 (p. 141).

Input (keyboard):

For each salesperson, prompt for and enter the following sales data:

> Salesperson number
> Salesperson name
> Monthly sales amount

Output (printer):

Print the monthly sales report shown in Figure 5.4.

Processing Requirements:

- Determine the sales commission based on the monthly sales (see the commission schedule).
- Determine the top salesperson and the top sales amount based on the highest monthly sales.
- At the end of the report, print the top salesperson and the top sales amount.

Pseudocode:

> START
> Clear screen
> Print report titles and headings
> Prompt and enter salesperson number
> LOOP until number = 0
>   Prompt and enter salesperson name
>   Prompt and enter monthly sales
>   Compute sales commission
>   Determine top salesperson
>   Print detail line
>   Prompt and enter salesperson number
> End LOOP
> Print top salesperson and sales
> END

Hierarchy Chart: See Figure 5.1.

Program Flowchart: See Figure 5.2 (p. 136).

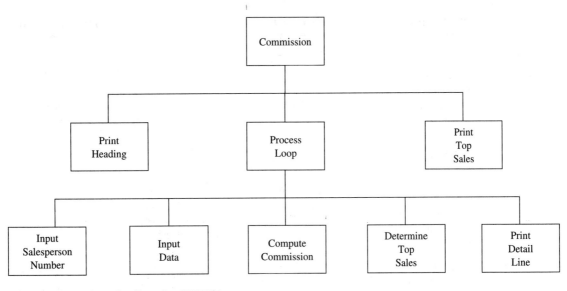

FIGURE 5.1 Hierarchy Chart for CHAP5A

Dissection of Sample Program CHAP5A

Walk through the program code shown in Figure 5.3. As usual, the preprocessing directives and the function prototypes are defined at the top of the program. However, the *PROGRAM SETUP* is organized a little differently. It is divided into three sections: One for the report titles and column headings, one for the input sales record, and one for the program constants and variables.

This particular arrangement makes the *PROGRAM SETUP* easier to read. Let's take a closer look at the processing performed by the input and calculation modules.

```
INPUT SALESPERSON NUMBER:

void InputNum(void)
{
    clrscr();
    cout << "Enter salesperson number('0' to quit): ";
    cin >> salesNum;
    cin.get();
    return;
}
```

The above statements prompt the user to enter the salesperson number. The *cin* statement gets the salesperson number, whereas the *cin.get()* removes the Enter key that was pressed and clears the input buffer.

If the buffer is not cleared at this point, the Enter key will be assigned to the salesperson's name when control branches to the *InputData* module.

Note: When in doubt, the safest rule to follow is to clear the keyboard buffer after each *cin* statement.

MAIN LINE

Start

Print
Headings

Process
Loop

Print
Top
Sales

End

PROCESS LOOP

Enter

Input
Number

(A)

Number ≠ 0 — Y → Input Data

N

Return

Compute
Commission

Determine
Top
Sales

Print
Detail
Line

Input
Number

(A)

PRINT HEADING

Enter

Print
Titles

Print
Headings

Return

PRINT DETAIL LINE

Enter

Print
Detail
Line

Return

PRINT TOP SALES

Enter

Print
Top
Name

Print
Top
Sales

Return

FIGURE 5.2 Program Flowchart for CHAP5A

COMPUTE COMMISSION

DETERMINE TOP SALES

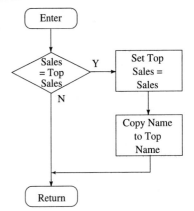

INPUT NUMBER

```
        Enter

    Prompt
    and Enter
    Number

       Return
```

INPUT DATA

```
        Enter

    Prompt
    and Enter
    Name

    Prompt
    and Enter
    Sales

       Return
```

FIGURE 5.2 *Continued*

```
INPUT SALES DATA:

void InputData(void)
{
    cout << "Enter salesperson name: ";
    cin.get(name, 20);
```

```
//---------- COMMISSION ----------------------------------
//    Compute and print a monthly sales commission report
//    for the Beale-Ross Corporation.
//
//             PROGRAM-ID: CHAP5A
//             PROGRAMMER: David M. Collopy
//             RUN DATE:   mm/dd/yy
//
//*************************************************************

#include<iostream.h>
#include<fstream.h>
#include<iomanip.h>
#include<conio.h>
#include<string.h>

//---------- FUNCTION PROTOTYPE ---------------------------

void PrnHeadings(void);         // print headings
void ProcessLoop(void);         // processing loop
void InputNum(void);            // input salesperson number
void InputData(void);           // input sales data
void CalcCommis(void);          // calculate commission
void FindTopPerson(void);       // find top salesperson
void PrnDetail(void);           // print detail line
void PrnTopPerson(void);        // print top salesperson

//---------- PROGRAM SETUP --------------------------------

//** H E A D I N G   L I N E S

char PT1[] = " B E A L E - R O S S   C O R P O R A T I O N";
char PT2[] = "            Monthly Sales Report";
char HL1[] = "S a l e s p e r s o n      Monthly      Earned";
char HL2[] = "Num    Name                Sales    Commission";
char HL3[] = "--------------------------------------------";
char SL1[] = "Top Salesperson: ";
char SL2[] = "      Top Sales: ";

//** S A L E S   R E C O R D
int    salesNum;                // salesperson number
char   name[21];                // salesperson name
float  sales;                   // monthly sales

//** P R O G R A M   V A R I A B L E S

float commission;               // sales commission
```

FIGURE 5.3 Sample Program CHAP5A: Compute and Print the Monthly Sales Report for the Beale-Ross Corporation

```
char   topName[21];                 // top salesperson
float topSales = 0.0;               // top sales amount

//** O P E N   P R I N T E R   F I L E

ofstream prnt("PRN");               // open printer file


//-----------------------------------------------------------
//             MAINLINE CONTROL
//-----------------------------------------------------------
main()
{
    PrnHeadings();                  // print headings
    ProcessLoop();                  // processing loop
    PrnTopPerson();                 // print top salesperson
    printer.close();                // close printer file
    return 0;
}
//-----------------------------------------------------------
//             PRINT HEADINGS
//-----------------------------------------------------------
void PrnHeadings(void)
{
    prnt << "\f";                   // reset to top of page
    prnt << PT1 << endl;            // print page title-1
    prnt << PT2 << endl;            // print page title-2
    prnt << "\n\n";                 // double space
    prnt << HL1 << endl;            // print heading line-1
    prnt << HT2 << endl;            // print heading line-2
    prnt << HL3 << endl;            // print heading line-3
    prnt << endl;                   // single space
    return;
}
//-----------------------------------------------------------
//             PROCESSING LOOP
//-----------------------------------------------------------
void ProcessLoop(void)
{
    InputNum();                     // input salesperson number
    while (salesNum != 0)  {
        InputData();                // input sales data
        CalcCommis();               // calculate commission
        FindTopPerson();            // find top salesperson
        PrnDetail();                // print detail line
        InputNum();                 // input salesperson number
    }
    return;
}
```

(continued on next page)

FIGURE 5.3   *Continued*

```
//-----------------------------------------------------------
//                INPUT SALESPERSON NUMBER
//-----------------------------------------------------------
void InputNum(void)
{
    clrscr();                         // clear screen
    cout << "Enter salesperson number('0' to quit): ";
    cin >> salesNum;                  // get salesperson number
    cin.get();                        // clear keyboard buffer
    return;
}
//-----------------------------------------------------------
//                INPUT SALES DATA
//-----------------------------------------------------------
void InputData(void)
{
    cout << "Enter salesperson name: ";
    cin.get(name, 20);                // get name only
    cout << "   Enter monthly sales: ";
    cin >> sales;                     // get monthly sales
    return;
}
//-----------------------------------------------------------
//                CALCULATE COMMISSION
//-----------------------------------------------------------
void CalcCommis(void)
{
    if (sales > 35000.00)
        commission = 2450.00 + 0.02 * (sales - 35000.00);
    else if (sales > 20000.00)
        commission = 1700.00 + 0.05 * (sales - 20000.00);
    else if (sales > 10000.00)
        commission = 1000.00 + 0.07 * (sales - 10000.00);
    else
        commission = sales * 0.10;
    return;
}
//-----------------------------------------------------------
//                FIND TOP SALESPERSON
//-----------------------------------------------------------
void FindTopPerson(void)
{
    if (sales > topSales)  {
        topSales = sales;
        strcpy(topName, name);
    return;
}
//-----------------------------------------------------------
```

FIGURE 5.3 *Continued*

```
//                  PRINT DETAIL LINE
//------------------------------------------------------------
void PrnDetail(void)
{
    prnt << salesNum << "   "
         << setiosflags(ios::left)      // left justify
         << setw(20) << name
         << resetiosflags(ios::left)    // right justify
         << setiosflags(ios::fixed)
         << setiosflags(ios::showpoint)
         << setw(9)  << setprecison(2) << sales
         << setw(11) << commission << endl;
    return;
}
//------------------------------------------------------------
//               PRINT TOP SALESPERSON
//------------------------------------------------------------
void PrnTopPerson(void)
{
    prnt << "\n\n";
    prnt << setiosflags(ios::left)      // left justify
         << SL1 << setw(20) << topName << endl;
    prnt << resetiosflags(ios::left)    // right justify
         << SL2 << setw(6) << topSales << endl;
    return;
}
```

FIGURE 5.3   *Continued*

```
    B E A L E - R O S S    C O R P O R A T I O N
              Monthly Sales Report

S a l e s p e r s o n       Monthly         Earned
Num     Name                Sales        Commissions
------------------------------------------------------
1000    Travis Coleman      34000.00      2400.00
2000    Katrina Lopez       50000.00      2750.00
3000    Mark Chen           25000.00      1950.00
4000    Erin Hessler        41200.00      2574.00
5000    Matt Wright         33170.00      2358.50


Top Salesperson:  Katrina Lopez
    Total Sales:  50000.00
```

FIGURE 5.4   Printer Output for CHAP5A

These statements (p. 137) mean: Prompt for and enter the salesperson's name. According to the *cin.get(name, 20)*, the input stream is read up to the Enter keycode (\n) and stored in the string variable called *name*.

```
cout << "   Enter monthly sales: ";
cin >> sales;
return;
}
```

The above statements prompt for and read the monthly sales. After reading the sales, control returns to the calling module.

CALCULATE COMMISSION:

```
void CalcCommis(void)
{
    if (sales > 35000.00)
        commission = 2450 + 0.02 * (sales - 35000.00);
    else if (sales > 20000.00)
        commission = 1700 + 0.05 * (sales - 20000.00);
    else if (sales > 10000.00)
        commission = 1000 + 0.07 * (sales - 10000.00);
    else
        commission = sales * 0.10;
    return;
}
```

The nested *if/else* starts by comparing *sales* to 35,000.00. If *sales* exceeds 35,000.00, then compute commission according to the formula given and skip to the return statement. Else, branch to the false path and compare *sales* to 20,000.00. This process continues until either a match is found or commission is assigned the default value.

FIND TOP SALESPERSON:

```
void TopSales(void)
{
    if (sales > topSales)   {
        topSales = sales;
        strcpy(topName, name);
    }
    return;
}
```

The above segment locates the top salesperson and sale. Since *topSales* was initially set to zero, the first comparison automatically assigns *sales* to *topSales*. Thereafter, *sales* is assigned to *topSales* only if it is the greater of the two.

The switch and break Statements

Format:

```
switch (expression)   {
case label1:
    statement(s);
```

```
        break;
case label2:
    statement(s);
    break;
  .....

case labeln:
    statement(s);
    break;
default:
    statement(s);
    break;
}
```

Purpose: To set up a multipath conditional branch. The *switch* statement allows the program to select one option from a given set of options. First, the integer or character *expression* is compared to the case labels. Each label is unique and identifies a processing option or case. A case may have multiple labels and the actual number of cases depends mostly on the application at hand.

Second, if a match is found, control performs the statement(s) corresponding to the case. The program executes the statement body of the case until *break* is encountered. The **break** statement marks the end of the case and causes control to exit the *switch* statement.

However, if a match is not found, control performs the statements specified by the **default** case (the case that's left when no other cases apply). Although default is shown at the end, it may be placed anywhere within the *switch* statement.

Examples:

```
1. int choice;
   .....

   cout << "Enter your choice... \n";
   cout << "Movie menu: 1-Action, 2-Comedy, 3-Drama\n";
   cin >> choice;
   switch (choice)  {
   case 1:
       cout << "Action movie fan\n";
       break;
   case 2:
       cout << "Comedy movie fan\n";
       break;
   case 3:
       cout << "Drama movie fan\n";
       break;
   default:
       cout << "Invalid choice\n";
       break;
   }
```

The user selects a choice from the menu line. A menu line displays the list of options available to the user. For example, if the third option (*choice* = 3) is selected, then the message Drama movie fan appears on the screen. Any selection other than 1–3 produces the error message Invalid choice.

```
2. char choice;
   .....

   cout << "Enter your choice... ";
   cout << "Movie menu: A/ction, C/omedy, D/rama";
   cin >> choice;
   switch (choice)  {
   case 'A':
   case 'a':
       cout << "Action movie fan\n";
       break;
   case 'C':
   case 'c':
       cout << "Comedy movie fan\n";
       break;
   case 'D':
   case 'd':
       cout << "Drama movie fan\n";
       break;
   default:
       cout << "Invalid choice\n";
       break;
   }
```

Here, the users enter the letters of their choices. To select a comedy video, they press either C or c. According to the labels, the selection may be in either uppercase or lowercase. Of course, any selection other than the options given will result in the error message `Invalid choice`.

The goto and label Statements

Format:

```
goto label;
label: statement;
```

Purpose: To transfer the program control. The *goto* statement causes an unconditional branch to a label within the current module. A **label** is an identifier that is attached to a program statement. The labeled statement may be placed anywhere in the body of the module that the *goto* appears. Both the *goto* and *label* statements end with semicolons.

Examples:

1. Clear the screen:

```
count = 1;
repeat:
    cout << "\n";
    count++;
if (count < 25)
    goto repeat;
```

OUTPUT: a blank screen

As long as *count* is less than 25, the looping *cin* statement pushes the lines upward and off the screen.

2. Loop until score falls below 60 points:

```
for (count = 1; count < 25; count++)  {
    cout << "Enter score: ";
    cin >> score;
    if (score < 60)
        goto failed;
}

failed:
    cout << "\n Since the class did not pass the test,";
    cout << "\n a retest will be given on Friday.";
```

OUTPUT: none—unless score is less than 60

Caution: It would be wise to avoid the *goto* statement altogether. Unconditional branching encourages a patchwork (spaghetti code) style of programming that leads to messy code and unreliable performance. A *goto*-riddled program destroys the benefits of top-down design and modular structured programming by making the code harder (if not impossible) to read, understand, and maintain.

Checkpoint 5B

1. Why should we avoid using the *goto* statement?
2. For the following code, what will print when *E* is selected?

```
char selection;
.....

cout << "Enter your selection...";
cout << "Dining Menu: S/ide Dish, E/ntree, D/essert";
cin >> selection;
switch(selection)  {
case 'S':
case 's':
    cout << "Bean, Broccoli, Chili, Potato\n";
    break;
case 'E':
case 'e':
    cout << "Fish, Poultry, Beef, Pork\n";
    break;
case 'D':
case 'd':
    cout << "Cake, Pie, Ice Cream, Cookie\n";
    break;
default:
    cout << "Invalid choice\n";
    break;
}
```

3. Using the code given in 2, what will print when *A* is selected?

4. Using the following code, what will print when *s* is selected? Why?

```cpp
char selection;
.....

cout << "Enter your selection...";
cout << "Dining Menu: S/ide Dish, E/ntree, D/essert";
cin >> selection;
switch(selection)  {
case 'S':
case 's':
    cout << "Bean, Broccoli, Chili, Potato\n";
case 'E':
case 'e':
    cout << "Fish, Poultry, Beef, Pork\n";
case 'D':
case 'd':
    cout << "Cake, Pie, Ice Cream, Cookie\n";
default:
    cout << "Invalid choice\n";
}
```

Sample Program CHAP5B

Mayesville wants to offer youth sport programs to the elementary school children. Bob Kesler, director of Parks and Recreations, surveyed the elementary schools to find out what sport activities the children would be interested in playing.

Write a program to tabulate the results of the survey and to print a report showing each sport and the number of children interested in playing. Sample program CHAP5B is shown in Figure 5.7 (p. 150); the program's output is shown in Figure 5.8 (p. 152).

Input (keyboard):

Prompt for and enter choice:

   1-Baseball, 2-Football, 3-Basketball, 4-Soccer

Output (printer):

Print the sports survey report shown in Figure 5.8.

Processing Requirements:

Accumulate totals for each sport.

Pseudocode:

   START
   Clear screen
   Print report titles
   Prompt and enter choice

LOOP until choice = 0
    Accumulate totals for each sport
    Prompt and enter choice
End LOOP
Print the results of the survey
END

Hierarchy Chart: See Figure 5.5.

Program Flowchart: See Figure 5.6.

Dissection of Sample Program CHAP5B

```
MAINLINE CONTROL:
```

```c
main()
{
    PrnTitles();
    ProcessLoop();
    PrnOutput();
    prnt.close();
    return 0;
}
```

The previous statements mean: Call and execute the modules in the order given. The last module, *PrnOutput*, prints the body of the report.

```
PROCESSING LOOP:
```

```c
void ProcessLoop(void)
{
    SelectSport();
    while (choice != 0)   {
```

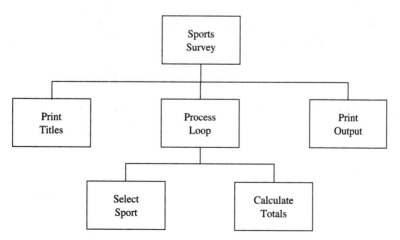

FIGURE 5.5   Hierarchy Chart for CHAP5B

```
        ComputeTotals();
        SelectSport();
    }
    return;
}
```

The above statements mean: Transfer control to *SelectSport* and prompt the user to select a sport. Compare the *choice* to 0. While *choice* is not 0, enter the loop. Else, skip the loop and return to the *MAINLINE*.

As long as *choice* is not 0, execute the calls in the order listed—*ComputeTotals* and *SelectSport*.

```
SELECT SPORT ACTIVITY:

void SelectSport(void)
{
    clrscr();
    cout << "\n\nSelect a sport or '0' to Quit: " <<endl;
    cout << "1-Baseball, 2-Football, 3-Basketball, 4-Soccer "
    <<endl;
    cin >> choice;
    cin.get();
    return;
}
```

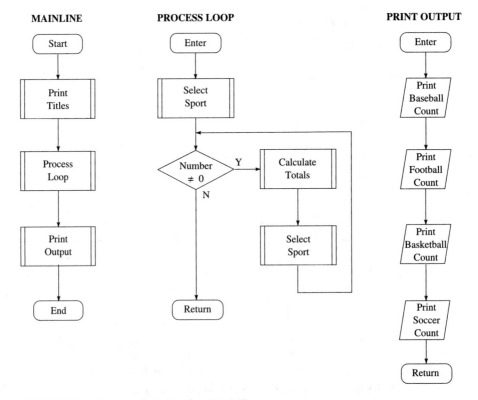

FIGURE 5.6   Program Flowchart for CHAP5B

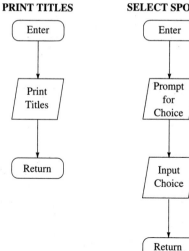

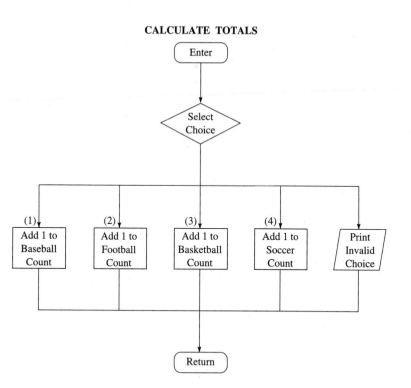

FIGURE 5.6   *Continued*

The previous statements prompt the user to either select a sport or enter 0 to quit. After the selection is assigned to *choice*, the program clears the keyboard buffer and control returns to the *ProcessLoop*.

```
//---------- SPORTS SURVEY -------------------------------
//     Compute and print the results of a sports survey.
//
//             PROGRAM-ID: CHAP5B
//             PROGRAMMER: David M. Collopy
//             RUN DATE:   mm/dd/yy
//
//*************************************************************

#include<iostream.h>
#include<fstream.h>
#include<iomanip.h>
#include<conio.h>
#include<string.h>


//---------- FUNCTION PROTOTYPE --------------------------

void PrnHeadings(void);          // print headings
void ProcessLoop(void);          // processing loop
void SelectSport(void);          // select sport activity
void CalcTotals(void);           // calculate sport totals
void PrnOutput(void);            // print report output

//---------- PROGRAM SETUP -------------------------------

//** H E A D I N G   L I N E S

char PT1[] = "  MAYESVILLE PARKS AND RECREATIONS DEPARTMENT";
char PT2[] = "              Youth Sports Survey";

//** P R O G R A M   R E C O R D
int   choice;                    // sports choice
      baseballCnt,               // baseball count
      footballCnt,               // football count
      basketballCnt,             // basketball count
      soccerCnt;                 // soccer count

//** O P E N   P R I N T E R   F I L E

ofstream prnt("PRN");            // open printer file


//--------------------------------------------------------
//             MAINLINE CONTROL
//--------------------------------------------------------
main()
{
    PrnTitles();                 // print titles
```

FIGURE 5.7 Sample Program CHAP5B: Compute and Print the Results of a Sports Survey

```
    ProcessLoop();              // processing loop
    PrnOutput();                // print report output
    prnt.close();               // close printer file
    return 0;
}
//------------------------------------------------------------
//              PRINT HEADINGS
//------------------------------------------------------------
void PrnHeadings(void)
{
    prnt << "\f";               // reset to top of page
    prnt << PT1 << endl;        // print page title-1
    prnt << PT2 << endl;        // print page title-2
    return;
}
//------------------------------------------------------------
//              PROCESSING LOOP
//------------------------------------------------------------
void ProcessLoop(void)
{
    SelectSport();              // select sport activity
    while (choice != 0)  {
        ComputeTotals();        // calculate sport totals
        SelectSport();          // select sport activity
    }
    return;
}
//------------------------------------------------------------
//              SELECT SPORT ACTIVITY
//------------------------------------------------------------
void SelectSport(void)
{
    clrscr();
    cout << "\n\nSelect a sport('0' to quit): "<< endl;
    cout << "1-Baseball, 2-Football, 3-Basketball, 4-Soccer "
        <<  endl;
    cin >> choice;              // get sport choice
    cin.get();                  // clear keyboard buffer
    return;
}
//------------------------------------------------------------
//              CALCULATE SPORT TOTALS
//------------------------------------------------------------
void CalcTotals(void)
{
    switch (choice)  {
```

(continued on next page)

FIGURE 5.7 *Continued*

```
        case 1:
            baseballCnt++;
            break;
        case 2:
            footballCnt++;
            break;
        case 3:
            basketballCnt++;
            break;
        case 4:
            soccerCnt++;
            break;
        default:
            cout << "\nError-invalid choice\n";
            break;
        }
    return;
    }
//----------------------------------------------------------
//              PRINT REPORT OUTPUT
//----------------------------------------------------------
void PrnOutput(void)
    {
        prnt << "\n\nBaseball:    " << setw(4) << baseballCnt;
        prnt << "\n\nFootball:    " << setw(4) << footballCnt;
        prnt << "\n\nBasketball: " << setw(4) << basketballCnt;
        prnt << "\n\nSoccer:      " << setw(4) << soccerCnt;
        return;
    }
```

FIGURE 5.7 *Continued*

```
        MAYESVILLE PARKS AND RECREATIONS DEPARTMENT
                   Youth Sports Survey

Baseball:    153

Football:    129

Basketball:  175

Soccer:      147
```

FIGURE 5.8 Printer Output for CHAP5B

```
CALCULATE SPORT TOTALS:

void ComputeTotals(void)
{
    switch (choice)  {
    case 1:
        baseballCnt++;
        break;
    case 2:
        footballCnt++;
        break;
    case 3:
        basketballCnt++;
        break;
    case 4:
        soccerCnt++;
        break;
    default:
        cout << "\nError-invalid choice\n";
        break;
    }
    return
}
```

The above statements mean: Compare *choice* to the labels. On a match, increment the sport count, skip to the end of the *switch* statement, and return to the *ProcessLoop*. If a match is not found, branch to *default* and print the error message.

Summary

1. The computer can be programmed to select and follow a particular course of action, depending on the comparative values of two data items.

2. An unconditional branch sends control directly to a specific location in the program. On the other hand, a conditional branch is taken only if a given condition is met.

3. The *if* decision performs the statement body only if the condition test is true. Otherwise, control skips to the first command after the *if* statement.

4. A nested *if* consists of at least one *if* inside the branch of another. The statement body is executed only if all conditions are true. Any time a condition is false, control exits the nested *if* statement.

5. The *if/else* decision statement selects one of two options. This function performs the statement body of the true path only if the condition test is true. Else, it performs the statement body of the false path.

6. A nested *if/else* consists of at least one *if* or *if/else* inside the false path of another. If a given condition is true, the program executes the statement body and skips to the first statement after the nested *if/else*.

7. A *goto* statement causes an unconditional jump to a label within the current module. A label is an identifier that is attached to a program statement. Overall, the use of the *goto* statement is considered poor programming.

8. The *switch* statement allows the program to select an option from a given set of options. A case may have more than one label. The *break* statement marks the end of a case and prevents control from falling through the body of the remaining cases.

Programming Projects

For each project, design the logic and write the modular structured program to produce the output. Model your program after the sample programs presented in the chapter. Verify your output.

Project 5–1   Overdue Accounts

Write a program to print a report for customers with account balances that are 90 days overdue.

Input (keyboard):

For each customer, prompt for and enter the following data:

Account Number	Customer Name	Days Overdue	Balance Due
1010	David Ryan	90	400.00
2450	Marie Hill	30	754.00
2730	Rita Fox	90	740.00
3100	Alvin Porter	90	550.00
4080	Corey Adkins	30	233.00
4890	Amy Wyatt	30	700.00
5260	Brian Knox	30	625.00
6350	Susan Cope	90	600.00
7720	Lisa Wilson	60	417.00
8540	Matt Hart	90	900.00
9200	Tori Landis	90	235.00
9630	Pat Rankin	60	342.00

Output (printer):

Print the following overdue accounts report:

```
Author           90-DAY OVERDUE ACCOUNTS           Page 01
                        mm/dd/yy


    Acct Number        Customer Name        Amount Due

        9999           X----------X           999.99
          :                 :                    :
          :                 :                    :
```

```
    9999              X-----------X           999.99

                                Total:    9999.99

   Number of overdue accounts:  99
   Number of accounts > 500.00: 99
```

Processing Requirements:

- Print a report of all accounts that are 90 days overdue.
- Accumulate a total for amount due.
- Count the number of 90-day overdue accounts.
- Count the number of 90-day overdue accounts with a balance greater than $500.00.

Project 5–2 Payroll

Write a program to calculate and print a weekly payroll roster. Hours worked over 40 are paid overtime. Assume the current federal income tax (FIT) rate is 15%.

Input (keyboard):

For each employee, prompt for and enter the following payroll data:

Employee Name	Hours Worked	Hourly Pay Rate
Tanya Bauer	40	7.50
Dana Clark	45	14.90
Sara Erickson	38	12.00
Scott Howard	42	9.75
Paul Irwin	48	8.72
Dale Miller	40	10.25
Bret Rossi	35	8.00
Karen Thomas	48	9.00
Tracy York	36	11.00

Output (printer):

Print the following payroll report:

```
Author                  WEEKLY PAYROLL REPORT                 Page 01
                             mm/dd/yy


Employee   Hours    Regular    Overtime   Gross
Name       Worked   Pay        Pay        Pay        FIT      Net Pay

X-------X    99     999.99     99.99      9999.99    99.99    999.99
    :        :         :          :          :         :         :
    :        :         :          :          :         :         :
X-------X    99     999.99     99.99      9999.99    99.99    999.99

        Totals:  9999.99     999.99     99999.99   999.99    9999.99
```

Processing Requirements:

- Compute the regular pay:
  If hours > 40,
      then regular pay = $40 \times$ pay rate
      else regular pay = hours $\times$ pay rate
- Compute the overtime pay:
  If hours > 40,
      then overtime pay = (hours $-$ 40) $\times$ 1.5 $\times$ pay rate else overtime pay = 0.
- Compute the gross pay:
  regular pay + overtime pay
- Compute the federal income tax:
  gross pay $\times$ FIT rate
- Compute the net pay:
  gross pay $-$ FIT
- Accumulate totals for regular pay, overtime pay, gross pay, FIT, and net pay.

Project 5–3   Sales Order

Write a program to calculate and print the customers' sales orders. Majestic Music Shop sells CDs at a discount when purchased in quantities. Assume the retail price for a single CD is $14.95 and the following discount schedule:

Quantity	Discount
2–6	10%
7–12	20%
13–24	30%
25–48	40%
49–up	50%

Input (keyboard):

For each customer, prompt for and enter the number of CDs purchased (or press '0' to quit). Enter the following purchase quantities: 7, 1, 26, 50, 2, 15, 12, and 24.

Output (screen):

For each customer, print the following sales order:

```
Author          MAJESTIC MUSIC SHOP         mm/dd/yy
                    Sales Order


Enter quantity purchased or '0' to Quit: 99

Discount rate = 0.99

You saved $999.99 on your order.
Please pay the cashier $999.99.
```

Processing Requirements:

- Determine the discount rate based on the quantity purchased (see the discount schedule).
- Compute the order total:
  quantity $\times$ 14.95
- Compute the discount amount:
  order total $\times$ discount rate
- Compute the bill:
  order total – discount amount

Project 5–4   Inventory

Write a program to compute and print an inventory reorder report.

Input (keyboard):

For each item, prompt for and enter the following inventory data:

Item Num	Description	Quantity on Hand	Reorder Point	Reorder Quantity	Unit Cost	Selling Price
1000	Hammers	24	12	24	4.75	9.49
2000	Saws	08	16	12	7.50	14.99
3000	Drills	10	12	18	7.83	15.95
4000	Screwdrivers	36	24	12	2.27	4.98
5000	Pliers	12	12	36	2.65	5.49

Output (printer):

Print the following inventory reorder report:

```
Author            INVENTORY REORDER REPORT        Page 01
                        mm/dd/yy


Item                          Quantity   Reorder   Item
Number    Description         on Hand    Quantity  Cost

 9999     X----------X          99         99      999.99
  :            :                 :          :        :
  :            :                 :          :        :
 9999     X----------X          99         99      999.99

                            Total Cost:      9999.99
```

Processing Requirements:

- Determine what items to reorder:
  Order the reorder quantity of an item when the quantity on hand is less than or equal to the reorder point.
- Compute the item cost:
  reorder quantity $\times$ unit cost
- Accumulate the total cost.

Project 5–5   Personnel

Write a program to print a salary report for the personnel department.

Input (keyboard):

For each employee, prompt for and enter the following personnel data:

Employee Number	Employee Name	Department Number	Sex Code	Annual Salary
1926	Dana Andrews	10	F	29000.00
2071	Scott Cooper	14	M	30250.00
3150	Todd Feldman	22	M	24175.00
3600	Amy Kwon	19	F	36025.00
4100	Derek Lowe	50	M	29120.00
4298	Lori Palmer	35	F	33400.00
5409	Bob Shields	47	M	27500.00
6552	Pam Wolfe	31	F	31773.00

Output (printer):

Print the following personnel report:

```
Author                SALARY REPORT            Page 01
                        mm/dd/yy


Employee                        Department    Annual
Number      Employee Name       Number        Salary

 9999       X-----------X           99        99999.99
  :              :                  :            :
  :              :                  :            :
 9999       X-----------X           99        99999.99

                                Average:      99999.99
```

Processing Requirements:

• Print a report of all female employees who are paid more than $30,000.00 a year.
• Accumulate a total for annual salary.
• Compute the average annual salary:
  total annual salary / number of female employees

Project 5–6   Accounts Payable

Write a program to compute and print an accounts payable report. Assume the following discount schedule applies to early payments (in days):

Paid By	Discount
1–10	12%
11–20	10%
21–30	8%
31–45	5%

Input (keyboard):

For each vendor, prompt for and enter the following data:

Vendor Number	Invoice Vendor Name	Number	Invoice Amount	Paid by
217	Metacraft	A1239	2309.12	10
349	IntraTell	T9823	670.00	25
712	Reylock	F0176	4563.78	33
501	Universal	W0105	1200.00	21
196	Northland	X2781	3429.34	45
414	MarxComm	H9205	913.87	18
659	Veston	D1776	5127.63	30

Output (printer):

Print the following accounts payable report:

```
Author                    ACCOUNTS PAYABLE              Page 01
                             mm/dd/yy


Vendor                  Invoice   Invoice   Discount   Amount
Number   Vendor Name    Number    Amount    Amount     Due

 999     X---------X    XXXX      9999.99   999.99     9999.99
  :          :           :          :         :          :
  :          :           :          :         :          :
 999     X---------X    XXXX      9999.99   999.99     9999.99

              Totals:             99999.99  9999.99    99999.99
```

Processing Requirements:

- Determine the discount rate based on early payment (see the discount schedule).
- Compute the discount amount:
  invoice amount × discount rate
- Compute the amount due:
  invoice amount – discount amount
- Accumulate totals for invoice amount, discount amount, and amount due.

Project 5–7 Production Output

Write a program to compute and print a production bonus report. Assume production workers are paid a bonus according to the number of units they produce over the quota. Use the following bonus pay schedule:

Units over Quota	Pay Rate Each
1–10	0.60
11–25	0.65
26–45	0.70
46+	0.75

Input (keyboard):

For each item, prompt for and enter the following production data:

Employee Name	Product Number	Quota	Units Produced
Kay Archer	P9511	65	65
Alan Baum	A1234	48	97
Marie Fitch	C4510	60	75
Lee Hildebrand	R0934	50	62
David Mullins	E3371	75	75
Chad Nelson	L8912	40	63
Bill Quinn	S0951	48	56
Nicole Renner	H9733	50	59
Erica Tate	Z0182	65	63
Terry West	A3235	70	116

Output (printer):

Print the following bonus report:

```
Author                  PRODUCTION BONUS REPORT             Page 01
                             mm/dd/yy

                    Product          Units     Over
Employee Name       Number   Quota   Produced  Quota   Bonus Pay

X----------X        XXXXX      99      99        99      999.99
     :                :         :       :         :         :
     :                :         :       :         :         :
X----------X        XXXXX      99      99        99      999.99

                         Totals:     999       999     9999.99
```

Processing Requirements:

- Compute the bonus pay based on units over quota (see the bonus pay schedule).
- Accumulate totals for units produced, units over quota, and bonus pay.

6   Using Menus

Overview

Learning Objectives

After you have read this chapter and completed the exercises, you should be able to:

- validate input data and prompt the user to correct data entry errors
- write menu-driven programs that allow the user to select an option from a list of available options
- design and create user-friendly menus that are easy to read and understand

- implement the menu selection process using nested *if/else* and *switch* statements
- use the getch() function to halt screen scrolling

Data Validation

Programs that interact with people should be user friendly. A **user-friendly** program is easy to use, tells the user exactly what to do, and catches data entry errors as they enter the system. It is the programmer's responsibility to ensure that the software is user friendly.

The purpose of **data validation** is to check the input data for errors. If the input is invalid, then the output will be invalid. When an error is detected, the program should alert the user to the error and prompt the user to re-enter the input. It is better to lock the user in the data entry routine until the data is correct than to let bad data enter the system.

Let's consider three common data validation techniques that we can write at this point. They include range checks, code checks, and cross-reference checks.

Range Checks: A **range check** determines if the data is reasonable and lies within a given range of values.

Examples:

1. Check a menu selection to ensure that it is within the range 1–4:

```
cout << "\nEnter choice (1 - 4) ===> ";
cin >> choice;
while (choice < 1 || choice > 4)  {
    cout << "\nERROR: Enter valid choice (1 - 4) ===> ";
    cin >> choice;
}
```

2. Check to ensure that no more than 263 (total number of employees) payroll checks were printed:

```
if (checkCount > 263)  {
    cout << "\nWARNING: The number of checks printed exceeds
            the employee count.";
}
```

Code Checks: A **code check** is used to determine if the input matches a set of predefined codes.

Examples:

1. Compare the size code to ensure that it matches one of the following values: SM, MD, LR:

```
while (strcmp(size, "SM") != 0 && strcmp(size, "MD") != 0
    && strcmp(size, "LR") != 0)  {
    cout << "\nERROR: Enter valid size codes: SM, MD, LR ";
}
```

2. Check the user's response for the values 0 or 1:

```
if (response == 0 || response == 1)  {
    cout << "\nResponse is OK";
```

```
else
    cout << "\nERROR: Invalid response detected";
}
```

Cross-Reference Checks: A **cross-reference check** is used to ensure that the relationship between two or more data items is consistent.

Examples:

1. Check the selling price of an item to ensure that it is greater than the cost:

```
if (price < cost)  {
    cout << "\nERROR: Price should exceed cost";
}
```

2. Check the size code; if it is SM or MD, then the only valid color codes are 1, 4, 5, and 8:

```
if (strcmp(size, "SM") != 0  && strcmp(size, "MD) ! = 0)   {
    if (color == 1 || color == 4 ||
        color == 5 || color == 8)    {
        cout << "\nSize and color code are OK";
    }
    else  {
        cout << "\nERROR: Bad size or color code;
    }

}
```

Menu-Driven Programs

In Chapter 5, we learned how to use a simple menu line to prompt the user to enter a choice. Whenever there are a variety of options available to the user, it would be simpler to display them on the screen with a menu. A **menu** prints a list of options and prompts the user to enter a choice.

For example, consider the **menu-driven** business processing system in Figure 6.1. At the main menu, the user is asked to select one of the five options. Assume the user selects the second option, the Inventory System. Next, the Inventory System menu appears and asks the user to make a further selection. Assume the user chooses the first option, "Add quantity received." Then another screen appears and prompts the user to enter the part number and quantity received.

This menu-driven system demonstrates how menus can be used to "walk" the user through a series of menus until the desired processing activity is found. Each menu leads to another until the final selection is made.

Guidelines for Creating Menus

There are a few simple guidelines the programmer should follow when designing user-friendly menus. The purpose of the guidelines is to provide a set of standards or procedures that help produce menus that are easy to use.

The following guidelines were used to design the menu-driven systems for the sample program presented in this chapter:

Make the Menu Easy to Read: A menu that is easy to read is also easy to use. When users understand what to do, they are inclined to make fewer errors and feel comfortable with the software.

Center the Menu: Center the titles and headings as well as the option list. Organize the contents of the menu from top to bottom, left to right—the normal way a person would read a page in a book.

Keep It Simple: Don't clutter the screen with information. Keep the selection process simple. Avoid putting too many options on one screen. If necessary, use two or more screens to show all the options.

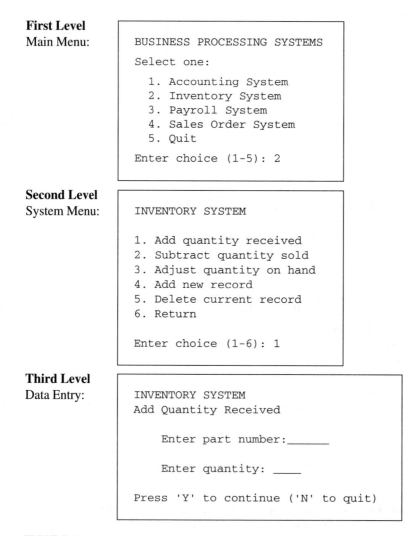

First Level
Main Menu:

```
BUSINESS PROCESSING SYSTEMS

Select one:

   1. Accounting System
   2. Inventory System
   3. Payroll System
   4. Sales Order System
   5. Quit

Enter choice (1-5): 2
```

Second Level
System Menu:

```
INVENTORY SYSTEM


1. Add quantity received
2. Subtract quantity sold
3. Adjust quantity on hand
4. Add new record
5. Delete current record
6. Return


Enter choice (1-6): 1
```

Third Level
Data Entry:

```
INVENTORY SYSTEM
Add Quantity Received


     Enter part number:_____


     Enter quantity: ____


Press 'Y' to continue ('N' to quit)
```

FIGURE 6.1 A Menu-Driven Business Processing System

Make the Choices Clear: After reading the menu, it should be obvious to the users what the options are and how to select the one they want. When possible, arrange the options either in numeric or alphabetic order.

Formatting and Printing Menus

Menus may vary in size and layout. Usually, the client has a rough idea of what the menu should look like, as well as the options it should contain. However, it may be necessary for the programmer to sit down and work with the client to design the ideal menu.

The menu in Figure 6.2 was designed to be user friendly. Look at the program code for the menu. Notice how the tabs(*\t)* are used in the *cout* statements to format the menu. Each tab moves the cursor to the right a fixed number of spaces. The program code prints the menu and prompts the user to select one of the five numeric options (1–5). Upon choosing an option, the *cin* statement assigns the selection to *choice*.

```
void PrnMainMenu(void);
{
    clrscr();
    cout << "\n\t\t BUSINESS PROCESSING SYSTEMS";
    cout << "\n\n\t\t  Select one:";
    cout << "\n\t\t     1. Accounting System";
    cout << "\n\t\t     2. Inventory System";
    cout << "\n\t\t     3. Payroll System";
    cout << "\n\t\t     4. Sales Order System";
    cout << "\n\t\t     5. Quit";
    cout << "\n\n\t\t  Enter choice (1-5): ";
    cin >> choice;
    cin.get();
    return;
}
```

Now look at the menu in Figure 6.2. Note the similarities between the program code and the screen menu.

```
BUSINESS PROCESSING SYSTEMS

  Select one:

     1. Accounting System
     2. Inventory System
     3. Payroll System
     4. Sales Order System
     5. Quit

     Enter choice (1-5):
```

FIGURE 6.2   Main Menu Using Numeric Codes

Menu Selection—Nested if/else Statements

After the user selects an option from the Business Processing Systems menu, the program evaluates the selection and branches to the module that corresponds to the user's choice. We can implement this selection process with nested *if/else* statements. The program code to evaluate and branch follows.

```
void ProcessLoop(void)
{
    PrnMainMenu();
    while (choice != 5)  {
        if (choice == 1)
            PrnAcctMenu();
        else if (choice == 2)
            PrnInvMenu();
        else if (choice == 3)
            PrnPayrollMenu();
        else
            PrnSalesMenu();
        PrnMainMenu();
    }
    return;
}
```

This module consists of a *while* loop that checks the user's selection (1–5) and, as long as *choice* is not equal to 5 (Quit), transfers control to the respective processing module.

Character Option Codes

By itself, a number bears little (if any) meaning or relationship to its corresponding menu choice, particularly when there are several options available. However, a letter, such as *I* that stands for Inventory, associates a specific meaning with a menu option. After all, it is easier to remember that *I* stands for the Inventory System than to recall what number 2 means.

Look at the second version of the Business Processing Systems menu in Figure 6.3. Notice that the option codes have been changed to letters. Now the user is prompted to enter the first letter of the desired option. Hence, the selection process had to be modified to handle character or nonnumeric option codes. This means that the numeric selection tests had to be changed to compare characters. The resulting program code is shown below.

```
void ProcessLoop(void)

{
    PrnMainMenu();
    while (strcmp(choice,'Q') != 0)  {
        if (strcmp(choice, 'A') == 0')
            PrnAcctMenu();
        else if (strcmp(choice, 'I') == 0)
            PrnInvMenu();
```

```
BUSINESS PROCESSING SYSTEMS

   Select one ( ):

      (A)ccounting System
      (I)nventory System
      (P)ayroll System
      (S)ales Order System
      (Q)uit

   Enter letter of choice:
```

FIGURE 6.3   Main Menu Using Character Codes

```
        else if (strcmp(choice, 'P') == 0)
            PrnPayrollMenu();
        else
            PrnSalesMenu();
        PrnMainMenu();
    }
    return;
}
```

The above code prompts the user to select the first letter of one of the five menu options (A, I, P, S, or Q) and then, as long as the *choice* is not equal to Q (Quit), transfers control to the corresponding processing module.

The getch() Function

Format:

```
identifier = getch();
```

Header File: *conio.h*

Purpose: To input a single character from the keyboard. As soon as a character is entered on the keyboard, it is passed to the identifier. The getch() function does not display the character on the screen, nor does it wait for the Enter key to be pressed. This means that once the character is typed, we may not go back and change it. The getch() function ends with a semicolon.

Examples:

```
1. cout << "Enter a grade (A-F) for the midterm and final\n";
   midterm = getch();
   final = getch();
   . . . . .
```

At the prompt, the user enters two letter grades, *AB*. The first letter grade, *A*, is assigned to *midterm* and the second letter grade, *B*, is assigned to *final*. Neither grade appears on the screen. Immediately after the second key is pressed, processing continues with the next program statement. Since getch() does not use the keyboard buffer, there is no need to clear it.

2.
```
cout << "\nThe first prize number is: 141959";
cout << "\n\nPress ENTER to continue...";
wait = getch();
.....
```

Upon displaying the message on the screen, the getch() function "holds" the screen and waits for the user to `Press ENTER to continue...` After pressing the Enter key, control continues with the next executable statement in the program.

Checkpoint 6A

1. List three common techniques for validating input data.
2. Identify four guidelines for creating menus.
3. (True or False) Letters as well as numbers can be used to make selections from a menu.
4. What does the getch() function do?

Sample Program CHAP6A

Sample Program CHAP6A (Figure 6.6, p. 172) illustrates an application of a menu system that displays the fall, winter, and spring computer science course offerings for Central State College. The menus are shown in Figures 6.7a and 6.7b (p. 175).

The following specifications apply to sample program CHAP6A:

Menu Choices:

1. Fall quarter
2. Winter quarter
3. Spring quarter
4. Quit

Input (internal):

Code the fall, winter, and spring quarter course offerings inside the program.

Output (screen):

Display the appropriate quarter course offerings (see Figure 6.7b).

Processing Requirements:

- Based on the quarter selected, display the corresponding course offerings on the screen.
- At the bottom of the screen, prompt the user to press Enter to continue—to return to the main menu.

Pseudocode:

```
START
Clear screen
Display main menu
```

       Prompt and enter choice (validate choice)
       LOOP until choice = quit
          Clear screen
          Display appropriate quarter course offerings
             choice 1 - display Fall
             choice 2 - display Winter
             choice 3 - display Spring
          Clear screen
          Display main menu
          Prompt and enter choice (validate choice)
       End LOOP
       END

Hierarchy Chart: See Figure 6.4.

Program Flowchart: See Figure 6.5.

Dissection of Sample Program CHAP6A

```
PROCESSING LOOP:

void ProcessLoop(void)
{
    PrnMainMenu();
    while (choice != 4)  {
        if (choice == 1)
            PrnFall();
        else if (choice == 2)
            PrnWinter();
        else
```

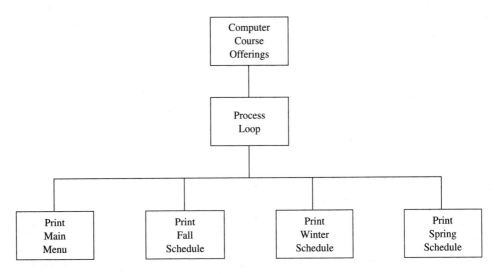

FIGURE 6.4   Hierarchy Chart for CHAP6A

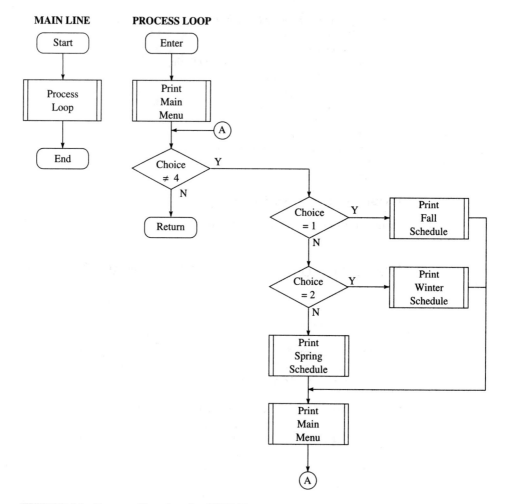

MAIN LINE   **PROCESS LOOP**

FIGURE 6.5   Program Flowchart for CHAP6A

```
        PrnSpring();
    PrnMainMenu();
  }
  return;
}
```

This module establishes a loop that clears the screen and prompts the user to select a choice (Fall, Winter, Spring, or Quit) and, as long as *choice* is not equal to 4 (Quit), transfers control to the appropriate processing module.

The following statements (pp. 175–176) display the main menu. For clarity purposes, the body of the menu is double spaced. Tabs are used to format the menu. The main menu prompts the user to either select a quarter (1–3) or 4 to quit. The *cin* statement assigns the user's selection to *choice*.

PRINT MAIN MENU

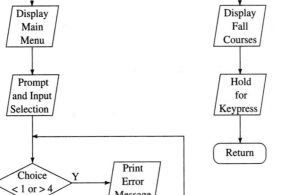

PRINT FALL SCHEDULE

PRINT WINTER SCHEDULE

PRINT SPRING SCHEDULE

Enter

Clear Screen

Display Spring Courses

Hold for Keypress

Return

FIGURE 6.5   *Continued*

```
//---------- COMPUTER COURSE OFFERINGS --------------------
//  Menu program shows computer course offerings by quarter
//
//            PROGRAM-ID: CHAP6A
//            PROGRAMMER: David M. Collopy
//            RUN DATE:   mm/dd/yy
//
//**********************************************************

#include<iostream.h>
#include<conio.h>


//---------- FUNCTION PROTOTYPE --------------------------

void PrnMainMenu(void);         // display main menu
void ProcessLoop(void);         // processing loop
void PrnFall(void);             // display fall courses
void PrnWinter(void);           // display winter courses
void PrnSpring(void);           // display spring courses


//---------- PROGRAM SETUP -------------------------------

//** H E A D I N G   L I N E S

char PT1[] = "  C E N T R A L   S T A T E   C O L L E G E";
char PT2[] = "        Computer Science Course Offerings";

//** P R O G R A M   V A R I A B L E S

int  choice;                    // menu choice
char wait;                      // wait for keypress


//-------------------------------------------------------
//            MAINLINE CONTROL
//-------------------------------------------------------
main()
{
    ProcessLoop();              // processing loop
    return 0;
}
//-------------------------------------------------------
//            PROCESSING LOOP
//-------------------------------------------------------
void ProcessLoop(void)
{
```

FIGURE 6.6   Sample Program CHAP6A: Menu Selections for Computer Science Course Offerings

```
    PrnMainMenu();                 // display main menu
    while (choice != 4)   {
        if (choice == 1)
            PrnFall();             // display fall courses
        else if (choice == 2)
            PrnWinter();           // display winter courses
        else
            PrnSpring();           // display spring courses
        PrnMainMenu();             // display main menu
    }
    return;
}
//------------------------------------------------------------
//              DISPLAY MAIN MENU
//------------------------------------------------------------
void PrnMainMenu(void)
{
    clrscr();
    cout << "\n\t", PT1;
    cout << "\n\t", PT2;
    cout << "\n\n\t              M A I N   M E N U";
    cout << "\n\n\n\t     Select one:";
    cout << "\n\n\t           1.  Fall quarter";
    cout << "\n\n\t           2.  Winter quarter";
    cout << "\n\n\t           3.  Spring quarter";
    cout << "\n\n\t           4.  Quit";
    cout << "\n\n\n\n\n\t     Enter choice (1 - 4) ===> ";
    cin >> choice;
    while (choice < 1 || choice > 4)   {
        cout << "\nERROR...re-enter choice (1 - 4) ===> ";
        cin >> choice;
    }
    return;
}
//------------------------------------------------------------
//              DISPLAY FALL COURSES
//------------------------------------------------------------
void PrnFall(void)
{
    clrscr()
    cout << "\n\t", PT1;
    cout << "\n\t", PT2;
    cout << "\n\n\t              - Fall Quarter -";
```

(continued on next page)

FIGURE 6.6 *Continued*

```
        cout << "\n\n\t CS 101      Introduction to Computers";
        cout << "\n\n\t CS 150      Programming and Design I";
        cout << "\n\n\t CS 201      COBOL Programming I";
        cout << "\n\n\t CS 300      Database Management Systems";
        cout << "\n\n\n\tPress ENTER to continue...";
        wait = getch();              // wait for keypress
        return;
}
//------------------------------------------------------------
//              DISPLAY WINTER COURSES
//------------------------------------------------------------
void PrnWinter(void)
{
        clrscr()
        cout << "\n\t", PT1;
        cout << "\n\t", PT2;
        cout << "\n\n\t                - Winter Quarter -";
        cout << "\n\n\t CS 101      Introduction to Computers";
        cout << "\n\n\t CS 151      Programming and Design II";
        cout << "\n\n\t CS 190      Operating Systems";
        cout << "\n\n\t CS 202      COBOL Programming II";
        cout << "\n\n\t CS 330      Systems Analysis and Design I";
        cout << "\n\n\n\tPress ENTER to continue...";
        wait = getch();              // wait for keypress
        return;
}
//------------------------------------------------------------
//              DISPLAY SPRING COURSES
//------------------------------------------------------------
void PrnSpring(void)
{
        clrscr()
        cout << "\n\t", PT1;
        cout << "\n\t", PT2;
        cout << "\n\n\t                - Spring Quarter -";
        cout << "\n\n\t CS 101      Introduction to Computers";
        cout << "\n\n\t CS 203      COBOL Application Project";
        cout << "\n\n\t CS 238      Assembler Programming";
        cout << "\n\n\t CS 273      Special Topics";
        cout << "\n\n\t CS 331      Systems Analysis and Design II";
        cout << "\n\n\n\tPress ENTER to continue...";
        wait = getch();              // wait for keypress
        return;
}
```

FIGURE 6.6 *Continued*

```
C E N T R A L    S T A T E    C O L L E G E
      Computer Science Course Offerings

           M A I N    M E N U

Select one:

    1.  Fall quarter

    2.  Winter quarter

    3.  Spring quarter

    4.  Quit


Enter choice (1 - 4) ===> __
```

FIGURE 6.7a   Main Menu for CHAP6A

```
C E N T R A L    S T A T E    C O L L E G E
      Computer Science Course Offerings

           -- Fall Quarter --

CS 101    Introduction to Computers

CS 150    Programming and Design I

CS 201    COBOL Programming I

CS 300    Database Management Systems


Press ENTER to continue...
```

FIGURE 6.7b   Fall Course Offerings for CHAP6A

DISPLAY MAIN MENU:

```
void PrnMainMenu(void)
{
    clrscr();
    cout << "\n\t", PT1;
```

```
cout << "\n\t", PT2;
cout << "\n\n\t                    M A I N     M E N U";
cout << "\n\n\n\t      Select one:";
cout << "\n\n\t          1.  Fall quarter";
cout << "\n\n\t          2.  Winter quarter";
cout << "\n\n\t          3.  Spring quarter";
cout << "\n\n\t          4.  Quit";
cout << "\n\n\n\n\n\t       Enter choice (1 - 4) ===> ";
cin >> choice;
```

The *while* loop performs a range check to ensure that *choice* is valid. If it is valid, control returns to the *Processing Loop*. If it is not, the user is prompted to re-enter a selection 1–4. Control will remain in the *while* loop until the user enters a valid choice.

```
while (choice < 1 || choice > 4)  {
    cout << "\nERROR...re-enter choice (1 - 4) ===> ";
    cin >> choice;
}
return;
}
```

Assuming that *choice* is 1, the following statements print the fall quarter course offerings on the screen. Notice that the last two commands "hold" the screen and tell the user what to do to continue. This setup gives the user time to read the course offerings before control returns to the main menu.

The last *cout* statement prompts the user to Press ENTER to continue. Upon pressing the Enter key, control returns to the calling module and redisplays the main menu. This looping process continues until the user selects 4 (Quit).

DISPLAY FALL COURSES:

```
void PrnFall(void)
{
    clrscr()
    cout << "\n\t", PT1;
    cout << "\n\t", PT2;
    cout << "\n\n\t              - Fall Quarter -";
    cout << "\n\n\t CS 101     Introduction to Computers";
    cout << "\n\n\t CS 150     Programming and Design I";
    cout << "\n\n\t CS 201     COBOL Programming I";
    cout << "\n\n\t CS 300     Database Management Systems";
    cout << "\n\n\n\tPress ENTER to continue...";
    wait = getch();
    return;
}
```

Menu Selection—The switch Statement

We may also implement the menu selection process with the *switch* statement. The modules that follow demonstrate the evaluate and branch process for both numeric and character selection codes.

Numeric Selection Codes

```
void ProcessLoop(void)
{
    PrnMainMenu();
    while (choice != 5) {
        switch(choice) {
        case 1:
            PrnAcctMenu();
            break;
        case 2:
            PrnInvMenu();
            break;
        case 3:
            PrnPayrollMenu();
            break;
        default:
            PrnSalesMenu();
            break;
        }
        PrnMainMenu();
    }
    return;
}
```

Character Selection Codes

```
void ProcessLoop(void)
{
    PrnMainMenu();
    while (strcmp(choice, 'Q') != 0) {
        switch(choice) {
        case 'A':
            PrnAcctMenu();
            break;
        case 'I':
            PrnInvMenu();
            break;
        case 'P':
            PrnPayrollMenu();
            break:
        default:
            PrnSalesMenu();
            break;
        }
        PrnMainMenu();
    }
    return;
}
```

For either module, the processing loop continues as long as *choice* is not equal to "Quit." When a selection is made, control branches to the corresponding processing module.

Sample Program CHAP6B

Sample program CHAP6B (Figure 6.10, p. 180) displays a menu of the daily flights scheduled for Wynfield Metro Airport. When the user selects a destination city, the program displays the departure times for the flights. The main menu and the departure times for the flights to New York are shown in Figures 6.11a (p. 184) and 6.11b (p. 185).

Menu Choices:

1. Atlanta
2. Boston
3. Los Angeles
4. Miami
5. New York
6. Quit

Input (internal):

Code the daily flight schedule inside the program.

Output (screen):

Display the appropriate flight schedule (Figure 6.11b).

Processing Requirements:

• Based on the city selected, display the corresponding flight schedule on the screen.
• At the bottom of the screen, prompt the user to press Enter to continue—return to the main menu.

Pseudocode:

```
START
Clear screen
Display main menu
Prompt and enter choice (validate choice)
LOOP until choice = quit
   Clear screen
   Display appropriate departure times
      choice 1 - Atlanta
      choice 2 - Boston
      choice 3 - Los Angeles
      choice 4 - Miami
      choice 5 - New York
   Clear screen
   Display main menu
   Prompt and enter choice (validate choice)
End LOOP
END
```

Hierarchy Chart: See Figure 6.8.

Program Flowchart: See Figure 6.9.

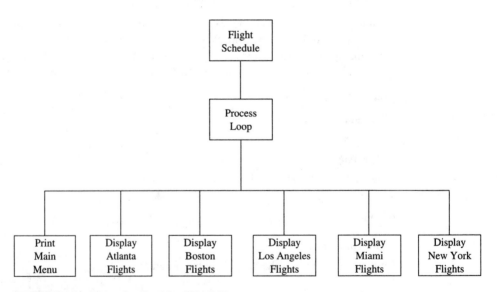

FIGURE 6.8   Hierarchy Chart for CHAP6B

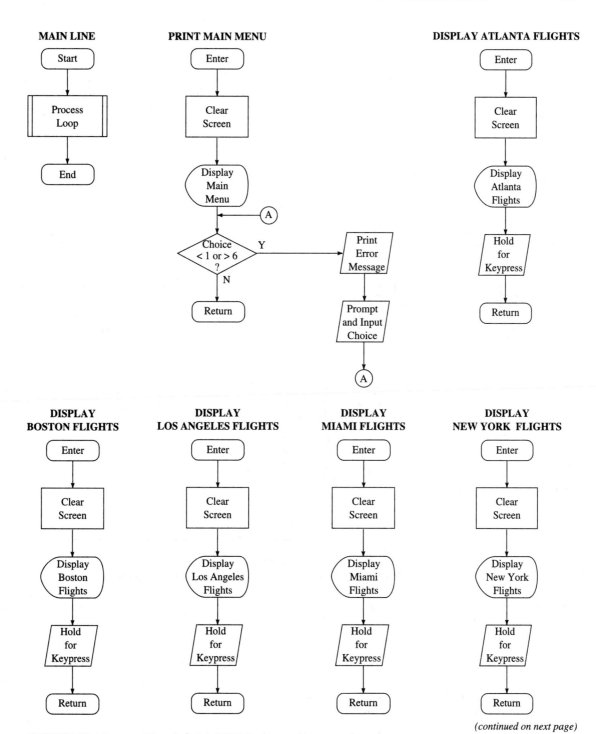

FIGURE 6.9   Program Flowchart for CHAP6B

(continued on next page)

PROCESS LOOP

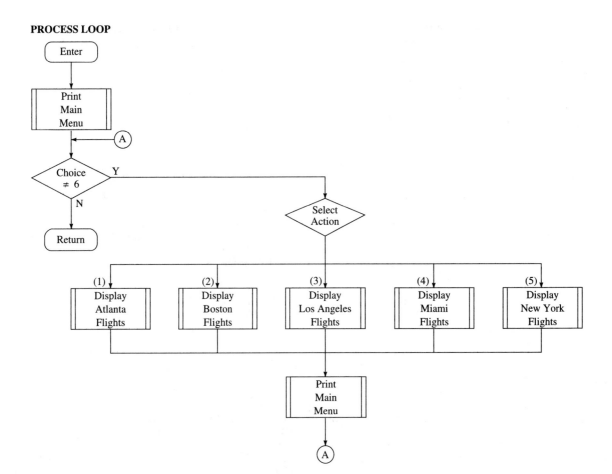

FIGURE 6.9   *Continued*

```
//---------- FLIGHT SCHEDULE --------------------------------
//   Menu flight schedule for Wynfield Metro Airport
//
//          PROGRAM-ID: CHAP6B
//          PROGRAMMER: David M. Collopy
//          RUN DATE:   mm/dd/yy
//
//**************************************************************

#include<iostream.h>
#include<conio.h>
```

FIGURE 6.10   Sample Program CHAP6B: Menu Flight Schedule for Wynfield Metro Airport

```
//---------- FUNCTION PROTOTYPE ----------------------------

void ProcessLoop(void);          // processing loop
void PrnMainMenu(void);          // display main menu
void Atlanta(void);              // Atlanta flights
void Boston(void);               // Boston flights
void LosAngeles(void);           // Los Angeles flights
void Miami(void);                // Miami flights
void NewYork(void);              // New York flights

//---------- PROGRAM SETUP --------------------------------

//** H E A D I N G   L I N E S

char PT1[] = " W Y N F I E L D   M E T R O   A I R P O R T";

//** P R O G R A M   V A R I A B L E S

int  choice;                     // menu choice
char wait;                       // wait for keypress


//---------------------------------------------------------
//              MAINLINE CONTROL
//---------------------------------------------------------
main()
{
    ProcessLoop();               // processing loop
    return 0;
}
//---------------------------------------------------------
//              PROCESSING LOOP
//---------------------------------------------------------
void ProcessLoop(void)
{
    PrnMainMenu();               // display main menu
    while (choice != 6)  {
        switch (choice)  {
        case 1:
            Atlanta();           // Atlanta flights
            break;
        case 2:
            Boston();            // Boston flights
            break;
        case 3:
            LosAngeles();        // Los Angeles flights
            break;
```

(continued on next page)

FIGURE 6.10   *Continued*

```
                case 4:
                        Miami();              // Miami flights
                        break;
                default:
                        NewYork();            // New York flights
                        break;
                }
                PrnMainMenu();                // display main menu
        }
        return;
}
//------------------------------------------------------------
//              DISPLAY MAIN MENU
//------------------------------------------------------------
void PrnMainMenu(void)
{
    clrscr();
    cout << "\n\t", PT1;
    cout << "\n\n\t             M A I N   M E N U";
    cout << "\n\n\n\t    Select one:";
    cout << "\n\n\t              1.  Atlanta";
    cout << "\n\n\t              2.  Boston ";
    cout << "\n\n\t              3.  Los Angeles ";
    cout << "\n\n\t              4.  Miami";
    cout << "\n\n\t              5.  New York";
    cout << "\n\n\t              6.  Quit";
    cout << "\n\n\n\n\n\t      Enter choice (1 - 6) ===> ";
    cin >> choice;
    while (choice < 1 || choice > 6)  {
        cout << "\nERROR...re-enter choice (1 - 6) ===> ";
        cin >> choice;
    }
    return;
}
//------------------------------------------------------------
//              ATLANTA FLIGHTS
//------------------------------------------------------------
void Atlanta(void)
{
    clrscr()
    cout << "\n\t", PT1;
    cout << "\n\n\t   Atlanta Flight Schedule";
    cout << "\n\n\t   --------------------------";
    cout << "\n\n\t   Flight#          Departure";
    cout << "\n\n\t     101              7:15 p.m.";
    cout << "\n\n\t     214              9:20 p.m.";
    cout << "\n\n\n\tPress ENTER to continue...";
```

FIGURE 6.10 *Continued*

```
        wait = getch();                    // wait for keypress
        return;
    }
    //-----------------------------------------------------------
    //              BOSTON FLIGHTS
    //-----------------------------------------------------------
    void Boston(void)
    {
        clrscr()
        cout << "\n\t", PT1;
        cout << "\n\n\t     Boston Flight Schedule";
        cout << "\n\n\t     --------------------------";
        cout << "\n\n\t     Flight#          Departure";
        cout << "\n\n\t       117             5:55 p.m.";
        cout << "\n\n\t       201             6:30 p.m.";
        cout << "\n\n\n\tPress ENTER to continue...";
        wait = getch();                    // wait for keypress
        return;
    }
    //-----------------------------------------------------------
    //              LOS ANGELES FLIGHTS
    //-----------------------------------------------------------
    void LosAngeles(void)
    {
        clrscr()
        cout << "\n\t", PT1;
        cout << "\n\n\t     Los Angeles Flight Schedule";
        cout << "\n\n\t     --------------------------";
        cout << "\n\n\t     Flight#          Departure";
        cout << "\n\n\t       122             3:10 p.m.";
        cout << "\n\n\t       205             4:30 p.m.";
        cout << "\n\n\n\tPress ENTER to continue...";
        wait = getch();                    // wait for keypress
        return;
    }
    //-----------------------------------------------------------
    //              MIAMI FLIGHTS
    //-----------------------------------------------------------
    void Miami(void)
    {
        clrscr()
        cout << "\n\t", PT1;
        cout << "\n\n\t     Miami Flight Schedule";
        cout << "\n\n\t     --------------------------";
        cout << "\n\n\t     Flight#          Departure";
        cout << "\n\n\t       102             1:25 p.m.";
        cout << "\n\n\t       204             4:00 p.m.";
```

(continued on next page)

FIGURE 6.10   *Continued*

```
        cout << "\n\n\n\tPress ENTER to continue...";
        wait = getch();                  // wait for keypress
        return;
}
//-----------------------------------------------------------
//              NEW YORK FLIGHTS
//-----------------------------------------------------------
void NewYork(void)
{
        clrscr()
        cout << "\n\t", PT1;
        cout << "\n\n\t    New York Flight Schedule";
        cout << "\n\n\t    --------------------------";
        cout << "\n\n\t    Flight#            Departure";
        cout << "\n\n\t      104                2:00 p.m.";
        cout << "\n\n\t      119                5:15 p.m.";
        cout << "\n\n\t      200                7:20 p.m.";
        cout << "\n\n\n\tPress ENTER to continue...";
        wait = getch();                  // wait for keypress
        return;
}
```

FIGURE 6.10 *Continued*

```
W Y N F I E L D   M E T R O   A I R P O R T

            M A I N   M E N U

Select one:

    1.  Atlanta

    2.  Boston

    3.  Los Angeles

    4.  Miami

    5.  New York

    6.  Quit


Enter choice (1 - 6) ===> __
```

FIGURE 6.11a Main Menu for CHAP6B

```
┌─────────────────────────────────────────────────┐
│                                                   │
│      W Y N F I E L D   M E T R O   A I R P O R T  │
│                                                   │
│     New York Flight Schedule:                     │
│                                                   │
│     -----------------------------                 │
│                                                   │
│     Flight#              Departure                │
│                                                   │
│       104                 2:00 p.m.               │
│                                                   │
│       119                 5:15 p.m.               │
│                                                   │
│       200                 7:20 p.m.               │
│                                                   │
│                                                   │
│     Press ENTER to continue...                    │
│                                                   │
└─────────────────────────────────────────────────┘
```

FIGURE 6.11b   New York Flight Schedule for CHAP6B

Dissection of Sample Program CHAP6B

With the exception of the *switch* statement, the processing performed by this sample program is similar to that performed by sample program CHAP6A.

PROCESSING LOOP:

```c
void ProcessLoop(void)
{
    PrnMainMenu();
    while (choice != 6)  {
        switch (choice)  {
        case 1:
            Atlanta();
            break;
        case 2:
            Boston();
            break;
        case 3:
            LosAngeles();
            break;
        case 4:
            Miami();
            break;
        default:
            NewYork();
            break;
        }
        PrnMainMenu();
    }
    return;
}
```

The above selection module compares the value of *choice* to the case labels. If a match is found, control branches to the processing module that corresponds to the label. If a match is not found, control defaults to New York and displays the New York Flight Schedule.

At first glance, it may appear that control defaults to New York for an invalid choice. This, of course, will not happen due to the range check placed at the end of the *PrnMain-Menu* module. A range check is used to ensure that the input is valid. For a choice outside the range 1–6, the user is prompted to re-enter a choice. Control will remain in the *while* loop until a valid selection is entered.

For example, if a 7 is entered on the keyboard, the program prompts the user to re-enter the choice. On the other hand, if a 1 is entered, the program displays the flight schedule for Atlanta. This looping process continues until the user selects 6 (Quit).

Summary

1. Interactive programs should be user friendly and catch input errors as they are entered at the keyboard.

2. The purpose of data validation is to check the input for errors. When an error is encountered, the program should prompt the user to re-enter the data. Data validation includes range checks, code checks, and cross reference checks.

3. A range check determines if the data is reasonable and lies within a given range of values.

4. Code checking is used to determine if the data matches a given set of codes.

5. A cross-reference check is used to ensure that the relationship between two or more data items is consistent.

6. Computer applications that require the user to choose from a variety of options can be easily implemented with menus.

7. A menu displays a list of options and prompts the user to enter a choice. A menu-driven system presents a series of menus that walk the user through the selection process.

8. Menus should be designed to be user friendly, easy to read, and simple to use.

9. Tabs \t are used with *cout* statements to format and print menus.

10. The menu selection process may be implemented with either the nested *if/else* or the *switch* statement. Both may use numeric or character codes to represent the menu choices.

11. Character selection codes remind the user of the menu options. They associate meaning with the options and are easier to remember.

12. The getch() function retrieves a character from the keyboard. It neither displays the character on the screen nor waits for the Enter key to be pressed. We may use this function to hold the screen until the user is ready to continue.

Programming Projects

For each project, design the logic and write the modular structured program to produce the output. Model your program after the sample programs presented in the chapter. Verify your output.

Project 6–1 **Overdue Accounts**

Write a menu program that allows the user to select different processing options for the overdue accounts reporting system.

Menu Choices:

1. 30 days overdue

2. 60 days overdue

3. 90 days overdue

4. Quit

Input (keyboard):

For each customer, prompt for and enter the following data:

Account Number	Customer Name	Days Overdue	Balance Due
1010	David Ryan	90	400.00
2450	Marie Hill	30	754.00
2730	Rita Fox	90	740.00
3100	Alvin Porter	90	550.00
4080	Corey Adkins	30	233.00
4890	Amy Wyatt	30	700.00
5260	Brian Knox	30	625.00
6350	Susan Cope	90	600.00
7720	Lisa Wilson	60	417.00
8540	Matt Hart	90	900.00
9200	Tori Landis	90	235.00
9630	Pat Rankin	60	342.00

Output (printer):

Print the appropriate overdue accounts report:

```
Author              90-DAY OVERDUE ACCOUNTS          Page 01
                          mm/dd/yy

  Acct Number         Customer Name          Amount Due

     9999             X----------X             999.99
      :                   :                      :
      :                   :                      :
     9999             X----------X             999.99

                                    Total:    9999.99

  Number of overdue accounts:   99
```

Processing Requirements:
- Based on the option selected, print the corresponding overdue accounts report.
- Accumulate a total for amount due.
- Count the number of overdue accounts.

Project 6–2   Payroll

Write a menu program that allows the user to select different processing options for the payroll reporting system.

Menu Choices:

1. Hourly employee

2. Salary employee

3. Contract services

4. Other

5. Quit

Input (keyboard):

Prompt for and enter the following payroll data:

ID Number	Employee Name	Pay Code	Gross Pay
1020	Tanya Bauer	3	300.00
3451	Dana Clark	2	670.50
2011	Sara Erickson	1	456.00
8192	Scott Howard	3	409.50
4500	Paul Irwin	4	418.56
5033	Dale Miller	2	410.00
2104	Bret Rossi	1	280.00
7909	Karen Thomas	4	432.00
6100	Tracy York	1	396.00

Output (printer):

Print the appropriate payroll report:

```
   Author              PAYROLL REPORT              Page 01
                       (Payroll Type)
                         mm/dd/yy


   ID Number        Employee Name              Gross Pay

     9999         X----------X                  999.99
        :                :                         :
        :                :                         :
     9999         X----------X                  999.99

                  Total Gross Pay:             9999.99
```

Processing Requirements:

- Write the input record to the payroll report when the pay code matches the processing option selected by the user.
- Include the payroll type on the report:

Options	Print
1	Hourly Employees
2	Salary Employees
3	Contract Services
4	Other

- Accumulate a total for gross pay.

Project 6–3   Sales Staff

Write a menu program that allows the sales manager to list the sales staff by region.

Menu Choices:

1. Northern Region

2. Southern Region

3. Eastern Region

4. Western Region

5. Quit

For each option 1–4, list the sales staff assigned to the region. The data shown below represent the salesperson's number, name, and monthly sales, respectively.

Options:

1.	1290	Karen Brown	7541.52
	2100	Bruce Lanning	15675.91
	3455	Nancy Reynolds	8435.75
2.	1657	Megan Andrews	10325.33
	3401	Mike Cruse	6123.81
	5022	Eric Hahn	12805.46
	7178	Linda Mauch	8127.62
	9010	Nikki Stevens	9310.16
3.	2455	Barb Ansel	6578.24
	4339	Gary Kline	16120.00
	6012	Keri Torbett	10451.69
	9120	Adam Yost	7823.45
4.	1042	Linda Arndt	12126.84
	2980	Kelly Fenton	8502.05
	5111	Dave Payton	10452.37
	7008	Nathan Sanders	14934.99
	8541	Beth Valentine	6152.86

Input (internal):

Code the sales staff data and monthly sales inside the program. (See sample programs CHAP6A and CHAP6B.)

Output (printer):

Print the appropriate sales staff report:

```
Author          SALES STAFF BY REGION        Page 01
                       (Region)
                      mm/dd/yy


Salesperson                              Monthly
Number          Salesperson Name          Sales

  9999        X---------------X          99999.99
   :                 :                       :
   :                 :                       :
  9999        X---------------X          99999.99
```

Processing Requirements:

• Based on the option selected, print the corresponding sales staff report.
• Include the region on the report:

Options	Print
1	Northern Region
2	Southern Region
3	Eastern Region
4	Western Region

Project 6–4   Inventory

Write a menu program that allows the user to list the status of any item in the inventory.

Menu Choices:

1. Hammers

2. Saws

3. Drills

4. Screwdrivers

5. Pliers

6. Quit

Input (keyboard):

For each item, prompt for and enter the following inventory data:

Item Number	Description	Quantity on Hand	Reorder Point	Reorder Quantity	Unit Cost	Selling Price
1000	Hammers	24	12	24	4.75	9.49
2000	Saws	08	16	12	7.50	14.99

3000	Drills	10	12	18	7.83	15.95
4000	Screwdrivers	36	24	12	2.27	4.98
5000	Pliers	12	12	36	2.65	5.49

Output (printer):

Print the appropriate inventory status report:

```
Author              INVENTORY SYSTEM          mm/dd/yy
                 Item Status Report


Item Number: 9999     Description: X------------X

Quantity on Hand: 99
   Reorder Point: 99
Reorder Quantity: 99

        Unit Cost: $99.99
    Selling Price: $99.99
```

Processing Requirements:

For the item selected, list the current status of the inventory.

Project 6–5   Personnel

Write a program that allows the user to list the employees by department.

Menu Choices:

1. Accounting
2. Programming
3. Sales
4. Payroll
5. Maintenance
6. Quit

Input (keyboard):

For each employee, prompt for and enter the following personnel data:

Employee Name	Department	Years of Service	Annual Salary
Dana Andrews	Accounting	2	25124.00
Scott Cooper	Maintenance	4	26400.00
Todd Feldman	Payroll	1	24300.00
Amy Kwon	Sales	5	36049.00
Derek Lowe	Programming	2	26225.00
Lori Palmer	Maintenance	2	22360.00
Bob Shields	Sales	3	30120.00
Pam Wolfe	Programming	6	34725.00

Output (printer):

Print the appropriate personnel report:

```
Author            PERSONNEL REPORT          Page 01
                    mm/dd/yy


Department: X---------X

                    Years of      Annual
      Employee Name  Service       Salary

      X----------X      2        99999.99
             :          :           :
             :          :           :
      X----------X      4        99999.99

                    Total:    999999.99

                    Employee count: 99
```

Processing Requirements:

- For the department selected, print the employee name, years of service, and annual salary.
- Accumulate a total for annual salary.
- Count the number of employees in the department.

Project 6–6   Accounts Payable

Write a menu program that allows the user to print the status of any of the vendor accounts listed below.

Menu Choices:

1. Metacraft
2. Reylock
3. Universal
4. Northland
5. Veston
6. Quit

Input (keyboard):

For each vendor, prompt for and enter the following data:

Vendor Number	Vendor Name	Invoice Number	Invoice Amount	Discount Rate
217	Metacraft	A1239	2309.12	0.10
712	Reylock	F0176	4563.78	0.12
501	Universal	W0105	1200.00	0.09
196	Northland	X2781	3429.34	0.10
659	Veston	D1776	5127.63	0.12

Output (printer):

Print the appropriate accounts payable status report:

```
Author              ACCOUNTS PAYABLE SYSTEM           mm/dd/yy
                        Status Report


Vendor No: 999        Vendor: X--------------X

        Invoice No: XXXXX
   Invoice Amount: $9999.99
  Discount Amount: $ 999.99
       Amount Due: $9999.99
```

Processing Requirements:

- For the option selected, print the current status of the vendor account.
- Compute the discount amount:
  invoice amount × discount rate
- Compute the amount due:
  invoice amount − discount amount

Project 6–7 Math Practice

Write a menu program that allows the user to practice addition, subtraction, multiplication, and division.

Menu Choices:

1. Addition
2. Subtraction
3. Multiplication
4. Division
5. Quit

Input (keyboard):

Prompt the user to enter two real numbers and the result of the selected operation.

Sample Output (screen):

Assume the user selected the first option (addition)—print the following output:

```
Author              MATH PRACTICE            mm/dd/yy

          ***  A D D I T I O N  ***

     First Number  =   79.3

     Second Number = 123.78

             Sum = 203.08   correct

  Press ENTER to continue...
```

Processing Requirements:

For the option selected, perform the corresponding arithmetic operation. Check the user's result: if it is correct, print the message "correct" next to the result; if the result is not correct, then print "incorrect" next to the user's result.

Options	Operations
1	Sum = number1 + number2
2	Difference = number1 − number2
3	Product = number1 × number2
4	Quotient = number1 / number2

7   Text Files

Overview

Learning Objectives

After you have read this chapter and completed the exercises, you should be able to:

- use a text editor to enter, edit, and save a data file
- use the *ifstream* file class to declare an input file stream

- open and close text files using the open() and close() member functions, respectively
- use the fail() member function to test for file open errors
- read a file and assign the input to the program variables using the get() member function
- test for the end-of-file condition using either the eof() member function or a trailer record

Files and Records

In Chapter 1, we learned that a program represents a set of instructions that accepts data, processes it, and provides output in the form of information. We also learned that data can be organized into files to facilitate processing by the computer.

By a previous definition, a file is a collection of related records that pertain to a specific application. In the example of a company that has a staff of 263 employees, the payroll file would consist of 263 records—one for each employee. Hence, a record is a collection of related fields. For instance, a payroll record would consist of all the fields necessary for computing the paycheck for a given employee.

Furthermore, a field is a collection of related character positions that form a single unit of information. For the payroll application, a field might include any one of the following items—employee number, name, pay rate, hours worked, and deductions.

Text Files

Consider a program that prompts the user to input inventory data until "Quit" is entered. Once a complete record is entered at the keyboard, it is processed by the program. Here the user is interactive with the program. **Interactive** means that the user communicates directly with the program as it executes; there is a dialog between the user and the computer.

There is, however, another way to input the program data. Instead of keying in one record at a time at the input prompts, we could enter all of the records into a file and save it on disk for later use by the program.

Let's assume that each line in the file represents a record that was previously entered one data item at a time. Therefore, each line consists of a set of constants (numeric and/or string) that make up a complete record. In other words, a text file represents a logically related set of constants that is read and processed by the program.

By definition, a **text file** consists of readable data that can be created with a text editor and saved on disk. In programming, there are two major types of files, **program** or **source code files** and **data files**. Both are text files and both can be read and modified by the programmer with a text editor (such as the one you are currently using to write your C++ programs).

In this chapter, we will see that text file processing involves the following activities: creating a file, declaring a file stream class, opening the file, reading and processing the data stored in the file, and closing the file.

Creating a Text File

A text file is created by using a text editor to enter, edit, and save data that will be processed by a program. Depending on the C++ compiler you are using, you may be able to create a text file with your program editor. Your instructor or supervisor will let you know which text editor to use.

Kelly Antonetz	70	50	98	80	65	85
Robert Cain	97	82	79	73	94	62
Karen Dehaven	81	87	94	85	93	89
Barry Harmon	76	77	80	81	75	92
Katrina Lang	99	93	89	83	94	90
Amanda Mohr	65	67	71	84	88	96
Mike Revell	90	87	78	52	76	89
Woody Synder	76	76	83	85	77	81

FIGURE 7.1   Grades Data File

Once in the editor, key in one record per line and press the Enter key. A record ends when you press the Enter key—the newline character \n. For example, Sample Program CHAP7A reads the grade file shown in Figure 7.1, processes the data, and prints a six-week grade report. The grades data file *grades.dat* was created and saved on disk. Each row in Figure 7.1 represents a record, and each column represents a constant that will be assigned to a program variable. According to Figure 7.1, each record consists of seven constants. When read by the program, the constants are assigned to the program variables *student*, *grade1*, *grade2*, *grade3*, *grade4*, *grade5*, and *grade6*.

Notice that the constants are separated by spaces. As you may recall, a blank space (white space) serves as a delimiter and tells the read statement that the input consists of multiple substrings or data items. Upon exiting the editor, an **end-of-file marker** is written after the last record. Later, this marker will be used by the program to detect the end of the file.

Although the constants are neatly aligned into columns, this is not necessary as long as they are separated by at least one blank space. Keep this in mind when keying in data for string constants. Since string constants require a fixed number of character positions, at times they may appear to have several spaces at the end of the field when actually they do not.

We will, however, continue to organize the data into columns and adopt this method as a standard. This convention makes it easier for us to read the data and make changes to it as needed.

Creating an Input File Stream

Format:

```
ifstream identifier;
```

Header File: *fstream.h*

Purpose: To create an input file stream. The *identifier* shown in the format is assigned to the input file stream (*ifstream*). The *identifier* is called the **file object name**. Be sure to include the *fstream.h* header file in your program. The header file defines the characteristics of the input file stream to the compiler. Each identifier must be unique. The file object name associates the identifier with the input file stream. The input file stream declaration ends with a semicolon.

Examples:

1. `ifstream gradeFile;`
2. `ifstream payroll;`

The first example assigns the identifier name, *gradeFile*, to the input file stream. The second declaration associates the file object name, *payroll*, with the input file stream.

Checkpoint 7A

1. What is a file? A record? A field?
2. What is a text file? How is it created?
3. Is it necessary to align the data in a text file into columns? Why or why not?
4. Give an example and show how to set up the input file stream.
5. What is the purpose of the file object name?

Opening a File

Format:

```
identifier.open("filename");
```

Header File: *fstream.h*

Purpose: To open a file. The **dot (.) operator** indicates that open() is a member function of the stream associated with the *identifier*. A file must be opened before it can be accessed by the program. According to the format, the *filename* argument refers to the name of the disk file.

When a file is successfully opened, the open() function passes the address of the file to the file object specified by the *identifier*. Otherwise, a zero (the null value) is passed to the identifier. Remember, an identifier is simply a variable name that is used to store the address of a specific file. Be sure to code one open() for each file required by the program. The open() function ends with a semicolon.

For now, we will open files to read data only. Later, in the chapters on file processing, we will have the opportunity to write and append data to the file.

The open() function performs the following activities:

1. Checks the disk directory for the file name. If the file is found, it returns the address of the file. If the file is not found, it returns the null pointer.
2. Sets up an input file buffer—a temporary storage area reserved in memory for holding the input.
3. Sets the file pointer to the beginning of the file and maintains the current position in the file as data is read and processed by the program.

Example:

```
gradeFile.open("a:grades.dat");
```

First, the grade file is opened for input. This means that data will be read from the "grades.dat" file; the data is stored on the disk that is in the A drive. Second, the address of the file is passed to the file object, *gradeFile*. Hence, it is assumed that the file object name has been declared prior to executing the open.

Reading a Record

Format:

```
identifier >> variable/s;
```

Header File: *fstream.h*

Purpose: To read data from the input file stream. According to the format, the statement uses the extraction operator to read and assign the input to the variable arguments. Multiple variables are separated by the extraction operator. The read() function ends with a semicolon.

This statement assigns the input to the variables given by the variable arguments. Since there is no inherent connection between the actual data in the file and the variable names specified by the input statement, it is up to the programmer to maintain a positional relationship and match them accordingly. Otherwise, a mismatch may occur and data may be incorrectly assigned to the program variables.

Examples:

1. `payroll >> emplNum >> regHours >> payRate;`

Example 1 reads three numeric values from the payroll file and assigns them to the program variables *emplNum*, *regHours*, and *payRate*, respectively.

2. `gradeFile.get(student, 16) >> grade1 >> grade2 >> grade3 >> grade4`
   `                    >> grade5 >> grade6;`

Example 2 reads the student's name and six grades from the input file stream and assigns them to the variables as shown. The get() member function reads the first 16 characters (including any white spaces) and assigns the input to the variable *student*.

3. `invFile >> itemNum ;`
   `  invFile.get(description, 20);`
   `  invFile >> quant << onOrder;`

Example 3 reads data from the inventory file and assigned the input to the variables *itemNum*, *description*, *quant*, and *onOrder*, respectively.

Testing for the End of File

Format:

```
identifier.eof();
```

Header File: *fstream.h*

Purpose: To test for the end-of-file condition. The empty parentheses indicates that the eof() member function takes no arguments. This function prevents the program from reading past the last record. It is commonly used with the *if* or *while* statement to test for the end of a file. If the file pointer is not pointing to the end of the file, the function returns a zero (false). Otherwise, it returns a nonzero value (true), indicating that the pointer is at the end of the file. The eof() function ends with a semicolon.

Examples:

1. `if (!gradeFile.eof())`
       `. . . . .`

2. `while (!gradeFile.eof())`

       `. . . . .`

Both examples test for the end-of-file condition. If the current position in the file is not equal to the end-of-file marker, then control enters the statement body. Otherwise, control skips to the first command after the *if* or *while* statement.

Closing a File

Format:

`identifier.close();`

Header File: *stdio.h*

Purpose: To close a file. A file should be closed prior to exiting the program. For an input stream file, the close() member function releases the input file buffer and closes the file associated with the identifier. For an output stream file (used later), the function clears the output file buffer by writing the remaining data to the disk before closing the file. The close() function ends with a semicolon.

Example:

`gradeFile.close();`

According to the example, the close() function releases the input file buffer and closes the file associated with the *gradeFile* identifier.

Checkpoint 7B

1. What three activities take place when the open() function is executed?
2. Code the open() function to open a file on the B drive. The file is called *employ.dat*. Use *employFile* as the file object name.
3. Code the statement to read a record from the *employ.dat* file. The fields are *employee number*, *employee's last name*, *pay rate*, and *hours worked*.
4. Code an *if* statement to test for the end of the *employ.dat* file.
5. Code the close() function to close the *employ.dat* file.

Sample Program CHAP7A

Sample program CHAP7A (Figure 7.4, p. 204) reads a grade file, processes the data, and prints a six-week grade report. Weekly test scores are totalled and averaged for each student. The output for sample program CHAP7A is shown in Figure 7.5 (p. 207).

The following specifications apply:

Input (text file):

For each student record, read and assign data to the following fields. Field size and type are shown in parentheses.

1. Student name   (15 char)
2. 1st week test score   (3 int)
3. 2nd week test score   (3 int)
4. 3rd week test score   (3 int)
5. 4th week test score   (3 int)
6. 5th week test score   (3 int)
7. 6th week test score   (3 int)

Text File (grades.dat):

Use the data given below to create the grades file. The numbers shown above the columns correspond to the fields described for the input.

1	2	3	4	5	6	7
Kelly Antonetz	70	50	98	80	65	85
Robert Cain	97	82	79	73	94	62
Karen Dehaven	81	87	94	85	93	89
Barry Harmon	76	77	80	81	75	92
Katrina Lang	99	93	89	83	94	90
Amanda Mohr	65	67	71	84	88	96
Mike Revell	90	87	78	52	76	89
Woody Synder	76	76	83	85	77	81

Output (screen):

Print the six-week grade report shown in Figure 7.5.

Processing Requirements:

- Read the grades file.
- Compute the grade total:
  $total = grade1 + grade2 + grade3 + grade4 + grade5 + grade6$
- Compute the average six-week grade:
  $average = total / 6$

Pseudocode:

```
START
Open file
If file opened
   Print report headings
   Read a record
   LOOP until end of file
      Compute grade total
      Compute average grade
      Print detail line
      Read a record
```

```
        End LOOP
        Close file
    END
```

Hierarchy Chart: See Figure 7.2.

Program Flowchart: See Figure 7.3.

Dissection of Sample Program CHAP7A

Let's focus our attention on the file-processing activities performed by sample program CHAP7A and start the dissection by looking at the file stream declaration and the structure of the input grade record.

```
INPUT GRADE RECORD

   ifstream gradeFile;
```

The above statement declares the file object name and assigns it to the input file stream. Hence, *gradeFile* will be used to hold the address of the grades data file.

As a standard, we will define the structure or format of the input record immediately after declaring the file stream and the identifier name. Hence, the variable declarations below define the fields belonging to the grades record.

When a record is read from the input file stream, data values are assigned to the fields defined for the grades record.

```
char    student[16];
```

The above statement defines the character string variable *student* and reserves 16 character positions for the input—15 for the data and 1 for the null character.

```
int    grade1;
int    grade2;
int    grade3;
int    grade4;
int    grade5;
int    grade6;
```

The above statements define six integer variables. They are used to hold the grades—one for each week in the six-week grading period.

```
PROGRAM VARIABLES

float    gradeTotal;
float    gradeAvr;
```

The above statements define two floating-point variables that are used to hold the six-week grade total and average, respectively.

```
OPEN PRINTER FILE

ofstream prnt("PRN");
```

The above statement defines the output file stream. Hence, the identifier name *prnt* is assigned to the *ofstream*. The device name *PRN* associates *prnt* with printer.

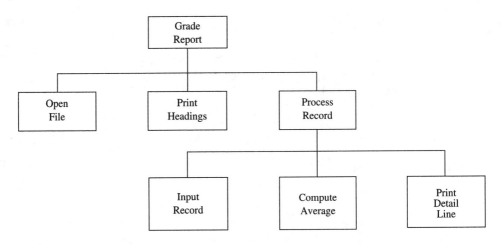

FIGURE 7.2   Hierarchy Chart for CHAP7A

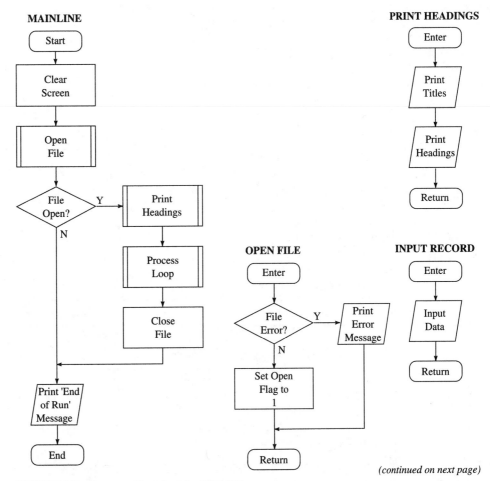

FIGURE 7.3   Program Flowchart for CHAP7A

(continued on next page)

PROCESS LOOP

COMPUTE AVERAGE

PRINT DETAIL

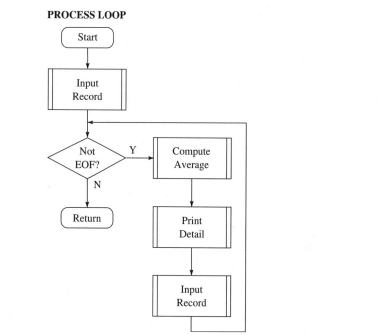

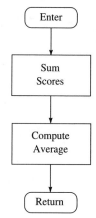

FIGURE 7.3 *Continued*

```
//---------- GRADE REPORT ---------------------------------
//   Read a file, compute the six-week grade average, and
//   print a six-week grade report.
//
//          PROGRAM-ID: CHAP7A
//          PROGRAMMER: David M. Collopy
//          RUN DATE:   mm/dd/yy
//*************************************************************

//---------- PREPROCESSING DIRECTIVES ----------------------
#include<iostream.h>
```

FIGURE 7.4 Sample Program CHAP7A: Compute and Print a Six-Week Grade Report

```
#include<fstream.h>
#include<iomanip.h>

//---------- FUNCTION PROTOTYPES --------------------------

void OpenFile(void);              // open grade file
void PrnHeadings(void);           // print headings
void ProcessLoop(void);           // processing loop
void InputRecord(void);           // input grade record
void ComputeAvr(void);            // compute grade average
void PrnDetail(void);             // print detail line

//---------- PROGRAM SETUP --------------------------------

//** H E A D I N G   L I N E S

char PT1[] = "    S I X   W E E K   G R A D E   R E P O R T";
char HL1[] = "  Student     T e s t   S c o r e s     Average";
char HL2[] = "--------------------------------------------";

//** I N P U T   G R A D E   R E C O R D

ifstream gradeFile;               // file object name
char student[16];                 // student name
int  grade1;                      // 1st week grade
int  grade2;                      // 2nd week grade
int  grade3;                      // 3rd week grade
int  grade4;                      // 4th week grade
int  grade5;                      // 5th week grade
int  grade6;                      // 6th week grade

//** P R O G R A M   V A R I A B L E S

float gradeTotal;                 // grade total
float gradeAvr;                   // grade average

//** O P E N   P R I N T E R   F I L E

ofstream prnt("PRN");

//---------------------------------------------------------
//            MAINLINE CONTROL
//---------------------------------------------------------
main()
{
    OpenFile();                   // open grade file
    if (!gradeFile.fail()) {
        PrnHeadings();            // print headings
```

(continued on next page)

FIGURE 7.4 *Continued*

```
        ProcessLoop();              // processing loop
        gradeFile.close();          // close grade file
    }
    cout << "\n-----<E N D   O F   R U N>-----";
    return 0;
}
//-------------------------------------------------------------
//              OPEN GRADE FILE
//-------------------------------------------------------------
void OpenFile(void)
{
    gradeFile.open("a:grades.dat");
    if (gradeFile.fail())
        cout << "Grade file open failed" << endl;
    return;
}
//-------------------------------------------------------------
//              PRINT HEADINGS
//-------------------------------------------------------------
void PrnHeadings(void)
{
    prnt << "\f";                   // reset to top of page
    prnt << PT1 << endl;            // print page title 1
    prnt << endl << endl;           // triple space
    prnt << HL1 << endl;            // print heading line 1
    prnt << HL2 << endl;            // print heading line 2
    return;
}
//-------------------------------------------------------------
//              PROCESSING LOOP
//-------------------------------------------------------------
void ProcessLoop(void)
{
    InputRecord();                  // input grade record
    while (!gradeFile.eof())  {
        ComputeAvr();               // compute average grade
        PrnDetail();                // print detail line
        InputRecord();              // input grade record
    }
    return;
}
//-------------------------------------------------------------
//              INPUT GRADE RECORD
//-------------------------------------------------------------
void InputRecord(void)
{
    gradeFile.get(student, 16)
        >> grade1 >> grade2 >> grade3
```

FIGURE 7.4 *Continued*

```
           >> grade4 >> grade5 >> grade6;
    gradeFile.get();              // clear input file buffer
    return;
}
//-----------------------------------------------------------
//             COMPUTE GRADE AVERAGE
//-----------------------------------------------------------
void ComputeAvr(void)
{
    gradeTotal = grade1 + grade2 + grade3 + grade4 + grade5 +
        grade6;
    gradeAvr = gradeTotal / 6;
    return;
}
//-----------------------------------------------------------
//             PRINT DETAIL LINE
//-----------------------------------------------------------
void PrnDetail(void)
{
    prnt << setw(15) << student << setw(4) << grade1
         << setw(4) << grade2 << setw(4) << grade3
         << setw(4) << grade4 << setw(4) << grade5
         << setw(40 << grade6 << setiosflags(ios::fixed)
         << setiosflags(ios::showpoint)
         << setw(10) << setprecision(2) << gradeAvr << endl;
    return;
}
```

FIGURE 7.4   *Continued*

```
    S I X   W E E K   G R A D E   R E P O R T


Student        T e s t   S c o r e s      Average
--------------------------------------------------
Kelly Antonetz 70  50  98  80  65  85     74.67
Robert Cain    97  82  79  73  94  62     81.17
Karen Dehaven  81  87  94  85  93  89     88.17
Barry Harmon   76  77  80  81  75  92     80.17
Katrina Lang   99  93  89  83  94  90     91.33
Amanda Mohr    65  67  71  84  88  96     78.50
Mike Revell    90  87  78  52  76  89     78.76
Woody Synder   76  76  83  85  77  81     79.67
```

FIGURE 7.5   Screen Output for CHAP7A

```
MAINLINE CONTROL:

main()
{
    OpenFile();
    if (!gradeFile.fail())  {
        PrnHeadings();
        ProcessLoop();
        gradeFile.close();
    }
    cout << "\n-----<E N D   O F   R U N>-----";
    return 0;
}
```

According to the *MAINLINE*, control passes to the subordinate modules only if the grades file can be opened. The *OpenFile* module attempts to open the file and returns the value 1 if the file can be opened.

Next the program tests the return value to determine whether to process the body of the *if* statement. If gradeFile.fail() equals 1, the main() calls the modules in the order shown—*PrnHeadings* and *ProcessLoop*. Otherwise, control skips the body of the *if* statement and prints the end of run message.

After processing the grades data, the file is closed. The gradeFile.close() function closes the grades file.

```
OPEN GRADE FILE:

void OpenFile(void)
{
    gradeFile.open("a:grades.dat");
    if (gradeFile.fail())
        cout << "Grade file open failed" << endl;
    return 0;
}
```

The above open statement attempts to open the *grades.dat* file. If the file is opened, then gradeFile.fail() returns a 0 (open successful) and the address of the file is assigned to the file object identifier. If the file is not opened, then gradeFile.fail() returns a 1 (open failed) and the error message `Grade file open failed` is displayed on the screen. Common open errors include misspelling the file name, forgetting to create the file, and inserting the wrong disk in the designated drive.

This is how the condition test works. If the file is opened, then `gradeFile.open()` returns the value 0 (open) to `gradeFile.fail()` function. Hence, the condition evaluates as false and control returns to the calling module. Otherwise, the error message is displayed on the screen.

```
PROCESSING LOOP:

void ProcessLoop(void)
{
    InputRecord();
```

The previous statement means: Transfer control to the *InputRecord* module and read the data for the first record.

```
    while (!gradeFile.eof())  {
```

The preceding statement means: As long as the current position in the grades file is not equal to the end-of-file marker, then execute the statements in the body of the loop. Otherwise, skip the statement body of the *while* loop.

```
        ComputeAvr();
        PrnDetail();
        InputRecord();
    }
    return;
}
```

The above statements mean: Execute the modules in the body of the loop in the order listed—*ComputeAvr, PrnDetail*, and *InputRecord*. After all the records in the grades file have been processed (end of file), return to the calling module.

```
INPUT GRADE RECORD:
void InputRecord(void)
{
    gradeFile.get(student, 16)
        >> grade1 >> grade2 >> grade3
        >> grade4 >> grade5 >> grade6;
    gradeFile.get();
    return;
}
```

The above statements mean: Read a record from the grades file and assign the data to the variables in the order listed—*student, grade1, grade2, grade3, grade4, grade5*, and *grade6*.

The first get() function tells the program to read the first 16 characters of the input file stream and store the resulting string in the variable *student*. The remainder of the first get() function tells the program to read the rest of the file stream and assign the data to the grade variables. The second get() function clears the input file stream buffer. After reading a record and clearing the buffer, control returns to the calling module.

Notice that the assignment of data to a variable is based on position only. That is, the first constant is assigned to the first variable, the second constant is assigned to the second variable, and so on.

Text File Processing Steps

Reading a file and assigning data to a program involves a series of activities that take place in different parts of the program. However, there is a relationship among a number of factors that we should clarify at this point.

Text file processing involves the following six-step process. Sample Program CHAP7A will be used to illustrate these steps.

Step 1: Create the file

Use a text editor to create the file. Key in one record per line and press the Enter key at the end of each line. After entering all of the data, save the file on your disk.

Step 2: Set up the input stream file

Declare the input file stream and assign an identifier name to the stream. The following declaration associates the identifier, *gradeFile*, with the input file stream:

```
ifstream gradeFile;
```

Step 3: Define the record format

Define the format of the input record. The following record structure defines the input fields (data types and names) belonging to the grades record:

```
char    student[16];
int     grade1;
int     grade2;
int     grade3;
int     grade4;
int     grade5;
int     grade6;
```

When data is read from the input file stream, it is assigned to the input fields.

Step 4: Open the file

Before a record can be retrieved from the input file stream, the file must be activated, or opened. The following open statement performs the necessary activities and prepares the *grades.dat* file for the read operation:

```
gradeFile.open("a:grades.dat");
```

Step 5: Read a record

The file object identifier, in conjunction with the get() function, reads data from the file and assigns the input stream to the program variables. According to the example, data is retrieved from the grades file and is assigned to the input fields *student, grade1, grade2, grade3, grade4, grade5,* and *grade6*, respectively. The second gradeFile.get() clears the input file buffer.

```
gradeFile.get(student, 16)
    >> grade1 >> grade2 >> grade3
    >> grade4 >> grade5 >> grade6;
gradeFile.get();
```

Step 6: Close the file

After a file has been read and processed, it is closed.

```
gradeFile.close();
```

The close() function closes the grades file and releases the input file buffer.

Using a Trailer Record

We may use the eof() function to test for the end-of-file condition, or we may use a trailer record. A **trailer record** is a special record that is placed at the end of the file (trails the data) by the programmer. It is not actually processed by the program but is instead used to determine when to stop reading data from the file. As an example, consider the simple inventory file shown in Figure 7.6, which consists of the following data—item number, item description, quantity on hand, and quantity on order. Look at the last record—the trailer record. When the program encounters the trailer record, it stops reading data from the inventory file.

As with the eof() function, the end-of-file test using a trailer record can be implemented with the *if* or *while* statement. The examples below illustrate this process.

Examples:

```
1. if (itemNumber != 0)
   .....

2. while (itemNumber != 0)
   .....
```

Both examples test for the end-of-file condition by comparing the item number of the input to 0. If the trailer record has not been read, control enters the statement body. Otherwise, control skips to the first command after the *if* or *while* statement.

Checkpoint 7C

1. List and briefly explain the six steps involved in defining a file and reading the input data.
2. What is a trailer record? What is its purpose?
3. Code a *while* statement that checks the input employee number for a trailer record value equal to zero. The *while* statement should continue looping as long as the employee number is not equal to zero.

Sample Program CHAP7B

Sample program CHAP7B (Figure 7.9, p. 214) reads an inventory file, processes the data, and produces a printed list of the sales activities for the past week. Quantities on hand and on order are totalled, and the results are printed at the end of the report. The output for sample program CHAP7B is shown in Figure 7.10 (p. 217).
    The following specifications apply:

Input (text file):

For each inventory record, read and assign data to the following fields. Field size and type are shown in parentheses.

1. Item number   (3 int)
2. Item description   (15 char)
3. Quantity on hand   (2 int)
4. Quantity on order   (2 int)

```
100 Hammer          10 20
200 Saw             24 00
300 Screwdriver     12 36
400 Pliers          40 00
500 Drill           24 12
600 Wrench          16 05
000 End of File     00 00
```

FIGURE 7.6   File with Trailer record

Text File (invent.dat):

Use the data given below to create the inventory file. The numbers shown above the columns correspond to the fields described for the input. Note the trailer record.

1	2	3	4
100	Hammer	10	20
200	Saw	24	00
300	Screwdriver	12	36
400	Pliers	40	00
500	Drill	24	12
600	Wrench	16	05
000	End of File	00	00

Output (printer):

Print the inventory report shown in Figure 7.10.

Processing Requirements:

- Read the inventory file.
- Accumulate the total quantity on hand.
- Accumulate the total quantity on order.

Pseudocode:

```
START
Open file
If file opened
    Print report headings
    Read a record
    LOOP until item number = 0
        Compute totals
        Print detail line
        Read a record
    End LOOP
    Print totals
    Close file
END
```

Hierarchy Chart: See Figure 7.7.
Program Flowchart: See Figure 7.8.

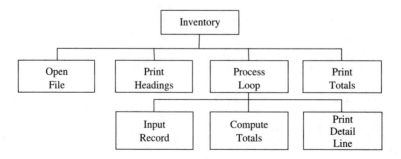

FIGURE 7.7   Hierarchy Chart for CHAP7B

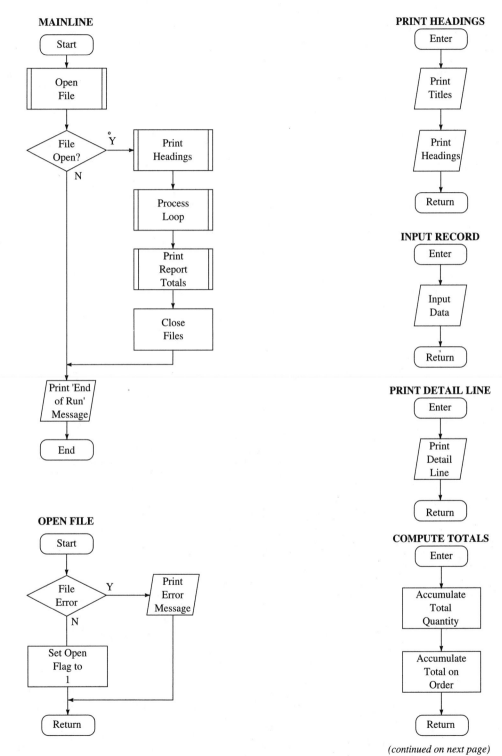

FIGURE 7.8   Program Flowchart for CHAP7B

(continued on next page)

PROCESS LOOP

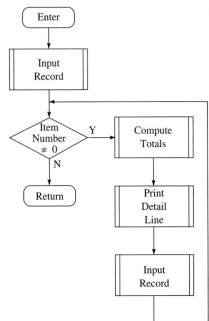

PRINT REPORT TOTALS

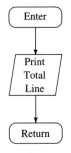

FIGURE 7.8   *Continued*

```
//---------- INVENTORY ------------------------------------
//    Read a file, compute totals for quanity on hand and
//    quantity on order, and print an inventory report. A
//    trailer record is used to detect the end of the file.
//
//          PROGRAM-ID: CHAP7B
//          PROGRAMMER: David M. Collopy
//          RUN DATE:   mm/dd/yy
//**********************************************************

//---------- PREPROCESSING DIRECTIVES ----------------------

#include<iostream.h>
#include<fstream.h>
#include<iomanip.h>


//---------- FUNCTION PROTOTYPES ---------------------------

void OpenFile(void);           // open inventory file
void PrnHeadings(void);        // print headings
```

FIGURE 7.9   Sample Program CHAP7B: Reads a File, Computes Totals, and Prints a Detail Line for Each Inventory Record Processed

```
void ProcessLoop(void);            // processing loop
void InputRecord(void);            // input inventory record
void ComputeTotals(void);          // compute totals
void PrnDetail(void);              // print detail line
void PrnTotals(void);              // print report totals

//---------- PROGRAM SETUP ------------------------------

//** H E A D I N G   L I N E S

char PT1[] = "          W O R K - L I N E   T O O L S        ";
char PT2[] = "              Inventory Report                 ";
char HL1[] = " Item                      Quantity  Quantity";
char HL2[] = "Number    Item Description  on Hand  on Order";
char HL3[] = "-------------------------------------------";
char TL[]  = "                    Totals: ";

//** I N P U T   I N V E N T O R Y   R E C O R D

ifstream invFile;                  // file object name
int  itemNum;                      // item number
char desc[16];                     // item description
int  quant;                        // quantity on hand
int  onOrder;                      // quantity on order

//** P R O G R A M   V A R I A B L E S

float totQuant;                    // total quantity on hand
float totOnOrder;                  // total quantity on order

//** O P E N   P R I N T E R   F I L E

ofstream prnt("PRN");

//------------------------------------------------------
//               MAINLINE CONTROL
//------------------------------------------------------
main()
{
    OpenFile();                    // open inventory file
    if (!invFile.fail()) {
        PrnHeadings();             // print headings
        ProcessLoop();             // processing loop
        PrnTotals();               // print report totals
        invFile.close();           // close inventory file
    }
    cout << "\n-----<E N D   O F   R U N>-----";
    return 0;
```

(continued on next page)

FIGURE 7.9 *Continued*

```
    }
    //-------------------------------------------------------------
    //              OPEN INVENTORY FILE
    //-------------------------------------------------------------
    void OpenFile(void)
    {
        invFile.open("a:invent.dat");
        if (invFile.fail())
            cout << "Inventory file open failed" << endl;
        return;
    }
    //-------------------------------------------------------------
    //              PRINT HEADINGS
    //-------------------------------------------------------------
    void PrnHeadings(void)
    {
        prnt << "\f";                   // reset to top of page
        prnt << PT1 << endl;            // print page title 1
        prnt << PT2 << endl;            // print page title 2
        prnt << endl;                   // double space
        prnt << HL1 << endl;            // print heading line 1
        prnt << HL2 << endl;            // print heading line 2
        prnt << HL3 << endl;            // print heading line 3
        return;
    }
    //-------------------------------------------------------------
    //              PROCESSING LOOP
    //-------------------------------------------------------------
    void ProcessLoop(void)
    {
        InputRecord();                  // input inventory record
        while (itemNum != 0)   {
            ComputeTotals();            // compute totals
            PrnDetail();                // print detail line
            InputRecord();              // input inventory record
        }
        return;
    }
    //-------------------------------------------------------------
    //              INPUT INVENTORY RECORD
    //-------------------------------------------------------------
    void InputRecord(void)
    {
        invFile >> itmNum;
        invFile.get(desc, 16) >> quant >> onOrder;
        gradeFile.get();                // clear input file buffer
        return;
    }
```

FIGURE 7.9   *Continued*

```
//------------------------------------------------------------
//              COMPUTE TOTALS
//------------------------------------------------------------
void ComputeTotals(void)
{
    totQuant = totQuant + quant;
    totOnOrder = totOnOrder + onOrder;
    return;
}
//------------------------------------------------------------
//              PRINT DETAIL LINE
//------------------------------------------------------------
void PrnDetail(void)
{
    prnt << setw(4) << itemNum << "      "
         << setiosflags(ios::left)        // left justify
         << setw(21) << desc
         << resetiosflags(ios::left)      // right justify
         << setw(5) << quant << setw(11) << onOrder << endl;
    return;
}
//------------------------------------------------------------
//              PRINT REPORT TOTALS
//------------------------------------------------------------
void PrnTotals(void)
{
    prnt << endl << TL << setw(6) << totQuant
         << setw(11) << totOnOrder << endl;
    return;
}
```

FIGURE 7.9 *Continued*

```
                W O R K - L I N E   T O O L S
                     Inventory Report
    Item                          Quantity    Quantity
    Number  Item Description      on Hand     on Order
    ------------------------------------------------------
     100    Hammer                   10          20
     200    Saw                      24           0
     300    Screwdriver              12          36
     400    Pliers                   40           0
     500    Drill                    24          12
     600    Wrench                   16           5

                        Totals:     126          73
```

FIGURE 7.10 Output Report for CHAP7B

Dissection of Sample Program CHAP7B

Overall, the file-processing activities performed by sample program CHAP7B are similar to those shown for CHAP7A. The only difference is that sample program CHAP7B uses a trailer record to mark the end of the file. Therefore, we will look at the end of file test performed by ProcessLoop.

```
PROCESSING LOOP:

void ProcessLoop(void)
{
    InputRecord();
```

The above statement means: Transfer control to the *InputRecord* module and read the first record.

```
    while (itemNum != 0)   {
```

The above statement means: As long as the input item number is not equal to 0 (the value specified by the trailer record), execute the statements in the body of the loop. If the item number is 0, then the file is empty and control skips the statement body of the loop.

```
        ComputeTotals();
        PrnDetail();
        InputRecord();
    }
    return;
}
```

The above statements mean: Call and execute the modules in the body of the loop in the order listed—*ComputeTotals, PrnDetail*, and *InputRecord*. After all the records have been processed (*itemNum* = 0), control returns to the calling module.

Summary

1. Data is organized into fields, records, and files to facilitate processing by the computer.
2. A text file consists of readable data that can be created with a text editor. Data constants, organized into records and stored on disk, are read from a file and processed by the program.
3. Text file processing involves the following activities: creating a file, setting up the input file stream, opening the file, reading and processing the data in the file, and closing the file.
4. A disk text file is created by using a text editor to enter, edit, and save data for later use by the program. Data is keyed into a file one record at a time. Each record ends with the newline character. The data constants should be organized into columns and separated by white space.
5. The file object name associates an identifier with the input file stream. Each file processed by the program must have a unique identifier name.

6. The open() member function opens a file. When a file is opened, the open() function passes the address of the disk file to the file identifier name.

7. The input statement uses the file identifier name to read data from the file stream and to assign the input to the program variables. Since there is no inherent connection between the data in the file and the variable names specified by the input statement, it is up to the programmer to maintain a positional relationship and match them accordingly.

8. In order to prevent the program from reading past the last record, the eof() function is used to test for the end-of-file condition. If the file pointer is not pointing to the end of the file, the eof() function returns a zero (false). Otherwise, it returns a nonzero value (true).

9. All files should be closed prior to exiting the program. The close() function clears and releases the file buffer and closes the file specified by the file identifier name.

10. We may use a trailer record to test for the end-of-file condition. A trailer record is a special record that is placed at the end of the file—it trails the data. It is used to signal that the program has reached the end of the file.

Programming Projects

For each project, design the logic and write the modular structured program to produce the output. Model your program after the sample programs presented in the chapter. Verify your output.

Project 7–1   Overdue Accounts

Write a program to read an overdue accounts file and print a report of the customers with account balances that are 90 days overdue.

Input (text file):

For each customer record, read and assign data to the following fields. Field size and type are shown in parentheses.

1. Account number   (4 int)
2. Customer name   (15 char)
3. Days overdue   (2 int)
4. Balance due   (6.2 float)

Text File (overdue.dat):

Use the data given below to create the overdue accounts file. The numbers shown above the columns correspond to the fields described for the input.

1	2	3	4
1010	David Ryan	90	400.00
2450	Marie Hill	30	754.00
2730	Rita Fox	90	740.00
3100	Alvin Porter	90	550.00

4080	Corey Adkins	30	233.00
4890	Amy Wyatt	30	700.00
5260	Brian Knox	30	625.00
6350	Susan Cope	90	600.00
7720	Lisa Wilson	60	417.00
8540	Matt Hart	90	900.00
9200	Tori Landis	90	235.00
9630	Pat Rankin	60	342.00

Output (printer):

Print the following 90-day overdue accounts report:

```
Author              90-DAY OVERDUE ACCOUNTS          Page 01
                          mm/dd/yy


   Acct Number         Customer Name         Amount Due

      9999             X----------X             999.99
       :                   :                      :
       :                   :                      :
      9999             X----------X             999.99

                                    Total:     9999.99


   Number of accounts overdue:   99
   Number of accounts > 500.00:  99
```

Processing Requirements:

- Read the overdue accounts file.
- Print a report of all accounts that are 90 days overdue.
- Accumulate a total for amount due.
- Count the number of 90-day overdue accounts.
- Count the number of 90-day overdue accounts that have a balance greater than $500.

Project 7–2 Payroll

Write a program to read a payroll file, calculate pay, and print a weekly payroll roster. Hours worked over 40 are paid overtime. Assume the current federal income tax (FIT) rate is 15%.

Input (text file):

For each payroll record, read and assign data to the following fields. Field size and type are shown in parentheses.

1. Employee name (15 char)

2. Hours worked   (2 int)

3. Hourly pay rate (5.2 float)

Text File (payroll.dat):

Use the data given below to create the payroll file. The numbers shown above the columns correspond to the fields described for the input.

1	2	3
Tanya Bauer	40	7.50
Dana Clark	45	14.90
Sara Erickson	38	12.00
Scott Howard	42	9.75
Paul Irwin	48	8.72
Dale Miller	40	10.25
Bret Rossi	35	8.00
Karen Thomas	48	9.00
Tracy York	36	11.00

Output (printer):

Print the following weekly payroll report:

```
Author                    WEEKLY  PAYROLL  REPORT              Page 01
                                mm/dd/yy


Employee    Hours     Regular    Overtime    Gross
Name        Worked    Pay        Pay         Pay        FIT      Net Pay

X-------X     99      999.99      99.99      9999.99    99.99     999.99
   :           :         :          :           :         :         :
   :           :         :          :           :         :         :
X-------X     99      999.99      99.99      9999.99    99.99     999.99

          Totals:  9999.99     999.99     99999.99   999.99    9999.99
```

Processing Requirements:

- Read the payroll file.
- Compute the regular pay:
  If hours > 40,
    then regular pay = *40 × pay rate*
    else regular pay = *hours × pay rate*
- Compute the overtime pay:
  If hours > 40,
    then overtime pay = *(hours – 40) × 1.5 × pay rate*
    else overtime pay = 0
- Compute the gross pay:
  regular pay + overtime pay
- Compute the federal income tax:
  gross pay × FIT rate
- Compute the net pay:
  gross pay – FIT
- Accumulate totals for regular pay, overtime pay, gross pay, FIT, and net pay.

Project 7–3   Sales Profit

Write a program to read a sales file, calculate profit per salesperson, and print a sales profit report.

Input (text file):

For each sales record, read and assign data to the following fields. Field size and type are shown in parentheses.

1. Salesperson name   (15 char)
2. Total sales   (8.2 float)
3. Cost of sales   (8.2 float)

Text File (sales.dat):

Use the data given below to create the sales file. The numbers shown above the columns correspond to the fields described for the input:

1	2	3
Lisa Conrad	8120.52	6450.71
Roy Hickle	2245.78	1072.49
Tara Perkins	12710.14	9735.38
Dennis Tian	4567.51	3119.22
Ann Zimmerman	5793.59	4204.45

Output (printer):

Print the following sales profit report:

```
Author              SALES PROFIT REPORT           Page 01
                         mm/dd/yy


Salesperson    Total Sales   Cost of Sales    Net Profit
--------------------------------------------------------
X---------X      99999.99       99999.99        99999.99
    :               :              :               :
    :               :              :               :
X---------X      99999.99       99999.99        99999.99

                                 Total:         999999.99

                                 Average:        99999.99
```

Processing Requirements:

- Read the sales file.
- Compute the net profit:
  total sales – cost of sales
- Count the number of salespeople.
- Accumulate a total for net profit.
- Compute average net profit:
  total net profit / number of salespeople

Project 7–4   Inventory

Write a program to read an inventory file and print an inventory reorder report.

Input (text file):

For each inventory record, read and assign data to the following fields:

1. Item number   (4 int)
2. Item description   (15 char)
3. Quantity on hand   (2 int)
4. Reorder point   (2 int)
5. Reorder quantity   (2 int)
6. Unit cost   (5.2 float)
7. Selling price   (5.2 float)

Text File (invent.dat):

Use the data given below to create the inventory file. The numbers shown above the columns correspond to the fields described for the input.

1	2	3	4	5	6	7
1000	Hammers	24	12	24	4.75	9.49
2000	Saws	08	16	12	7.50	14.99
3000	Drills	10	12	18	7.83	15.95
4000	Screwdrivers	36	24	12	2.27	4.98
5000	Pliers	12	12	36	2.65	5.49

Output (printer):

Print the following inventory reorder report:

```
Author              INVENTORY REORDER REPORT          Page 01
                         mm/dd/yy

Item                            Quantity   Reorder     Item
Number   Description            on Hand    Quantity    Cost

9999     X-----------X             99         99      999.99
  :           :                    :          :          :
  :           :                    :          :          :
9999     X-----------X             99         99      999.99

                                   Total Cost:        9999.99
```

Processing Requirements:

- Read the inventory file.
- Determine what items to reorder:
  Order the reorder quantity when the quantity on hand is less than or equal to the reorder point.
- Compute the item cost:
  reorder quantity × unit cost
- Accumulate the total cost.

Project 7–5   Personnel

Write a program to read a personnel file and print a salary report of all female employees who are paid more than $30,000 a year.

Input (text file):

For each employee record, read and assign data to the following fields. Field size and type are shown in parentheses.

1. Employee number   (4 int)
2. Employee name   (15 char)
3. Department number   (2 int)
4. Sex code   (1 char)
5. Annual Salary   (8.2 float)

Text File (persnel.dat):

Use the data given below to create the personnel file. The numbers shown above the columns correspond to the fields described for the record.

1	2	3	4	5
1926	Dana Andrews	10	F	29000.00
2071	Scott Cooper	14	M	30250.00
3150	Todd Feldman	22	M	24175.00
3600	Amy Kwon	19	F	36025.00
4100	Derek Lowe	50	M	29120.00
4298	Lori Palmer	35	F	33400.00
5409	Bob Shields	47	M	27500.00
6552	Pam Wolfe	31	F	31773.00

Output (printer):

Print the following personnel salary report:

```
Author                PERSONNEL SALARY REPORT           Page 01
                           mm/dd/yy
Employee                                Department         Annual
Number           Employee Name            Number           Salary

 9999            X-----------X              99            99999.99
   :                  :                      :               :
   :                  :                      :               :
 9999            X-----------X              99            99999.99

                                         Average:         99999.99
```

Processing Requirements:

- Read the personnel file.
- Print a report of all female employees who are paid more than $30,000 a year.
- Accumulate a total for annual salary.
- Compute the average annual salary:
  total annual salary / number of female employees

Project 7–6   Accounts Payable

Write a program to read a vendor file, compute amount due, and print an accounts payable report. Assume the following discount schedule applies to early payments:

Paid by (Days)	Discount
1 – 10	12%
11 – 20	10%
21 – 30	08%
31 – 45	05%

Input (text file):

For each vendor record, read and assign data to the following fields. Field size and type are shown in parentheses.

1. Vendor number   (3 int)
2. Vendor name   (12 char)
3. Invoice number   (5 char)
4. Invoice amount   (7.2 float)
5. Days paid by   (2 int)

Text File (vendor.dat):

Use the data given below to create the vendor file. The numbers shown above the columns correspond to the fields described for the input.

1	2	3	4	5
217	Metacraft	A1239	2309.12	10
349	IntraTell	T9823	670.00	25
712	Reylock	F0176	4563.78	33
501	Universal	W0105	1200.00	21
196	Northland	X2781	3429.34	45
414	MarxComm	H9205	913.87	18
659	Veston	D1776	5127.63	30

Output (printer):

Print the following accounts payable report:

```
Author                  ACCOUNTS PAYABLE REPORT              Page 01
                              mm/dd/yy


Vendor                   Invoice   Invoice   Discount   Amount
Number   Vendor Name     Number    Amount    Amount     Due

 999     X--------X      XXXX      9999.99    999.99    9999.99
  :          :            :           :         :          :
  :          :            :           :         :          :
 999     X--------X      XXXX      9999.99    999.99    9999.99

              Totals:             99999.99   9999.99   99999.99
```

Processing Requirements:

- Read the vendor file.
- Determine the discount rate based on early payment (see the discount schedule).
- Compute the discount amount:
  invoice amount × discount rate
- Compute the amount due:
  invoice amount − discount amount
- Accumulate totals for invoice amount, discount amount, and amount due.

Project 7–7   Production Output

Write a program to read a production file, compute bonus pay, and print a bonus pay report. Assume production workers are paid a bonus according to the number of units they produce over the quota. Use the following bonus pay schedule:

Units over Quota	Pay Rate Each
1 – 10	0.60
11 – 25	0.65
26 – 45	0.70
46 +	0.75

Input (text file):

For each production record, read and assign data to the following fields. Field size and type are shown in parentheses.

1. Employee name   (15 char)

2. Product number   (5 char)

3. Production quota   (3 int)

4. Units produced   (3 int)

Text File (prod.dat):

Use the data given below to create the production file. The numbers shown above the columns correspond to the fields described for the input.

1	2	3	4
Kay Archer	P9511	65	65
Alan Baum	A1234	48	97
Marie Fitch	C4510	60	75
Lee Hildebrand	R0934	50	62
David Mullins	E3371	75	75
Chad Nelson	L8912	40	63
Bill Quinn	S0951	48	56
Nicole Renner	H9733	50	59
Erica Tate	Z0182	65	63
Terry West	A3235	70	116

Output (printer):

Print the following bonus pay report:

```
Author                    BONUS PAY REPORT                  Page 01
                             mm/dd/yy


                   Product          Units      Over
Employee Name      Number    Quota  Produced   Quota   Bonus Pay

X----------X       XXXXX       99      99        99      999.99
     :               :         :       :         :         :
     :               :         :       :         :         :
X----------X       XXXXX       99      99        99      999.99

                          Totals:    999       999     9999.99
```

Processing Requirements:

- Read the production file.
- Compute the bonus pay based on units over quota (see the bonus pay schedule).
- Accumulate totals for units produced, units over quota, and bonus pay.

8   Page and Control Breaks

Overview

Learning Objectives

After you have read this chapter and completed the exercises, you should be able to:

- use line and page counters to construct page break (multipage report) programs
- explain why control break processing requires that the input data be arranged in control field order
- design and write one-level control break programs
- combine page break and control break processing techniques to develop multipage, one-level subtotal reports

Page Breaks

In business, computer-generated reports often consist of multipage output. **Multipage** indicates that the output consists of two or more pages. Each page of a multipage report should show the title and column headings printed across the top of the page. The body or contents of a report is different for each page and should be printed after the title and column headings.

For each page of the report, maintain a one-inch margin at the top and bottom, and print between 50 and 55 detail lines. Furthermore, when a page is full, we want the printer to stop, skip to the top of the next page, and resume printing.

In other words, a page break occurs when the number of lines printed equals the limit established for the page. Accordingly, the printer advances to a new page, prints the title and column headings, and continues with the body of the report.

The process for determining a **page break** requires the use of a line counter. The purpose of the **line counter** is to keep track of the number of detail lines printed per page. Each time a line is printed, the line counter is incremented and compared to the maximum number of lines allowed per page. If we are also numbering the pages, then we need an additional variable—a page counter. The purpose of the **page counter** is to keep track of the number of pages printed.

To further illustrate the concept of page breaks, let us look at the payroll report shown in Figure 8.1. Assume we are printing 40 lines per page. Once 40 detail lines have been printed, the line counter is set to 0, 1 is added to the page counter, the printer advances to the top of the next page; and the title, page number, and column heading line are printed. The pseudocode version of the page break routine is shown in Figure 8.2.

Given the limit of 40 lines per page, note the page and the line counters shown in Figure 8.2. For each page, the line counter advances from 1 to 40 as the detail lines are printed.

```
                    PAYROLL  REPORT                Page  1

       ID#    EMPLOYEE  NAME        PAY  RATE    HOURS  WORKED
      -----------------------------------------------------------
       101    Kami  Peyton            12.00          40
        :        :                      :             :
        :        :                      :             :
        :        :                      :             :
        :        :                      :             :
       140    David  Kerrington       10.00          39


                    PAYROLL  REPORT                Page  2

       ID#    EMPLOYEE  NAME        PAY  RATE    HOURS  WORKED
      -----------------------------------------------------------
       141    Kent  Broadwell         9.00          37
        :        :                      :             :
        :        :                      :             :
        :        :                      :             :
       165    Elinore  McLain        14.00          40
```

FIGURE 8.1 Payroll Report with Page Break

```
                                          Counters
                :                      Page    Line
If line count > 40
    Set line count to 0                 1     1-40
    Add 1 to page number                2     1-40
    Advance to the next page            3     1-40
    Print titles, page number, and      :      :
        column headings                 :      :
                :                        n     1-40
```

FIGURE 8.2   Page Break Logic

Checkpoint 8A

1. When does a page break occur?
2. What is the purpose of a page counter? A line counter?
3. Write the pseudocode that shows the steps involved in performing a page break.

Sample Program CHAP8A

This program demonstrates page break processing and prints a rental income report for Pernell Properties. Each detail line includes the location, rental agency, property manager, building number, apartment number, and monthly rent. Total monthly income is accumulated and printed at the end of the report. Sample program CHAP8A is shown in Figure 8.5 (p. 236); the program output is shown in Figures 8.6a (p. 239) and 8.6b (p. 240).

Input (text file):

For each rent record, read and assign data to the following fields. Field size and type are shown in parentheses.

1. Location   (5 char)
2. Agency number   (2 int)
3. Manager number   (3 int)
4. Building number   (2 int)
5. Apartment number   (1 int)
6. Monthly rent   (6.2 float)

Text File (rent.dat):

Use the data given below to create the rent file. The numbers shown above the columns correspond to the fields described for the input.

1	2	3	4	5	6
North	20	201	10	1	400.00
North	20	201	10	2	410.00
North	20	201	10	3	335.00

North	20	201	15	1	375.00
North	20	201	15	2	385.00
North	20	247	17	1	450.00
North	20	247	17	2	450.00
North	43	316	22	1	345.00
North	43	316	22	2	465.00
East	10	237	30	1	410.00
East	10	237	30	2	365.00
East	10	237	30	3	470.00
East	10	237	30	4	345.00
East	10	659	33	1	429.00
East	10	659	33	2	465.00
End	00	000	00	0	000.00 (trailer record)

Output (printer):

Print the page break report shown in Figures 8.6a and 8.6b.

Processing Requirements:

- Read the rent file.
- Print 12 detail lines per page.
- Accumulate a report total for rent.

Pseudocode:

```
START
Open file
If file opened
   Set line count to 0
   Add 1 to page number
   Advance to the next page
   Print titles, page number, and column heading
   Read a record
   LOOP until agency = 0
      Accumulate report total for rent
      If line count > 12
         Set line count to 0
         Add 1 to page number
         Advance to the next page
         Print titles, page number, and column heading
      Print detail line
      Add 1 to line count
      Read a record
   End LOOP
   Print total rent
   Close file
END
```

Hierarchy Chart: See Figure 8.3.

Program Flowchart: See Figure 8.4.

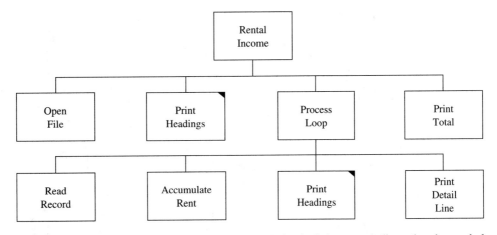

FIGURE 8.3 Hierarchy Chart for CHAP8A (*Note:* The shaded corners indicate that the symbol represents a module that is called by two or more modules in the program.)

Dissection of Sample Program CHAP8A

Let us examine the processing of sample program CHAP8A, beginning with the *PRINT HEADINGS* module. Note the activities performed by the module: It sets the line counter (*lineCnt*) to 0, increments the page number (*pageNum*), advances to the top of the next page, and prints the report titles and column headings.

From here, we enter the heart of the program: the *PROCESSING LOOP*. Overall, this module consists of a *while* loop that controls the reading of the file and the overall processing performed by the program.

```
PROCESSING LOOP:

void ProcessLoop(void)
{
    ReadRecord();
```

The priming read statement transfers control to the *ReadRecord* module; this module retrieves the first record from the rent file.

```
while (agency != 0)   {
```

The above statement means: As long as the agency number read from the file is not equal to 0 (the value specified by the trailer record), execute the statements in the body of the loop. If the agency number is 0, then the rent file is empty and control skips to the first executable statement after the *while* loop.

```
AccumRent();
```

The above statement means: Transfer control to the *AccumRent* module; this module adds the input rent income to the total rent.

```
if (lineCnt >= maxLines)
    PrnHeadings();
```

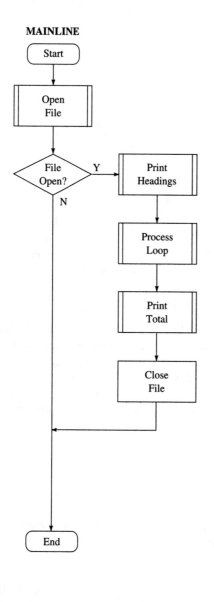

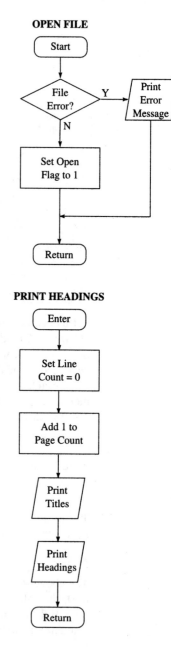

FIGURE 8.4   Program Flowchart for CHAP8A

PRINT REPORT TOTAL

Enter

Print
Report
Total

Return

READ RECORD

Enter

Read
Text
File

Return

PRINT DETAIL LINE

Enter

Print
Detail
Line

Add 1 to
Line Count

Return

PROCESS LOOP

Enter

Read
Record

(A)

Agency
≠ 0

Y → Accumulate
Rent

N

Return

Line
Count > Max
Lines

Y → Print
Headings

N

Print
Detail
Line

Read
Record

(A)

ACCUMULATE RENT

Enter

Accumulate
Total
Rent

Return

FIGURE 8.4   *Continued*

The preceding statement (p. 233) means: Compare the line counter (*lineCnt*) to the maximum number of lines (*maxLines*) allowed per page. If the line counter is greater than or equal to the maximum lines, then transfer control to the *PrnHeadings* module; this module prints the report title and column headings. Otherwise, fall through and continue with the next statement.

```
PrnDetail();
```

The above statement means: Transfer control to the *PrnDetail* module; this module prints the detail line.

```
        ReadRecord();
    }
    return;
}
```

```
//-------- RENTAL INCOME ------------------------------------
//     This program demonstrates page break processing for
//     Pernell rental properties.
//
//              PROGRAM-ID: CHAP8A
//              PROGRAMMER: David M. Collopy
//              RUN DATE:   mm/dd/yy
//***********************************************************

//**   PREPROCESSING DIRECTIVES

#include<iostream.h>
#include<fstream.h>
#include<iomanip.h>

//-------- FUNCTION PROTOTYPES ------------------------------

void OpenFile(void);            // open rent file
void PrnHeadings(void);         // print headings
void ProcessLoop(void);         // processing loop
void ReadRecord(void);          // read rent record
void AccumRent(void);           // accumulate rent
void PrnDetail(void);           // print detail line
void PrnTotal(void);            // print total rent

//-------- PROGRAM SETUP ------------------------------------

//**   H E A D I N G   L I N E S

char PT1[] = "P E R N E L L   P R O P E R T I E S    Page";
char PT2[] = "               Rental Income                ";
```

FIGURE 8.5 Sample Program CHAP8A: Print a Rental Income Report for Pernell Properties (Total rent is accumulated and printed at the end of the report.)

```
char HL[]  = "LOCATION  AGENCY  MGR  BLDG    APART#    RENT ";
char RTL[] = "                      ***** Report Total: $ ";

//**  I N P U T   R E N T   R E C O R D

ifstream rentFile;              // file object name
char  location[6];              // location code
int   agency;                   // agency number
int   mgr;                      // manager number
int   bldg;                     // building number
int   apart;                    // apartment number
float rent;                     // monthly rent income

//**  P R O G R A M   V A R I A B L E S

float rptTotal = 0.0;           // report total rent
int   pageNum = 0;              // page number
int   lineCnt;                  // detail line count
int   maxLines = 12;            // max detail lines per page

//**  O P E N   P R I N T E R   F I L E

ofstream prnt("PRN");           // open printer file

//-------------------------------------------------------------
//              MAINLINE CONTROL
//-------------------------------------------------------------
main()
{
    OpenFile();                 // open rent file
    if (!rentFile.fail())  {
        PrnHeadings();          // print headings
        ProcessLoop();          // processing loop
        PrnTotal();             // print total rent
        rentFile.close();       // close rent file
    }
    cout << "\n-----<E N D   O F   R U N>-----";
    return 0;
}
//-------------------------------------------------------------
//              OPEN RENT FILE
//-------------------------------------------------------------
void OpenFile(void)
{
    rentFile.open("a:rent.dat");
    if (rentFile.fail())
        cout << "Rent file open failed" << endl;
```

(continued on next page)

FIGURE 8.5   *Continued*

```
        return;
    }
    //------------------------------------------------------------
    //              PRINT HEADINGS
    //------------------------------------------------------------
    void PrnHeadings(void)
    {
        lineCnt = 0;                    // set line count to 0
        pageNum = pageNum + 1;          // add 1 to page number
        prnt << "\f";                   // reset to top of page
        prnt << PT1 << setw(2)
             << pageNum << endl;        // print page title 1
        prnt << PT2 << endl
             << endl;                   // print page title 2
        prnt << HL << endl
             << endl;                   // print heading line
        return;
    }
    //------------------------------------------------------------
    //              PROCESSING LOOP
    //------------------------------------------------------------
    void ProcessLoop(void)
    {
        ReadRecord();                   // read rent record
        while (agency != 0)  {
            AccumRent();                // accumulate rent
            if (lineCnt >= maxLines)
                PrnHeadings();          // print headings
            PrnDetail();                // print detail line
            ReadRecord();               // read rent record
        }
        return;
    }
    //------------------------------------------------------------
    //              READ RENT RECORD
    //------------------------------------------------------------
    void ReadRecord(void)
    {
        rentFile.get(location, 6) >> agency >> mgr
            >> bldg >> apart >> rent;
        rentFile.get();                 // clear input file buffer
        return;
    }
    //------------------------------------------------------------
    //              ACCUMULATE RENT
    //------------------------------------------------------------
    void AccumRent(void)
    {
```

FIGURE 8.5 *Continued*

```
      rptTotal = rptTotal + rent:
      return;
}
//------------------------------------------------------------
//              PRINT DETAIL LINE
//------------------------------------------------------------
void PrnDetail(void)
{
    prnt << setiosflags(ios::left)          // left justify
         << " " << setw(9) << location
         << resetiosflags(ios::left)        // right justify
         << setw(4) << agency << setw(7) << mgr
         << setw(5) << bldg << setw(7) << apart
         << "      $" << setiosflags(ios::fixed)
         << setiosflags(ios::showpoint) << setprecision(2)
         << setw(7) << rent << endl;
    lineCnt = lineCnt + 1;
    return;
}
//------------------------------------------------------------
//              PRINT TOTAL LINE
//------------------------------------------------------------
void PrnTotal(void)
{
    prnt << endl
         << RTL << setw(8) << rptTotal << endl;
    return;
}
```

```
P E R N E L L   P R O P E R T I E S      Page 1
               Rental Income


LOCATION  AGENCY  MGR  BLDG   APART#      RENT

  North      20   201   10      1      $ 400.00
  North      20   201   10      2      $ 410.00
  North      20   201   10      3      $ 335.00
  North      20   201   15      1      $ 375.00
  North      20   201   15      2      $ 385.00
  North      20   247   17      1      $ 450.00
  North      20   247   17      2      $ 450.00
  North      43   316   22      1      $ 345.00
  North      43   316   22      2      $ 465.00
  East       10   237   30      1      $ 410.00
  East       10   237   30      2      $ 365.00
  East       10   237   30      3      $ 470.00
```

FIGURE 8.6a   Program Output for CHAP8A

```
┌─────────────────────────────────────────────────────────┐
│                                                           │
│   P E R N E L L    P R O P E R T I E S      Page 2        │
│                   Rental Income                           │
│   LOCATION   AGENCY   MGR   BLDG    APART#      RENT       │
│     East       10     237    30       4      $  345.00    │
│     East       10     659    33       1      $  429.00    │
│     East       10     659    33       2      $  465.00    │
│                                                           │
│                ***** Report Total:   $ 6099.00           │
│                                                           │
└─────────────────────────────────────────────────────────┘
```

FIGURE 8.6b   Program Output for CHAP8A

The looping *read* statement (p. 236) transfers control to the *ReadRecord* module; this module retrieves the next record from the rent file.

The *return* statement sends control back to the *MAINLINE*, the calling module.

```
READ RENT RECORD:

void ReadRecord(void)
{
    rentFile.get(location, 6) >> agency >> mgr
        >> bldg >> apart >> rent;
    rentFile.get();
    return;
}
```

The above statements mean: Read a record from the rent file and assign the input to the variables in the order listed—*location, agency, mgr, bldg, apart*, and *rent*. The rentFile.get(location, 6) tells the program to read the first six characters and store them in the variable *location*. The second get() function clears the input file buffer.

After reading a record and clearing the buffer, control returns to the calling module.

```
PRINT DETAIL LINE:

void PrnDetail(void)
{
    prnt << setiosflags(ios::left)
        << " " << setw(9) << location
        << resetiosflags(ios::left)
        << setw(4) << agency << setw(7) << mgr
        << setw(5) << bldg << setw(7) << apart
        << "        $" << setiosflags(ios::fixed)
        << setiosflags(ios::showpoint) << setprecision(2)
        << setw(7) << rent << endl;
    lineCnt = lineCnt + 1;
    return;
}
```

The above statements mean: Set the line justification to left, print *location*, reset the line justification to right, print the rest of the detail line, and add 1 to the line count. Notice that *rent* is set up as a floating-point value with two decimal places. Control then returns to the calling module.

Control Breaks

Records arranged in either ascending or descending order according to a control field (such as customer number) can be processed in a special way to produce a subtotal or a group total. **Control break processing** involves grouping related records and then processing them together as a group. A **control field** is used to detect a change in the group and to determine when to print the subtotal before moving on to the next group. A **subtotal** is part of a report total that is accumulated and printed in relationship to a control group.

Thus, when the control field of the current record equals that of the previous one, the input is added to the subtotal for the related records. On the other hand, when a control break is encountered (the control field changes), the previous subtotal is printed and the input is added to the subtotal for the new control group.

As an example, look at Figure 8.7. Suppose that the previous and current customer numbers—the control fields—both equal 103. We add the current sales amount to the group subtotal for customer number 103, as shown.

However, a **control break** occurs when the customer number changes from 103 to 104. When the control break is detected, the group subtotal for customer 103 ($6,350.00) is printed. Then the subtotal field is reset to 0 in preparation for the next group (104).

After all the data has been processed, the subtotal for the last group (104) is printed, along with the report total ($8,650.00).

The pseudocode version of the control break routine is shown in Figure 8.8.

```
              CUSTOMER ACCOUNTS

CUSTOMER NUMBER              SALES AMOUNT
      103                     $1,400.00
      103                     $1,200.00
      103                     $2,000.00
      103                     $1,750.00
 Sales subtotal:             $6,350.00

      104                     $1,000.00
      104                     $1,300.00
 Sales subtotal:             $2,300.00
 * Report total:             $8,650.00
```

FIGURE 8.7   Control Break Processing

```
                    :
 If previous customer not = current customer
    Print customer subtotal
    Add 3 to line count
    Set previous customer = current customer
    Set customer subtotal to 0
                    :
```

FIGURE 8.8   Control Break Logic

Checkpoint 8B

1. What is a control field? What is the purpose of a control field?
2. Explain the concept of control break processing.
3. Why does control break processing require the input data to be arranged in control field order?
4. Write the pseudocode that shows the steps involved in performing a control break.

Sample Program CHAP8B

This program demonstrates application of both page and control break processing by producing a rental income report for Pernell Properties. Sample program CHAP8B is shown in Figure 8.11 (p. 246); the program's output is shown in Figures 8.12a (p. 250) and 8.12b (p. 251).

Notice that the input is the same as the input for sample program CHAP8A. However, sample program CHAP8B uses the building number as a control field to process the data. Note also that the input is arranged in ascending order by building number. This is significant to the operation of the program. Control break processing requires that the control fields be arranged in either ascending or descending order. Otherwise, a break will occur each time the control fields change values.

Input (text file):

For each rent record, read and assign data to the following fields. Field size and type are shown in parentheses.

1. Location   (5 char)
2. Agency number   (2 int)
3. Manager number   (3 int)
4. Building number   (2 int)
5. Apartment number   (1 int)
6. Monthly rent   (6.2 float)

Text File (rent.dat):

Use the data given below to create the rent file. The numbers shown above the columns correspond to the fields described for the input.

1	2	3	4	5	6
North	20	201	10	1	400.00
North	20	201	10	2	410.00
North	20	201	10	3	335.00
North	20	201	15	1	375.00
North	20	201	15	2	385.00
North	20	247	17	1	450.00
North	20	247	17	2	450.00
North	43	316	22	1	345.00
North	43	316	22	2	465.00
East	10	237	30	1	410.00
East	10	237	30	2	365.00
East	10	237	30	3	470.00

East	10	237	30	4	345.00
East	10	659	33	1	429.00
East	10	659	33	2	465.00
End	00	000	00	0	000.00 (trailer record)

Output (printer):

Print the control break report shown in Figures 8.12a and 8.12b. Notice the star (asterisk) on the building subtotal line. A single star indicates that the total represents a first-level subtotal. Multilevel totals are covered in Chapter 9.

Processing Requirements:

- Read the rent file.
- Print 21 detail lines per page.
- Subtotal rent by building.
- Accumulate a report total for rent.

Pseudocode:

```
START
Open file
If file opened
    Set line count to 0
    Add 1 to page number
    Advance to the next page
    Print titles, page number, and column heading
    Read a record
    Save building
    LOOP until agency = 0
        Subtotal rent by building
        Accumulate report total for rent
        If line count > 21
            Set line count to 0
            Add 1 to page number
            Advance to the next page
            Print titles, page number, and column heading
        Print detail line
        Read a record
        If input building not = previous building
            Print subtotal line
            Add 3 to line count
            Save building
            Set building subtotal to 0
    End LOOP
    Print report total
    Close file
END
```

Hierarchy Chart: See Figure 8.9.

Program Flowchart: See Figure 8.10.

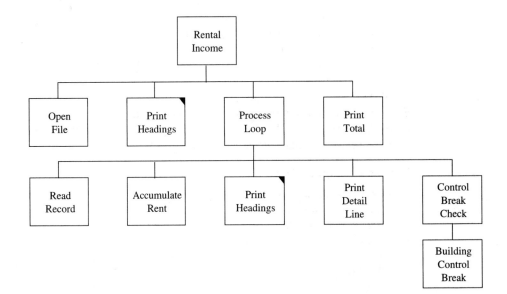

FIGURE 8.9   Hierarchy Chart for CHAP8B

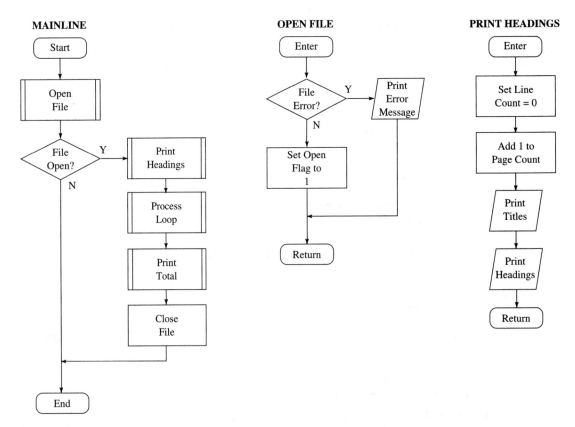

FIGURE 8.10   Program Flowchart for CHAP8B

PRINT REPORT TOTAL

Enter

↓

Print
Report
Total

↓

Return

READ RECORD

Enter

↓

Read
Text
File

↓

Return

PRINT DETAIL LINE

Enter

↓

Print
Detail
Line

↓

Add 1 to
Line Count

↓

Return

PROCESS LOOP

Enter

↓

Read
Record

↓

Save
Fields

↓ ←———(A)

Agency
≠ 0 ——Y——→ Accumulate
Rent

│N

Return

Accumulate Rent
↓

Line
Count > Max
Lines? ——Y——→ Print
Headings

│N ←————————┘

Print
Detail
Line

↓

Read
Record

↓

Control
Break
Check

↓

(A)

**BUILDING
CONTROL BREAK**

Enter

↓

Print
Building
Total

↓

Increment
Line
Count

↓

Save
Fields

↓

Reset
Building
Total to 0

↓

Return

(continued on next page)

FIGURE 8.10   *Continued*

ACCUMULATE RENT

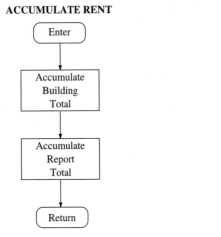

CONTROL BREAK CHECK

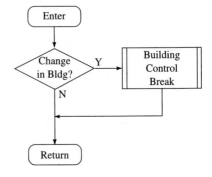

FIGURE 8.10   *Continued*

```
//---------- RENTAL INCOME --------------------------------
//  This rental program demonstrates page and control break
//  processing. A control break occurs on building number.
//
//          PROGRAM-ID: CHAP8B
//          PROGRAMMER: David M. Collopy
//          RUN DATE:   mm/dd/yy
//*************************************************************

//**  PREPROCESSING DIRECTIVES

#include<iostream.h>
#include<fstream.h>
#include<iomanip.h>


//---------- FUNCTION PROTOTYPES --------------------------

void OpenFile(void);           // open rent file
void PrnHeadings(void);        // print headings
void ProcessLoop(void);        // processing loop
void ReadRecord(void);         // read rent record
void AccumRent(void);          // accumulate rent totals
void CtlBreakCk(void);         // control break check
void BldgCtlBreak(void);       // building control break
void PrnDetail(void);          // print detail line
void PrnTotal(void);           // print total rent
```

FIGURE 8.11   Sample Program CHAP8B: Demonstrates Subtotal Processing for Pernell Properties
(Total rent is accumulated and printed at the end of the report.)

```
//----------- PROGRAM SETUP --------------------------------

//** H E A D I N G   L I N E S

char PT1[] = "P E R N E L L    P R O P E R T I E S    Page";
char PT2[] = "                    Rental Income            ";
char HL[]  = "LOCATION  AGENCY  MGR  BLDG    APART#    RENT ";
char CBL[] = "                         * Bldg Total:  $ ";
char RTL[] = "                    ***** Report Total: $ ";

//** I N P U T    R E N T    R E C O R D

ifstream rentFile;              // file object name
char   location[6];            // location code
int    agency;                 // agency number
int    mgr;                    // manager number
int    bldg;                   // building number
int    apart;                  // apartment number
float  rent;                   // monthly rent income

//** P R O G R A M    V A R I A B L E S

int    prevBldg;               // previous building number
float  rptTotal = 0.0;         // report total rent
float  bldgTotal = 0.0;        // building rent total
int    pageNum = 0;            // page number
int    lineCnt;                // detail line count
int    maxLines = 21;          // max detail lines per page

//** O P E N    P R I N T E R    F I L E

ofstream prnt("PRN");          // open printer file

//----------------------------------------------------------
//              MAINLINE CONTROL
//----------------------------------------------------------
main()
{
    OpenFile();                // open rent file
    if (!rentFile.fail())  {
        PrnHeadings();         // print headings
        ProcessLoop();         // processing loop
        PrnTotal();            // print total rent
        rentFile.close();      // close rent file
    }
    cout << "\n-----<E N D   O F   R U N>-----";
    return 0;
}
```

(continued on next page)

FIGURE 8.11 *Continued*

```
//-----------------------------------------------------------
//              OPEN RENT FILE
//-----------------------------------------------------------
void OpenFile(void)
{
    rentFile.open("a:rent.dat");
    if (rentFile.fail())
        cout << "Rent file open failed" << endl;
    return;
}
//-----------------------------------------------------------
//              PRINT HEADINGS
//-----------------------------------------------------------
void PrnHeadings(void)
{
    lineCnt = 0;                    // set line count to 0
    pageNum = pageNum + 1;          // add 1 to page number
    prnt << "\f";                   // reset to top of page
    prnt << PT1 << setw(2)
         << pageNum << endl;        // print page title 1
    prnt << PT2 << endl
         << endl;                   // print page title 2
    prnt << HL << endl
         << endl;                   // print heading line
    return;
}
//-----------------------------------------------------------
//              PROCESSING LOOP
//-----------------------------------------------------------
void ProcessLoop(void)
{
    ReadRecord();                   // read rent record
    prevBldg = bldg;                // save building number
    while (agency != 0)  {
        AccumRent();                // accumulate rent totals
        if (lineCnt >= maxLines)
            PrnHeadings();          // print headings
        PrnDetail();                // print detail line
        ReadRecord();               // read rent record
        CtlBreakCk();               // control break check
    }
    return;
}
```

FIGURE 8.11   *Continued*

```
//--------------------------------------------------------------
//                    READ RENT RECORD
//--------------------------------------------------------------
void ReadRecord(void)
{
    rentFile.get(location, 6) >> agency >> mgr
        >> bldg >> apart >> rent;
    rentFile.get();                   // clear input file buffer
    return;
}
//--------------------------------------------------------------
//                 ACCUMULATE RENT TOTALS
//--------------------------------------------------------------
void AccumRent(void)
{
    bldgTotal = bldgTotal + rent;
    rptTotal = rptTotal + rent;
    return;
}
//--------------------------------------------------------------
//                   PRINT DETAIL LINE
//--------------------------------------------------------------
void PrnDetail(void)
{
    prnt << setiosflags(ios::left)            // left justify
         << " " << setw(9) << location
         << resetiosflags(ios::left)          // right justify
         << setw(4) << agency << setw(7) << mgr
         << setw(5) << bldg << setw(7) << apart
         << "      $" << setiosflags(ios::fixed)
         << setiosflags(ios::showpoint) << setprecision(2)
         << setw(7) << rent << endl;
    lineCnt = lineCnt + 1;
    return;
}
//--------------------------------------------------------------
//                  CONTROL BREAK CHECK
//--------------------------------------------------------------
void CtlBreakCk(void)
{
    if (bldg != prevBldg)
        BldgCtlBreak();
    return;
}
//--------------------------------------------------------------
//                 BUILDING CONTROL BREAK
//--------------------------------------------------------------
void BldgCtlBreak(void)
```

(continued on next page)

FIGURE 8.11   *Continued*

```
{
    prnt << endl
        << CBL << setw(8) << bldgTotal << endl << endl;
    lineCnt = lineCnt + 3;
    prevBldg = bldg;
    bldgTotal = 0.0;
    return;
}
//------------------------------------------------------------
//              PRINT TOTAL LINE
//------------------------------------------------------------
void PrnTotal(void)
{
    prnt << endl
        << RTL << setw(8) << rptTotal << endl;
    return;
}
```

FIGURE 8.11 *Continued*

```
P E R N E L L    P R O P E R T I E S        Page 1
              Rental Income

LOCATION  AGENCY  MGR  BLDG   APART#      RENT
North       20    201   10      1      $ 400.00
North       20    201   10      2      $ 410.00
North       20    201   10      3      $ 335.00

                   *  Bldg Total:    $ 1145.00

North       20    201   15      1      $ 375.00
North       20    201   15      2      $ 385.00

                   *  Bldg Total:    $  760.00

North       20    247   17      1      $ 450.00
North       20    247   17      2      $ 450.00

                   *  Bldg Total:    $  900.00

North       43    316   22      1      $ 345.00
North       43    316   22      2      $ 465.00

                   *  Bldg Total:    $  810.00
```

FIGURE 8.12a Program Output for CHAP8B

```
P E R N E L L   P R O P E R T I E S      Page 2
              Rental Income

LOCATION   AGENCY   MGR   BLDG    APART#      RENT

  East       10     237    30       1     $  410.00
  East       10     237    30       2     $  365.00
  East       10     237    30       3     $  470.00
  East       10     237    30       4     $  345.00

                      *   Bldg Total:      $ 1590.00

  East       10     659    33       1     $  429.00
  East       10     659    33       2     $  465.00

                      *   Bldg Total:      $  894.00

                  *****   Report Total:    $ 6099.00
```

FIGURE 8.12b   Program Output for CHAP8B

Dissection of Sample Program CHAP8B

Review the program carefully. Notice the similarities between this program and sample program CHAP8A. In order to implement the subtotal processing, two modules were added to the control break program: *CONTROL BREAK CHECK* and *BUILDING CONTROL BREAK*.

Let us look at the program code and see how it all fits together.

```
PROCESSING LOOP:

void ProcessLoop(void)
{
    ReadRecord();
```

The priming *read* statement transfers control to the *ReadRecord* module; this module retrieves the first record from the rent file.

```
    prevBldg = bldg;
```

The above statement means: Save the control field for later use. This "sets the stage" for subsequent processing. For example, the first record has no previous building number. By copying the current control field to the previous control field, we can avoid an untimely break on the first record.

```
    while (agency != 0)  {
```

The above statement means: As long as the agency number is not equal to 0 (the value specified by the trailer record), execute the statements in the body of the loop. If the agency number is 0, then the file is empty and control skips to the first executable statement after the *while* loop.

```
        AccumRent();
```

The above statement means: Transfer control to the *AccumRent* module and perform the processing given there; this module accumulates totals for the rent.

```
        if (lineCnt >= maxLines)
            PrnHeadings();
```

The above statement means: Compare the line counter to the maximum number of lines allowed per page. If the line counter is greater than or equal to the maximum lines, then transfer control to the *PrnHeadings* module; this module prints the report titles and column headings. Otherwise, fall through and continue with the next statement.

```
            ReadRecord();
```

The looping read statement transfers control to the *ReadRecord* module; this module retrieves the next record from the rent file.

```
            CtlBreakCk();
        }
        return;
}
```

The above statements mean: Transfer control to the *CtlBreakCk* module and perform the processing given there; this module checks for a control break.

The *return* statement sends control back to the *MAINLINE*, the calling module.

```
ACCUMULATE RENT TOTALS:

void AccumRent(void)
{
    bldgTotal = bldgTotal + rent;
    rptTotal = rptTotal + rent;
    return;
}
```

The above statements mean: Add the rent to the building subtotal and to the report total. Control then returns to the calling module.

```
CONTROL BREAK CHECK:

void CtlBreakCk(void)
{
    if (bldg != PrevBldg)
        BldgCtlBreak();
    return;
}
```

The above statements mean: Compare the previous building number to the input building number. If they are not equal, transfer control to *BldgCtlBreak* and perform the control break processing activities given there. Otherwise, skip the control break and return to the calling module.

```
BUILDING CONTROL BREAK:

void BldgCtlBreak(void)
{
    prnt << endl
        << CBL << setw(8) << bldgTotal << endl<< endl;
    lineCnt = lineCnt + 3;
```

The above statements mean: Advance to a new line, print the building subtotal, advance two lines, and add 3 to the line counter (1 for the blank line before, 1 for the subtotal line, and 1 for the blank line after).

The CBL stands for *Control Break Line*; it specifies the format of the subtotal line. CBL is defined in the *PROGRAM SETUP* section of the program.

```
    prevBldg = bldg;
```

The above statement means: Save the current building number for later use. This is done to set up processing for the next building group.

```
    bldgTotal = 0;
    return;
}
```

The above statements mean: Reset the building subtotal to 0. This is done in preparation for the next building subtotal. Control then returns to the calling module.

Summary

1. A page break occurs when the number of lines printed equals the limit established for the page.
2. Line count is used to determine when to perform a page break. Each time a line is printed, line count is incremented and compared to the maximum number of lines allowed per page. If the count equals the limit, then the program performs a page break.
3. Page count is used to keep track of the number of pages printed. Each time a page is printed, page count is incremented.
4. When a page break is encountered, the printer advances to a new page, prints the title and column headings, and continues with the body of the report.
5. A control field is a special field in the input record that is used to arrange the records in either ascending or decending order. The value of the control field is used by the program to determine when to perform a control break.
6. Records arranged in control field order can be processed to produce a subtotal. A subtotal is part of a total that is accumulated and printed in relationship to a control group.
7. A control break involves grouping related records and processing them together as a single unit.
8. A program executes a control break when the value of the current control field does not equal the value of the previous control field.

9. When a control break is encountered, the previous subtotal is printed and the input is added to the subtotal for the new control group.

10. After the data has been read and processed, the subtotal for the last group is printed, along with the report total.

Programming Projects

For each project, design the logic and write the modular structured program to produce the output. Model your program after the sample programs presented in the chapter. Verify your output.

Project 8–1   Payroll-1

Write a page break program to read a payroll file, calculate gross pay, and print a weekly payroll report. Assume overtime is not computed.

Input (text file):

For each payroll record, read and assign data to the following fields. Field size and type are shown in parentheses.

1. Branch number   (1 int)
2. Division number   (2 int)
3. Department number   (3 int)
4. Employee name   (20 char)
5. Hours worked   (2 int)
6. Hourly pay rate   (5.2 float)

Text File (payroll.dat):

Use the data given below to create the payroll file. The numbers shown above the columns correspond to the fields described for the input.

1	2	3	4	5	6
1	10	100	Tanya Bauer	40	7.50
1	10	100	Diane Dixon	40	9.75
1	10	106	Randy Karns	37	8.55
1	20	112	Dana Clark	45	14.90
1	20	112	Nick Larson	43	7.72
1	20	112	Colleen Norris	40	11.35
1	20	123	Sara Erickson	38	12.00
1	40	117	Scott Howard	42	9.75
2	10	105	Paul Irwin	48	8.72
2	10	105	Cyndi Olson	45	15.10
2	18	144	Dale Miller	40	10.25
3	23	121	Bret Rossi	35	8.00
3	23	121	Karen Thomas	48	9.00
3	23	137	Cheryl Dietz	42	7.50

```
      3      23      137    Neil Kenney      38     7.25
      3      34      150    Tracy York       36    11.00
      0      00      000    Trailer Record   00     0.00
```

Output (printer):

Print the following page break report:

```
Author              C O M P A N Y   P A Y R O L L         Page 99

                         Gross Pay Report
                            mm/dd/yy


Branch     Division     Department     Employee Name      Gross Pay

  9          99           999          X------------ X     999.99
  :           :            :                 :              :
  :           :            :                 :              :
  9          99           999          X------------X      999.99

                                 ****  Report Total:      9999.99
```

Processing Requirements:

- Read the payroll file.
- Print 10 detail lines per page.
- Compute the gross pay:
  hours worked × pay rate
- Accumulate a report total for gross pay.

Project 8–2   Payroll-2

Modify the program in Project 8–1 to include control break processing. Group and list employee gross pay by department and print the department subtotal for each group. Print a blank line before and after the subtotal. Be sure to include the blank lines in the line count. Print 28 detail lines per page. Model the logic after sample program CHAP8B.

Print the following control break report:

```
Author              C O M P A N Y   P A Y R O L L         Page 99

                         Gross Pay Report
                            mm/dd/yy


Branch     Division     Department     Employee Name      Gross Pay

  9          99           999          X--------------X    999.99
  :           :            :                 :              :
  :           :            :                 :              :
  9          99           999          X--------------X    999.99

                                    *  Department Total:   9999.99
              . . . . .                          . . . . .
                                 ****  Report Total:      99999.99
```

Project 8–3   Sales Analysis-1

Write a page break program to read a sales file, accumulate total customer sales, and print a sales analysis report.

Input (text file):

For each sales record, read and assign data to the following fields. Field size and type are shown in parentheses.

1. Region number   (1 int)
2. State code   (2 int)
3. Store number   (3 int)
4. Salesperson number (3 int)
5. Customer number   (4 int)
6. Sales amount   (7.2 float)

Text File (sales.dat):

Use the data given below to create the sales file. The numbers shown above the columns correspond to the fields described for the input.

1	2	3	4	5	6
1	OH	100	190	1180	380.00
1	OH	100	190	3100	273.00
1	OH	100	225	2510	161.00
1	OH	210	287	5090	492.00
1	IN	198	338	4200	185.00
1	IN	198	412	6100	200.00
1	IN	198	412	9430	300.00
2	KY	279	206	2900	563.00
2	KY	279	490	3000	175.00
2	KY	300	640	3100	100.00
2	KY	313	110	7170	400.00
3	PA	121	720	1200	369.00
3	PA	239	378	2600	349.00
3	PA	239	600	5500	200.00
0	XX	000	000	0000	000.00 (trailer record)

Output (printer):

Print the following page break report:

```
Author              SALES ANALYSIS REPORT          Page 99
                         mm/dd/yy

Region   State   Store   Salesperson   Customer   Sales
---------------------------------------------------------
  9       XX      999        999         9999     999.99
  :        :       :          :            :        :
  :        :       :          :            :        :
  9       XX      999        999         9999     999.99

                 *****  Report Total:            9999.99
```

Processing Requirements:
- Read the sales file.
- Print 10 detail lines per page.
- Accumulate a report total for customer sales.

Project 8–4   Sales Analysis-2

Modify the program in Project 8–3 to include control break processing. Group and list customer sales by salesperson and print the salesperson subtotal for each group. Print a blank line before and after the subtotal. Be sure to include the blank lines in the line count. Print 30 detail lines per page. Model the logic after sample program CHAP8B.

Print the following control break report:

```
Author                SALES ANALYSIS REPORT              Page 99
                           mm/dd/yy


Region    State    Store    Salesperson    Customer    Sales
---------------------------------------------------------------
  9        XX       999         999          9999      999.99
  :         :        :           :             :          :
  :         :        :           :             :          :
  9        XX       999         999          9999      999.99

                             *    Salesperson Total: 9999.99
         . . . . .                         . . . . .
                          *****   Report Total:      9999.99
```

Project 8–5   Inventory-1

Write a page break program to read an inventory file, accumulate total quantity on hand, and print an inventory analysis report.

Input (text file):

For each inventory record, read and assign data to the following fields. Field size and type are shown in parentheses.

1. Region number   (1 int)
2. State code   (2 char)
3. Location number   (2 int)
4. Warehouse number   (3 int)
5. Item number   (5 char)
6. Quantity on hand   (2 int)

Text File (invent.dat):

Use the data given below to create the inventory file. The numbers shown above the columns correspond to the fields described for the input.

1	2	3	4	5	6
1	OH	43	101	A7100	24
1	OH	43	101	B0340	12
1	OH	43	101	D0019	35

1	OH	43	340	C1970	48
1	OH	43	340	H0120	16
1	OH	66	220	F3170	96
1	OH	66	220	K8800	24
1	IN	27	125	C5510	12
1	IN	27	125	I1700	36
2	KY	18	107	B1776	24
2	KY	18	107	D0011	30
2	KY	18	130	F0910	36
2	KY	18	130	L7650	96
2	KY	18	130	P0150	15

Output (printer):

Print the following page break report:

```
Author            INVENTORY ANALYSIS REPORT            Page 99
                        mm/dd/yy


Region    State    Location    Warehouse    Item#    Quantity

  9        XX         99          999        XXXXX       99
  :         :          :           :           :          :
  :         :          :           :           :          :
  9        XX         99          999        XXXXX       99


                         *****  Report Total:          999
```

Processing Requirements:

- Read the inventory file.
- Print 10 detail lines per page.
- Accumulate a report total for quantity on hand.

Project 8–6   Inventory-2

Modify the program in Project 8–5 to include control break processing. Group and list the quantity on hand by warehouse and print the warehouse subtotal for each group. Print a blank line before and after the subtotal. Be sure to include the blank lines in the line count. Print 21 detail lines per page. Model the logic after sample program CHAP8B.

Print the following control break report:

```
Author            INVENTORY ANALYSIS REPORT            Page 99
                        mm/dd/yy


Region    State    Location    Warehouse    Item#    Quantity

  9        XX         99          999        XXXXX       99
  :         :          :           :           :          :
  :         :          :           :           :          :
  9        XX         99          999        XXXXX       99


                                  *  Warehouse Total:   999
             . . . . .                     . . . .
                         *****  Report Total:          999
```

Project 8–7   Personnel-1

Write a page break program to read a personnel file, count the number of employees, and print a personnel report.

Input (text file):

For each record, read and assign data to the following fields. Field size and type are shown in parentheses.

1. Branch number   (1 int)
2. Division number   (2 int)
3. Department number   (3 int)
4. Manager number   (2 int)
5. Supervisor number   (4 int)
6. Employee count   (2 int)

Text File (persnel.dat):

Use the data given below to create the personnel file. The numbers shown above the columns correspond to the fields described for the input.

1	2	3	4	5	6
1	10	101	20	2010	08
1	10	101	20	2025	12
1	10	101	30	3050	16
1	10	101	30	3055	12
1	10	101	30	3060	10
1	10	120	45	4520	14
1	10	120	45	4530	12
1	20	206	12	1210	07
1	20	206	12	1220	12
2	15	115	22	2210	15
2	15	115	22	2230	12
2	15	210	33	3340	18
2	15	210	33	3360	16
2	15	210	45	4510	10
2	15	210	45	4550	12
2	27	108	26	2630	12
2	27	108	26	2640	16
2	27	108	26	2680	14
0	00	000	00	0000	00 (trailer record)

Output (printer):

Print the following page break report:

```
Author              P E R S O N N E L   R E P O R T          Page 99
                            Employee Count
                              mm/dd/yy

 Branch   Division   Department   Manager   Supervisor   Employees
   9         99         999         99         9999          99
   :          :          :          :           :            :
```

```
    :          :            :          :           :            :
    9         99           999        99         9999          99

                             *****   Report Total:            999
```

Processing Requirements:

- Read the personnel file.
- Print 10 detail lines per page.
- Accumulate a report total for employee count.

Project 8–8 Personnel-2

Modify the program in Project 8–7 to include control break processing. Group and list the employee count by manager and print the manager subtotal for each group. Print a blank line before and after the subtotal. Be sure to include the blank lines in the line count. Print 25 detail lines per page. Model the logic after sample program CHAP8B.

Print the following control break report:

```
Author            P E R S O N N E L    R E P O R T           Page 99

                             Employee Count
                               mm/dd/yy

    Branch  Division  Department  Manager  Supervisor  Employees

      9        99         999        99        9999          99
      :         :          :          :          :            :
      :         :          :          :          :            :
      9        99         999        99        9999          99

                                      *   Manager Total:      999
                       . . . . .                 . . . . .
                                    *****  Report Total:      999
```

9 Multilevel Control Breaks

Overview

Learning Objectives

After you have read this chapter and completed the exercises, you should be able to:

- arrange the input data in ascending control field order to prepare for multilevel control break processing
- design and write multilevel control break programs
- combine page break and control break processing techniques to develop multipage, multilevel subtotal reports

Multilevel Control Breaks

This chapter expands upon the control break processing techniques introduced in Chapter 8. As you recall, sample program CHAP8B printed a simple one-level rental income report for Pernell Properties. The program executed a single control break and printed a subtotal line each time the building number (the control field) changed. The format of the income report is shown in Figure 9.1.

Some business applications require reports that contain multilevel control totals or subtotals. Such totals may go two, three, four, or more levels deep; the actual number of levels depends mostly on the application at hand.

In general, a **multilevel control break** consists of two or more subtotals. For example, in Figure 9.1, we could accumulate the rent by manager and building. Or we could accumulate the rent by agency, manager, and building. Actually, there are four levels of totals that we could accumulate for the rent income: location total, agency total, manager total, and building total. Hence, a four-level control break report would show the rent by location, agency, manager, and building.

Chapter 9 presents a structured approach to designing multilevel control break reports. In the sections that follow, we will see how to develop a two-level and a four-level control break program for Pernell Properties. Once you understand the logic behind this approach, you will be able to apply it to other control break applications as well.

Planning a Two-Level Control Break Program

Assume that management wants us to develop a two-level control break program that lists the rent income for Pernell Properties by manager and building. The planning process involves the following steps. First, use a printer spacing chart to design the output; be sure to include the subtotal lines. Second, arrange the data in ascending order by manager and building. Third, develop the logic required to force the program to break when either control field changes value.

```
 P E R N E L L    P R O P E R T I E S        Page 9
                 Rental  Income

 LOCATION  AGENCY  MGR  BLDG   APART#      RENT

   X---X      99   999    99      9      $  999.99
     :         :     :     :       :          :
     :         :     :     :       :          :
   X---X      99   999    99      9      $  999.99

                      *   Bldg Total:   $ 9999.99
       .  .  .  .  .            .  .  .  .  .
                   *****  Report Total:  $ 9999.99
```

FIGURE 9.1 A One-Level Control Break Report

Essentially, we want the report to show the rent by manager and building. That is, we want the building subtotal to print when the building number changes, and we want the building and manager subtotals to print when the manager number changes.

A two-level control break (Figure 9.2) contains a major and a minor control field. For the rental income application, manager number is the major control field and building number is the minor control field. A break on the **major control field** forces the program to print the minor control total first, followed by the major control total. A break on the **minor control field** forces the program to print only the minor control total. Notice that a two-level control break provides three levels of totals, one for the manager, one for the building, and one for the report. The stars shown in Figure 9.2 correspond to the level numbers of the totals; * indicates the first level, ** indicates the second level, and so on. Look at the five stars shown next to the report total. This indicates that the report total represents the fifth level.

Since a break may occur on the manager number or the building number, the program logic must be designed to execute a break on either control field. Here is how it works. According to the logic in Figure 9.3, when a control break is detected for the building number, the program prints the building subtotal, increments the line counter, saves the input data for later use, and sets the building subtotal to 0 in preparation for the next building group.

However, when a control break is detected for the manager number, first the program branches and executes a building control break. Upon returning, the program then prints the manager subtotal, increments the line counter, and sets the manager subtotal to 0 in preparation for the next manager group.

The important thing to remember is that when a major control break occurs, the program executes the minor control break first. Hence, for a break on manager, the program must print the building subtotal before it prints the manager subtotal. This must be done this way, because the building subtotal "belongs to," or is part of, the previous manager subtotal.

```
PERNELL    PROPERTIES          Page 9
              Rental Income


   LOCATION   AGENCY   MGR   BLDG   APART#      RENT

    X---X       99     999    99       9      $ 999.99
      :          :      :      :       :         :
      :          :      :      :       :         :
    X---X       99     999    99       9      $ 999.99


                        *    Bldg Total:   $ 9999.99
                       **    Mgr Total:    $ 9999.99
         . . . . .              . . . . .
                      *****   Report Total:  $ 9999.99
```

FIGURE 9.2   A Two-Level Control Break Report

```
MANAGER CONTROL BREAK
   1. Do building control break
   2. Print manager subtotal
   3. Increment line count
   4. Set manager subtotal to 0

BUILDING CONTROL BREAK
   1. Print building subtotal
   2. Increment line count
   3. Save the input
   4. Set building subtotal to 0
```

FIGURE 9.3 Two-Level Control Break Logic

Sample Program CHAP9A

This program demonstrates application of a two-level control break to produce the rental income report for Pernell Properties. Sample program CHAP9A is shown in Figure 9.6 (p. 269); the program's output is shown in Figures 9.7a (p. 274) and 9.7b (p. 275).

Once again, the input has been arranged in ascending order to facilitate control break processing. Sample Program CHAP9A uses the manager number as the major control field and the building number as the minor control field.

The following specifications apply:

Input (text file):

For each record, read and assign data to the following fields. Field size and type are shown in parentheses.

1. Location   (5 char)
2. Agency number   (2 int)
3. Manager number   (3 int)
4. Building number   (2 int)
5. Apartment number   (1 int)
6. Monthly rent   (6.2 float)

Text File (rent.dat)

Use the data given below to create the rent file. The numbers shown above the columns correspond to the fields described for the input.

1	*2*	*3*	*4*	*5*	*6*
North	20	201	10	1	400.00
North	20	201	10	2	410.00
North	20	201	10	3	335.00
North	20	201	15	1	375.00
North	20	201	15	2	385.00

North	20	247	17	1	450.00
North	20	247	17	2	450.00
North	43	316	22	1	345.00
North	43	316	22	2	465.00
East	10	237	30	1	410.00
East	10	237	30	2	365.00
East	10	237	30	3	470.00
East	10	237	30	4	345.00
East	10	659	33	1	429.00
East	10	659	33	2	465.00
End	00	000	00	0	000.00 (trailer record)

Output (printer):

Print the two-level control break report shown in Figures 9.7a and 9.7b.

Processing Requirements:

- Read the rent file.
- Print 23 detail lines per page.
- Subtotal rent by building.
- Subtotal rent by manager.
- Accumulate a report total for the rent.

Pseudocode:

Two new conventions introduced in the following logic design require explanation. First, any statement enclosed within parentheses specifies a call to the named module. Second, a block of pseudocode beginning with ENTER and ending with RETURN represents a module.

```
START
Open file
If file opened
   (Print Headings)
   Read a record
   Save manager number
   Save building number
   LOOP until agency number = 0
      Accumulate building rent subtotal
      Accumulate manager rent subtotal
      Accumulate report rent total
      If line counter > 23
      (Print Headings)
      Print detail line
      Read a record
      If input manager not = previous manager
         (Manager Control Break)
      else if input building not = previous building
         (Building Control Break)
   End LOOP
   Print report rent total
```

```
    Close file
END

ENTER: Print Headings
Set line counter to 0
Add 1 to page number
Advance to the next page
Print titles, page number, and column headings
RETURN

ENTER: Manager Control Break
(Building Control Break)
Print manager subtotal
Add 2 to line count
Set manager subtotal to 0
RETURN

ENTER: Building Control Break
Print building subtotal
Add 2 to line count
Save manager number
Save building number
Set building subtotal to 0
RETURN
```

Hierarchy Chart: See Figure 9.4.

Program Flowchart: See Figure 9.5.

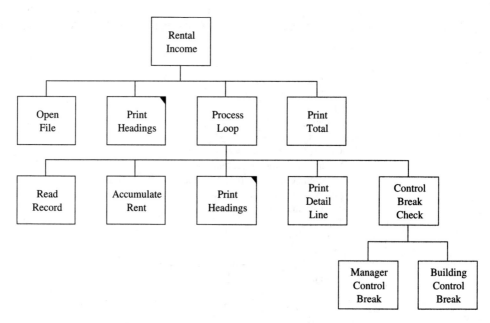

FIGURE 9.4   Hierarchy Chart for CHAP9A

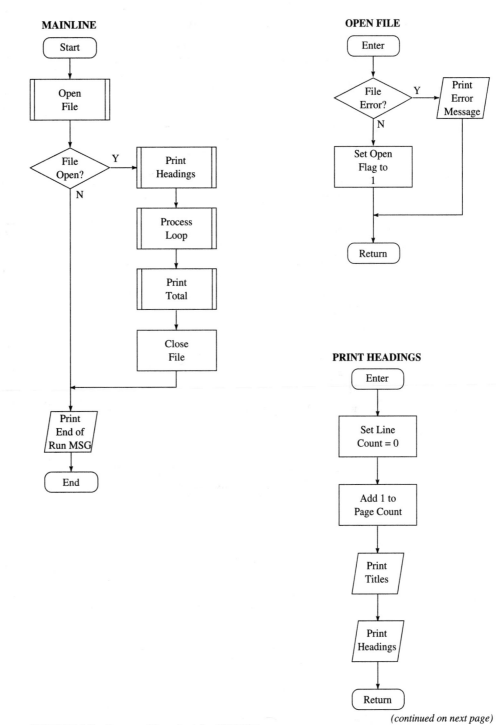

FIGURE 9.5   Program Flowchart for CHAP9A

(continued on next page)

PRINT REPORT TOTAL

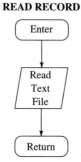

READ RECORD

PRINT DETAIL LINE

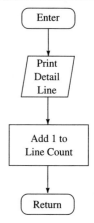

PROCESS LOOP

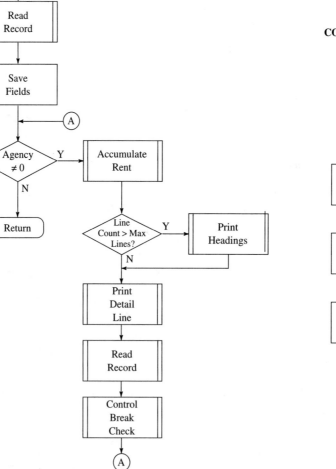

BUILDING CONTROL BREAK

FIGURE 9.5 *Continued*

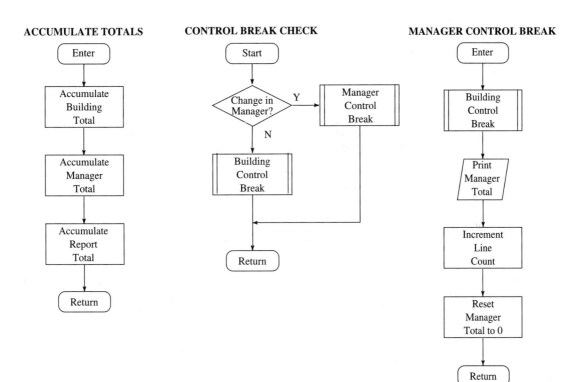

ACCUMULATE TOTALS **CONTROL BREAK CHECK** **MANAGER CONTROL BREAK**

FIGURE 9.5 *Continued*

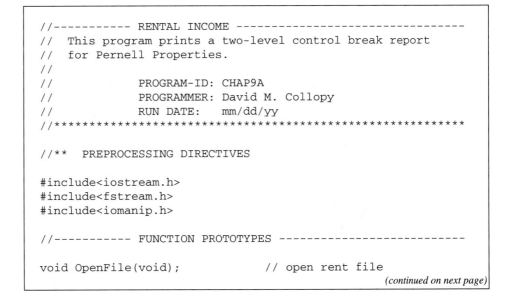

```
//----------- RENTAL INCOME --------------------------------
//  This program prints a two-level control break report
//  for Pernell Properties.
//
//          PROGRAM-ID: CHAP9A
//          PROGRAMMER: David M. Collopy
//          RUN DATE:   mm/dd/yy
//*************************************************************

//**   PREPROCESSING DIRECTIVES

#include<iostream.h>
#include<fstream.h>
#include<iomanip.h>

//----------- FUNCTION PROTOTYPES --------------------------

void OpenFile(void);                // open rent file
```
(continued on next page)

FIGURE 9.6 Sample Program CHAP9A: A Two-Level Control Break Report for Pernell Properties

```
void PrnHeadings(void);          // print headings
void ProcessLoop(void);          // processing loop
void ReadRecord(void);           // read rent record
void AccumRent(void);            // accumulate rent totals
void CtlBreakCk(void);           // control break check
void MgrCtlBreak(void);          // manager control break
void BldgCtlBreak(void);         // building control break
void PrnDetail(void);            // print detail line
void PrnTotal(void);             // print total line

//---------- PROGRAM SETUP -------------------------------

//** H E A D I N G   L I N E S
char PT1[] = "P E R N E L L    P R O P E R T I E S    Page";
char PT2[] = "                Rental Income              ";
char HL[]  = "LOCATION  AGENCY  MGR  BLDG    APART#    RENT ";
char CB1[] = "                     * Bldg Total:    $";
char CB2[] = "                    ** Mgr Total:     $";
char RTL[] = "                ***** Report Total: $";

//** I N P U T   R E N T   R E C O R D
ifstream rentFile;               // file object name
char  location[6];               // location code
int   agency;                    // agency number
int   mgr;                       // manager number
int   bldg;                      // building number
int   apart;                     // apartment number
float rent;                      // monthly rent income

//** P R O G R A M   V A R I A B L E S
int   prevMgr;                   // previous manager number
int   prevBldg;                  // previous building number
float mgrTotal = 0.0;            // manager rent total
float bldgTotal = 0.0;           // building rent total
float rptTotal = 0.0;            // report total rent
int   pageNum = 0;               // page number
int   lineCnt;                   // detail line count
int   maxLines = 23;             // max detail lines per page

//** O P E N   P R I N T E R   F I L E
ofstream prnt("PRN");            // open printer file

//-------------------------------------------------------
//              MAINLINE CONTROL
//-------------------------------------------------------
main()
{
```

FIGURE 9.6 *Continued*

```
        OpenFile();                    // open rent file
        if (!rentFile.fail())  {
            PrnHeadings();             // print headings
            ProcessLoop();             // processing loop
            PrnTotal();                // print total line
            rentFile.close();          // close rent file
        }
        cout << "\n-----<E N D   O F   R U N>-----";
        return 0;
}
//------------------------------------------------------------
//              OPEN RENT FILE
//------------------------------------------------------------
void OpenFile(void)
{
        rentFile.open("a:rent.dat");
        if (rentFile.fail())
            cout << "Rent file open failed" << endl;
        return;
}
//------------------------------------------------------------
//              PRINT HEADINGS
//------------------------------------------------------------
void PrnHeadings(void)
{
        lineCnt = 0;                   // set line count to 0
        pageNum = pageNum + 1;         // add 1 to page number
        prnt << "\f";                  // reset to top of page
        prnt << PT1 << setw(2)
             << pageNum << endl;       // print page title 1
        prnt << PT2 << endl
             << endl;                  // print page title 2
        prnt << HL << endl
             << endl;                  // print heading line
        return;
}
//------------------------------------------------------------
//              PROCESSING LOOP
//------------------------------------------------------------
void ProcessLoop(void)
{
        ReadRecord();                  // read rent record
        prevMgr = mgr;                 // save manager number
        prevBldg = bldg;               // save building number
        while (agency != 0)  {
```

(continued on next page)

FIGURE 9.6 *Continued*

```
        AccumRent();                    // accumulate rent totals
        if (lineCnt >= maxLines)
            PrnHeadings();              // print headings
        PrnDetail();                    // print detail line
        ReadRecord();                   // read rent record
        CtlBreakCk();                   // control break check
    }
    return;
}
//-------------------------------------------------------------
//              READ RENT RECORD
//-------------------------------------------------------------
void ReadRecord(void)
{
    rentFile.get(location, 6) >> agency >> mgr
        >> bldg >> apart >> rent;
    rentFile.get();                     // clear input file buffer
    return;
}
//-------------------------------------------------------------
//              ACCUMULATE RENT TOTALS
//-------------------------------------------------------------
void AccumRent(void)
{
    bldgTotal = bldgTotal + rent;
    mgrTotal = mgrTotal + rent:
    rptTotal = rptTotal + rent:
    return;
}
//-------------------------------------------------------------
//              PRINT DETAIL LINE
//-------------------------------------------------------------
void PrnDetail(void)
{
    prnt << endl;
    prnt << setiosflags(ios::left)              // left justify
        << " " << setw(9) << location
        << resetiosflags(ios::left)             // right justify
        << setw(4) << agency << setw(7) << mgr
        << setw(5) << bldg << setw(7) << apart
        << "      $" << setiosflags(ios::fixed)
        << setiosflags(ios::showpoint) << setprecision(2)
        << setw(7) << rent;
    lineCnt = lineCnt + 1;
    return;
}
```

FIGURE 9.6   *Continued*

```
//-----------------------------------------------------------
//               CONTROL BREAK CHECK
//-----------------------------------------------------------
void CtlBreakCk(void)
{
    if (mgr != prevMgr)
        MgrCtlBreak();
    else if (bldg != prevBldg)
        BldgCtlBreak();
    return;
}
//-----------------------------------------------------------
//               MANAGER CONTROL BREAK
//-----------------------------------------------------------
void MgrCtlBreak(void)
{
    BldgCtlBreak();
    prnt << CB2 << setw(8) << mgrTotal << endl;
    lineCnt = lineCnt + 2;
    mgrTotal = 0.0;
    return;
}
//-----------------------------------------------------------
//               BUILDING CONTROL BREAK
//-----------------------------------------------------------
void BldgCtlBreak(void)
{
    prnt << endl << endl
         << CB1 << setw(8) << bldgTotal << endl;
    lineCnt = lineCnt + 2;
    prevMgr = mgr;
    prevBldg = bldg;
    bldgTotal = 0.0;
    return;
}
//-----------------------------------------------------------
//               PRINT TOTAL LINE
//-----------------------------------------------------------
void PrnTotal(void)
{
    prnt << endl << endl
         << RTL << setw(8) << rptTotal << endl;
    return;
}
```

FIGURE 9.6   *Continued*

```
  P E R N E L L   P R O P E R T I E S        Page 1
                 Rental Income

  LOCATION   AGENCY   MGR   BLDG   APART#      RENT

  North        20     201    10      1      $  400.00
  North        20     201    10      2      $  410.00
  North        20     201    10      3      $  335.00

                        *  Bldg Total:      $ 1145.00

  North        20     201    15      1      $  375.00
  North        20     201    15      2      $  385.00

                        *  Bldg Total:      $  760.00
                       **  Mgr  Total:      $ 1905.00

  North        20     247    17      1      $  450.00
  North        20     247    17      2      $  450.00

                        *  Bldg Total:      $  900.00
                       **  Mgr  Total:      $  900.00

  North        43     316    22      1      $  345.00
  North        43     316    22      2      $  465.00

                        *  Bldg Total:      $  810.00
                       **  Mgr  Total:      $  810.00
```

FIGURE 9.7a   Program Output for CHAP9A

Dissection of Sample Program CHAP9A

Overall, the logic used for sample program CHAP9A is similar in structure to that shown in Sample Program CHAP8B. A few modifications were made to include the control break on manager number. For example, the program computes a manager subtotal for rent and checks for a change in manager number—the major control field. When the manager numbers change, the program performs a control break and prints the building subtotal and the manager subtotal.

```
ACCUMULATE RENT TOTALS:
void AccumRent(void)
{
    bldgTotal = bldgTotal + rent;
    mgrTotal = mgrTotal + rent;
    rptTotal = rptTotal + rent;
    return;
}
```

```
P E R N E L L    P R O P E R T I E S        Page 2
                 Rental Income

LOCATION   AGENCY   MGR   BLDG    APART#        RENT

  East       10     237    30       1      $  410.00
  East       10     237    30       2      $  365.00
  East       10     237    30       3      $  470.00
  East       10     237    30       4      $  345.00

                     *    Bldg Total:     $ 1590.00
                    **    Mgr Total:      $ 1590.00

  East       10     659    33       1      $  429.00
  East       10     659    33       2      $  465.00

                     *    Bldg Total:     $   894.00
                    **    Mgr Total:      $   894.00


                  *****   Report Total:   $  6099.00
```

FIGURE 9.7b   Program Output for CHAP9A

The previous statements mean: Add the rent to the building and manager subtotals and to the report total. Control returns to the processing loop.

CONTROL BREAK CHECK:

```
void CtlBreakCk(void)
{
    if (mgr != prevMgr)
        MgrCtlBreak();
```

The above statements mean: Compare the previous manager number to the input manager number. If they are not equal, transfer control to *MgrCtlBreak*. Otherwise, skip to the next statement.

```
    else if (bldg != prevBldg)
        BldgCtlBreak();
    return;
}
```

Control branches here only if the manager numbers are equal. The above statements mean: Compare the previous building number to the input building number. If they are not equal, transfer control to *BldgCtlBreak* and perform the processing activities given there. Otherwise, return to the processing loop.

MANAGER CONTROL BREAK:

```
void MgrCtlBreak(void)
```

```
{
    BldgCtlBreak();
    prnt << CB2 << setw(8) << mgrTotal << endl;
    lineCnt = lineCnt + 2;
```

The above statements mean: Transfer control to the *BldgCtlBreak* module; this module prints the building subtotal line, saves the control fields for later use, and resets the building subtotal to 0. Upon returning, the program prints the manager subtotal line and adds 2 to the line counter (1 for the manager subtotal line and 1 for the blank line after).

The CB2 (Control Break 2) in the output statement specifies the format of the manager subtotal line and is defined in the *PROGRAM SETUP* section of the program.

```
    mgrTotal = 0.0;
    return;
}
```

The above statements mean: Reset the manager subtotal to 0. This is done in preparation for the next manager subtotal. Control then returns to the processing loop.

Checkpoint 9A

1. Explain why it is important to be able to develop multilevel control break programs.
2. List the steps involved in planning a multilevel control break program.
3. How many totals will a two-level control break program produce? A three-level? A four-level? A 10-level?
4. Show the four steps involved in performing a two-level control break on the major and minor control fields.

Planning a Four-Level Control Break Program

Now management would like to see the rent income broken down by location, agency, manager, and building. The format of the report is shown in Figure 9.8. Once again, the data must be arranged in ascending order by control fields to facilitate processing by the program. That is, the input must be ordered by location. Within each location, the input must be ordered by agency number. Within each agency, the input must be ordered by manager number. And within each manager, the input must be ordered by building number. At first, the logic may seem more complicated than it really is.

For this application, the program has four control fields: location, agency, manager, and building. Location represents the major control field, agency and manager represent the intermediate, and building represents the minor control field. An **intermediate control field** represents a control field between the major and minor control fields.

Notice that a four-level control break provides five totals, one for each control field and one for the report. Again, the stars shown on the report (Figure 9.8) correspond to the level numbers (1–5) of the totals.

Since a control break may occur at any one of the four levels, the program logic must be designed to print the subtotals from the "inside out." Thus, the minor subtotal (building) must be printed before the intermediate subtotals (manager and agency), and the intermediate subtotals must be printed before the major subtotal (location). This is done this way because the inner subtotals are actually part of the outer subtotals.

In order to see how this works, let us consider a control break on agency number. According to the logic in Figure 9.9, a break on *agency* sends the program to the *manager* control break module, which in turn sends it to the *building* control break module. Here, the program executes a *building* control break and returns, or "backs out," to the *manager* control break module. Next the program executes a manager control break and finally returns to execute the *agency* control break.

For a multilevel control break program, it is important to realize that each time a break occurs, the program executes the minor control break first. As the program "backs out" of the lower level modules, it executes the remaining control breaks "inside out."

Sample Program CHAP9B

Sample Program CHAP9B illustrates application of a four-level control break to produce the rental income report for Pernell Properties. Sample Program CHAP9B is shown in Figure 9.12 (p. 285); the program's output is shown in Figures 9.13a (p.290) and 9.13b (p. 291).

```
P E R N E L L    P R O P E R T I E S      Page 9
             Rental Income


LOCATION  AGENCY  MGR  BLDG  APART#      RENT

  X---X      99    999   99     9     $ 999.99
   :          :     :     :      :        :
   :          :     :     :      :        :
  X---X      99    999   99     9     $ 999.99

                    *   Bldg Total:    $ 9999.99
                   **   Mgr Total:     $ 9999.99
                  ***   Agency Total:  $ 9999.99
                 ****   Loc Total:     $ 9999.99


     .  .  .  .  .              .  .  .  .  .


               *****   Report Total:  $ 9999.99
```

FIGURE 9.8 A Four-Level Control Break Report

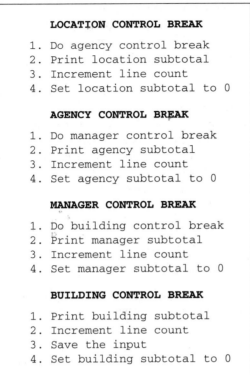

LOCATION CONTROL BREAK

1. Do agency control break
2. Print location subtotal
3. Increment line count
4. Set location subtotal to 0

AGENCY CONTROL BREAK

1. Do manager control break
2. Print agency subtotal
3. Increment line count
4. Set agency subtotal to 0

MANAGER CONTROL BREAK

1. Do building control break
2. Print manager subtotal
3. Increment line count
4. Set manager subtotal to 0

BUILDING CONTROL BREAK

1. Print building subtotal
2. Increment line count
3. Save the input
4. Set building subtotal to 0

FIGURE 9.9   Four-Level Control Break Logic

Sample program CHAP9B uses four control fields—location, agency number, manager number, and building number—to produce the rental income report.

The following specifications apply:

Input (text file):

For each record, read and assign data to the following fields. Field size and type are shown in parentheses.

1. Location   (5 char)
2. Agency number   (2 int)
3. Manager number   (3 int)
4. Building number   (2 int)
5. Apartment number   (1 int)
6. Monthly rent   (6.2 float)

Text File (rent.dat)

Use the data given below to create the rent file. The numbers shown above the columns correspond to the fields described for the input.

1	2	3	4	5	6
North	20	201	10	1	400.00
North	20	201	10	2	410.00
North	20	201	10	3	335.00
North	20	201	15	1	375.00
North	20	201	15	2	385.00
North	20	247	17	1	450.00
North	20	247	17	2	450.00
North	43	316	22	1	345.00
North	43	316	22	2	465.00
East	10	237	30	1	410.00
East	10	237	30	2	365.00
East	10	237	30	3	470.00
East	10	237	30	4	345.00
East	10	659	33	1	429.00
East	10	659	33	2	465.00
End	00	000	00	0	000.00 (trailer record)

Output (printer):

Print the four-level control break report shown in Figures 9.13a and 9.13b.

Processing Requirements:

- Read the rent file.
- Print 26 detail lines per page.
- Subtotal rent by building.
- Subtotal rent by manager.
- Subtotal rent by agency.
- Subtotal rent by location.
- Accumulate a report total for the rent.

Pseudocode:

```
START
Open file
If file opened
   (Print Headings)
   Read a record
   Save location
   Save agency number
   Save manager number
   Save building number
   LOOP until agency number = 0
      Accumulate building rent subtotal
      Accumulate manager rent subtotal
      Accumulate agency rent subtotal
      Accumulate location rent subtotal
      Accumulate report rent total
      If line counter > 26
         (Print Headings)
      Print detail line
      Read a record
```

```
                    If input location not = previous location
                        (Location Control Break)
                    else if input agency not = previous agency
                        (Agency Control Break)
                    else if input manager not = previous manager
                        (Manager Control Break)
                    else if input building not = previous building
                        (Building Control Break)
                End LOOP
                Print report rent total
                Close file
            END

            ENTER: Print Headings
            Set line counter to 0
            Add 1 to page number
            Advance to the next page
            Print titles, page number, and column headings
            RETURN

            ENTER: Location Control Break
            (Agency Control Break)
            Print location subtotal
            Add 2 to line count
            Set location subtotal to 0
            RETURN

            ENTER: Agency Control Break
            (Manager Control Break)
            Print agency subtotal
            Add 2 to line count
            Set agency subtotal to 0
            RETURN

            ENTER: Manager Control Break
            (Building Control Break)
            Print manager subtotal
            Add 2 to line count
            Set manager subtotal to 0
            RETURN

            ENTER: Building Control Break
            Print building subtotal
            Add 2 to line count
            Save location
            Save agency number
            Save manager number
            Save building number
            Set building subtotal to 0
            RETURN
```

Hierarchy Chart: See Figure 9.10.

Program Flowchart: See Figure 9.11.

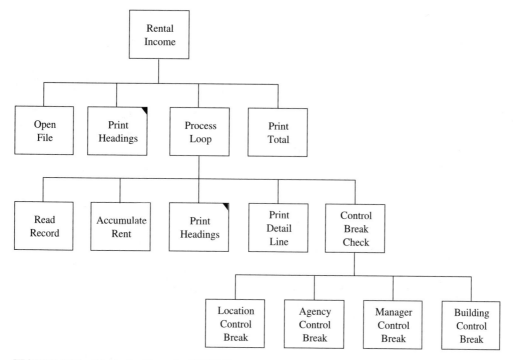

FIGURE 9.10   Hierarchy Chart for CHAP9B

Dissection of Sample Program CHAP9B

The logic and structure for sample program CHAP9B are similar to Sample Program CHAP9A. Therefore we will focus on the activities associated with performing the location and agency control breaks.

```
ACCUMULATE RENT TOTALS:
void AccumRent(void)
{
    bldgTotal = bldgTotal + rent;
    mgrTotal = mgrTotal + rent;
    agencyTotal = agencyTotal + rent;
    locTotal = locTotal + rent;
    rptTotal = rptTotal + rent;
    return;
}
```

The above statements mean: Add the input rent to the program subtotals—building, manager, agency, and location; the rent is also added to the report total. Control then returns to the processing loop *ProcessLoop*.

```
CONTROL BREAK CHECK:
void CtlBreakCk(void)
{
    if (strcmp(location, prevLoc) != 0)
        LocCtlBreak();
```

MAINLINE

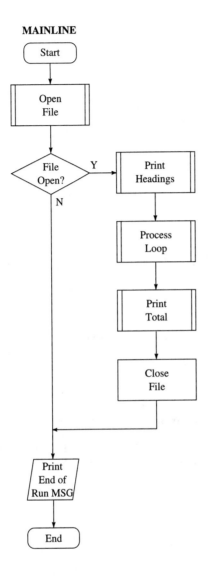

OPEN FILE

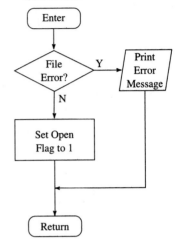

PRINT HEADINGS

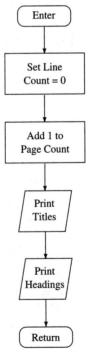

FIGURE 9.11   Program Flowchart for CHAP9B

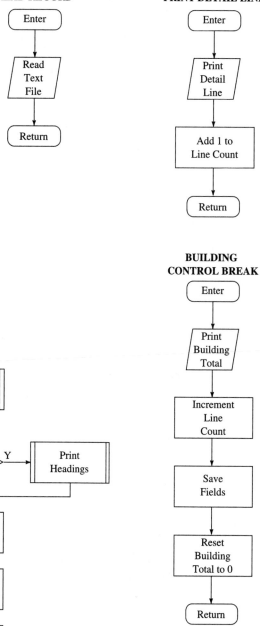

FIGURE 9.11   *Continued*

(continued on next page)

**MANAGER
CONTROL BREAK**

Enter

Building
Control
Break

Print
Manager
Total

Increment
Line
Count

Reset
Manager
Total to 0

Return

**ACCUMULATE
RENT**

Enter

Accumulate
Building
Total

Accumulate
Manager
Total

Accumulate
Agency
Total

Accumulate
Location
Total

Accumulate
Report
Total

Return

**LOCATION
CONTROL BREAK**

Enter

Agency
Control
Break

Print
Location
Total

Increment
Line
Count

Reset
Location
Total to 0

Return

**AGENCY
CONTROL BREAK**

Enter

Manager
Control
Break

Print
Agency
Total

Increment
Line
Count

Reset
Agency
Total to 0

Return

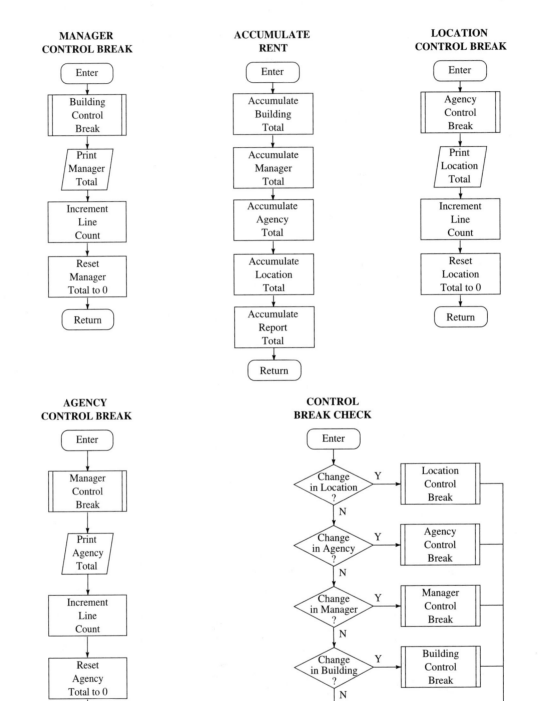

**CONTROL
BREAK CHECK**

Enter

Change
in Location
? —Y→ Location
Control
Break

N

Change
in Agency
? —Y→ Agency
Control
Break

N

Change
in Manager
? —Y→ Manager
Control
Break

N

Change
in Building
? —Y→ Building
Control
Break

N

Return

FIGURE 9.11   *Continued*

```
//---------- RENTAL INCOME --------------------------------
//  This program prints a four-level control break report
//  for Pernell Properties.
//
//              PROGRAM-ID: CHAP9B
//              PROGRAMMER: David M. Collopy
//              RUN DATE:   mm/dd/yy
//***********************************************************

//**   PREPROCESSING DIRECTIVES

#include<iostream.h>
#include<fstream.h>
#include<iomanip.h>
#include<string.h>

//---------- FUNCTION PROTOTYPES --------------------------

void OpenFile(void);            // open rent file
void PrnHeadings(void);         // print headings
void ProcessLoop(void);         // processing loop
void ReadRecord(void);          // read rent record
void AccumRent(void);           // accumulate rent totals
void CtlBreakCk(void);          // control break check
void LocCtlBreak(void);         // location control break
void AgencyCtlBreak(void);      // agency control break
void MgrCtlBreak(void);         // manager control break
void BldgCtlBreak(void);        // building control break
void PrnDetail(void);           // print detail line
void PrnTotal(void);            // print total line

//---------- PROGRAM SETUP --------------------------------

//**  H E A D I N G    L I N E S

char PT1[] = "P E R N E L L    P R O P E R T I E S     Page";
char PL2[] = "                Rental Income                ";
char HL[]  = "LOCATION  AGENCY  MGR   BLDG   APART#    RENT ";
char CB1[] = "                  * Bldg Total:    $";
char CB2[] = "                 ** Mgr Total:     $";
char CB3[] = "                *** Agency Total: $";
char CB4[] = "               **** Loc Total:     $";
char RTL[] = "              ***** Report Total: $";

//**  I N P U T   R E N T   R E C O R D

ifstream rentFile;              // file object name
char   location[6];             // location code
int    agency;                  // agency number
int    mgr;                     // manager number
int    bldg;                    // building number
int    apart;                   // apartment number
float  rent;                    // monthly rent income

//**  P R O G R A M   V A R I A B L E S
```

(continued on next page)

FIGURE 9.12 Sample Program CHAP9B: A Four-Level Control Break Report for Pernell Properties

```
char  prevLoc[6];              // previous location code
int   prevAgency;             // previous agency number
int   prevMgr;                // previous manager number
int   prevBldg;               // previous building number
float locTotal = 0.0;         // location rent total
float agencyTotal = 0.0;      // agency rent total
float mgrTotal = 0.0;         // manager rent total
float bldgTotal = 0.0;        // building rent total
float rptTotal = 0.0;         // report total rent
int   pageNum = 0;            // page number
int   lineCnt;                // detail line count
int   maxLines = 26;          // max detail lines per page

//**  O P E N   P R I N T E R   F I L E

ofstream prnt("PRN");          // open printer file

//-------------------------------------------------------------
//              MAINLINE CONTROL
//-------------------------------------------------------------
main()
{
    OpenFile();                // open rent file
    if (!rentFile.fail())  {
        PrnHeadings();         // print headings
        ProcessLoop();         // processing loop
        PrnTotal();            // print total line
        rentFile.close();      // close rent file
    }
    cout << "\n-----<E N D   O F   R U N>-----";
    return 0;
}
//-------------------------------------------------------------
//              OPEN RENT FILE
//-------------------------------------------------------------
void OpenFile(void)
{
    rentFile.open("a:rent.dat");
    if (rentFile.fail())
        cout << "Rent file open failed" << endl;
    return;
}
//-------------------------------------------------------------
//              PRINT HEADINGS
//-------------------------------------------------------------
void PrnHeadings(void)
{
    lineCnt = 0;               // set line count to 0
    pageNum = pageNum + 1;     // add 1 to page number
    prnt << "\f";              // reset to top of page
    prnt << PT1 << setw(2)
         << pageNum << endl;   // print page title 1
    prnt << PT2 << endl
         << endl;              // print page title 2
}
```

FIGURE 9.12 *Continued*

```
       prnt << HL << endl
            << endl;                    // print heading line
       return;
}
//------------------------------------------------------------
//              PROCESSING LOOP
//------------------------------------------------------------
void ProcessLoop(void)
{
    ReadRecord();                       // read rent record
    strcpy(prevLoc = loc);              // save location code
    prevAgency = agency;                // save agency number
    prevMgr = mgr;                      // save manager number
    prevBldg = bldg;                    // save building number
    while (agency != 0)  {
        AccumRent();                    // accumulate rent totals
        if (lineCnt >= maxLines)
            PrnHeadings();              // print headings
        PrnDetail();                    // print detail line
        ReadRecord();                   // read rent record
        CtlBreakCk();                   // control break check
    }
    return;
}
//------------------------------------------------------------
//              READ RENT RECORD
//------------------------------------------------------------
void ReadRecord(void)
{
    rentFile.get(location, 6) >> agency >> mgr
        >> bldg >> apart >> rent;
    rentFile.get();                     // clear input file buffer
    return;
}
//------------------------------------------------------------
//              ACCUMULATE RENT TOTALS
//------------------------------------------------------------
void AccumRent(void)
{
    bldgTotal = bldgTotal + rent;
    mgrTotal = mgrTotal + rent:
    agencyTotal = agencyTotal + rent:
    locTotal = locTotal + rent:
    rptTotal = rptTotal + rent:
    return;
}
//------------------------------------------------------------
//              PRINT DETAIL LINE
//------------------------------------------------------------
void PrnDetail(void)
{
    prnt << endl;
    prnt << setiosflags(ios::left)              // left justify
```
(continued on next page)

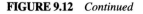

FIGURE 9.12 *Continued*

```
                    << " " << setw(9) << location
                    << resetiosflags(ios::left)        // right justify
                    << setw(4) << agency << setw(7) << mgr
                    << setw(5) << bldg << setw(7) << apart
                    << "       $" << setiosflags(ios::fixed)
                    << setiosflags(ios::showpoint) << setprecision(2)
                    << setw(7) << rent;
        lineCnt = lineCnt + 1;
        return;
}
//------------------------------------------------------------
//              CONTROL BREAK CHECK
//------------------------------------------------------------
void CtlBreakCk(void)
{
        if (strcmp(location, prevLoc) != 0)
            LocCtlBreak();
        else if (agency != prevAgency)
            AgencyCtlBreak();
        else if (mgr != prevMgr)
            MgrCtlBreak();
        else if (bldg != prevBldg)
            BldgCtlBreak();
        return;
}
//------------------------------------------------------------
//              LOCATION CONTROL BREAK
//------------------------------------------------------------
void LocCtlBreak(void)
{
        AgencyCtlBreak();
        prnt << CB4 << setw(8) << locTotal << endl;
        lineCnt = lineCnt + 2;
        locTotal = 0.0;
        return;
}
//------------------------------------------------------------
//              AGENCY CONTROL BREAK
//------------------------------------------------------------
void AgencyCtlBreak(void)
{
        MgrCtlBreak();
        prnt << CB3 << setw(8) << agencyTotal << endl;
        lineCnt = lineCnt + 2;
        agencyTotal = 0.0;
        return;
}
//------------------------------------------------------------
//              MANAGER CONTROL BREAK
//------------------------------------------------------------
void MgrCtlBreak(void)
{
        BldgCtlBreak();
```

FIGURE 9.12 *Continued*

```
        prnt << CB2 << setw(8) << mgrTotal << endl;
        lineCnt = lineCnt + 2;
        mgrTotal = 0.0;
        return;
}
//----------------------------------------------------------
//              BUILDING CONTROL BREAK
//----------------------------------------------------------
void BldgCtlBreak(void)
{
        prnt << endl << endl
             << CB1 << setw(8) << bldgTotal << endl;
        lineCnt = lineCnt + 2;
        strcpy(prevLoc, location);
        prevAgency = agency;
        prevMgr = mgr;
        prevBldg = bldg;
        bldgTotal = 0.0;
        return;
}
//----------------------------------------------------------
//              PRINT TOTAL LINE
//----------------------------------------------------------
void PrnTotal(void)
{
        prnt << endl << endl
             << RTL << setw(8) << rptTotal << endl;
        return;
}
```

FIGURE 9.12   *Continued*

The preceding statements (on p. 281) mean: Compare the previous location to the input location. If they are not equal, transfer control to *LocCtlBreak*. Otherwise, skip to the next statement.

```
    else if (agency != prevAgency)
        AgencyCtlBreak();
```

Control branches here only if the locations are equal. The above statements mean: Compare the previous agency number to the input agency number. If they are not equal, transfer control to *AgencyCtlBreak*. Otherwise, skip to the next statement.

```
    else if (mgr != prevMgr)
        MgrCtlBreak();
```

Control branches here only if the agency numbers are equal. The above statements mean: Compare the previous manager number to the input manager number. If they are not equal, transfer control to *MgrCtlBreak*. Otherwise, skip to the next statement.

```
    else if (bldg != prevBldg)
        BldgCtlBreak();
    return;
}
```

```
P E R N E L L   P R O P E R T I E S        Page 1
              Rental Income

LOCATION  AGENCY  MGR   BLDG   APART#       RENT

 North      20    201    10      1      $  400.00
 North      20    201    10      2      $  410.00
 North      20    201    10      3      $  335.00

                   *   Bldg Total:      $ 1145.00

 North      20    201    15      1      $  375.00
 North      20    201    15      2      $  385.00

                   *   Bldg Total:      $  760.00
                  **   Mgr Total:       $ 1905.00

 North      20    247    17      1      $  450.00
 North      20    247    17      2      $  450.00

                   *   Bldg Total:      $  900.00
                  **   Mgr Total:       $  900.00
                 ***   Agency Total:    $ 2805.00

 North      43    316    22      1      $  345.00
 North      43    316    22      2      $  465.00

                   *   Bldg Total:      $  810.00
                  **   Mgr Total:       $  810.00
                 ***   Agency Total:    $  810.00
                ****   Loc Total:       $ 3615.00
```

FIGURE 9.13a Program Output for CHAP9B

Control branches here only if the manager numbers are equal. The preceding statements mean: Compare the previous building number to the input building number. If they are not equal, transfer control to *BldgCtlBreak*. Otherwise, return to the processing loop.

```
LOCATION CONTROL BREAK:

void LocCtlBreak(void)
{
    AgencyCtlBreak();
    prnt << CB4 << setw(8) << locTotal << endl;
    lineCnt = lineCnt + 2;
    locTotal = 0.0;
    return;
}
```

```
P E R N E L L   P R O P E R T I E S       Page 2
               Rental Income

LOCATION   AGENCY   MGR   BLDG   APART#        RENT

  East       10     237    30      1      $  410.00
  East       10     237    30      2      $  365.00
  East       10     237    30      3      $  470.00
  East       10     237    30      4      $  345.00

                      *   Bldg Total:      $ 1590.00
                     **   Mgr Total:       $ 1590.00

  East       10     659    33      1      $  429.00
  East       10     659    33      2      $  465.00

                      *   Bldg Total:      $  894.00
                     **   Mgr Total:       $  894.00
                    ***   Agency Total:    $ 2484.00
                   ****   Loc Total:       $ 2484.00


                  *****   Report Total:    $ 6099.00
```

FIGURE 9.13b   Program Output for CHAP9B

The preceding statements mean: Transfer control to *AgencyCtlBreak*. Upon returning, print the location subtotal line and add 2 to the line counter (1 for the manager location subtotal line and 1 for the blank line after).

The CB4 (Control Break 4) specifies the format of the location subtotal line and is defined in *PROGRAM SETUP* section of the program.

```
AGENCY CONTROL BREAK:

void AgencyCtlBreak(void)
{
    MgrCtlBreak();
    prnt << CB3 << setw(8) << agencyTotal << endl;
    lineCnt = lineCnt + 2;
    agencyTotal = 0.0;
    return;
}
```

The above statements mean: Transfer control to *MgrCtlBreak*; this module prints the manager subtotal line and resets the manager subtotal to 0. Upon returning, the program prints the agency subtotal line and adds 2 to the line counter (1 for the agency subtotal line and 1 for the blank line after).

The CB3 (Control Break 3) specifies the format of the agency subtotal line and is defined in the *PROGRAM SETUP* section of the program.

Checkpoint 9B

1. What is a major control field? An intermediate control field? A minor control field?

2. Explain what it means to design the program logic so the subtotals print from the "inside out."

3. Show the four steps involved in performing a three-level control break that contains a major, an intermediate, and a minor control field.

Summary

1. Business applications often require reports that contain multilevel control totals or subtotals.

2. Control totals may go two, three, four, or more levels deep; the actual number of levels depends mostly on the application at hand.

3. Designing multilevel reports involves grouping subtotals within subtotals.

4. Planning a multilevel control break involves the following: formatting the report on a printer spacing chart, arranging the data in sequential order by control fields, and developing the logic to force the program to break when the control fields change values.

5. A two-level control break contains a major and a minor control field.

6. A two-level control break program accumulates and prints three levels of totals: one for the major control field, one for the minor, and one for the report.

7. Stars are printed next to the total lines to specify the level number of each total. One star indicates the first level, two stars indicate the second level, and so on.

8. A four-level control break program has four control fields: one major, two intermediate, and one minor.

9. A four-level control break program provides five totals: one for each control field and one for the report.

10. For a multilevel control break, the program always executes the minor control break first. Then as the program "backs out" of the other modules one by one, it executes the remaining control breaks "inside out."

Programming Projects

For each project, design the logic and write the modular structured program to produce the output. Model your program after the Sample Programs presented in the chapter. Verify your output.

Project 9–1   Payroll-1

Write a program to read a payroll file, calculate gross pay, and print a two-level control total payroll report. Assume overtime is not computed.

Input (text file):

For each payroll record, read and assign data to the following fields. Field size and type are shown in parentheses.

1. Branch number   (1 int)
2. Division number   (2 int)
3. Department number   (3 int)
4. Employee name   (20 char)
5. Hours worked   (2 int)
6. Hourly pay rate   (5.2 float)

Text File (payroll.dat):

Use the data given below to create the payroll file. The numbers shown above the columns correspond to the fields described for the input.

1	2	3	4	5	6
1	10	100	Tanya Bauer	40	7.50
1	10	100	Diane Dixon	40	9.75
1	10	106	Randy Karns	37	8.55
1	20	112	Dana Clark	45	14.90
1	20	112	Nick Larson	43	7.72
1	20	112	Colleen Norris	40	11.35
1	20	123	Sara Erickson	38	12.00
1	40	117	Scott Howard	42	9.75
2	10	105	Paul Irwin	48	8.72
2	10	105	Cyndi Olson	45	15.10
2	18	144	Dale Miller	40	10.25
3	23	121	Bret Rossi	35	8.00
3	23	121	Karen Thomas	48	9.00
3	23	137	Cheryl Dietz	42	7.50
3	23	137	Neil Kenney	38	7.25
3	34	150	Tracy York	36	11.00
0	00	000	Trailer Record	00	0.00

Output (printer):

Print the following two-level control break report:

```
Author            C O M P A N Y   P A Y R O L L        Page 99
                        Gross Pay Report
                          mm/dd/yy
Branch    Division    Department    Employee Name        Gross Pay
   9         99          999        X------------X        999.99
   :          :           :              :                  :
   :          :           :              :                  :
   9         99          999        X------------X        999.99

                              *   Department Total:     9999.99
                             **   Division Total:       9999.99
            . . . . .                    . . . . .
                           ****   Report Total:         9999.99
```

Processing Requirements:

- Read the payroll file.
- Print 31 detail lines per page.
- Compute the gross pay:
  regular pay + overtime pay
- Subtotal gross pay by department.
- Subtotal gross pay by division.
- Accumulate a report total for gross pay.

Project 9–2   Payroll-2

Modify the program in Project 9–1 to include a three-level control break. Group and list employee gross pay by department, division, and branch, and print the appropriate subtotal for each group. Print 32 detail lines per page. Model the logic after Sample Program CHAP9B.

Print the following three-level control break report:

```
Author            C O M P A N Y   P A Y R O L L        Page 99
                         Gross Pay Report
                           mm/dd/yy

Branch    Division   Department    Employee Name      Gross Pay
   9         99         999        X-------------X      999.99
   :          :          :              :                :
   :          :          :              :                :
   9         99         999        X-------------X      999.99
                                *  Department Total:    9999.99
                               **  Division Total:      9999.99
                              ***  Branch Total:        9999.99
            . . . . .                   . . . . .
                             ****  Report Total:       99999.99
```

Project 9–3   Sales Analysis-1

Write a program to read a sales file, accumulate total customer sales, and print a three-level control total sales report.

Input (text file):

For each sales record, read and assign data to the following fields. Field size and type are shown in parentheses.

1. Region number   (1 int)
2. State code   (2 int)
3. Store number   (3 int)
4. Salesperson number   (3 int)
5. Customer number   (4 int)
6. Sales amount   (7.2 float)

Text File (sales.dat):

Use the data given below to create the sales file. The numbers shown above the columns correspond to the fields described for the input.

1	2	3	4	5	6
1	OH	100	190	1180	380.00
1	OH	100	190	3100	273.00
1	OH	100	225	2510	161.00
1	OH	210	287	5090	492.00
1	IN	198	338	4200	185.00
1	IN	198	412	6100	200.00
1	IN	198	412	9430	300.00
2	KY	279	206	2900	563.00
2	KY	279	490	3000	175.00
2	KY	300	640	3100	100.00
2	KY	313	110	7170	400.00
3	PA	121	720	1200	369.00
3	PA	239	378	2600	349.00
3	PA	239	600	5500	200.00
0	XX	000	000	0000	000.00 (trailer record)

Output (printer):

Print the following three-level control break report:

```
Author                SALES ANALYSIS REPORT              Page 99
                          mm/dd/yy

Region    State   Store    Salesperson    Customer    Sales
---------------------------------------------------------------
  9        XX      999         999          9999      999.99
  :        :       :           :             :          :
  :        :       :           :             :          :
  9        XX      999         999          9999      999.99

                           *   Salesperson Total: 9999.99
                          **   Store Total:        9999.99
                         ***   State Total:        9999.99
        . . . . .                           . . . . .
                       *****   Report Total:       9999.99
```

Processing Requirements:

- Read the sales file.
- Print 35 detail lines per page.
- Subtotal sales by salesperson.
- Subtotal sales by store.
- Subtotal sales by state.
- Accumulate a report total for sales.

Project 9–4   Sales Analysis-2

Modify the program in Project 9–3 to include a four-level control break. Group and list customer sales by salesperson, store, state, and region, and print the appropriate sales subtotal for each group. Print 36 detail lines per page. Model the logic after Sample Program CHAP9B.

Print the following control break report:

```
Author              SALES ANALYSIS REPORT            Page 99
                         mm/dd/yy


Region    State   Store   Salesperson   Customer   Sales
-------------------------------------------------------------
   9       XX      999        999          9999     999.99
   :        :       :          :             :         :
   :        :       :          :             :         :
   9       XX      999        999          9999     999.99

                            *   Salesperson Total: 9999.99
                           **   Store Total:        9999.99
                          ***   State Total:        9999.99
                         ****   Region Total:       9999.99
           . . . . .                    . . . . .
                        *****   Report Total:       9999.99
```

Project 9–5   Inventory-1

Write a program to read an inventory file, accumulate total quantity on hand, and print a three-level control total inventory report.

Input (text file):

For each inventory record, read and assign data to the following fields. Field size and type are shown in parentheses.

1. Region number   (1 int)
2. State code   (2 char)
3. Location number   (2 int)
4. Warehouse number   (3 int)
5. Item number   (5 char)
6. Quantity on hand   (2 int)

Text File (invent.dat):

Use the data given below to create the inventory file. The numbers shown above the columns correspond to the fields described for the input.

1	2	3	4	5	6
1	OH	43	101	A7100	24
1	OH	43	101	B0340	12
1	OH	43	101	D0019	35

```
1      OH     43     340     C1970     48
1      OH     43     340     H0120     16
1      OH     66     220     F3170     96
1      OH     66     220     K8800     24
1      IN     27     125     C5510     12
1      IN     27     125     I1700     36
2      KY     18     107     B1776     24
2      KY     18     107     D0011     30
2      KY     18     130     F0910     36
2      KY     18     130     L7650     96
2      KY     18     130     P0150     15
0      XX     00     000     XXXXX     00 (trailer record)
```

Output (printer):

Print the following three-level control break report:

```
Author            INVENTORY ANALYSIS REPORT           Page 99
                        mm/dd/yy

Region    State    Location    Warehouse    Item#    Quantity
  9        XX         99          999       XXXXX       99
  :         :          :           :           :          :
  :         :          :           :           :          :
  9        XX         99          999       XXXXX       99

                              *   Warehouse Total:    999
                             **   Location Total:     999
                            ***   State Total:        999
           . . . . .                   . . . . .
                          *****   Report Total:       999
```

Processing Requirements:

- Read the inventory file.
- Print 25 detail lines per page.
- Subtotal quantity by warehouse.
- Subtotal quantity by location.
- Subtotal quantity by state.
- Accumulate a report total for quantity on hand.

Project 9–6   Inventory-2

Modify the program in Project 9–5 to include a four-level control break. Group and list the quantity on hand by warehouse, location, and state, and print the appropriate subtotal for each group. Print 26 detail lines per page. Model the logic after Sample Program CHAP9B.

Print the following four-level control break report:

```
Author            INVENTORY ANALYSIS REPORT           Page 99
                        mm/dd/yy

Region    State    Location    Warehouse    Item#    Quantity
  9        XX         99          999       XXXXX       99
  :         :          :           :           :          :
  :         :          :           :           :          :
```

```
9         XX        99          999       XXXXX      99
                              *    Warehouse Total:   999
                             **    Location Total:    999
                            ***    State Total:       999
                           ****    Region Total:      999
         . . . . .                    . . . . .
                          *****    Report Total:      999
```

Project 9–7   Personnel-1

Write a program to read a personnel file, count the number of employees, and print a two-level control total personnel report.

Input (text file):

For each record, read and assign data to the following fields. Field size and type are shown in parentheses.

1. Branch number   (1 int)
2. Division number   (2 int)
3. Department number   (3 int)
4. Manager number   (2 int)
5. Supervisor number   (4 int)
6. Employee count   (2 int)

Text File (persnel.dat):

Use the data given below to create the personnel file. The numbers shown above the columns correspond to the fields described for the input.

1	2	3	4	5	6
1	10	101	20	2010	08
1	10	101	20	2025	12
1	10	101	30	3050	16
1	10	101	30	3055	12
1	10	101	30	3060	10
1	10	120	45	4520	14
1	10	120	45	4530	12
1	20	206	12	1210	07
1	20	206	12	1220	12
2	15	115	22	2210	15
2	15	115	22	2230	12
2	15	210	33	3340	18
2	15	210	33	3360	16
2	15	210	45	4510	10
2	15	210	45	4550	12
2	27	108	26	2630	12
2	27	108	26	2640	16
2	27	108	26	2680	14
0	00	000	00	0000	00 (trailer record)

Output (printer):

Print the following two-level control break report:

```
Author              P E R S O N N E L   R E P O R T           Page 99

                         Employee Count
                            mm/dd/yy

  Branch   Division   Department   Manager   Supervisor   Employees
    9         99         999         99         9999          99
    :          :          :          :           :            :
    :          :          :          :           :            :
    9         99         999         99         9999          99
                                      *   Manager Total:      999
                                     **   Department Total:   999
            . . . . .                            . . . . .
                                  *****   Report Total:       999
```

Processing Requirements:

- Read the personnel file.
- Print 29 detail lines per page.
- Subtotal employee count by manager.
- Subtotal employee count by department.
- Accumulate a report total for employee count.

Project 9–8   Personnel–2

Modify the program in Project 9–7 to include a four-level control break. Group and list the employee count by manager, department, division, and branch, and print the appropriate subtotal for each group. Print 32 detail lines per page. Model the logic after sample program CHAP9B.

Print the following four-level control break report:

```
Author              P E R S O N N E L   R E P O R T           Page 99

                         Employee Count
                            mm/dd/yy

  Branch   Division   Department   Manager   Supervisor   Employees
    9         99         999         99         9999          99
    :          :          :          :           :            :
    :          :          :          :           :            :
    9         99         999         99         9999          99
                                      *   Manager Total:      999
                                     **   Department Total:   999
                                    ***   Division Total:     999
                                   ****   Branch Total:       999
            . . . . .                            . . . . .
                                  *****   Report Total:       999
```

10 Arrays and Sorting

Learning Objectives

After you have read this chapter and completed the exercises, you should be able to:
- understand the purpose of arrays and the use of subscripts
- define and load numeric and character arrays
- manipulate and print data stored in arrays
- define and load data into parallel arrays

- search and update data stored in parallel arrays
- sort (rearrange) the elements in an array in ascending and descending order

Arrays

An **array** represents a set of values that is given one name. Each item in the array is called an **element**, and each element has identical data types. Collectively, the elements resemble a list of related objects, such as test scores, close friends, best-selling book titles, paid holidays, top-rated TV shows, and so forth.

In this chapter, we will learn how to define two types of arrays: character and numeric. **Character arrays** hold nonnumeric or string data, whereas **numeric arrays** hold integer or floating-point values. Integer and floating-point values are stored in separate arrays.

For example, in Figure 10.1, *quantity* is an integer array that consists of seven elements, and *mileage* is a floating-point array that consists of five elements. Hence, an **integer array** consists of a set of integers, and a **floating-point array** consists of a set of floating-point elements.

Like single variables, array variables (elements) are used to store data in memory. This means that once an array is loaded—values assigned to the elements—the data can be processed repeatedly without requiring the program to reenter it.

As an example, assume a series of 36 test scores are loaded into an array. The program could access the scores from the array and print them on the screen. Next the program could access the scores a second time and compute the class average. Furthermore, the program could access the scores a third time and "curve" them by adding six points to each score before printing them on the printer.

Creating an Array

Arrays are defined by specifying a data type, a name, and a size. Data type refers to the kind of data the array will hold—numeric or character. Name refers to the identifier assigned to the array. And size specifies the number of elements reserved for the array. Size is enclosed within square brackets [].

```
quantity                    mileage
   12                         78.5
   36                         94.2
   68    ←— elements —→       86.9
   09                         68.0
   44                         75.3
   51
   87
```

FIGURE 10.1   Numeric Arrays

Both numeric and character data may be stored in arrays.

Numeric Arrays: Numeric data is stored in either integer or floating-point arrays. Declarations that define numeric arrays allocate storage spaces for numeric data items.

Examples of numeric array declarations are:

```
int    quantity[7];
float  mileage[5];
float  area[12], amountDue[36], int colorCode[10];
int    points[12],
       location[50],
       units[24];
```

We may define one or more arrays on the same line. Multiple array declarations are separated by commas. We may also list the arrays down the page. Each declaration begins with a data type and ends with a semicolon.

The above declarations define the following numeric arrays:

quantity	7 elements	(int)
mileage	5 elements	(float)
area	12 elements	(float)
amountDue	36 elements	(float)
colorCode	10 elements	(int)
points	12 elements	(int)
location	50 elements	(int)
units	24 elements	(int)

The data types are shown in parentheses.

Character Arrays: String data is stored in character arrays. Declarations that define character arrays allocate storage for string data items. For character arrays, we not only specify the size of the array, we also specify the size of the elements.

Examples of character arrays are:

```
char day[7][10];
char jobTitle[30][20];
char studentRank[100][10], building[5][25];
char supplier[40][30],
     description[200][50],
     magazine[15][35];
```

Consider the declaration for *day*. It reserves enough storage space for seven elements, each of which may hold up to a maximum of nine characters of data. The last position is reserved for the null character.

The above declarations define the following character arrays:

day	7 elements	(10)
jobTitle	30 elements	(20)
studentRank	100 elements	(10)
building	5 elements	(25)
supplier	40 elements	(30)

description	200 elements	(50)
magazine	15 elements	(35)

The lengths of the elements are shown in parentheses.

Checkpoint 10A

1. What is an array? What is an element?
2. Identify two types of arrays and explain each.
3. What is the benefit of using arrays?
4. What information is specified when creating a numeric array?
5. Using the following definitions, code the statement to define each numeric array.
   a. *amount*   48 elements   (float)
   b. *qtyOnHand*   450 elements   (int)
   c. *price*   25 elements   (float)
6. In addition to data type, array name, and size, what other information is needed to define a character array?
7. Using the following definitions, code the statement to define each character array.
   a. *employeeName*   268 elements   (20 characters)
   b. *address*   100 elements   (30 characters)
   c. *socSecNbr*   50 elements   (11 characters)

Subscripts

Since one name applies to the entire array, how can we reference the individual elements? The answer is by using a subscript. Each element can be accessed by appending a subscript to the array name. A **subscript** is an integer value that is used to reference a specific element in the array. Consequently, an element is called a **subscripted variable**. Accordingly, the arrays shown in Figure 10.2 consist of a set of subscripted variables that are numbered from first to last, starting with 0. Zero is always assigned to the first element in the array. This is an important convention to remember—the first subscript is always 0, not 1. Hence the elements stored in the day array contain the following data: *day[0]*: Sunday, *day[1]*: Monday, *day[2]*: Tuesday, and so on; the elements stored in the mileage array contain the following data: *mileage[0]*: 78.5, *mileage[1]*: 94.2, *mileage[2]*: 86.9, and so on.

Another important thing to know about subscripts is that they may not be negative or exceed the size of the array minus 1 (size − 1). Hence, in Figure 10.2, the only valid subscripts for *day* are 0–6. Therefore, a reference to either *day[10]* or *day[−2]* would cause the compiler to produce an error message indicating that the subscript is invalid.

Subscripts may be expressed as integer constants or variables. Subscripted variables allow the program to access or print the value of a specific element or to perform a variety of arithmetic operations on one or more elements stored in an array.

Constants: An integer constant is a whole number that directly references a given element. Any element stored in an array may be directly referenced by specifying its subscripts as an integer constant.

```
char day[7][10]              float mileage[5]

day[0]    Sunday             mileage[0]    78.5
day[1]    Monday             mileage[1]    94.2
day[2]    Tuesday            mileage[2]    86.9
day[3]    Wednesday          mileage[3]    68.0
day[4]    Thursday           mileage[4]    75.3
day[5]    Friday
day[6]    Saturday
```

FIGURE 10.2   Arrays and Subscripts

Examples of constant subscripts are:

```
cout << "Grade = " << grade[0];

total = grade[0] + grade[1] + grade[2] + grade[3] + grade[4];

grade[2] = grade[2] + 6.0;

strcpy(day[2], "TUESDAY");

mileage[3] = 95.0;
```

Variables: Variable subscripts may be written as either a single variable or as an arithmetic expression. Variable subscripts allow the programmer to tap into the full power of arrays and array processing techniques.

Examples of variable subscripts are:

```
cin >> grade[i];

cout << "Grade = " << grade[n];

grade[sub] = grade[sub] + 6.0;

strcpy(day[x], "TUESDAY");

mileage[sub+1] = 95.0;
```

Checkpoint 10B

1. What is a subscript?

2. (True or False) An element is also referred to as a subscripted variable.

3. What integer subscript is always assigned to the first element in an array?

4. (True or False) Subscripts may be negative, and they may exceed the size of the array.

5. What is the value of using a variable as a subscript as opposed to using an integer constant?

Loading an Array

Array declarations do not automatically assign data to the elements. It is up to the programmer to decide how to fill the arrays. Essentially, there are three methods of assigning data to an array: (1) initialize the elements when the array is declared; (2) prompt the user to enter the data at the keyboard; and (3) load the data from a file.

Initializing Data: Data may be assigned to an array when it is defined. For character arrays, this is the only time that a string can be directly assigned to an element using the equal sign.

Examples of initializing data are:

```
char  day[7][10] = {"Sunday", "Monday", "Tuesday",
                    "Wednesday", "Thursday", "Friday",
                    "Saturday"};

float mileage[5] = {78.5, 94.2, 86.9, 68.0, 75.3};
```

The first declaration assigns a set of names to the *day* array; each element may hold up to nine characters of data. String constants are enclosed within double quotation marks and are separated by commas. Syntax requires that the set of constants be enclosed within braces { }.

Similarly, the second declaration assigns a set of floating-point values to the *mileage* array. Numeric values are not enclosed within double quotation marks. Both declarations end with a semicolon.

Interactive Input: Data may be assigned to an array by prompting the user to enter the input at the keyboard. The examples shown below use a counter-controlled loop to prompt for the input. The input is assigned to the elements as it is entered at the keyboard.

```
//----- LOAD DAY ARRAY -------
for (i = 0; i < 7; i++)  {
    cout << "Enter the day: ";
    cin >> day[i];
}
```

Although *day* has two subscripts, we use only one to load data into the array. Here we need only to specify the elements we intend to load into the array.

```
//----- LOAD MILEAGE ARRAY -------
for (i = 0; i < 5; i++)  {
    cout << "Enter the mileage: ";
    cin >> mileage[i];
}
```

File Input: Data can be read from a file and loaded directly into an array. The examples shown below use a conditional loop to read the data from a file. As long as the end-of-file marker has not been read, the input is assigned to the elements as it is read from the file.

Note that the input file buffer is cleared after reading a string of characters. This is done to remove the Enter key code from the buffer. Otherwise, the next get() function would load the Enter key code into the *day* array.

```
//----- LOAD DAY ARRAY -------
i = 0;
while(!inputFile.eof())  {
    inputFile.get(day[i], 10);
    inputFile.get();
    i = i + 1;
}

//----- LOAD MILEAGE ARRAY -----
i = 0;
while(!milesFile.eof())  {
    milesFile >> mileage[i];
    i = i + 1;
}
```

Printing an Array

Array data is stored in memory. Since the data was assigned directly to the elements, we have no way of knowing for sure what was placed in the array. We cannot see the elements. Therefore, it would be wise to verify the contents of the array. We can do this by reading the array and printing a copy of the elements.

The code shown below prints the contents of the *day* and *mileage* arrays.

```
//----- PRINT DAY ARRAY -----------------
for (i = 0; i < 7; i++)  {
    cout << setiosflags(ios::left)
         << setw(10) << day[i] << endl;
}

//----- PRINT MILEAGE ARRAY --------------------
for (i = 0; i < 5; i++)  {
    cout << setiosflags(ios::fixed)
         << setiosflags(ios::showpoint) << setw(4)
         << setprecision(1) << mileage[i] << endl;
}
```

Processing an Array

Data stored in an array can be processed much like data stored in a single variable. The only difference is that array variables are subscripted. Other than that, we can perform normal arithmetic operations and logical comparisons, determine high and low values, update elements, compute totals, calculate averages, and so on.

High and Low Values: The first *for* loop locates the high mileage stored in the array, while the second locates the low.

```
float mileage[5] = {78.5, 94.2, 86.9, 68.0, 75.3};
float high = 0.0;
float low = 1000.0;
  . . . . .
```

```
//----- FIND HIGH MILEAGE -----
for (i = 0; i < 5; i++)  {
    if (mileage[i] > high)
        high = mileage[i];
}

//----- FIND LOW MILEAGE -----
for (i = 0; i < 5; i++)  {
    if (mileage[i] < low)
        low = mileage[i];
}
```

Notice that *high* is initialized to 0. This "sets the stage" for subsequent comparisons by forcing the first element into the high position. Inside the loop, the elements are compared one by one to the high value. If an element is greater than the current high value, then it becomes the new high value. See if you can follow the logic for finding the low value.

Totals and Averages: The body of the *for* loop computes a total for the elements stored in the array. Upon exiting the loop, the program computes the average.

```
float mileage[5] = {78.5, 94.2, 86.9, 68.0, 75.3};
float total = 0;
float average;
  . . . . .

//----- TOTAL THE MILEAGE -----
for (i = 0; i < 5; i++)  {
    total = total + mileage[i];
}
average = total/5;
```

Parallel Arrays

Parallel arrays consist of two or more single arrays that are related in some way. That is, the elements in one array correspond to the elements in another. Parallel arrays have the same number of elements defined for each array in the parallel set. Figure 10.3 shows two arrays, *driver* and *mileage*. The names in the first array correspond to the miles driven in the second. Hence, Vicki drove 78.5 miles, David drove 94.2 miles, Karen drove 86.9 miles, Matt drove 68.0 miles, and Heather drove 75.3 miles.

Follow the sample code shown below. The first two modules demonstrate how to load the parallel arrays using interactive and file input. The third module prints the contents of the *driver* and *mileage* arrays.

```
//----- LOAD FROM USER INPUT -----
for (i = 0; i < 5; i++)  {
    cout << "  Enter driver: ";
    cin.get(driver[i], 15);
    cin.get();
    cout << "  Enter miles: ";
    cin >> mileage[i];
}
```

	driver		mileage
(0)	Vicki Cho	(0)	78.5
(1)	David Nelson	(1)	94.2
(2)	Karen Sims	(2)	86.9
(3)	Matt Andrews	(3)	68.0
(4)	Heather Karr	(4)	75.3

FIGURE 10.3   Parallel Arrays

```
//----- LOAD FROM FILE INPUT ----------------
for (i = 0; i < 5; i++)  {
    dataFile.get(driver[i], 15) >> mileage[i];
    dataFile.get();
}

//----- PRINT PARALLEL ARRAYS -----
for (i = 0; i < 5; i++)  {
    cout << setiosflags(ios::left)
         << setw(15) << driver[i]
         << resetiosflags(ios::left)
         << setiosflags(ios::fixed)
         << setiosflags(ios::showpoint)
         << setw(4) << setprecision(1)
         << mileage[i] << endl;
}
```

Checkpoint 10C

1. What three methods may be used to load an array with data?
2. Which of the two statements will cause an error? Why?

```
char text[5][7] = {"This", "is", "some", "sample", "text."};
text[2] = "some";
```

3. Why is it good practice to print an array after loading it?
4. What is the difference between processing data stored in arrays and processing data stored in a single variable?
5. Explain the concept of parallel arrays.
6. Code the statements to load two parallel arrays with the data shown in the following table. (*Note:* The data will be entered at the keyboard.) Then code the statements to print the arrays to verify that they were loaded correctly. Assume the following definitions:

```
int    i;
char   employee[5][20];
float hourlyRate[5];
```

Employee	Hourly Rate
John Smith	10.75
George Thomas	9.50
Sue Blackstone	9.75
Joan Banner	8.45
Todd Nichols	7.00

Sample Program CHAP10A

Sample program CHAP10A (Figure 10.6, p. 312) loads employee names and production data into parallel arrays and prints a production report from the arrays. Figured 10.7 (p. 314) shows the data entered by the user and Figure 10.8 (p. 314) shows the program's output.

The following specifications apply:

Input (keyboard):

For each employee, prompt for and enter the following data:

Employee name
Production output

Output (screen):

Print the production report shown in Figure 10.8.

Processing Requirements:

- Prompt for and enter the employee names and production output.
- Load the input into the name and production arrays, respectively.
- Read and print the contents of the arrays.

Pseudocode:

```
START
Create name and production arrays
LOOP while employee count < 5
    Prompt for and enter employee name and production
    Store input in arrays
End LOOP
LOOP while employee count < 5
    Read data from arrays
    Print employee name and corresponding production
End LOOP
END
```

Hierarchy Chart: See Figure 10.4.

Program Flowchart: See Figure 10.5.

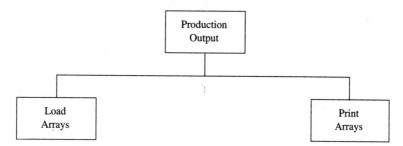

FIGURE 10.4   Hierarchy Chart for CHAP10A

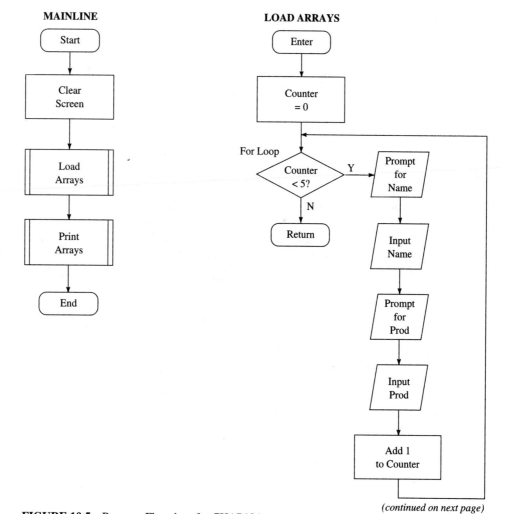

FIGURE 10.5   Program Flowchart for CHAP10A

(continued on next page)

PRINT ARRAYS

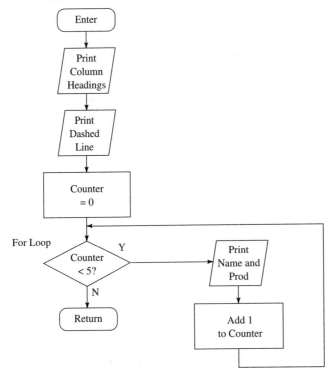

FIGURE 10.5 *Continued*

```
//---------- PRODUCTION OUTPUT ----------------------------
//  This program loads data into parallel arrays and prints
//  the contents of the arrays.
//
//          PROGRAM-ID: CHAP10A
//          PROGRAMMER: David M. Collopy
//          RUN DATE:   mm/dd/yy
//**********************************************************

//---------- PREPROCESSING DIRECTIVES ----------------------

#include<iostream.h>
#include<iomanip.h>
#include<conio.h>

//---------- FUNCTION PROTOTYPES ---------------------------

void LoadArrays(void);          // load data into arrays
void PrintArrays(void);         // print array data
```

FIGURE 10.6 Sample Program CHAP10A: Loads and Prints Data Stored in Parallel Arrays

```
//---------- PROGRAM SETUP --------------------------------
//**  P R O G R A M   V A R I A B L E S
char  name[5][21];              // 5 element 21 char name array
int   prod[5];                  // 5 element production array
int   i;                        // array subscript

//------------------------------------------------------------
//              MAINLINE CONTROL
//------------------------------------------------------------
main()
{
    clrscr();                   // clear the screen
    LoadArrays();               // load data into arrays
    PrintArrays();              // print array data
    return 0;
}
//------------------------------------------------------------
//              LOAD DATA INTO ARRAYS
//------------------------------------------------------------
void LoadArrays(void)
{
    for (i = 0; i < 5, i++)  {
        cout << "Enter employee name " << (i + 1) << ": ";
        cin.get(name[i], 21);   // get name only
        cin.get();              // clear keyboard buffer
        cout << "  Enter production " << (i + 1) << ": ":
        cin >> prod[i];         // get production data
        cin.get();              // clear keyboard buffer
    }
    return;
}
//------------------------------------------------------------
//              PRINT ARRAY DATA
//------------------------------------------------------------
void PrintArrays(void)
{
    cout << "\nEMPLOYEE NAME              PRODUCTION";
    cout << "\n---------------------------------";
    for (i = 0; i < 5; i++)  {
        cout << endl << setiosflags(ios::left)
             << setw(20) << name[i]
             << resetiosflags(ios::left)
             << setw(10) << prof[i];
    }
    return;
}
```

FIGURE 10.6 *Continued*

```
Enter employee name 1: Melia Sanchez
    Enter production 1: 15
Enter employee name 2: Jason Kimm
    Enter production 2: 16
Enter employee name 3: Nanci Parker
    Enter production 3: 25
Enter employee name 4: Randy Wade
    Enter production 4: 23
Enter employee name 5: Cindy Brown
    Enter production 5: 17
```

FIGURE 10.7 Data Entry Screen for CHAP10A

```
EMPLOYEE NAME                 PRODUCTION
---------------------------------------
Melia Sanchez                    15
Jason Kimm                       16
Nanci Parker                     25
Randy Wade                       23
Cindy Brown                      17
```

FIGURE 10.8 Program Output for CHAP10A

Dissection of Sample Program CHAP10A

PROGRAM VARIABLES:

```
char   name[5][21];
```

The above statement means: Define a five-element character array called *name* and allocate 20 characters of storage for each name.

```
int    prod[5];
int    i;
```

The above statements mean: Define a five-element integer array called *prod* and the subscript *i*.

LOAD DATA INTO ARRAYS:

```
void LoadArrays(void)
{
    for (i = 0; i < 5; i++)  {
        cout << "Enter employee name " << (i + 1) << ": ";
        cin.get(name[i], 21);
```

```
        cin.get();
        cout << "    Enter production " << (i + 1) << ": ";
        cin >> prod[i];
        cin.get();
    }
    return;
}
```

The preceding statements mean: As long as the subscript is less than 5, prompt the user to enter the employee's name and production data. The first *cin* statement reads up to 21 characters of input or until the Enter key code is encountered and stores the employee name in the *i*th element of the *name* array. The third *cin* statement reads the input and stores the production in the *i*th element of the prod array. The cin.get() statements clear the keyboard buffer after each read.

```
PRINT ARRAY DATA:

void PrintArrays(void)
{
    cout << "\nEMPLOYEE NAME          PRODUCTION";
    cout << "\n-----------------------------";
```

The above statements mean: Print two column heading lines.

```
    for (i = 0; i < 5; i++)  {
        cout << endl << setiosflags(ios::left)
             << setw(20) << name[i]
             << resetiosflags(ios::left)
             << setw(10) << prof[i];
    }
    return;
}
```

The above statements mean: As long as the current value of the subscript is less than 5, print the employee's name and the corresponding production output from the arrays.

Array Lookup

At times, it may be necessary to locate (look up) certain data items in an array to either display or update the contents. Hence, **array lookup** is the process of locating data stored in an array. In this section, we will learn how to perform array lookup using direct reference and sequential search. Direct reference uses subscripts to directly locate data, whereas sequential search scans each element until the data is found.

Direct Reference: **Direct reference** assumes that there is a direct relationship between the user's input and the array subscripts. That is, the input entered at the keyboard is used by the program to access the data stored in the array.

For example, in direct reference, the part number of an inventory item (entered at the keyboard) may be used to directly access the quantity on hand for that item. Similarly, when the user enters a sales number, it may be used as the subscript to update the sales data stored in the array.

Direct reference lookup is illustrated below. Salesperson number is used as a subscript to access the sales data and to add the input to the sales total stored in the array.

```
float sales[5] = {85.95, 134.72, 57.10, 250.00, 76.43};
int    num;
float amount;
    .  .  .  .  .


//----- DIRECT REFERENCE LOOKUP ----------------------
cout << "\nEnter salesperson number '-1' to Quit: ";
cin >> num;
while (num != -1)  {
    cout << "\nEnter sales amount: ";
    cin >> amount;
    sales[num] = sales[num] + amount;
    cout << "\nEnter salesperson number '-1' to Quit: ";
    cin >> num;
}
```

According to the code, if the user enters the salesperson number 2 and the sales amount 30.00, then the salesperson number is used as the subscript to add the sales amount to the current value stored in the array. Hence, *sales[2]* = 57.10 + 30.00.

Sequential Search: Sequential search requires, at minimum, two parallel arrays: one for holding the record keys (item number, salesperson number, etc.) and one for holding the corresponding data (quantity on hand, total sales, etc.). **Sequential search** compares the input—the search key—to each element in the key array until a match is found or the end of the array has been encountered. For a match, the subscript of the key array is used to access the corresponding element stored in the data array.

Sequential search lookup is illustrated below. Assume that the salesperson numbers (100, 200, 300, 400, and 500) are stored in the key array and that the corresponding sales totals are stored in the *sales* array. Once the user enters the search key (*salesNum*) and the sales income (*salesAmt*), the search begins.

```
//----- SEQUENTIAL SEARCH LOOKUP -------
i = 0;
sub = -1;
while (i < 5 && sub == -1)  {
    if (salesNum == key[i])  {
        sub = i;
    }
    i = i + 1;
}
```

The variables, *i* and *sub*, are set to 0 and –1, respectively. As long as the condition test is true, the search key is compared to the elements stored in the *key* array. If a match is found, *sub* is set to *i*, the value of the subscript where the search key was found.

```
//----- CHECK FOR A MATCH -------------
if (sub == -1)  {
    cout << "\nEmployee not found";
```

```
    }
    else   {
        sales[sub] = sales[sub] + salesAmt;
    }
```

If *sub* equals –1, the message Employee not found is printed. Otherwise, the program uses *sub* as the subscript and adds the sales income to the total stored in the *sales* array.

Checkpoint 10D

1. Define *array lookup*. Why is it useful?
2. Identify two array lookup or search techniques and briefly explain each.
3. Code the statements to input data. Then sequentially search the description array until a match is found. Finally, update the *qtyOnHand* array to add the input data to the current quantity on hand. Assume the following declarations:

```
char description[5][15];
int  qtyOnHand[5];
char inputDesc[15];
int  newQty;
int  i;
int  sub;
```

Note: The user will enter the description into the identifier *inputDesc*. The user will also enter the update quantity into the identifier *newQty*.

Element	Description
0	Hammer
1	Saw
2	Pliers
3	Screwdriver
4	Wrench

Element	Quantity on Hand
0	25
1	13
2	8
3	16
4	22

Sample Program CHAP10B

Sample program CHAP10B (Figure 10.11, p. 311) allows the user to update the production data stored in parallel arrays. Figures 10.12 (p. 324) and 10.13 (p. 324) show the program's input and output, respectively.

The following specifications apply:

Input (keyboard):

For each update, prompt for and enter the following data:

Employee name
Production output

Output (screen):

Print the output shown in Figure 10.13.

Processing Requirements:

- Define and initialize the name and production arrays.
- Prompt for and enter the employee name and the production update.
- Look up employee name:
  No match—print "Name not found" and continue.
  Match—update the production array.
- After the updates, print the contents of the arrays.

Pseudocode:

```
START
Define and initialize the name and production arrays
Clear the screen
Enter employee name
LOOP until employee name = quit
   Enter production output
   Lookup employee name
      If name not found
         Print error message and continue
      Else
         Update production array
      Enter employee name
End LOOP
LOOP while employee count < 5
   Print employee name and production
End LOOP
END
```

Hierarchy Chart: See Figure 10.9.

Program Flowchart: See Figure 10.10.

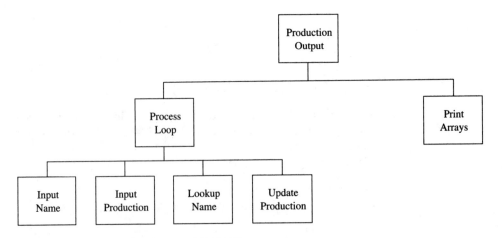

FIGURE 10.9   Hierarchy Chart for CHAP10B

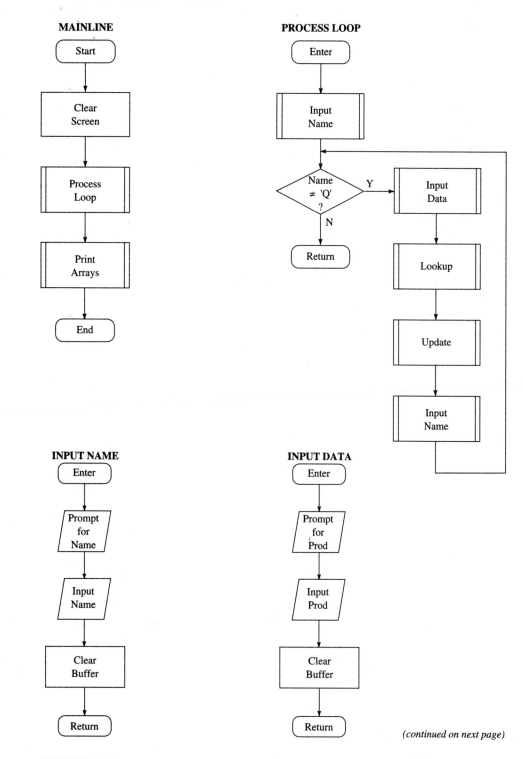

FIGURE 10.10   Program Flowchart for CHAP10B

(continued on next page)

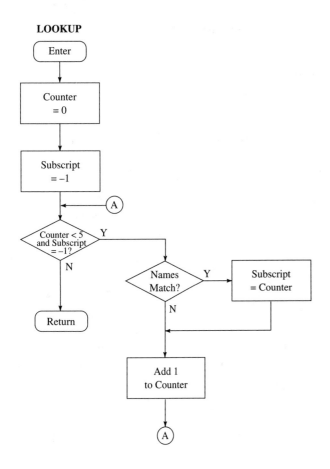

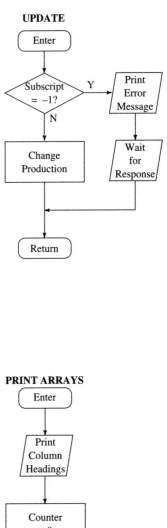

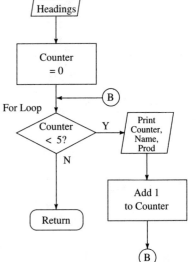

FIGURE 10.10   *Continued*

```
//----------- PRODUCTION OUTPUT ----------------------------
//  This program loads data into parallel arrays and prints
//  the contents of the arrays.
//
//              PROGRAM-ID: CHAP10B
//              PROGRAMMER: David M. Collopy
//              RUN DATE:   mm/dd/yy
//************************************************************

//----------- PREPROCESSING DIRECTIVES ---------------------

#include<iostream.h>
#include<iomanip.h>
#include<conio.h>
#include<string.h>

//----------- FUNCTION PROTOTYPES --------------------------

void ProcessLoop(void);        // processing loop
void InputName(void);          // input update name
void InputData(void);          // input update data
void LookUp(void);             // locate employee name
void Update(void);             // update production
void PrintArrays(void);        // print array data

//----------- PROGRAM SETUP --------------------------------

//**  P R O G R A M   V A R I A B L E S

char  name[5][21] = {"Melia Sanchez", "Jason Kimm",
                     "Nanci Parker", "Randy Wade",
                     "Cindy Brown"};

                        // 5 element 21 char name array

int   prod[5] = {15, 16, 25, 23, 17};

                        // 5 element production array

int   i;                // array subscript
char  iname[21];        // input employee name
int   iprod;            // input production
char  wait;             // wait for Enter key to be pressed
int   sub;              // subscript of match

//----------------------------------------------------------
//              MAINLINE CONTROL
//----------------------------------------------------------
main()
{
    clrscr();                   // clear the screen
    ProcessLoop();              // processing loop
    PrintArrays();              // print array data
```

(continued on next page)

FIGURE 10.11   Sample Program CHAP10B: Load and Update Data Stored in Parallel Arrays

```
        return 0;
    }
    //-----------------------------------------------------------
    //               PROCESSING LOOP
    //-----------------------------------------------------------
    void ProcessLoop(void)
    {
        InputName();
        while (strcmp(iname, "Q") != 0)  {
            InputData();
            LookUp():
            Update();
            InputName():
        }
        return;
    }
    //-----------------------------------------------------------
    //               INPUT UPDATE NAME
    //-----------------------------------------------------------
    void InputName(void)
    {
        cout << "Enter employee name or 'Q' to QUIT: ";
        cin.get(iname, 21);         // get name only
        cin.get();                  // clear keyboard buffer
        return;
    }
    //-----------------------------------------------------------
    //               INPUT UPDATE DATA
    //-----------------------------------------------------------
    void InputData(void)
    {
        cout << "              Change production to: ";
        cin >> iprod;               // get production
        cin.get();                  // clear keyboard buffer
        return;
    }
    //-----------------------------------------------------------
    //               LOCATE EMPLOYEE NAME
    //-----------------------------------------------------------
    void LookUp(void)
    {
        i = 0;
        sub = -1;
        while (i < 5 && sub == -1)  {
            if (strcmp(iname, name[i]) == 0)  {
                sub = i;             // found name
            }
            i = i + 1;
```

FIGURE 10.11   *Continued*

```
        }
    return;
}
//------------------------------------------------------------
//              UPDATE PRODUCTION
//------------------------------------------------------------
void Update(void)
{
    if (sub == -1)  {
        cout << "\nName not found-"
            << "press ENTER to continue\n";
        wait = getch();          // wait for response
    }
    else
        prod[sub] = iprod;
    return;
}
//------------------------------------------------------------
//              PRINT ARRAY DATA
//------------------------------------------------------------
void PrintArray(void)
{
    cout << "\nSUB  EMPLOYEE NAME              PRODUCTION";
    cout << "\nSUB--------------------------------";
    for (i = 0; i < 5; i++)  {
        cout << endl << setiosflags(ios::left)
            << setw(20) << name[i]
            << resetiosflags(ios::left)
            << setw(10) << prof[i];
    }
    return;
}
```

FIGURE 10.11 *Continued*

Dissection of Sample Program CHAP10B

PROCESSING LOOP:

```
void ProcessLoop(void)
{
    InputName();
    while (strcmp(iname, "Q") != 0)  {
        InputData();
        LookUp();
        Update();
        InputName();
    }
    return;
}
```

```
Enter employee name or 'Q' to QUIT: Jason Kimm
              Change production to: 29

Enter employee name or 'Q' to QUIT: Drew Lanick
              Change production to: 30

Name not found--press ENTER to continue

Enter employee name or 'Q' to QUIT: Q
```

FIGURE 10.12   Program Input for CHAP10B

```
SUB   EMPLOYEE NAME          PRODUCTION
----------------------------------------
 0    Melia Sanchez              15
 1    Jason Kimm                 29
 2    Nanci Parker               25
 3    Randy Wade                 23
 4    Cindy Brown                17
```

FIGURE 10.13   Program Output for CHAP10B

The preceding statements mean: Transfer control to *InputName* and prompt the user to input the employee's name. As long as the name is not equal to *Q*, enter the *while* loop and execute the modules in the order listed.

Control returns to the calling module when the user enters *Q* for the employee name.

INPUT UPDATE NAME:

```
void InputName(void)
{
    cout << "Enter employee name or 'Q' to QUIT: ";
    cin.get(iname, 20);
    cin.get();
    return;
}
```

The above statements mean: Prompt the user to enter the employee name or *Q* to quit. The first cin.get() reads up to 21 characters or until the Enter key code is encountered and assigns the result to *iname*. The second cin.get() clears the keyboard buffer.

At the end of the module, control returns to the calling environment.

INPUT UPDATE DATA:

```
void InputData(void)
{
```

```
        cout << "                    Change production to: ";
        cin >> iprod;
        cin.get();
        return;
}
```

The above statements mean: Prompt the user to enter the change in production. Read the input, convert it to an integer, and assign the result to the production array. The cin.get() removes the Enter key code from the keyboard buffer.

After clearing the buffer, control returns to the calling module.

LOCATE EMPLOYEE NAME:

```
void LookUp(void)
{
    i = 0;
```

The above statement means: Initialize the subscript to 0. This forces the program to begin the search with the first element in the array.

```
    sub = -1;
```

The above statement means: Initialize the *sub* to –1. A –1 tells the program that a match was not found for the employee name. Any value other than –1 tells the program where the match was found.

```
    while (i < 5 && sub == -1)  {
```

The above statement means: As long as the subscript is less than 5 and a match has not been found, enter the body of the loop.

```
        if (strcmp(iname, name[i]) == 0)  {
            sub = i;

        }
```

The above statements mean: If the employee name matches the data stored in the current element, then assign the value of the subscript to *sub*.

```
        i = i + 1;
    }
```

The above statements mean: Increment the subscript. This statement adds one to the current value of *i*.

```
    return;
}
```

The above statement means: Return to the calling module. Control returns either upon finding a match or upon encountering the end of the array.

UPDATE PRODUCTION:

```
void Update(void)
```

```
{
    if (sub == -1)  {
        cout << "\nName not found-"
             << "press ENTER to continue\n";
        wait = getch();
    }
```

The above statements mean: If the employee name was not found in the array, print the message enclosed within double quotation marks and wait for the user to press the Enter key.

```
    else
        prod[sub] = iprod;
    return;
}
```

The preceding statements mean: If the employee name was found, then assign the input production to the array element indexed by *sub* and return to the calling module.

PRINT ARRAY DATA:

```
void PrintArrays(void)
{
    cout << "\nSUB  EMPLOYEE NAME               PRODUCTION";
    cout << "\n-----------------------------------------";
    for (i = 0; i < 5; i++)  {
        cout << endl << setiosflags(ios::left)
             << setw(20) << name[i]
             << resetiosflags(ios::left)
             << setw(10) << prof[i];
    }
    return;
}
```

The above statements mean: Print the contents of the parallel arrays. This is done to verify that the updates were correctly applied to the production array.

Sorting

Sorting is the process of arranging data in a given order. The contents of an array may be used to arrange the elements in either ascending or descending order. Usually, data is loaded into an array in the order that it is received. Yet we may want to show a list of names in alphabetic order or a series of numbers in ascending order. Sorting allows us to do this.

Although many sort algorithms have been developed for the computer, we will focus on two basic techniques that are relatively easy to use: the bubble sort and the Shell sort.

The Bubble Sort: For long lists, the bubble sort is not too efficient. It does, however, work quite well for short lists. The **bubble sort** works by repeatedly comparing and exchanging elements until they are arranged in the specified order.

The example below demonstrates the bubble sort. A list of five items is arranged in ascending order. Walk through the steps. Note that it takes, at most, five passes to arrange the list in ascending order. In general, it takes, at most, *n* passes to sort a list of *n* elements.

BEFORE (unsorted list):   90 20 80 60 10

Pass 1: Compare Elements	*Action*
[90 20] 80 60 10	exchange 90 and 20
20 **[90 80]** 60 10	exchange 90 and 80
20 80 **[90 60]** 10	exchange 90 and 60
20 80 60 **[90 10]**	exchange 90 and 10

Pass 2: Compare Elements	*Action*
[20 80] 60 10 90	no exchange
20 **[80 60]** 10 90	exchange 80 and 60
20 60 **[80 10]** 90	exchange 80 and 10
20 60 10 **[80 90]**	no exchange

Pass 3: Compare Elements	*Action*
[20 60] 10 80 90	no exchange
20 **[60 10]** 80 90	exchange 60 and 10
20 10 **[60 80]** 90	no exchange
20 10 60 **[80 90]**	no exchange

Pass 4: Compare Elements	*Action*
[20 10] 60 80 90	exchange 20 and 10
10 **[20 60]** 80 90	no exchange
10 20 **[60 80]** 90	no exchange
10 20 60 **[80 90]**	no exchange

Pass 5: Compare Elements	*Action*
[10 20] 60 80 90	no exchange
10 **[20 60]** 80 90	no exchange
10 20 **[60 80]** 90	no exchange
10 20 60 **[80 90]**	no exchange

AFTER (sorted list):   10 20 60 80 90

On the last pass, no exchanges were made. This tells us that the list is now in ascending order. For each pass, the elements enclosed within square brackets [] are compared and exchanged only if the first element is greater than the second. During the sort, the low values "ripple" to the left (top) of the list, and the high values "ripple" to the right (bottom). Because of this, the bubble sort is also known as the **ripple sort**.

Example:

The bubble sort shown below rearranges an array of five elements in ascending order.

```
swap = 1;
while (swap == 1)  {
    swap = 0;
    for (i = 0; i < 5; i++)  {
        if (num[i] > num[i+1])  {
            temp = num[i];
            num[i] = num[i+1];
            num[i+1] = temp;
            swap = 1;
```

```
            }
        }
    }
```

Dissection: In order to enter the *while* loop, *swap* is set to 1. The swap flag is used to determine whether to continue or to terminate the sort. Zero indicates that no exchanges (swaps) were made on the last pass—the sort is complete; 1 indicates that at least one exchange occurred on the last pass—the sort continues.

Inside the *while* loop, the flag is set to 0. This is done in preparation *for* the next pass. Control now enters the *for* loop. Here the *if* statement compares adjacent elements and exchanges them only if the first is greater than the second. For an exchange, the flag is reset to 1.

During an exchange, the first element is temporarily copied to *temp*, and the second element is assigned to the first. Next the value stored at *temp* is reassigned to the second element. This, of course, completes the exchange.

As long as an exchange is made (*swap* = 1), the *while* loop continues to compare and exchange elements. Otherwise, the elements are in order and the sort stops.

The Shell Sort: The Shell sort, developed by Donald Shell, provides a faster and more efficient sort algorithm. For a small list of 10 items or so, the execution times for the bubble sort and the Shell sort are comparable. However, for longer lists, the execution times are significantly different. For example, it takes the bubble sort five times longer to sort a list of 100 items than it does the Shell sort; it takes about 30 times longer to sort a list of 1,000 items.

Like the bubble sort, the **Shell sort** compares and exchanges elements. However, it compares the elements over a gap. A **gap** is the distance between two elements. The Shell sort works by repeatedly comparing and exchanging elements over a series of gaps until the array is arranged in the specified order.

On the first pass, the gap is computed by dividing the size of the array by 2 (i.e., gap = size / 2). Subsequent gaps are computed by dividing the previous gap by 2 (i.e., gap = gap / 2), until the length of the gap equals 1.

The example below demonstrates how the Shell sort works. Walk through the process as the elements are compared and exchanged over the gaps.

BEFORE (unsorted list): 90 20 80 60 10 70 40 50
Compute the first gap: gap = size / 2 or gap = 4.

Compare Elements	Action
90 20 80 60 **10** 70 40 50	exchange 90 and 10
10 **20** 80 60 90 **70** 40 50	no exchange
10 20 **80** 60 90 70 **40** 50	exchange 80 and 40
10 20 40 **60** 90 70 80 **50**	exchange 60 and 50

Compare and exchange elements over the gap until no exchanges are made on a pass.
Compute the next gap: gap = gap / 2 or gap = 2.

Compare Elements	Action
10 20 **40** 50 90 70 80 60	no exchange

```
10 20 40 50 90 70 80 60          no exchange
    ^    ^
10 20 40 50 90 70 80 60          no exchange
       ^    ^
10 20 40 50 90 70 80 60          no exchange
          ^    ^
10 20 40 50 90 70 80 60          exchange 90 and 80
             ^    ^
10 20 40 50 80 70 90 60          exchange 70 and 60
                ^    ^
```

Compare and exchange elements over the gap until no exchanges are made on a pass.

Compute the next gap: gap = gap / 2 or gap = 1.

For gap = 1, the Shell sort works like the bubble sort.
When no exchanges are made on a pass, the sort is complete.

Example:

The Shell sort shown below rearranges an array of eight elements in ascending order.

```
size = 8;
  . . . . .
gap = size/2;
while (gap > 0) {
    swap = 1;
    while (swap == 1)  {
        swap = 0;
        for (i = 0; i < size - gap; i++)  {
            if (num[i] > num[i+gap])  {
                temp = num[i];
                num[i] = num[i+gap];
                num[i+gap] = temp;
                swap = 1;
            }
        }
    }
    gap = gap/2;
}
```

Dissection: Processing begins by setting the initial *gap* to *size*/2. Basically, the Shell sort consists of a three-level nested loop. The first loop determines whether to continue or to terminate the sort. As long as the gap is greater than 0, *swap* is set to 1 and the sort continues.

The second loop determines when to change the gap. As long as *swap* equals 1, the flag is reset to 0 (in preparation for the next pass), and control enters the *for* loop to compare elements. But if *swap* equals 0, then the elements are in order for the current gap, and it is time to exit the second loop and change the gap.

Note that the third loop establishes a sort range of 0 to *size – gap*. This tells the program how many times to compare elements. Here the body of the *for* loop compares the elements and exchanges them only if the first element is greater than the second. For each exchange, the flag is reset to 1.

As long as the gap is greater than 0, the sort continues. Otherwise, the elements are in order and the sort stops.

Checkpoint 10E

1. What is *sorting*?
2. Identify two sorting methods and briefly explain each.
3. For the Shell sort, how is the gap calculated for:
   a. the first pass?
   b. subsequent passes?
4. Using the Shell sort, code the statements that will arrange the following array values in descending (high to low) order.

```
int list[10] = {30, 80, 68, 42, 79, 90, 43, 51, 25, 100};
```

Sample Program CHAP10C

Sample program CHAP10C (Figure 10.16, p. 333) uses the Shell sort to arrange the random data stored in parallel arrays in ascending order. Figure 10.17 shows the unsorted data output (p. 336) and Figure 10.18 (p. 336) shows the program's final output.

The following specifications apply:

Input (internal):

Initialize the parallel arrays to the values given below:

Employee Number	Employee Name	Production
303	Adams	20
400	Wyler	19
510	Brownfield	23
237	Caluci	17
120	Stein	24
101	Nichols	21
100	Perkins	22

Output (screen):

Print the unsorted and sorted production reports shown in Figures 10.17 and 10.18, respectively.

Processing Requirements:

- Create and initialize three parallel arrays—employee number, employee name, and production output.
- Set the size of each array to 7.
- Print the unsorted data stored in the arrays.
- Sort the arrays and arrange the elements in ascending order by employee number.
- Print the sorted data stored in the arrays.

Pseudocode:

```
START
Clear screen
LOOP while subscript < 7
   Print unsorted data
End LOOP
Set gap = size/2
LOOP while gap > 0
   Set swap to 1
   LOOP while swap = 1
      Set swap = 0
      LOOP while subscript < size – gap
         If employee number1 > employee number2
         Exchange gap elements
         Set swap = 1
      End LOOP
   End LOOP
   Set gap = gap/2
End LOOP
LOOP while subscript < 7
   Print sorted data
End LOOP
END
```

Hierarchy Chart: See Figure 10.14.

Program Flowchart: See Figure 10.15.

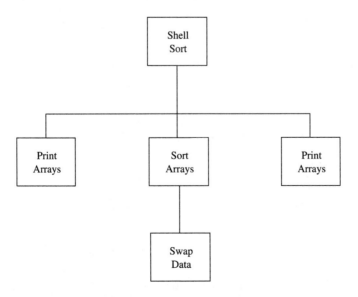

FIGURE 10.14   Hierarchy Chart for CHAP10C

MAINLINE

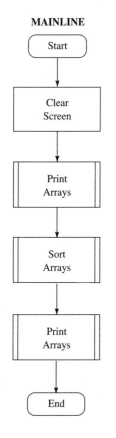

Start

Clear
Screen

Print
Arrays

Sort
Arrays

Print
Arrays

End

PRINT ARRAYS

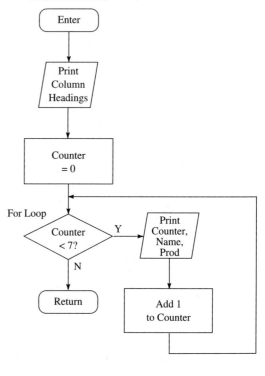

Enter

Print
Column
Headings

Counter
= 0

For Loop

Counter
< 7?

Y → Print
Counter,
Name,
Prod

Add 1
to Counter

N

Return

SWAP DATA

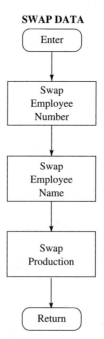

Enter

Swap
Employee
Number

Swap
Employee
Name

Swap
Production

Return

FIGURE 10.15   Program Flowchart for CHAP10C

SORT ARRAYS

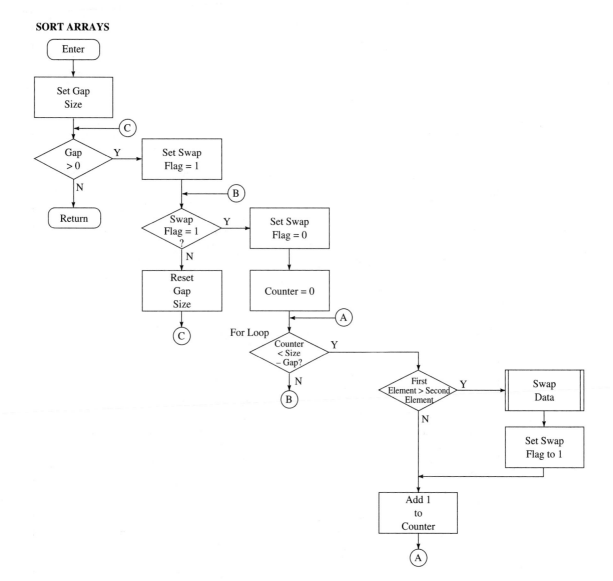

FIGURE 10.15 *Continued*

```
//---------- SHELL SORT ------------------------------------
//    This program uses the Shell sort to arrange the data
//    stored in parallel arrays in ascending order.
//
//          PROGRAM-ID: CHAP10C
//          PROGRAMMER: David M. Collopy
//          RUN DATE:   mm/dd/yy
```
(continued on next page)

FIGURE 10.16 Sample Program CHAP10C: Application of the Shell Sort

```
//*************************************************************

//---------- PREPROCESSING DIRECTIVES ---------------------

#include<iostream.h>
#include<iomanip.h>
#include<conio.h>
#include<string.h>

//---------- FUNCTION PROTOTYPES --------------------------

void PrintArrays(void);          // print array data
void SortArrays(void);           // sort array data
void SwapData(void);             // swap elements

//---------- PROGRAM SETUP --------------------------------

//**  P R O G R A M   V A R I A B L E S

int   num[7] = {303, 400, 510, 237, 120, 101, 100};
char  name[5][21] = {"Adams", "Wyler", "Brownfield",
                     "Caluci", "Stein", "Nichols",
                     "Perkins"};
int   prod[7] = {20, 19, 23, 17, 24, 21, 22};

int   i;                         // array subscript
char  temp1;                     // numeric temporary storage
int   temp2[21];                 // string temporary storage
int   swap;                      // swap flag
int   size = 7;                  // array size
int   gap;                       // gap size

//--------------------------------------------------------
//               MAINLINE CONTROL
//--------------------------------------------------------
main()
{
    clrscr();                    // clear the screen
    PrintArrays();               // print array data
    SortArrays();                // sort array data
    PrintArrays();               // print array data
    return 0;
}
//--------------------------------------------------------
//               PRINT ARRAY DATA
//--------------------------------------------------------
void PrintArrays(void)
{
```

FIGURE 10.16 *Continued*

```
      cout << "\nEmp#  Employee Name              Production";
      cout << "\n----------------------------------------";
      for (i = 0; i < 7; i++)  {
           cout << endl << setw(3) << num[i] << "    "
                << setiosflags(ios::left)
                << setw(20) << name[i]
                << resetiosflags(ios::left)
                << setw(10) << prof[i];
      }
      return;
}
//----------------------------------------------------------------
//              SORT ARRAY DATA
//----------------------------------------------------------------
void SortArrays(void)
{
    gap = size/2                       // set gap size
    while (gap > 0)  {
        swap = 1;                      // set to yes
        while (swap == 1)  {
            swap = 0;                  // set to no
            for (i = 0; i < size-gap; i++;  {
                if (num[i] > num[i+gap];  {
                    SwapData();        // swap elements
                    swap = 1;          // set to yes
                }
            }
        }
        gap = gap/2;                   // reset gap size
    }
    return;
}
//----------------------------------------------------------------
//              SWAP ELEMENTS
//----------------------------------------------------------------
void SwapData(void)
{
    temp1 = num[i];                    // swap employee number
    num[i] = num[i+gap];
    num[i+gap] = temp1;
    strcpy(temp2, name[i]);            // swap employee name
    strcpy(name[i], name[i+gap]);
    strcpy(name[i+gap], temp2);
    temp1 = prod[i];                   // swap production
    prod[i] = prod[i+gap];
    prod[i+gap] = temp1;
    return;
}
```

FIGURE 10.16 *Continued*

```
Emp#   Employee Name      Production

303    Adams                 20
400    Wyler                 19
510    Brownfield            23
237    Caluci                17
120    Stein                 24
101    Nichols               21
100    Perkins               22
```

FIGURE 10.17   Unsorted Data for CHAP10C

```
Emp#   Employee Name      Production

100     Perkins               22
101     Nichols               21
120     Stein                 24
237     Caluci                17
303     Adams                 20
400     Wyler                 19
510     Brownfield            23
```

FIGURE 10.18   Sorted Output for CHAP10C

Dissection of Sample Program CHAP10C

Three arrays are declared and initialized in the *PROGRAM SETUP*. Although other declarations are also coded there, the two that require further explanation are *temp1* and *temp2*. Both define temporary holding areas that are used to exchange elements when a swap is detected by the program. The first one, *temp1*, is used to hold numeric data (employee number and production output), whereas the second is used to hold the employee name.

Sample program CHAP10C prints the arrays twice: once before the sort to show the original order of the elements, and once after the sort to verify that the elements were successfully arranged in ascending order.

The heart of the processing takes place in the *SortArrays* module. So let us pick up the program dissection there.

```
SORT ARRAY DATA:

void SortArrays(void)
{
    gap = size/2;
```

The preceding statement means: Compute the initial gap by dividing the number of elements in the array by 2.

```
while (gap > 0)   {
    swap = 1;
```

The above statement means: As long as the gap is greater than 0, enter the loop and set the swap flag to 1. The flag is set to 1 in order to enter the next *while* loop. But when the gap is 0, the sort is finished and control returns to the calling module.

```
    while (swap == 1)   {
```

The above statement means: As long as the flag equals 1, enter the loop. Otherwise, skip the body of the loop and compute the next gap. One indicates that at least one exchange was made on the last pass, and the elements are not yet in order for the current gap.

```
        swap = 0;
```

The above statement means: Reset the swap flag to 0. Zero represents the initial setting of the flag. This is done in preparation for the next pass.

```
        for (i = 0; i < size-gap; i++)   {
```

The above statement means: Initialize the array subscript to 0 and test for the ending condition. As long as the subscript is less than *size–gap*, control enters the body of the loop. The expression *size–gap* specifies the number of times to compare the elements.

```
            if (num[i] > num[i+1])   {
                SwapData();
                swap = 1;
            }
```

The above statements mean: If the first element is greater than the second, then perform *SwapData* and set *swap* to 1. Otherwise, skip the body of the *if* statement.

```
        }
    }
    gap = gap/2;
}
```

The above statement means: Calculate the next gap and go back to the first *while* statement.

```
    return;
}
```

The above statement means: Return to the calling module.

```
SWAP ELEMENTS:

void SwapData(void)
{
    temp1 = num[i];
```

The above statement means: Copy the first element (the high value) to temporary storage, *temp1*.

```
    num[i] = num[i+gap];
```

The preceding statement means: Assign the second element (the low value) to the first, *num[i]*.

```
num[i+gap] = temp1;
```

The above statement means: Assign the high value stored at *temp1* to the second element, *num[i+gap]*. This completes the exchange.

```
strcpy(temp2, name[i]);
strcpy(name[i], name[i+gap]);
strcpy(name[i+gap], temp2);
```

The above statements mean: Exchange the employee names over the current gap.

```
temp1 = prod[i];
prod[i] = prod[i+gap];
prod[i+gap] = temp1;
return;
}
```

The above statements mean: Exchange the employee production over the current gap.

Summary

1. An array represents a set of variables that is given one name. Each item in the array is called an element, and each element has identical data types.

2. Character arrays store nonnumeric or string data, and numeric arrays store integer or floating-point values. Integer and floating-point data are stored in separate arrays.

3. Data assigned to an array can be processed repeatedly without requiring the program to reload the array.

4. Arrays are defined by specifying the data type, the name, and the number of elements. For character arrays, the size of the elements is also declared.

5. A subscript is used to uniquely identify or reference a specific element in an array. Subscripts represent integer values that may be expressed as either constants or variables.

6. Subscripts are numbered starting with 0. A subscript may not be negative or exceed the size of the array minus 1.

7. Data may be assigned to an array by initializing the elements when the array is declared, prompting the user to enter the data at the keyboard, or reading the data from a file.

8. Data stored in an array can be processed much like data stored in a single variable. We can perform arithmetic operations and logical comparisons, determine high and low values, compute totals, and so forth.

9. Parallel arrays consist of two or more single arrays that are processed together. The elements in one array are related and correspond to the elements in another.

10. Array lookup pertains to the process of locating a specific element stored in an array.

11. Direct reference lookup uses a subscript to directly locate the data stored in the array. This method assumes that there is a direct relationship between user input and the subscripts.

12. Sequential search lookup requires at minimum two parallel arrays—one for the record keys and one for the data. This method compares the input, the search key, to each element in the key array.

13. Sorting is the process of rearranging the elements of an array in a specific order.

14. The bubble sort rearranges small lists of items. It works by repeatedly comparing and exchanging elements until the array is arranged in the desired order.

15. The Shell sort rearranges large lists of items. It works by repeatedly comparing and exchanging elements over a series of gaps until the array is arranged in the desired order. A gap is defined as the distance between two elements.

Programming Projects

For each project, design the logic and write the modular structured program to produce the output. Model your program after the sample programs presented in the chapter. Verify your output.

Project 10–1   Overdue Accounts-1

Write a program to read a file, load the input into parallel arrays, and print a report of all customers with account balances 90 days overdue.

Input (text file):

For each customer, read a record and load the data into the following arrays. Array types are shown in parentheses.

account	(int)
name	(char)
overdue	(int)
balance	(float)

Set the size of each array to 12. Allow for a maximum of 15 characters of data for the elements in the *name* array.

Text File (overdue.dat):

Create the overdue accounts file from the data given below. Enter the records in the order shown.

Account Number	Customer Name	Days Overdue	Balance Due
4080	Corey Adkins	30	233.00
2730	Rita Fox	90	740.00
7720	Lisa Wilson	60	417.00
3100	Alvin Porter	90	550.00
9630	Pat Rankin	60	342.00
9200	Tori Landis	90	235.00

1010	David Ryan	90	400.00
4890	Amy Wyatt	30	700.00
5260	Brian Knox	30	625.00
2450	Marie Hill	30	754.00
8540	Matt Hart	90	900.00
6350	Susan Cope	90	600.00

Ouput (printer):

Print the following 90-day overdue accounts report:

```
Author              90-DAY OVERDUE ACCOUNTS           Page 01
                           mm/dd/yy


  Acct Number         Customer Name            Amount Due

     9999             X-----------X              999.99
       :                   :                       :
       :                   :                       :
     9999             X-----------X              999.99

                               Total:          9999.99
```

Processing Requirements:

- Read and load the file input into the arrays.
- Print the unsorted data stored in the arrays.
- Sort the arrays and arrange the data in ascending order by account number.
- Print the sorted data stored in the arrays.
- Read the arrays and print a report of all the accounts 90 days overdue.
- Accumulate and print a report total for the amount due.

Project 10–2   Overdue Accounts-2

Modify the program in Project 10–1 to allow the user to update the data stored in the parallel arrays. Prompt for and enter the updates given below. Search for a match on account number (Enter '-1' to quit). If a match is not found, print the message Account not found - press ENTER to continue. Add the lookup and update logic to the program after the arrays are sorted.

Enter the updates in the order shown.

Account Number	Customer Name	Days Overdue	Balance Due
5260	Brian Knox	30	872.00
2459	Marie Hill	90	700.00
6350	Susan Cope	60	610.00
1023	David Ryan	90	435.00
7720	Lisa Wilson	60	495.00
4081	Corey Adkins	30	249.00

Project 10–3   Payroll-1

Write a program to compute and print a weekly payroll roster. Read the data from a file, load the input into parallel arrays, and process the data stored in the arrays. Assume the current federal income tax (FIT) rate is 15% and overtime is not computed.

Input (text file):

For each employee, read a record and load the data into the following arrays. Array types are shown in parentheses.

    name   (char)
    hours   (int)
    rate   (float)

Set the size of each array to 9. Allow for a maximum of 15 characters of data for the elements in the *name* array.

Text File (payroll.dat):

Create the payroll file from the data given below. Enter the records in the order shown.

Employee Name	Hours	Pay Rate
Tracy York	36	11.00
Dale Miller	40	10.25
Sara Erickson	38	12.00
Karen Thomas	48	9.00
Paul Irwin	48	8.72
Dana Clark	45	14.90
Tanya Bauer	40	7.50
Bret Rossi	35	8.00
Scott Howard	42	9.75

Ouput (printer):

Print the following weekly payroll report:

```
Author                WEEKLY PAYROLL REPORT              Page 01
                          mm/dd/yy


Employee   Hours     Pay Rate    Gross Pay     FIT      Net Pay

X-------X    99       99.99        999.99      99.99     999.99
    :         :          :            :          :          :
    :         :          :            :          :          :
X-------X    99       99.99        999.99      99.99     999.99

                     Totals:       9999.99     999.99    9999.99
```

Processing Requirements:

- Read and load the file input into the arrays.
- Print the unsorted data stored in the arrays.

- Sort the arrays and arrange the data in alphabetic order by employee name.
- Print the sorted data stored in the arrays.
- Compute the gross pay:
  hours × pay rate
- Compute the federal income tax:
  gross pay × FIT rate
- Compute the net pay:
  gross pay – FIT
- Accumulate totals for gross pay, FIT, and net pay.

Project 10–4   Payroll-2

Modify the program in Project 10–3 to allow the user to update the payroll data stored in the parallel arrays. Prompt for and enter the updates given below. Search for a match on employee name (Enter 'Q' to quit). If a match is not found, print the message Name not found - press ENTER to continue. Add the lookup and update logic to the program after the arrays are sorted.

Enter the payroll updates in the order shown.

Employee Name	Hours	Pay Rate
Karen Thomas	44	9.00
Darla Clark	40	10.60
Tracy York	39	11.50
Diane Reeves	38	7.90
Scott Howard	42	10.00
Patsy Ireland	40	8.45

Project 10–5   Sales Profit-1

Write a program to calculate the profit generated by each salesperson and print a sales profit report. Read the data from a file, load the input into parallel arrays, and process the data stored in the arrays.

Input (text file):

For each sales representative, read a record and load the data into the following arrays. Array types are shown in parentheses.

    name   (char)
    sales   (float)
    cost   (float)

Set the size of each array to 5. Allow for a maximum of 15 characters of data for the elements in the *name* array.

Text File (sales.dat):

Create the sales file from the data given below. Enter the records in the order shown.

Salesperson	Total Sales	Cost of Sales
Ann Zimmerman	5793.59	4204.45
Tara Perkins	12710.14	9735.38
Dennis Tian	4567.51	3119.22

Roy Hickle	2245.78	1072.49
Lisa Conrad	8120.52	6450.71

Ouput (printer):

Print the following sales profit report:

```
Author                SALES PROFIT REPORT              Page 01
                          mm/dd/yy

Salesperson   Total Sales   Cost of Sales   Net Profit
----------------------------------------------------------
X--------X     99999.99       99999.99       99999.99
    :             :              :              :
    :             :              :              :
X--------X     99999.99       99999.99       99999.99

                             Total:         999999.99
```

Processing Requirements:

- Read and load the file input into the arrays.
- Print the unsorted data stored in the arrays.
- Sort the arrays and arrange the data in alphabetic order by salesperson name.
- Print the sorted data stored in the arrays.
- Compute the net profit:
  total sales – cost of sales
- Accumulate and print a report total for net profit.

Project 10–6 Sales Profit-2

Modify the program in Project 10–5 to allow the user to update the sales data stored in the parallel arrays. Prompt for and enter the updates given below. Search for a match on salesperson name (Enter 'Q' to quit). If a match is not found, print the message Name not found - press ENTER to continue. Add the lookup and update logic to the program after the arrays are sorted.

Enter the sales updates in the order shown.

Salesperson	Total Sales	Cost of sales
Tara Perkins	13944.70	10378.59
Lisa Conrad	8001.03	6392.53
Holly Winkler	4316.22	2975.65
Ann Zimmerman	6090.00	4354.64
Roy Hickle	2368.99	1139.16
Barbara Rider	7605.42	4321.28

Project 10–7 Inventory

Write a program to read an inventory file, load the input into parallel arrays, and print an inventory profit report.

Input (text file):

For each inventory item, read a record and load the data into the following arrays. Array types are shown in parentheses.

itemNum	(int)
description	(char)
quantity	(int)
cost	(float)
price	(float)

Set the size of each array to 5. Allow for a maximum of 15 characters of data for the elements in the *description* array.

Text File (invent.dat):

Create the inventory file from the data given below. Enter the data in the order shown.

Item Number	Description	Quantity on Hand	Unit Cost	Selling Price
4000	Screwdrivers	36	2.27	4.98
3000	Drills	10	7.83	15.95
5000	Pliers	12	2.65	5.49
2000	Saws	08	7.50	14.99
1000	Hammers	24	4.75	9.49

Ouput (printer):

Print the following inventory profit report:

```
Author            INVENTORY PROFIT REPORT        Page 01
                        mm/dd/yy


Item Number     Description        Quantity     Item Profit

   9999         X----------X          99          999.99
    :               :                  :             :
    :               :                  :             :
   9999         X----------X          99          999.99

                         Total Profit:     9999.99
```

Processing Requirements:

- Read and load the file input into the arrays.
- Print the unsorted data stored in the arrays.
- Sort the arrays and arrange the data in ascending order by item number.
- Print the sorted data stored in the arrays.
- Compute the item cost:
  quantity × unit cost
- Compute the item income:
  quantity × selling price
- Compute the item profit:
  item income – item cost
- Accumulate a report total for the item profit.

Project 10-8 Personnel

Write a program to compute and print the annual salary report for the personnel department. Read the data from a file, load the input into parallel arrays, and process the data stored in the arrays.

Input (text file):

For each employee, read a record and load the data into the following arrays. Array types are shown in parentheses.

enum	(int)
name	(char)
deptNum	(int)
salary	(float)
increase	(float)

Set the size of each array to 8. Allow for a maximum of 15 characters of data for the elements in the *name* array.

Text File (persnel.dat):

Create the personnel file from the data given below. Enter the data in the order shown.

Employee Number	Employee Name	Department Number	Annual Salary	Percent Increase
5409	Bob Shields	47	27500.00	0.08
2071	Scott Cooper	14	30250.00	0.12
6552	Pam Wolfe	31	31773.00	0.10
4100	Derek Lowe	50	29120.00	0.07
3600	Amy Kwon	19	36025.00	0.09
1926	Dana Andrews	10	29000.00	0.10
4298	Lori Palmer	35	33400.00	0.11
3150	Todd Feldman	22	24175.00	0.07

Ouput (printer):

Print the following personnel report:

```
Author                PERSONNEL ANNUAL SALARY REPORT            Page 01
                            mm/dd/yy


Employee                        Dept.     Old       Dollar      New
Number     Employee Name        Number    Salary    Increase    Salary

 9999      X-----------X          99     99999.99   9999.99    99999.99
  :             :                 :          :         :           :
  :             :                 :          :         :           :
 9999      X-----------X          99     99999.99   9999.99    99999.99

                                        Total:                 999999.99
```

Processing Requirements:

- Read and load the file input into the arrays.
- Print the unsorted data stored in the arrays.
- Sort the arrays and arrange the data in ascending order by employee number.

- Print the sorted data stored in the arrays.
- Compute the dollar increase:
  old salary × percent increase
- Compute the new salary:
  old salary + dollar increase
- Accumulate a report total for annual salary.

Project 10–9 Accounts Payable

Write a program to compute and print an accounts payable report. Read the data from a file, load the input into parallel arrays, and process the data stored in the arrays.

Input (text file):

For each vendor, read a record and load the data to the following arrays. Array types are shown in parentheses.

vnum	(int)
vendor	(char)
invoiceNum	(char)
invoiceAmt	(float)
discRate	(int)

Set the size of each array to 7. Allow for a maximum of 12 character positions for the elements in the *vendor* array and 5 for the elements in the *invoiceNum* array.

Text File (vendor.dat):

Create the vendor file from the data given below. Enter the records in the order shown.

Vendor Number	Vendor Name	Invoice Number	Invoice Amount	Discount Rate
217	Metacraft	A1239	2309.12	0.10
349	IntraTell	T9823	670.00	0.09
712	Reylock	F0176	4563.78	0.12
501	Universal	W0105	1200.00	0.09
196	Northland	X2781	3429.34	0.10
414	MarxComm	H9205	913.87	0.05
659	Veston	D1776	5127.63	0.08

Ouput (printer):

Print the following accounts payable report:

```
Author                ACCOUNTS PAYABLE REPORT            Page 01
                            mm/dd/yy


Vendor               Invoice   Invoice    Discount    Amount
Number  Vendor Name  Number    Amount     Amount      Due

 999    X---------X   XXXX      9999.99    999.99      9999.99
```

```
    :        :         :          :          :          :
    :        :         :          :          :          :
   999     X--------X     XXXX     9999.99     999.99     9999.99

                  Totals:         99999.99    9999.99    99999.99
```

Processing Requirements:

- Read and load the file input into the arrays.
- Print the unsorted data stored in the arrays.
- Sort the arrays and arrange the data in ascending order by vendor number.
- Print the sorted data stored in the arrays.
- Compute the discount amount:
  invoice amount × discount rate
- Compute the amount due:
  invoice amount – discount amount
- Accumulate report totals for the invoice amount, discount amount, and amount due.

Project 10–10 Production Cost

Write a program to compute and print a production cost report. Read the data from a file, load the input into parallel arrays, and process the data stored in the arrays.

Input (text file):

For each production record, read and load the data into the following arrays. Array types are shown in parentheses.

ename	(char)
product	(char)
units	(int)
cost	(float)

Set the size of each array to 10. Allow for a maximum of 15 character positions for the elements in the *ename* array and 5 for the elements in the *product* array.

Text File (prod.dat):

Create the production file from the data given below. Enter the data in the order shown.

Employee Name	Product Number	Units Produced	Unit Cost
Kay Archer	P9511	42	2.98
Alan Baum	A1234	24	5.50
Marie Fitch	C4510	36	7.94
Lee Hildebrand	R0934	18	6.75
David Mullins	E3371	36	3.79
Chad Nelson	L8912	20	4.33
Bill Quinn	S0951	48	5.65
Nicole Renner	H9733	24	4.25
Erica Tate	Z0182	27	8.10
Terry West	A3235	30	2.95

Ouput (printer):

Print the following production cost report:

```
Author              PRODUCTION COST REPORT           Page 01
                         mm/dd/yy


                    Product   Units      Unit        Production
Employee Name       Number    Produced   Cost        Cost

X----------X        XXXXX        99      99.99        999.99
     :                 :         :         :             :
     :                 :         :         :             :
X----------X        XXXXX        99      99.99        999.99

                    Totals:     999     999.99       9999.99
```

Processing Requirements:

- Read and load the file input into the arrays.
- Print the unsorted data stored in the arrays.
- Sort the arrays and arrange the data in alphabetic order by employee name.
- Print the sorted data stored in the arrays.
- Compute the production cost:
  units produced × unit cost
- Accumulate report totals for the unit produced, unit cost, and production cost.

11   Multidimension Arrays

Learning Objectives

After you have read this chapter and completed the exercises, you should be able to:

- define and load two-dimension arrays
- manipulate and print data stored in two-dimension arrays
- search and update two-dimension arrays
- understand the purpose and use of multidimension arrays

Two-Dimension Arrays

This chapter expands upon the arrays processing techniques introduced in the previous chapter. As you may recall, sample program CHAP10A printed the data stored in two parallel arrays. The output, reproduced in Figure 11.1, consists of a list of employee names and their corresponding production output.

An array that defines a list or a single set of items is called a **one-dimension array**. All of the arrays presented in Chapter 10 are one-dimension arrays. The arrays shown in Figure 11.1 represent two one-dimension arrays—a list of employee names and a list of units produced.

Some data processing applications require that certain data be stored in **two-dimension arrays**, or **tables**. Consider the example shown in Figure 11.2. The table consists of three rows and five columns. A **row** represents a set of values across the table, whereas a **column** represents a set of values down the table. Hence, row 0 represents the values 15, 17, 14, 20, and 19, whereas column 0 represents the values 15, 16, and 25. The table shown in Figure 11.2 is also called a 3 by 5 or **3 × 5 array**.

Any item stored in a two-dimension array can be referenced by specifying the appropriate row and column subscript. In general, *prod[r][c]* refers to the data stored in the *prod* array at row *r* and column *c*.

In other words, an element of a two-dimension array can be directly accessed by coding two subscripts. For example, the data stored in the production array can be referenced accordingly: *prod[0][0]*: 15; *prod[0][1]*: 17; *prod[0][2]*: 14; *prod[0][3]*: 20; *prod[0][4]*: 19; *prod[1][0]*: 16; *prod[1][1]*: 16; *prod[1][2]*: 15; and so forth.

According to Figure 11.3, the subscripts for the 3 × 5 array are row, 0–2; column, 0–4. Once again, the subscripts are numbered from first to last, starting with 0.

```
EMPLOYEE NAME              PRODUCTION
-----------------------------------
Melia Sanchez                 15
Jason Kimm                    16
Nanci Parker                  25
Randy Wade                    23
Cindy Brown                   17
```

FIGURE 11.1 Program Output for CHAP10A

```
                    C o l u m n s

              0    1    2    3    4
      R     -----------------------
      o   0 | 15   17   14   20   19
      w   1 | 16   16   15   17   18
      s   2 | 25   23   24   20   18
```

FIGURE 11.2 Two-Dimension Production Array

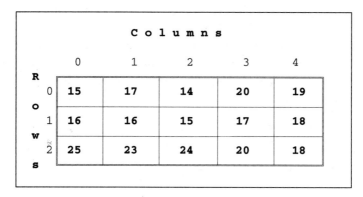

FIGURE 11.3   Production Array with Subscripts

Furthermore, a subscript may not be negative or exceed the size established for either the row or column. Hence, any reference to a subscript outside the row or column range will cause the compiler to produce an error message.

The row and/or column subscripts of a two-dimension array may be expressed as integer constants or variables.

Creating a Two-Dimension Array

A two-dimension array is defined by specifying a data type, a name, and the size of the row and column subscripts. For example, a 3 × 5 array reserves storage space for 15 elements. Similarly, a 10 × 8 array reserves storage for 80 elements.

Examples of two-dimension array declarations are:

```
int    quantity[7][3];
float mileage[5][4];
float area[12][3], amountDue[36][2];
int    points[12][16],
        samples[10][4];
```

We may, of course, define one or more arrays on the same line. Multiple array declarations are separated by commas. We may also list the arrays down the page. Be sure to end each declaration with a semicolon.

The above declarations define the following arrays:

quantity	21 elements	(int)
mileage	20 elements	(float)
area	36 elements	(float)
amountDue	72 elements	(float)
points	192 elements	(int)
samples	40 elements	(int)

The data types are shown in parentheses.

Checkpoint 11A

1. A _____ represents a set of values listed across or horizontally in the table while a _____ represents a set of values listed down or vertically in the table.

2. Using the following table, how would you reference the value 8 stored in the *nbr* array?

10	20	30	40	50
5	15	25	35	45
2	4	6	8	12
3	7	9	11	13

3. Can a two-dimension array be referenced with one subscript?

4. Refer to the table in Excercise 2. Are the following references valid or invalid? If invalid, explain the problem.
   a. nbr [4][3];
   b. nbr [2][-1];
   c. nbr [0][0];

Loading a Two-Dimension Array

A two-dimension array may be loaded by initializing the elements as the array is defined, prompting the user to enter the data at the keyboard, or reading the data from a file.

Initializing Data: Data may be assigned to a table as it is declared. This method is frequently used to load an array with data that remains stable or relatively constant over time.

An example of initializing data is:

```
//----- INITIALIZING DATA ------------
int prod[3][5] = {15, 17, 14, 20, 19,
                  16, 16, 15, 17, 18,
                  25, 23, 24, 20, 18};
```

The declaration assigns a set of 15 integer values to the *prod* array. For convenience, the data is arranged in tabular form. This makes it easier to read and understand.

Interactive Input: Data may be assigned to a table by prompting the user to enter it at the keyboard. Interactive input is used when the data assigned to a table changes frequently over time.

An example of interactive input is:

```
//----- INTERACTIVE INPUT ------------
int prod[3][5];
    . . . . .

for (row = 0; row < 3; row++)  {
    for ( col = 0; col < 5; col++)  {
        cout << "Enter production: ";
        cin >> prod[row][col];
    }
}
```

This example uses a nested counter-controlled loop to prompt for the input. As long as *row* is less than 3 and *column* is less than 5, the input is assigned to the *prod[row][col]* element.

Notice that the column subscript advances from 0–4 for each row subscript. Hence, the table is loaded one row at a time.

File Input: Data can be read from a file and loaded into a table. File input saves time by eliminating the data entry step during the program run. This method may be used to load a table with data that remains constant or changes frequently.

An example of file input is:

```
//----- FILE INPUT -------------------------------
ifstream inFile;
int prod[3][5];
     . . . . .
while(!inputFile.eof())  {
    for (row = 0; row < 3; row++)  {
        for (col = 0; col < 5; col++)  {
            inFile >> prod[row][col];
        }
    }
}
```

This example uses a nested loop to read data from the file and store it in the table. As long as the end-of-file marker is not encountered, the input is assigned to the *prod[row][col]* element.

Printing a Two-Dimension Array

Once an array has been loaded, it is always a good idea to print the array to verify that the data was correctly loaded. The code shown below prints the contents of a two-dimension production array.

```
for (row = 0; row < 3; row++)  {
    for ( col = 0; col < 5; col++)  {
        cout << prod[row][col];
    }
}
```

Checkpoint 11B

1. What three items are specified when defining a two-dimension array?
2. Draw the table that is defined with the statement int students[6][2];
3. Load the *student* table (from Exercise 2) with the following values: 8, 6, 15, 12, 20, 19, 7, 4, 10, 9, 3, and 1. Load the array by initializing the data elements.
4. What other two methods may be used to load a two-dimension array?
5. Code the statements to print the contents of the *student* array on the screen.

Sample Program CHAP11A

Sample program CHAP11A (Figure 11.6, p. 356) loads and processes the data stored in parallel arrays and computes the daily and weekly production totals. Figure 11.7 (p. 359) shows the data entry screen for the program and Figure 11.8 (p. 359) shows the output report.

The following specifications apply:

Input (keyboard):

For each employee, prompt for and enter the following data:

> Employee name
> Production output

Output (screen):

Print the weekly production report shown in Figure 11.8.

Processing Requirements:

- Prompt for and enter the employee names and the daily production output.
- Load the input into the name and production arrays.
- Compute the daily and weekly production totals.
- Print the weekly production report.

Pseudocode:

```
START
Clear the screen
LOOP for row < 3
   Prompt and enter employee name
   LOOP for day < 5
      Prompt and enter production
   End LOOP
End LOOP
LOOP for row < 3
   LOOP for day < 5
      Accumulate weekly production
      Accumulate daily production
   End LOOP
End LOOP
Print report headings
LOOP for row < 3
   Print employee name and weekly production total
End LOOP
Print daily production totals
END
```

Hierarchy Chart: See Figure 11.4.

Program Flowchart: See Figure 11.5.

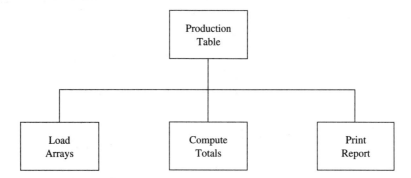

FIGURE 11.4   Hierarchy Chart for CHAP11A

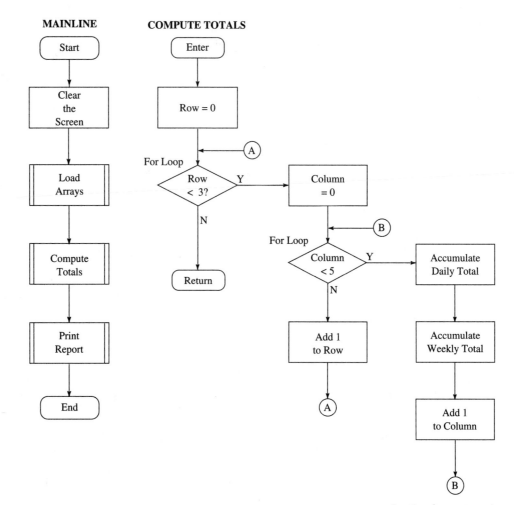

FIGURE 11.5   Program Flowchart for CHAP11A

(continued on next page)

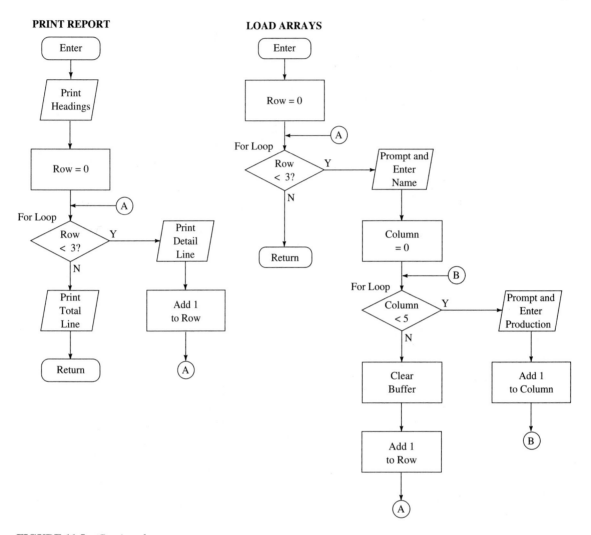

FIGURE 11.5   *Continued*

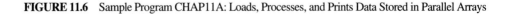

```
//-------- PRODUCTION TABLE --------------------------------
// This program demonstrates application of a two-dimension
// array to compute the daily and weekly production totals.
//
//          PROGRAM-ID: CHAP11A
//          PROGRAMMER: David M. Collopy
//          RUN DATE:   mm/dd/yy
//************************************************************
```

FIGURE 11.6   Sample Program CHAP11A: Loads, Processes, and Prints Data Stored in Parallel Arrays

```
//-------- PREPROCESSING DIRECTIVES ------------------------

#include<iostream.h>
#include<iomanip.h>
#include<conio.h>

//-------- FUNCTION PROTOTYPES -----------------------------

void LoadArrays(void);          // load data into arrays
void ComputeTotals(void);       // compute production totals
void PrintReport(void);         // print production report

//-------- PROGRAM SETUP -----------------------------------

//**  P R O G R A M   V A R I A B L E S

char  name[3][21];       // 3 element 21 char name array
int   prod[3][5];        // 3 × 5 production array
int   dayTotal[5];       // 5 element daily production array
int   weekTotal[3];      // 3 element weekly production array
int   r;                 // row subscript
int   c;                 // column subscript

//---------------------------------------------------------
//              MAINLINE CONTROL
//---------------------------------------------------------
main()
{
    clrscr();                    // clear the screen
    LoadArrays();                // load data into arrays
    ComputeTotals();             // compute production totals
    PrintReport();               // print production report
    return 0;
}
//---------------------------------------------------------
//            LOAD DATA INTO ARRAYS
//---------------------------------------------------------
void LoadArrays(void)
{
    for (r = 0; r < 3, r++)  {
        cout << "Enter employee name: ";
        cin.get(name[r], 21);
        for (c = 0; c < 5, c++)  {
            cout << "  Enter production: ";
            cin >> prod[r][c];
        }
```

(continued on next page)

FIGURE 11.6 *Continued*

```
            cin.get();                      // clear keyboard buffer
        }
    return;
}
//-----------------------------------------------------------
//              COMPUTE PRODUCTION TOTALS
//-----------------------------------------------------------
void ComputeTotals(void)
{
    for (r = 0; r < 3, r++)  {
        for (c = 0; c < 5, c++)  {
            dayTotal[c] = dayTotal[c] + prod[r][c];
            weekTotal[r] = weekTotal[r] + prod[r][c];
        }
    }
    return;
}
//-----------------------------------------------------------
//              PRINT PRODUCTION REPORT
//-----------------------------------------------------------
void PrintReport(void)
{
    cout << "\n\n  EMPLOYEE NAME          MON TUE WED THR FRI"
         << " TOTALS";
    cout << "\n-------------------------------------------"
         << "--------";
    for (r = 0; r < 3; r++)  {
        cout << endl << setiosflags(ios::left)
             << setw(20) << name[r]
             << resetiosflags(ios::left)
             << setw(4) << prod[r][0]
             << setw(4) << prod[r][1]
             << setw(4) << prod[r][2]
             << setw(4) << prod[r][3]
             << setw(4) << prod[r][4]
             << setw(6) << weekTotal[r];
    }
    cout << "\n\n          Totals: "
         << setw(4) << dayTotal[0] << setw(4) << dayTotal[1]
         << setw(4) << datTotal[2] << setw(4) << dayTotal[3]
         << setw(4) << dayTotal[4];
    return;
}
```

FIGURE 11.6 *Continued*

```
Enter employee name: Melia Sanchez
   Enter production: 15
   Enter production: 17
   Enter production: 14
   Enter production: 20
   Enter production: 19
Enter employee name: Jason Kimm
   Enter production: 16
            :           :
            :           :
```

FIGURE 11.7   Data Entry Screen for CHAP11A

```
    EMPLOYEE NAME        MON TUE WED THR FRI TOTALS
-----------------------------------------------------
    Melia Sanchez        15  17  14  20  19    85
    Jason Kimm           16  16  15  17  18    82
    Nanci Parker         25  23  24  20  18   110

         Totals:         56  56  53  57  55
```

FIGURE 11.8   Production Output Report for CHAP11A

Dissection of Sample Program CHAP11A

PROGRAM VARIABLES

char name[3][21];

The above statement means: Define a three-element character array called *name* and allocate 20 characters of storage to each name. One position is reserved for the null character.

int prod[3][5];

The above statement means: Define a 3×5 integer array called *prod*. This declaration allocates storage for 15 elements.

int dayTotal[5];

The above statement means: Define a five-element integer array called *dayTotal*. This array will be used to hold the daily production totals.

int weekTotal[3];

The preceding statement means: Define a three-element integer array called *weekTotal*. This array will be used to hold the weekly production total for the employees.

```
int   r;
int   c;
```

The above statements mean: Define the row *r* and column *c* subscripts.

LOAD DATA INTO ARRAYS

```
void LoadArrays(void)
{
    for (r = 0; r < 3, r++)   {
        cout << "Enter employee name: ";
        cin.get(name[r], 21);
        for (c = 0; c < 5, c++)   {
            cout << "   Enter production: ";
            cin >> prod[r][c];
        }
        cin.get();
    }
    return;
}
```

The above statements mean: First, as long as the row subscript is less than 3, prompt the user to enter the employee's name. Second, as long as the column subscript is less than 5, prompt the user to enter the weekly production output one day at a time.

For each increment of the row subscript, the column subscript advances from 0 to 4 and prompts the user to enter five days of production work.

Notice that each time control leaves the inner loop, the cin.get() clears the keyboard buffer of the last Enter key that was pressed. This prepares the buffer to receive the next employee name.

COMPUTE PRODUCTION TOTALS

```
void ComputeTotals(void)
{
    for (r = 0; r < 3; r++)   {
        for (c = 0; c < 5; c++)   {
            dayTotal[c] = dayTotal[c] + prod[r][c];
            weekTotal[r] = weekTotal[r] + prod[r][c];
        }
    }
    return;
}
```

The above statements mean: Accumulate a daily (column) total for the production output and a weekly production (row) total for each employee. The relationship between the production table and the two one-dimension arrays is illustrated in Figure 11.9.

prod[r][c]   weekTotal[r]

15	17	14	20	19
16	16	15	17	18
25	23	24	20	18

85
82
110

dayTotal[c]

56	56	53	57	55

FIGURE 11.9   Relationship Between Production Table and Arrays for CHAP11A

The process begins by setting the row and column subscripts to 0. Each time the row subscript is incremented, the column subscript advances from 0 to 4. Notice that elements in the *dayTotal* array are computed by adding the column elements in the *prod* array.

```
dayTotal[c] = dayTotal[c] + prod[r][c];
```

And the elements in the *weekTotal* array are computed by adding the row elements in the *prod* array.

```
weekTotal[r] = weekTotal[r] + prod[r][c];
```

```
PRINT PRODUCTION REPORT:

void PrintReport(void)
{
    cout << "\n\n      EMPLOYEE NAME        MON TUE WED THR FRI";
    cout << " TOTALS";
    cout << "\n-----------------------------------------------";
    cout << "--------";
```

The above statements mean: Print two column heading lines.

```
    for (r = 0; r < 3; r++)  {
        cout << endl << setiosflags(ios::left)
             << setw(20) << name[r]
             << resetiosflags(ios::left)
             << setw(4) << prod[r][0]
             << setw(4) << prod[r][1]
             << setw(4) << prod[r][2]
             << setw(4) << prod[r][3]
             << setw(4) << prod[r][4]
             << setw(6) << weekTotal[r];
    }
```

The preceding statements mean: As long as the current value of the row subscript is less than 3, print the employee's name, the production output, and the weekly total. This is accomplished by holding the column subscript constant while incrementing the row subscripts from 0 to 2.

```
    cout << "\n\n          Totals: "
        << setw(4) << dayTotal[0] << setw(4) << dayTotal[1]
        << setw(4) << datTotal[2] << setw(4) << dayTotal[3]
        << setw(4) << dayTotal[4];
    return;
}
```

The above statements mean: Print the five-day production totals. The column subscripts are coded as constants in order to print all of the elements at the same time.

Searching and Updating Tables

From Chapter 10, we know that array lookup is the process of locating data stored in an array. To find a given element in a two-dimension array, we specify the row and column subscripts. In this section, we will learn how to perform table lookup using direct reference or sequential search.

Direct Reference: Direct reference assumes that there is a direct relationship between the user's input and the subscripts. For a two-dimension array, the row and column subscripts are entered at the keyboard and are used by the program to access the data stored in the table.

Consider a programming application that records the points scored during a basketball game. The points are recorded at the end of each quarter and stored in a 2×4 table called *points*. According to the code shown below, the team number and quarter are used as the row and column subscripts to access and display the score on the screen.

```
int points[2][4] = {19, 17, 20, 16,
                     14, 18, 19, 15};
int team, qtr;
  . . . . .


//----- DIRECT REFERENCE LOOKUP ---------------------
cout << "\nEnter team number (1-2) or '-1' to Quit: ";
cin >> team;
while (team != -1)  {
    cout << "\nEnter quarter (1-4): ";
    cin >> qtr;
    cout << "\nScore = " << points[team-1][qtr-1];
    cout << "\nEnter team number (1-2) or '-1' to Quit: ";
    cin >> team;
}
```

For example, if the user enters 2 for the team and 4 for the quarter, then the program displays the score 15 on the screen; *score[team–1][qtr–1] = score[1][3]* = 15. Remember that the subscript, row or column, always begins with 0.

Sequential Search: For a two-dimension array, sequential search requires, at most, two one-dimension arrays: one for holding the row keys and one for holding the column keys. Sequential search is used when there is no direct relationship between the user's input and

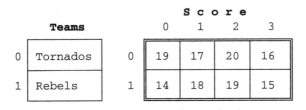

FIGURE 11.10   Relationship Between Score Table and Team Array

one or more of the array subscripts. Consequently, the program compares the input to the elements in the key array until a match is found or the end of the array is encountered. For a match, the subscript of the key array is used to access the corresponding element stored in the two-dimension table.

In Figure 11.10, assume that the user has entered the team name and the quarter.

```
//----- SEQUENTIAL SEARCH LOOKUP ----------
r = 0;
row = -1
while (r < 2 && row == -1)  {
    if (strcmp(inputTeam, team[r]) == 0)  {
        row = r;
    }
    r = r + 1;
}
```

The search begins by setting the variables *r* and *row* to 0 and –1, respectively. As long as the *while* condition test is true, the search key *inputTeam* is compared to the elements stored in the *team* array. If a match is found, *row* is set to *r*, the value of the subscript where the team name was found.

```
/------ CHECK FOR TEAM MATCH ----------------
if (row == -1)  {
    count << "\nTeam not found";
}
else  {
    cout << "Score = " << points[row][qtr-1];
}
```

For example, if the user enters Tornados for the team and 2 for the second quarter, then the program displays the score 17 on the screen; *score[0][2–1] = 17*. Of course, if a match is not found, the program prints the message Team not found on the screen.

Checkpoint 11C

1. Explain the difference between direct reference and sequential search.

2. Using the following table and direct reference lookup, code the statements to find a specific piece of data in the *price* table. (*Note:* The rows represent the type of item [e.g., blender, toaster, mixer] and the columns represent prices of various models.)

27.50	32.45	48.29	54.63
19.12	24.81	36.21	47.40
10.53	21.14	31.16	44.78

3. Using the code segment written in Exercise 2, if the user enters 2 for the item and 3 for the model, what will print as the price?

4. Using the following arrays and serial search, code the statements to search the item table for a specific household appliance and the price table for the specific model number (e.g., 1, 2, 3, or 4).

	Price			
Item	Model1	Model2	Model3	Model4
Blender	27.50	32.45	48.29	54.63
Toaster	19.12	24.81	36.21	47.40
Mixer	10.53	21.14	31.16	44.78

Sample Program CHAP11B

Sample program CHAP11B (Figure 11.13, p. 369) updates data stored in parallel arrays. It also computes the weekly and daily production output and prints a simple production report. Figure 11.14 (p. 373) shows the update entry prompts and Figure 11.15 (p. 373) shows the updated output.

The following specifications apply:

Input (keyboard):

For each update, prompt for and enter the following data:

    Employee name
    Work day
    Production update

Output (screen):

Print the weekly production report shown in Figure 11.15.

Processing Requirements:

* Define and initialize the following arrays:

    | Employee names | (5 rows) |
    | Production output | (5 × 5 table) |
    | Work days | (5 columns) |
    | Daily totals | (5 columns) |
    | Weekly totals | (5 rows) |

* Prompt for and enter the employee's name, work day, and production update.
* Look up and update data stored in the production array.

- Compute the daily and weekly production totals and store them in one-dimension arrays.
- After the updates, print the production output report.

Pseudocode:

```
START
Clear the screen
Enter employee name
LOOP until employee name = quit
   Enter work day
   Enter production update
   Look up employee name
   Look up work day
   Update production output
      If employee name not found
         Print error message and continue
      else if work day not found
         Print error message and continue
      else
         Update production
   Enter employee name
End LOOP
LOOP for count < 5
   LOOP for day < 5
      Accumulate weekly production
      Accumulate daily production
   End LOOP
End LOOP
Print report headings
LOOP for count < 5
   Print employee name and weekly production total
End LOOP
Print daily production totals
END
```

Hierarchy Chart: See Figure 11.11.

Program Flowchart: See Figure 11.12.

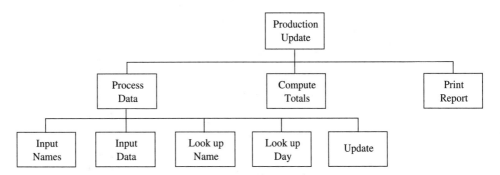

FIGURE 11.11   Hierarchy Chart for CHAP11B

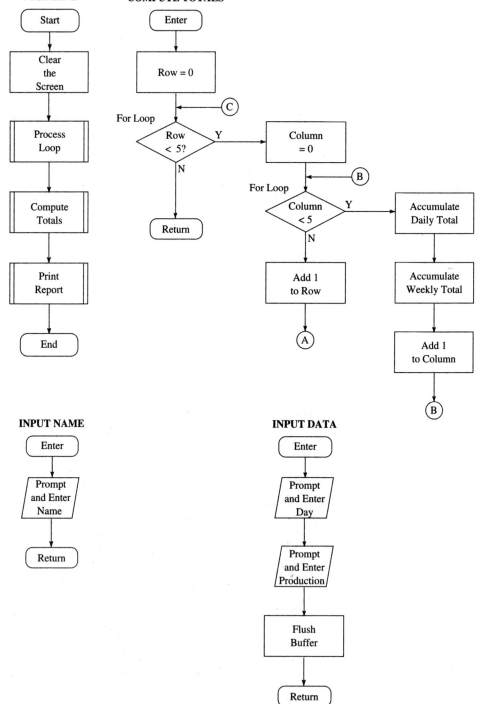

FIGURE 11.12　Program Flowchart for CHAP11B

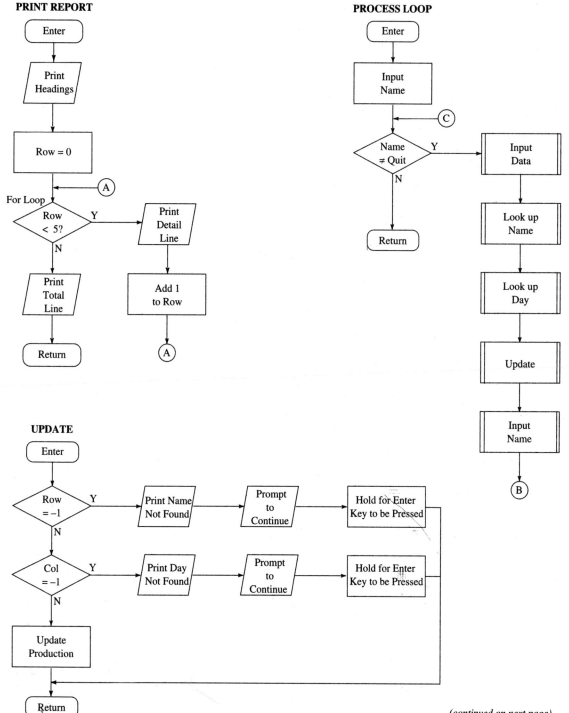

PRINT REPORT

Enter

Print Headings

Row = 0

(A)

For Loop
Row < 5?   Y →   Print Detail Line

N

Print Total Line

Return   Add 1 to Row

(A)

PROCESS LOOP

Enter

Input Name

(C)

Name ≠ Quit   Y →   Input Data

N

Return   Look up Name

Look up Day

Update

Input Name

(B)

UPDATE

Enter

Row = −1   Y →   Print Name Not Found →   Prompt to Continue →   Hold for Enter Key to be Pressed

N

Col = −1   Y →   Print Day Not Found →   Prompt to Continue →   Hold for Enter Key to be Pressed

N

Update Production

Return

(continued on next page)

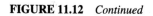

FIGURE 11.12   *Continued*

LOOKUP NAME

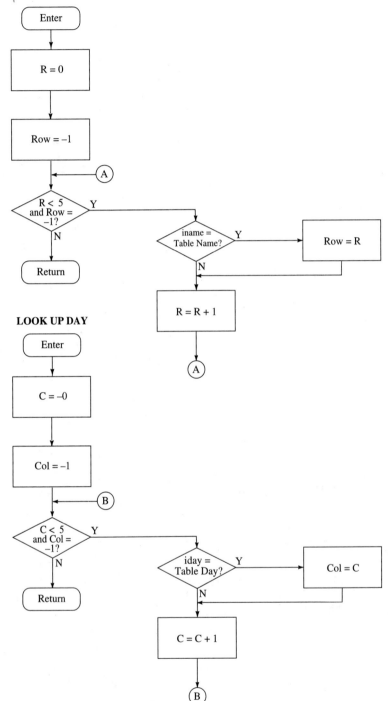

LOOK UP DAY

FIGURE 11.12   *Continued*

```
//---------- PRODUCTION TABLE ------------------------------
// This program uses sequential search to locate and update
// the daily production stored in a two-dimension array.
//
//           PROGRAM-ID: CHAP11B
//           PROGRAMMER: David M. Collopy
//           RUN DATE:   mm/dd/yy
//**********************************************************

//---------- PREPROCESSING DIRECTIVES ---------------------

#include<iostream.h>
#include<iomanip.h>
#include<conio.h>
#include<string.h>

//---------- FUNCTION PROTOTYPES --------------------------

void ProcessLoop(void);        // processing loop
void InputName(void);          // input employee name
void InputData(void);          // input update data
void LookupName(void);         // locate employee name
void LookupDay(void);          // locate production day
void Update(void);             // update production data
void ComputeTotals(void);      // compute production totals
void PrintReport(void);        // print production report

//---------- PROGRAM SETUP --------------------------------

//**  P R O G R A M   V A R I A B L E S

char   name[5][21] ={"Melia Sanchez", "Jason Kimm",
                     "Nanci Parker", "Randy Wade",
                     "Cindy Brown"};
int    prod[5][5] = {15, 17, 14, 20, 19
                     16, 16, 15, 17, 18,
                     25, 23, 24, 20, 18,
                     23, 16, 17, 19, 15,
                     17, 19, 17, 16, 20};
int    dayTotal[5];
int    weekTotal[5]
char   day[5][4] = {"MON", "TUE", "WED", "THR", "FRI"};
int    r;                      // row subscript
int    c;                      // column subscript
int    row;                    // row lookup match
int    col;                    // column lookup match
chat   iname[21];              // input employee name
char   iday[4];                // input work day
```

(continued on next page)

FIGURE 11.13   Sample Program CHAP11B: Updates Data Stored in a Two-Dimension Array

```
int    iprod;                  // input production update
char   wait;                   // wait for Enter key to be pressed

//-----------------------------------------------------------
//                  MAINLINE CONTROL
//-----------------------------------------------------------
main()
{
    clrscr();                  // clear the screen
    ProcessLoop();             // processing loop
    ComputeTotals();           // compute production totals
    PrintReport();             // print production report
    return 0;
}
//-----------------------------------------------------------
//                  PROCESSING LOOP
//-----------------------------------------------------------
void ProcessLoop(void)
{
    InputName();
    while (strcmp(iname, "quit") != 0)  {
        InputData();
        LookupName();
        LookupDay();
        Update();
        InputName();
    }
    return;
}
//-----------------------------------------------------------
//                  INPUT EMPLOYEE NAME
//-----------------------------------------------------------
void InputName(void)
{
    cout << "Enter employee name or 'quit' to STOP: ";
    cin.get(iname, 21);        // get name
    cin.get();                 // clear keyboard buffer
    return;
}
//-----------------------------------------------------------
//                  INPUT UPDATE DATA
//-----------------------------------------------------------
void InputData(void)
{
    cout << "  Enter day - MON, TUE, WED, THR, FRI: ";
    cin.get(iday, 4);          // get work day
    cout << "                    Enter production update: ":
```

FIGURE 11.13 *Continued*

```
    cin >> iprod;            // get production
    cin.get();               // clear keyboard buffer
    return;
}
//-----------------------------------------------------------
//              LOCATE EMPLOYEE NAME
//-----------------------------------------------------------
void LookupName(void)
{
    r = 0;
    row = -1;
    while (r < 5 && row == -1)  {
        if (strcmp(iname, name[r]) == 0)  {
            row = r;           // found name
        }
        r = r + 1;
    }
    return;
}
//-----------------------------------------------------------
//              LOCATE PRODUCTION DAY
//-----------------------------------------------------------
void LookupDay(void)
{
    c = 0;
    col = -1;
    while (c < 5 && col == -1)  {
        if (strcmp(iday, day[c]) == 0)  {
            col = c;           // found day
        }
        c = c + 1:
    }
    return;
}
//-----------------------------------------------------------
//              UPDATE PRODUCTION DATA
//-----------------------------------------------------------
void Update(void)
{
    if (row == -1)  {
        cout << "\nEMPLOYEE NAME NOT FOUND"
             << " - Press 'ENTER' to continue...";
        wait = getch();        // wait for Enter key to be pressed
    {
    else if (col == -1)  {
        cout << "\nUPDATE DAY NOT FOUND"
```

(continued on next page)

FIGURE 11.13 *Continued*

```
                      <<  " - Press 'ENTER' to continue.":
           wait = getch();        // wait for Enter key to be pressed
       }
       else  {
           prod[row][col] = production[row][col] + iprod;
       }
       return;
    }
    //------------------------------------------------------------
    //               COMPUTE PRODUCTION TOTALS
    //------------------------------------------------------------
    void ComputeTotals(void)
    {
        for (r = 0; r < 5, r++)  {
            for (c = 0; c < 5, c++)  {
                dayTotal[c] = dayTotal[c] + prod[r][c];
                weekTotal[r] = weekTotal[r] + prod[r][c];
            }
        }
        return;
    }
    //------------------------------------------------------------
    //               PRINT PRODUCTION REPORT
    //------------------------------------------------------------
    void PrintReport(void)
    {
        cout << "\n\n  EMPLOYEE NAME         MON TUE WED THR FRI"
             << " TOTALS";
        cout << "\n---------------------------------------------"
             << "--------";
        for (r = 0; r < 5; r++)  {
            cout << endl << setiosflags(ios::left)
                 << setw(20) << name[r]
                 << resetiosflags(ios::left)
                 << setw(4) << prod[r][0]
                 << setw(4) << prod[r][1]
                 << setw(4) << prod[r][2]
                 << setw(4) << prod[r][3]
                 << setw(4) << prod[r][4]
                 << setw(6) << weekTotal[r];
        }
        cout << "\n\n          Totals: "
             << setw(4) << dayTotal[0] << setw(4) << dayTotal[1]
             << setw(4) << datTotal[2] << setw(4) << dayTotal[3]
             << setw(4) << dayTotal[4];
        return;
    }
```

FIGURE 11.13 *Continued*

```
Enter employee name or 'quit' to STOP: Tim Mohr
   Enter day - MON, TUE, WED, THR, FRI: TUE
               Enter production update: 7

EMPLOYEE NAME NOT FOUND - press ENTER to continue...

Enter employee name or 'quit' to STOP: Nanci Parker
   Enter day - MON, TUE, WED, THR, FRI: FRI
               Enter production update: 3

Enter employee name or 'quit' to STOP: quit
```

FIGURE 11.14   Update Prompts for CHAP11B

```
    EMPLOYEE NAME        MON TUE WED THR FRI TOTALS
---------------------------------------------------
    Melia Sanchez         15  17  14  20  19    85
    Jason Kimm            16  16  15  17  18    82
    Nanci Parker          25  23  24  20  21   113
    Randy Wade            23  16  17  19  15    90
    Cindy Brown           17  19  17  16  20    89

           Totals:        96  91  87  92  93
```

FIGURE 11.15   Updated Production Report for CHAP11B

Dissection of Sample Program CHAP11B

The following statements (continued on p. 374) mean: Transfer control to the *InputName* module and prompt the user to enter the employee's name. As long as the input name is not equal to *quit*, control enters the *while* loop and executes the modules in the order listed.

PROCESSING LOOP

```
void ProcessLoop(void)
{
    InputName();
    while (strcmp(iname, "quit") != 0)  {
        InputData();
        LookupName();
        LookupDay();
        Update();
        InputName();
    }
    return;
}
```

INPUT EMPLOYEE NAME

```
void InputName(void)
{
    cout << "Enter employee name or 'quit' to STOP: ";
    cin.get(iname, 21);
    cin.get();
    return;
}
```

The above statements mean: Prompt the user to enter the employee's name or "quit" to stop. The input is assigned to *iname*, and the keyboard buffer is cleared.

INPUT UPDATE DATA

```
void InputData(void)
{
    cout << "  Enter day - MON, TUE, WED, THR, FRI: ";
    cin.get(iday, 4);
    cout << "            Enter production update: ":
    cin >> iprod;
    cin.get();
    return;
}
```

The above statements mean: Prompt the user to enter the work day and production update. The work day is assigned to *iday*, and the production update is assigned to *iprod*. Once again, the keyboard buffer is cleared.

LOCATE EMPLOYEE NAME

```
void LookupName(void)
{
    r = 0;
    row = -1;
    while (r < 5 && row == -1)  {
        if (strcmp(iname, name[r]) == 0)  {
            row = r;
        }
        r = r + 1;
    }
    return;
}
```

The above statements mean: As long as the subscript *r* is less than 5 and a match has not been found, control enters the body of the loop. If the search key *iname* matches the employee name stored in the current element of the name array, then assign the value of the subscript *r* to *row*. Otherwise, continue until either the name is found or the end of the array is encountered.

LOCATE PRODUCTION DAY

```
void LookupDay(void)
{
    c = 0;
    col = -1;
    while (c < 5 && col == -1)  {
```

```
        if (strcmp(iday, day[c]) == 0)  {
            col = c;
        }
        c = c + 1;
    }
    return;
}
```

The above statements mean: As long as the subscript *c* is less than 5 and a match has not been found, control enters the body of the loop. If the search key *iday* matches the work day stored in the current element of the *day* array, then assign the value of the subscript *c* to *col*. Otherwise, continue until either the work day is found or the end of the array is encountered.

UPDATE PRODUCTION DATA

```
void Update(void)
{
    if (row == -1)  {
        cout << "\nEMPLOYEE NAME NOT FOUND"
             << " - Press 'ENTER' to continue...";
        wait = getch();
    {
    else if (col == -1)  {
        cout << "\nUPDATE DAY NOT FOUND"
             << " - Press 'ENTER' to continue...":
        wait = getch();
    }
    else  }
        prod[row][col] = production[row][col] + iprod;
    }
    return;
}
```

The above statements mean: If the employee's name was not found in the *name* array, then print the name error message and wait for the user to continue. Else, if the work day was not found in the *day* array, then print the day error message and wait for the user to continue.

However, if the employee's name and work day are found, then add the production update to the element indexed by the *row* and *col* subscripts and return to the calling module.

COMPUTE PRODUCTION TOTALS

```
void ComputeTotals(void)
{
    for (r = 0; r < 5; r++)  {
        for (c = 0; c < 5; c++)  {
            dayTotal[c] = dayTotal[c] + prod[r][c];
            weekTotal[r] = weekTotal[r] + prod[r][c];
        }
    }
    return;
}
```

The previous statements mean: Accumulate a daily (column) total for the production output and a weekly production (row) total for each employee. The nested for() loop forces the column subscript to increment from 0 to 4 for each iteration of the row subscript.

PRINT PRODUCTION REPORT

```
void PrintReport(void)
{
    cout << "\n\n  EMPLOYEE NAME              MON TUE WED THR FRI"
         << " TOTALS";
    cout << "\n---------------------------------------------"
         << "--------";
    for (r = 0; r < 5; r++)  {
        cout << endl << setiosflags(ios::left)
             << setw(20) << name[r]
             << resetiosflags(ios::left)
             << setw(4) << prod[r][0]
             << setw(4) << prod[r][1]
             << setw(4) << prod[r][2]
             << setw(4) << prod[r][3]
             << setw(4) << prod[r][4]
             << setw(6) << weekTotal[r];
    }
    cout << "\n\n          Totals: "
         << setw(4) << dayTotal[0] << setw(4) << dayTotal[1]
         << setw(4) << dayTotal[2] << setw(4) << dayTotal[3]
         << setw(4) << dayTotal[4];
    return;
}
```

The above statements mean: As long as the current value of the row subscript is less than 5, print the employee's name, daily production output, and the weekly total. At the end of the report, print the total daily production output.

Multidimension Arrays

So far we have seen examples of one- and two-dimension arrays. Actually, arrays may consist of three, four, or more dimensions; the actual number depends mostly on the application at hand. However, not many applications would go beyond three dimensions.

Consider the basketball scorekeeping application presented earlier where the points are recorded at the end of each quarter for team 1 (home) and team 2 (visitors) in a 2×4 array. The two-dimension array is shown in Figure 11.16.

For the subscripts t and q, the statement *points[t][q]* represents the points scored by the t-team in the q-quarter. Hence, *points[1][3]* refers to the points scored by the visitors in the fourth quarter.

Assume that games are played at three different schools; school 1 (Adams), school 2 (Lincoln), and school 3 (Washington). The three-dimension array is shown in Figure 11.17.

For the subscripts s, t, and q, the statement *points[s][t][q]* represents the points scored during the game played at s-school by the t-team in the q-quarter. Hence, *points[2][1][3]*

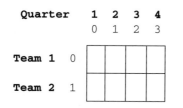

FIGURE 11.16   Two-Dimension Array

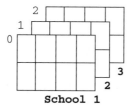

FIGURE 11.17   Three-Dimension Array

refers to the points scored during the game played at Washington High School by the visitors in the fourth quarter.

Furthermore, assume that nine games are played during the week at three high schools located in three different cities; city 1 (Millersburg), city 2 (Rosedale), and city 3 (Westport). The four-dimension array is shown in Figure 11.18.

For the subscripts *c, s, t,* and *q,* the statement *points[c][s][t][q]* represents the points scored in *c*-city during the game played at *s*-school by the *t*-team in the *q*-quarter. Hence, *points[0][2][1][3]* refers to the points scored in Millersburg during the game played at Washington High School by the visitors in the fourth quarter.

At first, the concept of multidimension arrays may seem confusing and somewhat difficult to visualize. However, it may be helpful to think of a two-dimension array as a table, a three-dimension array as a sequence of pages, and a four-dimension array as a group of pages organized into chapters.

For example, look at the array shown in Figure 11.16 as a table; the arrays shown in Figure 11.17 as a sequence of pages (each school represents a page); and the arrays shown in Figure 11.18 as chapters (each city represents a chapter).

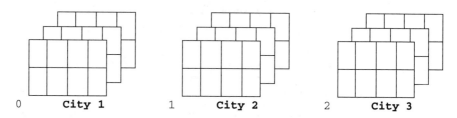

FIGURE 11.18   Four-Dimension Array

Checkpoint 11D

1. Code the statement to dimension the integer array shown in the following illustration.

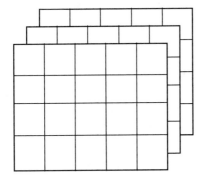

2. The array shown in the illustration in Excercise 1 is referred to as a _____-dimension array.

3. Although multidimension arrays can have several dimensions, for most applications, we seldom go beyond _____ dimensions.

4. A four-dimension array requires _____ subscripts to locate a specific element stored in the array.

Summary

1. Many data processing applications require that certain data be stored in tables, or two-dimension arrays.

2. A two-dimension array consists of a finite number of rows and columns. A row represents a set of values across the table, and a column represents a set of values down the table.

3. A two-dimension array is defined by specifying a data type, a name, and a size. Size refers to the number of rows and columns reserved for the array. For example, a 5 by 6 array reserves storage space for 30 (5×6) elements.

4. Individual elements stored in a two-dimension array are referenced by specifying a row and a column subscript. In other words, any element can be accessed by appending two subscripts to the array name.

5. A subscript may not be negative or exceed the size established for either the row or column. Any reference to a subscript outside the row or column range will cause the compiler to produce an error message.

6. The subscripts of a two-dimension array may be expressed as integer constants or variables.

7. For a two-dimension array, direct reference lookup requires a row and a column subscript to directly locate the data stored in the table. Direct reference uses the subscripts entered at the keyboard to directly access the data stored in the table.

8. For a two-dimension array, sequential search requires, at most, two one-dimension arrays: one for holding the row subscripts and one for holding the column subscripts. Sequential search uses the data entered at the keyboard to search the one-dimension array(s) to determine the subscript(s) of the data stored in the table.

9. Multidimension arrays allow the program to store data in two, three, four, or more dimensions.

10. A three-dimension array requires three subscripts to locate a specific element stored in the array. As a rule, an *n*-dimension array requires *n* subscripts to locate a given element stored in the array.

Programming Projects

For each project, design the logic and write the modular structured program to produce the output. Model your program after the sample programs presented in the chapter. Verify your output.

Project 11–1 Overdue Accounts-1

Write a program to read a file, load the input into arrays, and print a report of the overdue accounts.

Input (text file):

For each customer, read a record and load the data into to the following arrays. Array types are shown in parentheses.

1. Name array (char)
2. 12 × 3 overdue account array (float)
   columns: 30 days, 60 days, and 90 days

Set the row size of each array to 12. Allow for a maximum of 15 characters of data for the elements in the *name* array.

Text File (overdue.dat):

Create the overdue accounts file from the data given below. Enter the records in the order shown.

Customer Name	30 Days Overdue	60 Days Overdue	90 Days Overdue
Corey Adkins	233.00	0.00	0.00
Rita Fox	0.00	135.00	740.00
Lisa Wilson	119.00	417.00	0.00
Alvin Porter	100.00	154.00	550.00
Pat Rankin	0.00	342.00	218.00
Tori Landis	0.00	0.00	235.00
David Ryan	100.00	200.00	400.00
Amy Wyatt	700.00	400.00	100.00
Brian Knox	625.00	0.00	0.00
Marie Hill	754.00	122.00	0.00
Matt Hart	136.00	340.00	900.00
Susan Cope	100.00	300.00	600.00

Output (printer):

Print the following overdue accounts report:

```
Author            OVERDUE ACCOUNTS REPORT        Page 01
                        mm/dd/yy

                     30 Days    60 Days    90 Days
Customer Name        Overdue    Overdue    Overdue

X----------X          999.99     999.99     999.99
     :                  :          :          :
     :                  :          :          :
X----------X          999.99     999.99     999.99

         Totals:     9999.99    9999.99    9999.99
```

Processing Requirements:

- Read and load the file into the arrays.
- Read the arrays and print a report of all the customers with overdue accounts.
- Accumulate totals for the 30-day, 60-day, and 90-day overdue accounts.

Project 11–2 Overdue Accounts-2

Modify the program in Project 11–1 to allow the user to update the data stored in the arrays. Prompt for and enter the updates given below. Search for a match on employee name or `Enter 'Q' to quit`. If a match is not found, print the message `Account not found - press ENTER to continue`.

Enter the updates in the order shown.

Customer Name	Days Overdue	Balance Overdue
Brian Knox	30	872.00
Marie Hill	90	700.00
Susan Cope	60	610.00
David Ryan	90	435.00
Lisa Wilcox	60	495.00
Corey Adkins	30	249.00
Tori Landis	30	112.00

Project 11–3 Payroll-1

Write a program to compute and print a weekly payroll roster. Read the data from a file, load the input into arrays, and process the data stored in the arrays. Do not compute overtime. Assume that the current federal income tax (FIT) rate is 15%.

Input (text file):

For each employee, read a record and load the data into the following arrays. Array types are shown in parentheses.

1. Name array (char)
2. 9×2 payroll data array (float)
   columns: hours and rate

Set the row size of each array to 9. Allow for a maximum of 15 characters of data for the elements in the *name* array.

Text File (payroll.dat):

Create the payroll file from the data given below. Enter the records in the order shown.

Employee Name	Hours	Pay Rate
Tracy York	36.1	11.00
Dale Miller	40.0	10.25
Sara Erickson	38.7	12.00
Karen Thomas	48.0	9.00
Paul Irwin	48.5	8.72
Dana Clark	45.3	14.90
Tanya Bauer	40.0	7.50
Bret Rossi	35.9	8.00
Scott Howard	42.2	9.75

Output (printer):

Print the following weekly payroll report:

```
Author              WEEKLY  PAYROLL  REPORT           Page 01
                         mm/dd/yy


Employee    Hours     Pay Rate    Gross Pay     FIT      Net Pay

X-------X     99       99.99       999.99      99.99     999.99
   :          :          :           :          :          :
   :          :          :           :          :          :
X-------X     99       99.99       999.99      99.99     999.99

            Totals:               9999.99     999.99    9999.99
```

Processing Requirements:

- Read and load the file input into the arrays.
- Compute the gross pay:
  hours × pay rate
- Compute the federal income tax:
  gross pay × FIT rate
- Compute the net pay:
  gross pay – FIT
- Accumulate totals for gross pay, FIT, and net pay.

Project 11–4 Payroll-2

Modify the program in Project 11–3 to allow the user to update the payroll data stored in the arrays. Prompt for and enter the updates given below. Search for a match on employee name or Enter 'Q' to quit. If a match is not found, print the message Name not found - press ENTER to continue.

Enter the payroll updates in the order shown.

Employee Name	Hours	Pay Rate
Karen Thomas	44.1	9.00
Darla Clark	40.0	10.60
Tracy York	39.5	11.50
Diane Reeves	38.3	7.90
Scott Howard	42.2	10.00
Patsy Ireland	40.0	8.45

Project 11–5 Sales Profit-1

Write a program to calculate the profit generated by each salesperson and print a sales profit report. Read the data from a file, load the input into arrays, and process the data stored in the arrays.

Input (text file):

For each sales representative, read a record and load the data into the following arrays. Array types are shown in parentheses.

1. Name array (char)
2. 5 × 2 sales data array (float)
   columns: sales and cost

Set the row size of each array to 5. Allow for a maximum of 15 characters of data for the elements in the *name* array.

Text File (sales.dat):

Create the sales file from the data given below. Enter the records in the order shown.

Salesperson	Total Sales	Cost of Sales
Ann Zimmerman	5793.59	4204.45
Tara Perkins	12710.14	9735.38
Dennis Tian	4567.51	3119.22
Roy Hickle	2245.78	1072.49
Lisa Conrad	8120.52	6450.71

Output (printer):

Print the following sales profit report:

```
Author               SALES PROFIT REPORT            Page 01
                         mm/dd/yy



Salesperson   Total Sales   Cost of Sales   Net Profit
--------------------------------------------------------
X--------X     99999.99        99999.99       99999.99
    :             :               :              :
    :             :               :              :
X--------X     99999.99        99999.99       99999.99

                              Total:          999999.99
```

Processing Requirements:

- Read and load the file input into the arrays.
- Compute the net profit:
  total sales – cost of sales
- Accumulate and print a report total for net profit.

Project 11–6 Sales Profit-2

Modify the program in Project 11–5 to allow the user to update the sales data stored in the arrays. Prompt for and enter the updates given below. Search for a match on salesperson name or Enter `'Q'` to quit. If a match is not found, print the message `Name not found - press ENTER to continue`.

Enter the sales updates in the order shown.

Salesperson	Total Sales	Cost of Sales
Tara Perkins	13944.70	10378.59
Lisa Conrad	8001.03	6392.53
Holly Winkler	4316.22	2975.65
Ann Zimmerman	6090.00	4354.64
Roy Hickle	2368.99	1139.16
Barbara Rider	7605.42	4321.28

Project 11–7 Inventory-1

Write a program to read an inventory file, load the input into arrays, and print an inventory profit report.

Input (text file):

For each inventory item, read a record and load the data into the following arrays. Array types are shown in parentheses.

1. Description array (char)

2. Quantity array (int)

3. 5 × 2 cost-price array (float)
   columns: unit cost and selling price

Set the row size of each array to 5. Allow for a maximum of 15 characters of data for the elements in the *description* array.

Text File (invent.dat):

Create the inventory file from the data given below. Enter the data in the order shown.

Description	Quantity on Hand	Unit Cost	Selling Price
Screwdrivers	36	2.27	4.98
Drills	10	7.83	15.95
Pliers	12	2.65	5.49
Saws	08	7.50	14.99
Hammers	24	4.75	9.49

Output (printer):

Print the following inventory profit report:

```
Author           INVENTORY PROFIT REPORT           Page 01
                       mm/dd/yy


    Description            Quantity        Item Profit

    X-----------X             99            999.99
         :                     :               :
         :                     :               :
    X-----------X             99            999.99


                       Total Profit:    9999.99
```

Processing Requirements:

- Read and load the file input into the arrays.
- Compute the item cost:
  quantity × unit cost
- Compute the item income:
  quantity × selling price
- Compute the item profit:
  item income – item cost
- Accumulate a report total for the item profit.

Project 11–8 Inventory-2

Modify the program in Project 11–7 to allow the user to update the inventory data stored in the arrays. Prompt for and enter the updates given below. Search for a match on item description or Enter 'Q' to quit. If a match is not found, print the message Item not found - press ENTER to continue.

Enter the inventory updates in the order shown.

Description	Quantity on Hand	Unit Cost	Selling Price
Screwdrivers	48	2.49	5.29
Hatchets	12	4.49	9.99
Pliers	24		
Saws		7.95	
Hammers			9.99

Project 11–9 Proficiency Test-1

Write a program to read data from a file, load the input into arrays, and print a report of the fourth-grade proficiency results for the Hartford County suburban school districts.

Input (text file):

For each school, read a record and load the data into the following arrays. Array types are shown in parentheses.

1. School district array (char)
2. 10×4 proficiency array (int)
   columns: citizenship, math, reading, and writing

Set the row size of each array to 10. Allow for a maximum of 25 characters of data for the elements in the *district* array.

Text File (results.dat):

Create the school file from the data given below. Enter the data in the order shown.

School District	Citizenship	Math	Reading	Writing
Adamsburg	94	85	89	90
Davidson	96	89	91	92
Claymore	93	78	92	91
Hamilton	85	81	86	83
Newland	90	84	88	80
Piketon	92	90	92	93
Reynolds	96	85	95	95
Southford	93	82	89	84
Stockdale	80	75	81	82
Winslow	91	80	90	92

Output (printer):

Print the following proficiency test report:

```
Author                H A R T F O R D   C O U N T Y        Page 01
                        SUBURBAN SCHOOL DISTRICTS


                   Fourth-Grade Proficiency Results
                             mm/dd/yy

School District  Citizenship  Math  Reading  Writing  Average

X-----------X        99        99      99       99       99
       :              :         :       :        :        :
       :              :         :       :        :        :
X-----------X        99        99      99       99       99
```

Processing Requirements:

- Read and load the file input into the arrays.
- Compute the proficiency average:
  (citizenship + math + reading + writing) / 4
- Print the detail line on the report.

Project 11–10 Proficiency Test-2

Modify the program in Project 11–9 to allow the user to update the data stored in the arrays. Prompt for and enter the updates given below. Search for a match on school district or Enter 'Q' to quit. If a match is not found, print the message District not found - press ENTER to continue.

Enter the updates in the order shown.

School District	Citizenship	Math	Reading	Writing
Davis	90	87	89	91
Claymore	95	83	90	90
Newland		80		84
Pike	87	92		
Southford	91	85	90	86
Stockdale		77	85	
Winslow			93	94

12 Sequential Files

Overview

Learning Objectives

After you have read this chapter and completed the exercises, you should be able to:

- explain the purpose and use of sequential files
- create a sequential file
- read and print the data stored in a sequential file
- append data to a sequential file

Files, Records, and Keys

As we have seen in previous chapters, data is organized into fields, records, and files to facilitate processing by the computer. A file is a collection of related records that pertain to a specific data processing application—accounts receivable, payroll, sales, inventory, and so on. A record is a collection of related data items or fields that contain information about a single unit in the file—a customer, an employee, a sales rep, an inventory item, and so on. A field is a collection of characters that describe a single unit of data—account number, name, address, ZIP code, telephone number, and so on.

A special field called a **record key** or **key field** is used to uniquely identify the records in the file. Examples of key fields are account number, social security number, salesperson number, part number, and so forth. A key field is used to access records and to arrange the records of a file in a specific order. Because the key field is used to store, retrieve, and access the records in the file, the record keys must be unique.

Sequential File Organization

Sequential file organization stores records on disk or tape in key field order. It offers the advantage of efficient use of storage, since the records are stored one after another. For applications that require access to all or most of the records in the file, sequential file organization provides fast and efficient processing and allows the programmer to tap into the real power of file processing—sequential file updating. Chapter 13 presents the fundamentals of updating sequential files.

However, sequential file access can be a time-consuming process for applications that require access to only a small number of records at any given time. It can be compared to selecting a song recorded on a cassette tape. The user must manually skip through the other songs until the correct one is found.

For example, in order to access record number 100, the program must first search through all of the records up to record 100. The program actually reads 99 records before it finds the one it is looking for. This, of course, can be a rather lengthy process for a file that contains thousands upon thousands of records.

Creating a Sequential File

Consider an application that requires a sequential file for the courses offered at the branch campus of Central State College. Once administration has decided what information is required for the course offering system, a file is created. Data is collected for each course offered at the branch campus and stored on disk for future reference.

Since each record in the file contains information about one course, we will need some way of organizing the file so that any record can be accessed and processed by the computer. We will use the call number as the key field to uniquely identify each record. Hence, the records in the course file will be stored sequentially in ascending (low to high) order according to the key field—the call number.

Creating a sequential file involves the following process:

1. Declare the file name and assign it to the output file stream.
2. Define the record format—the fields of the record.

3. Open the file.
4. Prompt for and enter the file data.
5. Write the data to the file.
6. Close the file.

This process is illustrated in sample program CHAP12A. The course file is created from the data entered at the keyboard.

Checkpoint 12A

1. Describe the organization of data, in order, from the smallest unit to the largest unit. Briefly discuss each.
2. Define a *record key* or *key field*.
3. Explain the concept of sequential file organization.
4. What are the advantages of sequential file organization?
5. List the six steps involved in creating a sequential file.

Sample Program CHAP12A

Sample program CHAP12A (Figure 12.3, p. 392) creates a sequential file for the courses offered at the branch campus of Central State College. The data is entered by the user in ascending key order. The data entry screen is shown in Figure 12.4 (p. 393). The specifications, logic design, and program listing follow.

Input (keyboard):

For each course, prompt for and enter the following data. Field size and types are shown in parentheses.

Call number	(3 int)
Department & number	(15 char)
Student enrollment	(2 int)

Output (course.fil):

The sequential file is shown in Figure 12.5 (p. 393).

Processing Requirements:

* Open the file for output.
* Prompt for and enter the data.
* Write the data to the file.
* Close the file.

Pseudocode:

```
START
Clear the screen
Open file
```

If file opened
    Prompt and enter the call number
    LOOP until call number = −1
        Prompt and enter the rest of the data
        Write the input to the file
        Prompt and enter the call number
    End LOOP
    Close file
END

Hierarchy Chart:　　See Figure 12.1.

Program Flowchart:　　See Figure 12.2.

Dissection of Sample Program CHAP12A

OUTPUT COURSE RECORD

```
ofstream outFile;
int   callNum;
char dept[15];
int   enroll;
```

The above statements mean: Declare the output file stream and the record fields *callNum*, *dept*, and *enroll*. The file identifier name *outFile* is assigned to the output file stream. Hence, *outFile* associates a name with the output file stream.

MAINLINE CONTROL

```
main()
{
    clrscr();
    OpenFile();
```

The preceding statements mean: Clear the screen and branch to open the course file. The *OpenFile* module attempts to open the course file for output.

```
        if (!outFile.fail())   {
            LoadFile();
```

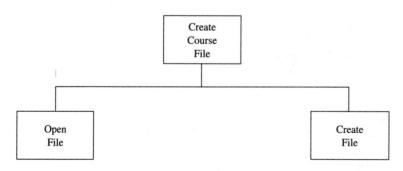

FIGURE 12.1　Hierarchy Chart for CHAP12A

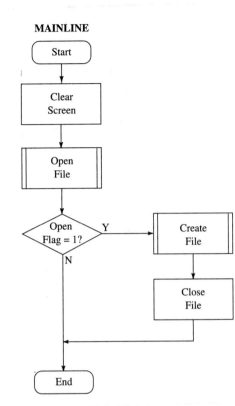

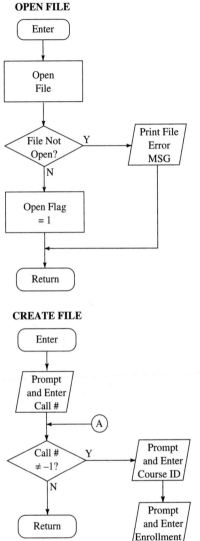

FIGURE 12.2 Program Flowchart for CHAP12A

```
//---------- CREATE COURSE FILE----------------------------
//  This program accepts data from the keyboard and creates
//  a sequential disk file for the courses offered at the
//  branch campus of Central State College.
//
//           PROGRAM-ID: CHAP12A
//           PROGRAMMER: David M. Collopy
//           RUN DATE:   mm/dd/yy
//**********************************************************

//---------- PREPROCESSING DIRECTIVES ----------------------

#include<iostream.h>
#include<fstream.h>
#include<conio.h>

//---------- FUNCTION PROTOTYPES ---------------------------

void OpenFile(void);            // open course file
void LoadFile(void);            // load course file data

//---------- PROGRAM SETUP ---------------------------------

//**  O U T P U T   C O U R S E   R E C O R D

ofstream outFile;          // file object name
int  callNum;              // call number
char dept[15];             // department & number
int  enroll;               // student enrollment

//---------------------------------------------------------
//                 MAINLINE CONTROL
//---------------------------------------------------------
main()
{
    clrscr();                  // clear the screen
    OpenFile();                // open course file
    if (!outFile.fail())  {
        LoadFile();            // load course file data
        outFile.close()        // close course file
    }
    return 0;
}
//---------------------------------------------------------
//                 OPEN COURSE FILE
//---------------------------------------------------------
void OpenFile(void)
{
```

FIGURE 12.3   Sample Program CHAP12A: Creates a Sequential Disk File from User Input

```
        outFile.open("a:course.fil");    // open course file
        if (outFile.fail())  {
            cout << "Course file open failed " << endl;
        }
        return;
    }
    //------------------------------------------------------------
    //              LOAD COURSE FILE DATA
    //------------------------------------------------------------
    void LoadFile(void)
    {
        cout << "\nEnter call number or '-1' to quit: ";
        cin >> callNum;
        cin.get();                       // clear keyboard buffer
        while (callNum != -1)  {
            cout << "            Enter department & number: ";
            cin.get(dept, 15);
            cout << "            Enter student enrollment: ";
            cin >> enroll;
            outFile << callNum << " " << dept << " "
                    << enroll << endl;
            cout << "\nEnter call number or '-1' to quit: ";
            cin >> callNum;
            cin.get();                   // clear keyboard buffer
        }
        return;
    }
```

FIGURE 12.3 *Continued*

```
Enter call number or '-1' to quit: 100
        Enter department & number: ACCT101
          Enter student enrollment: 24
Enter call number or '-1' to quit: 200
            :                :
            :                :
```

FIGURE 12.4   Data Entry Screen for CHAP12A

```
100 ACCT101 24
200 BIOL101 19
300 CHEM201 21
400 ENG200 16
500 HIST225 33
600 MGT330 29
```

FIGURE 12.5   Disk File Output for CHAP12A

```
            outFile.close();
        }
        return 0;
}
```

The preceding statements (starting on p. 390) mean: If the open was successful, then branch to the *LoadFile* module and perform the processing activities given there. After the course data is loaded, the file is closed.

OPEN COURSE FILE

```
void OpenFile(void)
{
    outFile.open("a:course.fil");
    if (outFile.fail())  {
        cout << "Course file open failed " << endl;
    }
    return;
}
```

The above statements mean: Open the course file. If the file is opened, the outFile.open() statement establishes an address for the file and associates it with the identifier name *outFile*. However, if the file is not opened, the error message is displayed on the screen.

LOAD COURSE FILE DATA

```
void LoadFile(void)
{
    cout << "\nEnter call number or '-1' to quit: ";
    cin >> callNum;
    cin.get();
    while (callNum != -1)  {
        cout << "              Enter department & number: ";
        cin.get(dept, 15);
        cout << "              Enter student enrollment: ";
        cin >> enroll;
        outFile << callNum << " " << dept << " "
                << enroll << endl;
        cout << "\nEnter call number or '-1' to quit: ";
        cin >> callNum;
        cin.get();
    }
    return;
}
```

The above statements mean: As long as the call number is not equal to −1, enter the course department/number and enrollment, and write the record to the file. Otherwise, control exits the module and returns to the *MAINLINE*.

Reading and Printing a Sequential File

The course file created in the previous section was stored on disk. Since the records were written directly to the disk, we have no way of knowing for sure what was actually placed there. We didn't see the output. Therefore, it would be wise to look at the file and verify the contents. Although some compilers allow the programmer to look at the data stored on disk, others may not. In any case, we can look at the data by simply writing a program to read the file and print the records.

Reading and printing a sequential file involves the following process:

1. Declare the file name and assign it to the input file stream.
2. Define the record fields.
3. Open the file.
4. Read the records from the file.
5. Display the records on the screen.
6. Close the file.

This process is illustrated in sample program CHAP12B. The program reads the course file and prints a copy of the records stored on disk.

Checkpoint 12B

1. List the steps necessary to read and print the contents of a sequential file.
2. Code the module to read and print the records in a file. The fields are Name (15 characters), Hourly Pay Rate (float), and Hours Worked (integer).

Sample Program CHAP12B

Sample program CHAP12B (Figure 12.8, p. 398) reads and prints the course file created in sample program CHAP12A. Each record is read from the disk and written to the output report. Figure 12.9 (p. 399) shows the output.

The following specifications apply:

Input (course.fil):

For each record, read the following data from the course file. Field size and type are shown in parentheses.

Call number	(3 int)
Department & number	(15 char)
Student enrollment	(2 int)

Output (screen):

The output report is shown in Figure 12.9.

Processing Requirements:
- Open the file for input.
- Read the course file.
- Write the records to the output report.
- Close the file.

Pseudocode:

```
START
Clear the screen
Open file
If file opened
   Print the heading line
   Read a record
   LOOP until no more data
      Print a record
      Read a record
   End LOOP
   Close file
END
```

Hierarchy Chart: See Figure 12.6.

Program Flowchart: See Figure 12.7.

Dissection of Sample Program CHAP12B

```
INPUT COURSE RECORD
ifstream inFile;
int  callNum;
char dept[15];
int  enroll;
```

The above statements mean: Declare the input file stream and the record format. The identifier *inFile* is assigned to the input file stream. The file name is mnemonic; it reminds us that data is input from the file.

```
READ AND PRINT COURSE DATA

void ReadFile(void)
{
    prnt << "\nCall#  Dept-Number#          Enrollment\n";
```

The above statement means: Print the report heading line.

```
    inFile >> callNum >> dept >> enroll:
    inFile.get();
```

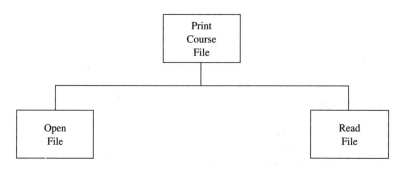

FIGURE 12.6   Hierarchy Chart for CHAP12B

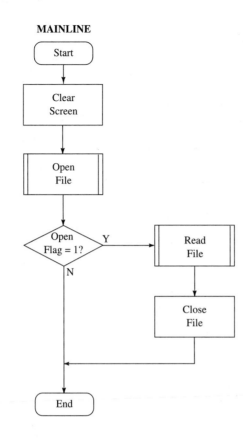

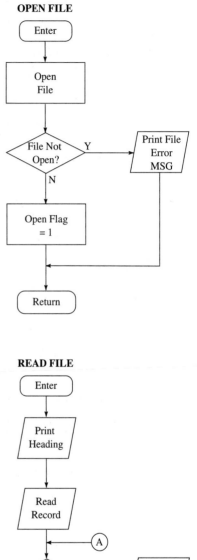

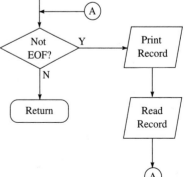

FIGURE 12.7   Program Flowchart for CHAP12B

```
//---------- PRINT COURSE FILE-----------------------------
//    This program reads and prints the contents of the
//    sequential course file.
//
//            PROGRAM-ID: CHAP12B
//            PROGRAMMER: David M. Collopy
//            RUN DATE:   mm/dd/yy
//**********************************************************

//---------- PREPROCESSING DIRECTIVES ----------------------

#include<iostream.h>
#include<fstream.h>
#include<iomanip.h>
#include<conio.h>

//---------- FUNCTION PROTOTYPES ---------------------------

void OpenFile(void);        // open course file
void ReadFile(void);        // read & print course data

//---------- PROGRAM SETUP ---------------------------------

//**  I N P U T   C O U R S E   R E C O R D

ifstream inFile;         // file object name
int  callNum;            // call number
char dept[15];           // department & number
int  enroll;             // student enrollment

//**  O P E N   P R I N T E R   F I L E

ofstream prnt("PRN");    // open printer file

//-----------------------------------------------------------
//              MAINLINE CONTROL
//-----------------------------------------------------------
main()
{
    clrscr();                   // clear the screen
    OpenFile();                 // open course file
    if (!inFile.fail()) {
        ReadFile();             // read & print course data
        inFile.close()          // close course file
    }
    return 0;
}
```

FIGURE 12.8 Sample Program CHAP12B: Reads a Sequential Disk File and Prints an Output Report

```
}
//------------------------------------------------------------
//              OPEN COURSE FILE
//------------------------------------------------------------
void OpenFile(void)
{
    inFile.open("a:course.fil");   // open course file
    if (inFile.fail())  {
        cout << "Course file open failed " << endl;
    }
    return;
}
//------------------------------------------------------------
//            READ AND PRINT COURSE DATA
//------------------------------------------------------------
void ReadFile(void)
{
    prnt << "\nCall#  Dept-Number#          Enrollment\n";
    inFile >> callNum >> dept >> enroll;
    inFile.get();                    // clear file buffer
    while (!inFile.eof())  {
        prnt << endl << setw(4) << callNum << "    "
             << setiosflags(ios::left)
             << setw(15) << dept
             << resetiosflags(ios::left)
             << setw(14) << enroll;
        inFile >> callNum >> dept >> enroll;
        inFile.get();                // clear file buffer
    }
    prnt << endl;                    // reset printer
    return;
}
```

FIGURE 12.8 *Continued*

```
Call#   Dept-Number#           Enrollment

100    ACCT101                 24
200    BIOL101                 19
300    CHEM201                 21
400    ENG200                  16
500    HIST225                 33
600    MGT330                  29
```

FIGURE 12.9 Screen Output for CHAP12B

The above statements mean: Read a record from the course file and assign the data to the variables in the order listed—*callNum, dept*, and *enroll*. The inFile.get() clears the newline character from the input file buffer.

```
while (!inFile.eof())) {
```

The above statement means: As long as the current position in the course file is not equal to the end-of-file marker, execute the statements in the body of the loop. Otherwise, skip the loop and return to the *MAINLINE*.

```
        prnt << endl << setw(4) << callNum << "    "
             << setiosflags(ios::left)
             << setw(15) << dept
             << resetiosflags(ios::left)
             << setw(14) << enroll;
        inFile >> callNum >> dept >> enroll;
        inFile.get();
    }
    prnt << endl;
    return;
}
```

The above statements mean: Format and print the call number, course department/number, and student enrollment. Control reads a record from the file, returns to the *while* statement, and tests for the end-of-file condition.

Appending Records to a Sequential File

We can add records to the course file created earlier by specifying *append* for the open statement. For example, the following statement opens the course file in *append* mode; app indicates append:

```
outFile.open("a:course.fil", ios::app);
```

This feature allows the program to add records to the end of a sequential file.

Appending records to a sequential file involves the following process:

1. Declare the file name and assign it to the output stream.
2. Define the record fields.
3. Open the file in *append* mode.
4. Prompt for and enter the file data.
5. Write the new data to the end of the file.
6. Close the file.

This process is illustrated in sample program CHAP12C.

Checkpoint 12C

1. How are records added to the end of a sequential file?
2. Code the statement to open the file called *test.dat* on the A drive in *append* mode.
3. List six steps that are performed when appending records to a sequential file.

Sample Program CHAP12C

Sample program CHAP12C (Figure 12.12, p. 403) appends records at the end of the course file. The output is shown in Figure 12.13 (p. 404).

The following specifications apply:

Input (keyboard):

For each new course, prompt for and enter the following data. Field size and type are shown in parentheses.

Call number	(3 int)
Department & number	(15 char)
Student enrollment	(2 int)

Output (course.fil):

The appended file is shown in Figure 12.13.

Processing Requirements:

- Open the file in *append* mode.
- Prompt for and enter the data.
- Write the new records to the file.
- Close the file.

Pseudocode:

```
START
Clear the screen
Open file
If file opened
   Prompt and enter the call number
   LOOP until call number = -1
      Prompt and enter the rest of the data
      Write the input to the file
      Prompt and enter the call number
   End LOOP
   Close file
END
```

Hierarchy Chart: See Figure 12.10.

Program Flowchart: See Figure 12.11.

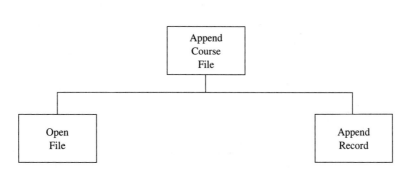

FIGURE 12.10   Hierarchy Chart for CHAP12C

MAINLINE

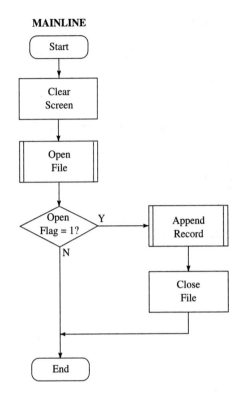

OPEN FILE

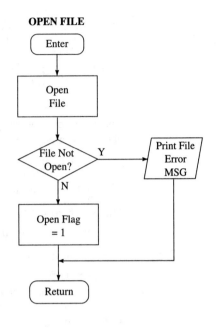

APPEND RECORD

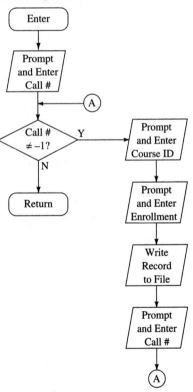

FIGURE 12.11   Program Flowchart for CHAP12C

```
//---------- APPEND COURSE FILE --------------------------
//     This program appends records at the end of the
//     sequential file.
//
//              PROGRAM-ID: CHAP12C
//              PROGRAMMER: David M. Collopy
//              RUN DATE:   mm/dd/yy
//********************************************************

//---------- PREPROCESSING DIRECTIVES ---------------------

#include<iostream.h>
#include<fstream.h>
#include<conio.h>

//---------- FUNCTION PROTOTYPES --------------------------

void OpenFile(void);          // open course file
void AppendRec(void);         // append records to file

//---------- PROGRAM SETUP --------------------------------

//** O U T P U T   C O U R S E   R E C O R D

ofstream outFile;        // file object name
int  callNum;            // call number
char dept[15];           // department & number
int  enroll;             // student enrollment
//--------------------------------------------------------
//              MAINLINE CONTROL
//--------------------------------------------------------
main()
{
    clrscr();                 // clear the screen
    OpenFile();               // open course file
    if (!outFile.fail())  {
        AppendRec();          // append records to file
        outFile.close()       // close course file
    }
    return 0;
}
```

(continued on next page)

FIGURE 12.12   Sample Program CHAP12C: Appends Records to the Course File

```
//------------------------------------------------------------
//               OPEN COURSE FILE
//------------------------------------------------------------
void OpenFile(void)
{
    outFile.open("a:course.fil", ios::app);    // open-append
    if (outFile.fail())  {
        cout << "Course file open failed " << endl;
    }
    return;
}
//------------------------------------------------------------
//               APPEND RECORDS TO FILE
//------------------------------------------------------------
void AppendRec(void)
{
    cout << "\nEnter call number or '-1' to quit: ";
    cin >> callNum;
    cin.get();                       // clear keyboard buffer
    while (callNum != -1)  {
        cout << "          Enter department & number: ";
        cin.get(dept, 15);
        cout << "          Enter student enrollment: ";
        cin >> enroll;
        outFile << callNum << " " << dept << " "
                << enroll << endl;
        cout << "\nEnter call number or '-1' to quit: ";
        cin >> callNum;
        cin.get();                   // clear keyboard buffer
    }
    return;
}
```

FIGURE 12.12 *Continued*

```
100 ACCT101 24
200 BIOL101 19
300 CHEM201 21
400 ENG200 16
500 HIST225 33
600 MGT330 29
700 MATH120 14    ← new records
800 PHYS251 20      appended here
900 SPAN111 12
```

FIGURE 12.13 Disk File Output for CHAP12C

Dissection of Sample Program CHAP12C

Essentially, the program consists of a three-step process. First, the output file stream and the record fields are declared. Second, the open statement specifies *append* mode. Third, the program prompts the user to enter the additional courses and adds them to the end of the file.

The *Append* module is shown below.

```
APPEND RECORDS TO FILE

void AppendRec(void)
{
    cout << "\nEnter call number or '-1' to quit: ";
    cin >> callNum;
    cin.get();
    while (callNum != -1)  {
        cout << "            Enter department & number: ";
        cin.get(dept, 15);
        cout << "            Enter student enrollment: ";
        cin >> enroll;
        outFile << callNum << " " << dept << " "
                << enroll << endl;
        cout << "\nEnter call number or '-1' to quit: ";
        cin >> callNum;
        cin.get();
    }
    return;
}
```

The above statements mean: As long as the call number is not equal to –1, enter the course data, and write the record to the file. Otherwise, control exits the module and returns to the *MAINLINE.*

Summary

1. Data represents facts that are used to describe a data processing application; data is organized into fields, records, and files.

2. A file is a collection of related records that pertain to a specific data processing application. A record is a collection of related data items or fields that contain information about a single unit in the file. A field is a collection of characters that describe a single unit of data.

3. A key field is used to uniquely identify the records in a file. It is used to access or arrange the records in ascending or descending order.

4. In sequential file organization, the records are stored on disk or tape in key field order.

5. Sequential file organization offers the advantage of efficient use of storage; the records are stored one after another in a specific order.

6. Sequential file organization provides fast and efficient processing for applications that require access to all or most of the records in the file. However, this method can be time consuming for applications that require access to only a small number of records at any given time.

7. Creating a sequential file involves the following six-step process: (1) declare the file name and the output stream, (2) define the record format, (3) open the file, (4) enter the file data, (5) write the data to the file, and (6) close the file.

8. The contents of a sequential file can be verified by reading the file and copying the records to a report.

9. Records may be added to a sequential file by specifying the *append* mode in the open statement. *Append* attaches the new records to the end of the file.

Programming Projects

For each project, design the logic and write the modular structured program to produce the output. Model your program after the sample programs presented in the chapter. Verify your output.

Project 12–1   Overdue Accounts

Write a program to prompt for the input and create a sequential file for the overdue accounts. Then read the file and print a report of the customers with account balances 90 days overdue.

Part I: Create the sequential file.

Input (keyboard):

For each customer record, prompt for and enter the following data. Field size and type are shown in parentheses.

1. Account number   (4 int)
2. Customer name   (15 char)
3. Days overdue   (2 int)
4. Balance due   (6.2 float)

File Data:

Use the data given below to create the overdue accounts file. The numbers shown above the columns correspond to the fields described for the input.

1	2	3	4
1010	David Ryan	90	400.00
2450	Marie Hill	30	754.00
2730	Rita Fox	90	740.00
3100	Alvin Porter	90	550.00
4080	Corey Adkins	30	233.00
4890	Amy Wyatt	30	700.00
5260	Brian Knox	30	625.00
6350	Susan Cope	90	600.00
7720	Lisa Wilson	60	417.00
8540	Matt Hart	90	900.00
9200	Tori Landis	90	235.00
9630	Pat Rankin	60	342.00

Output (overdue.fil):

Sequential disk file

Processing Requirements:

- Open the file for output.
- Prompt for and enter the data.
- Write the data to the file.
- Close the file.

Part II: Read the file, process the data, and print the report.

Input (overdue.fil):

Sequential disk file

Output (printer):

Print the following 90-day overdue accounts report:

```
Author              90-DAY OVERDUE ACCOUNTS          Page 01
                          mm/dd/yy

    Acct Number         Customer Name          Amount Due

       9999          X-----------X              999.99
        :                 :                       :
        :                 :                       :
       9999          X-----------X              999.99

                             Total:            9999.99
```

Processing Requirements:

- Open the file for input.
- Read the overdue accounts.
- Print a report of all accounts that are 90 days overdue.
- Accumulate a total for the amount due and print it at the end of the report.
- Close the file.

Project 12-2 Payroll

Write a program to prompt for the input data and create a sequential file for the payroll department. Then read the file, calculate pay, and print the weekly payroll roster. Hours worked over 40 are paid overtime. Assume the current federal income tax (FIT) rate is 15%.

Part I: Create the sequential file.

Input (keyboard):

For each payroll record, prompt for and enter the following data. Field size and type are shown in parentheses.

1. Employee number   (4 int)
2. Employee name   (15 char)

3. Hours worked   (2 int)
4. Hourly pay rate   (5.2 float)

File Data:

Use the data given below to create the payroll file. The numbers shown above the columns correspond to the fields described for the input.

1	2	3	4
1000	Tanya Bauer	40	7.50
1200	Dana Clark	45	14.90
1400	Sara Erickson	38	12.00
2000	Scott Howard	42	9.75
3000	Paul Irwin	48	8.72
3100	Dale Miller	40	10.25
3500	Bret Rossi	35	8.00
4000	Karen Thomas	48	9.00
4200	Tracy York	36	11.00

Output (payroll.fil):

Sequential disk file

Processing Requirements:

- Open the file for output.
- Prompt for and enter the data.
- Write the data to the file.
- Close the file.

Part II: Read the file, process the data, and print the report.

Input (payroll.fil):

Sequential disk file

Output (printer):

Print the following weekly payroll report:

```
Author                  WEEKLY PAYROLL REPORT             Page 01
                             mm/dd/yy


Employee             Hours   Hourly    Gross
Number   Employee    Worked  Pay Rate   Pay       FIT      Net Pay

9999     X--------X    99    99.99    9999.99    99.99     999.99
            :          :       :         :         :         :
            :          :       :         :         :         :
9999     X--------X    99    99.99    9999.99    99.99     999.99

                          Totals:    99999.99   999.99    9999.99
```

Processing Requirements:

- Open the file for input.
- Read the payroll records.
- Compute the regular pay:
  If hours > 40,
    then regular pay = *40 × pay rate*
    else regular pay = *hours × pay rate*
- Compute the overtime pay:
  If hours > 40,
    then overtime pay = *(hours – 40) × 1.5 × pay rate*
    else overtime pay = 0
- Compute the gross pay:
  regular pay + overtime pay
- Compute the federal income tax:
  gross pay × FIT rate
- Compute the net pay:
  gross pay – FIT
- Accumulate totals for gross pay, FIT, and net pay;
  print them at the end of the report.
- Close the file.

Project 12–3 Sales Profit

Write a program to prompt for the input and create a sequential file for the sales department. Then read the file, calculate profit per salesperson, and print a sales profit report.

Part I: Create the sequential file.

Input (keyboard):

For each sales record, prompt for and enter the following data. Field size and type are shown in parentheses.

1. Salesperson number   (3 int)

2. Salesperson name   (15 char)

3. Total sales   (8.2 float)

4. Cost of sales   (8.2 float)

File Data:

Use the data given below to create the sales file. The numbers shown above the columns correspond to the fields described for the input.

1	2	3	4
100	Lisa Conrad	8120.52	6450.71
300	Roy Hickle	2245.78	1072.49
400	Tara Perkins	12710.14	9735.38
700	Dennis Tian	4567.51	3119.22
900	Ann Zimmerman	5793.59	4204.45

Output (sales.fil):

Sequential disk file

Processing Requirements:

- Open the file for output.
- Prompt for and enter the data.
- Write the data to the file.
- Close the file.

Part II: Read the file, process the data, and print the report.

Input (sales.fil):

Sequential disk file

Output (printer):

Print the following sales profit report:

```
Author                  SALES PROFIT REPORT              Page 01
                             mm/dd/yy

                        Total           Cost of         Net
Num    Salesperson      Sales           Sales           Profit
----------------------------------------------------------------
999    X---------X      99999.99        99999.99        99999.99
  :        :               :               :               :
  :        :               :               :               :
999    X---------X      99999.99        99999.99        99999.99

                                        Total:          999999.99
```

Processing Requirements:

- Open the file for input.
- Read the sales records.
- Compute the net profit:
  total sales – cost of sales
- Accumulate a total for the net profit and print it at the end of the report.
- Close the file.

Project 12–4 Inventory

Write a program to prompt for the input and create a sequential file for the inventory department. Then read the file and print an inventory reorder report.

Part I: Create the sequential file.

Input (keyboard):

For each inventory record, prompt for and enter the following data. Field size and type are shown in parentheses.

1. Item number   (4 int)

2. Item description   (15 char)

3. Quantity on hand   (2 int)

4. Reorder point   (2 int)
5. Reorder quantity   (2 int)
6. Unit cost   (5.2 float)
7. Selling price   (5.2 float)

File Data:

Use the data given below to create the inventory file. The numbers shown above the columns correspond to the fields described for the input.

1	2	3	4	5	6	7
1000	Hammers	24	12	24	4.75	9.49
2000	Saws	08	16	12	7.50	14.99
3000	Drills	10	12	18	7.83	15.95
4000	Screwdrivers	36	24	12	2.27	4.98
5000	Pliers	12	12	36	2.65	5.49

Output (invent.fil):

Sequential disk file

Processing Requirements:

- Open the file for output.
- Prompt for and enter the data.
- Write the data to the file.
- Close the file.

Part II: Read the file, process the data, and print the report.

Input (invent.fil):

Sequential disk file

Output (printer):

Print the following inventory reorder report:

```
    Author              INVENTORY REORDER REPORT          Page 01
                            mm/dd/yy


    Item                          Quantity   Reorder    Item
    Number    Description         on Hand    Quantity   Cost

    9999      X-----------X          99         99       999.99
      :           :                  :          :          :
      :           :                  :          :          :
    9999      X-----------X          99         99       999.99

                                   Total Cost:          9999.99
```

Processing Requirements:

- Open the file for input.
- Read the inventory records.
- Determine what items to reorder:
  Order reorder quantity of an item when the quantity on hand is less than or equal to the reorder point.

- Compute the item cost:

  reorder quantity × *unit cost*
- Accumulate the total cost and print it at the end of the report.
- Close the file.

Project 12–5 Personnel

Write a program to prompt for the input and create a sequential file for the personnel department. Then read the file and print a salary report of all female employees who earn more than $30,000 a year.

Part I: Create the sequential file.

Input (keyboard):

For each employee record, prompt for and enter the following data. Field size and type are shown in parentheses.

1. Employee number   (4 int)

2. Employee name   (15 char)

3. Department number   (2 int)

4. Gender code   (1 char)

5. Annual salary   (8.2 float)

File Data:

Use the data given below to create the personnel file. The numbers shown above the columns correspond to the fields described for the record.

1	*2*	*3*	*4*	*5*
1900	Dana Andrews	10	F	29000.00
2070	Scott Cooper	14	M	30250.00
3150	Todd Feldman	22	M	24175.00
3600	Amy Kwon	19	F	36025.00
4100	Derek Lowe	50	M	29120.00
4290	Lori Palmer	35	F	33400.00
5400	Bob Shields	47	M	27500.00
6500	Pam Wolfe	31	F	31773.00

Output (persnel.fil):

Sequential disk file

Processing Requirements:

- Open the file for output.
- Prompt for and enter the data.
- Write the data to the file.
- Close the file.

Part II: Read the file, process the data, and print the report.

Input (persnel.fil):

Sequential disk file

Output (printer):

Print the following personnel salary report:

```
Author              PERSONNEL  SALARY  REPORT          Page 01
                          mm/dd/yy


Employee                            Department      Annual
Number         Employee Name          Number        Salary

 9999         X------------X            99         99999.99
  :                :                    :              :
  :                :                    :              :
 9999         X------------X            99         99999.99

                                     Average:      99999.99
```

Processing Requirements:

- Open the file for input.
- Read the personnel records.
- Print a report of all female employees who earn over $30,000 a year.
- Accumulate a total for annual salary.
- Compute the average annual salary and print it at the end of the report:
  total annual salary / number of female employees
- Close the file.

Project 12–6 Accounts Payable

Write a program to prompt for the data and create a sequential file for the accounts payable. Then read the file, compute the amount due, and print an accounts payable report. Assume the following discount schedule applies to early payments:

Paid by (Days)	Discount
1–10	12%
11–20	10%
21–30	8%
31–45	5%

Part I: Create the sequential file.

Input (keyboard):

For each vendor record, prompt for and enter the following data. Field size and type are shown in parentheses.

1. Vendor number   (3 int)
2. Vendor name   (12 char)
3. Invoice number   (5 char)

4. Invoice amount   (7.2 float)

5. Days paid by   (2 int)

File Data:

Use the data given below to create the vendor file. The numbers shown above the columns correspond to the fields described for the input.

1	2	3	4	5
340	IntraTell	T9823	670.00	25
410	MarxComm	H9205	913.87	18
420	Metacraft	A1239	2309.12	10
500	Northland	X2781	3429.34	45
600	Reylock	F0176	4563.78	33
830	Universal	W0105	1200.00	21
950	Veston	D1776	5127.63	30

Output (vendor.fil):

Sequential disk file

Processing Requirements:

- Open the file for output.
- Prompt for and enter the data.
- Write the data to the file.
- Close the file.

Part II: Read the file, process the data, and print the report.

Input (vendor):

Sequential disk file

Output (printer):

Print the following accounts payable report:

```
Author                ACCOUNTS PAYABLE REPORT            Page 01
                            mm/dd/yy


Vendor                  Invoice   Invoice   Discount   Amount
Number   Vendor Name    Number    Amount    Amount     Due

 999     X---------X     XXXX     9999.99    999.99    9999.99
  :          :            :          :         :          :
  :          :            :          :         :          :
 999     X---------X     XXXX     9999.99    999.99    9999.99

              Totals:            99999.99   9999.99   99999.99
```

Processing Requirements:

- Open the file for input.
- Read the vendor records.
- Determine the discount rate based on early payment (see the discount schedule).
- Compute the discount amount:
  invoice amount × discount rate

- Compute the amount due:
  invoice amount – discount amount
- Accumulate totals for invoice amount, discount amount, and amount due.
  Print the totals at the end of the report.
- Close the file.

Project 12–7 Production Output

Write a program to prompt for the input and create a sequential file for the production output. Then read the file, compute bonus pay, and print a bonus pay report. Assume production workers are paid a bonus according to the number of units produced over the quota. Use the following bonus pay schedule:

Units over Quota	Pay Rate Each
1–10	0.60
11–25	0.65
26–45	0.70
46+	0.75

Part I: Create the sequential file.

Input (keyboard):

For each production record, prompt for and enter the following data. Field size and type are shown in parentheses.

1. Employee number   (3 int)
2. Employee name   (15 char)
3. Product number   (5 char)
4. Production quota   (3 int)
5. Units produced   (3 int)

File Data:

Use the data given below to create the production file. The numbers shown above the columns correspond to the fields described for the input.

1	2	3	4	5
110	Kay Archer	P9511	65	65
200	Alan Baum	A1234	48	97
300	Marie Fitch	C4510	60	75
370	Lee Hildebrand	R0934	50	62
430	David Mullins	E3371	75	75
460	Chad Nelson	L8912	40	63
540	Bill Quinn	S0951	48	56
600	Nicole Renner	H9733	50	59
810	Erica Tate	Z0182	65	63
930	Terry West	A3235	70	116

Output (prod.fil):

Sequential disk file

Processing Requirements:

- Open the file for output.
- Prompt for and enter the data.
- Write the data to the file.
- Close the file.

Part II: Read the file, process the data, and print the file.

Input (prod.fil):

Sequential disk file

Output (printer):

Print the following bonus pay report:

```
Author                    BONUS PAY REPORT                Page 01
                            mm/dd/yy


Employee                  Product       Units   Over
Number    Employee        Number  Quota  Made   Quota   Bonus Pay

999       X----------X    XXXXX    99    99     99      999.99
             :              :      :     :      :          :
             :              :      :     :      :          :
999       X----------X    XXXXX    99    99     99      999.99

                          Totals:  999   999    999     9999.99
```

Processing Requirements:

- Open the file for input.
- Read the production records.
- Compute the bonus pay based on units over quota (see the bonus pay schedule).
- Accumulate totals for quota, units produced, units over quota, and bonus pay. Print the totals at the end of the report.
- Close the file.

13 Updating Sequential Files

Overview

Learning Objectives

After you have read this chapter and completed the exercises, you should be able to:

- understand why data files are maintained
- explain the process of updating a sequential file

- create a transaction file and a master file
- use transaction codes to update the master file
- read a transaction file, check for input errors, and update the master file

Sequential File Maintenance

Most organizations require information about their customers, employees, products, services, creditors, and so forth. Data processing applications provide this information. Files are created and maintained to reflect the current business situation or financial conditions of the company.

In this book, we learned that data is organized into files to facilitate processing by the computer. In business, there are two major types of files: master files and transaction files. A **master file** contains permanent information about a particular application. A **transaction file** contains temporary information that is used to update the master file. Sequential file maintenance is the process of maintaining information stored in the master file. It consists of the following activities: creating the master and transaction files, updating the master file, and processing the data stored in the master file.

Creating a File

Consider the course scheduling master file *course.fil* for Central State College, created in sample program CHAP12A. This file contains information about the courses offered at the branch campus. As you may recall, the courses were written in the file in ascending key order by call number.

Updating a File

Even though the master file is a permanent repository of information, the data stored in the file must be updated to reflect day-to-day changes. File updating refers to the process of changing the master file to include new information.

Once the course master file for Central State College has been created, the records can be maintained to reflect the current course offerings at the branch campus. Periodically, new courses are added, old courses are deleted, and changes are made to existing courses. When a student registers for a course, the enrollment stored in the master file must be adjusted to reflect the change. Similarly, when a new course is offered, a new record must be added to the master file.

For large files that require updates to only a few records at a time, updating can be a rather lengthy process. However, transactions are normally batched (daily, weekly, monthly, etc.) before they are applied to the master file. This, of course, saves both time and resources. Student enrollments, as well as other course-related activities, are batched to form a transaction file that can be used to make changes to the master file.

Once the transactions are arranged (sorted) by call number, they are applied to the old master file to produce the new or updated master file. If errors are detected during the update, they are written to the course error log (Figure 13.1).

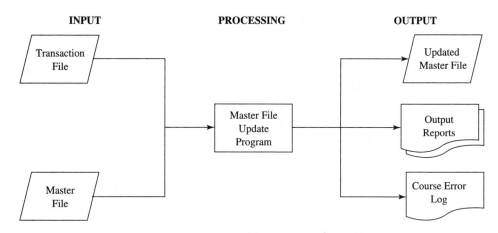

FIGURE 13.1   Sequential File Updating

Processing a File

When the master file is updated, various reports are produced by the program. Management uses information from the reports to monitor the operation and progress of the business. For example, the course update program could provide the following information about the course registration system:

- student enrollment per course
- closed courses
- income generated per course for a specific quarter
- transactions processed for the current week
- waiting lists for closed courses
- male and female enrollment figures

The administration could use this information to monitor the course registration system and to make decisions about opening and closing classes. For instance, the registrar could use the number of students on the waiting list to determine whether to open another session.

Checkpoint 13A

1. Identify two major types of files and briefly explain each.
2. Briefly explain sequential file maintenance.
3. Define file updating.
4. Draw a sketch to illustrate the sequential file update process.

Sample Program CHAP13A (Creating the Master File)

Sample program CHAP13A (Figure 13.4, p. 422) creates the course master file for Central State College; the logic is similar to that of sample program CHAP12A. The data is entered at the keyboard in ascending key order as shown in Figure 13.5 (p. 424).

The specifications, logic design, and program listing follow.

Input (keyboard):

For each course, prompt for and enter the following data. Field size and type are shown in parentheses.

Call number	(3 int)
Department & number	(15 char)
Student enrollment	(2 int)

Output (course.mst):

The master file output is shown in Figure 13.6 (p. 424).

Processing Requirements:

- Open the master file for output.
- Prompt for and enter the master file data.
- Write the input data to the master file.
- After creating the master file, write a trailer record to mark the end of the data stored in the file.

Pseudocode:

```
START
Clear the screen
Open file
If file opened
   Prompt and enter the call number
   LOOP until call number = –1
      Prompt and enter the rest of the data
      Write the input to the master file
      Prompt and enter the call number
   End LOOP
   Write the trailer record to the master file
   Close file
END
```

Hierarchy Chart: See Figure 13.2.

Program Flowchart: See Figure 13.3.

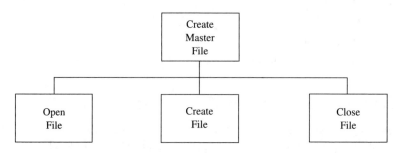

FIGURE 13.2   Hierarchy Chart for CHAP13A

MAINLINE

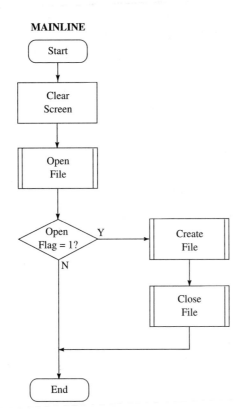

OPEN FILE

CLOSE FILE

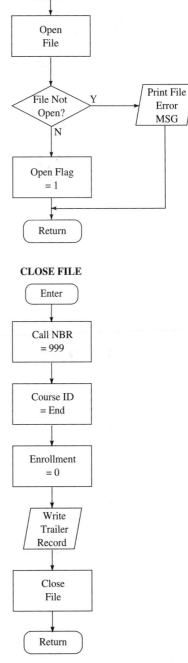

(continued on next page)

FIGURE 13.3   Program Flowchart for CHAP13A

CREATE FILE

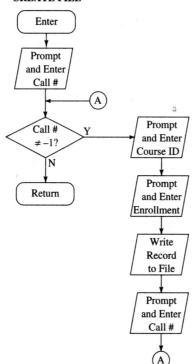

FIGURE 13.3 *Continued*

```
//---------- CREATE MASTER FILE---------------------------
//   This program accepts input from the keyboard and creates
//   the course master file.
//
//           PROGRAM-ID: CHAP13A
//           PROGRAMMER: David M. Collopy
//           RUN DATE:   mm/dd/yy
//***********************************************************

//---------- PREPROCESSING DIRECTIVES ---------------------
#include<iostream.h>
#include<fstream.h>
#include<conio.h>
#include<string.h>
//---------- FUNCTION PROTOTYPES ---------------------------

void OpenFile(void);              // open master file
void LoadFile(void);              // load master file
void CloseFile(void);             // close master file
```

FIGURE 13.4   Sample Program CHAP13A: Creates Course Master File from User Input

```
//---------- PROGRAM SETUP ---------------------------------

//** C O U R S E   M A S T E R   R E C O R D

ofstream outMF;          // file object name
int  callNum;            // call number
char dept[15];           // department & number
int  enroll;             // student enrollment


//-------------------------------------------------------------
//              MAINLINE CONTROL
//-------------------------------------------------------------
main()
{
    clrscr();                     // clear the screen
    OpenFile();                   // open master file
    if (!outMF.fail())  {
        LoadFile();               // load master file
        CloseFile()               // close master file
    }
    return 0;
}
//-------------------------------------------------------------
//              OPEN MASTER FILE
//-------------------------------------------------------------
void OpenFile(void)
{
    outMF.open("a:course.mst");    // open for output
    if (outMF.fail())  {
        cout << "Master file open failed " << endl;
    }
    return;
}
//-------------------------------------------------------------
//              LOAD MASTER FILE
//-------------------------------------------------------------
void LoadFile(void)
{
    cout << "\nEnter call number or '-1' to quit: ";
    cin >> callNum;
    cin.get();                    // clear keyboard buffer
    while (callNum != -1)  {
        cout << "          Enter department & number: ";
        cin.get(dept, 15);
        cout << "          Enter student enrollment: ";
        cin >> enroll;
        outMF << callNum << " " << dept << " "
              << enroll << endl;
        cout << "\nEnter call number or '-1' to quit: ";
```

(continued on next page)

FIGURE 13.4 *Continued*

```
        cin >> callNum;
        cin.get();                    // clear keyboard buffer
    }
    return;
}
//-----------------------------------------------------------
//                CLOSE MASTER FILE
//-----------------------------------------------------------
void CloseFile(void)
{
    callNum = 999;
    strcpy(dept, "END");
    enroll = 0;
    outMF << callNum << " " << dept << " " << enroll << endl;
    outMF.close();
    return;
}
```

FIGURE 13.4 *Continued*

```
Enter call number or '-1' to quit: 100
        Enter department & number: BIOL101
          Enter student enrollment: 24
Enter call number or '-1' to quit: 200
                :                 :
                :                 :
```

FIGURE 13.5 Master File Data Entry Screen for CHAP13A

```
100 ACCT101 24
200 BIOL101 19
300 CHEM201 21
400 ENG200 16
500 HIST225 33
600 MGT330 29
700 MATH120 14
800 PHYS251 20
900 SPAN111 12
999 END 0          ◄——— trailer record
```

FIGURE 13.6 Master File Output for CHAP13A

Dissection of Sample Program CHAP13A

First, the output file stream and the record fields are declared. The identifier name *outMF* indicates that data is written (output) to the master file.

Second, the *MAINLINE* clears the screen and branches to the module that opens the master file. If the file can be opened, the program creates the master file from the data entered at the keyboard. But if the file cannot be opened, the program prints an error message and stops the run.

Third, after the data is entered, the program attaches a trailer record to the end of the file. Later the update program uses the trailer record to control the update process.

CLOSE MASTER FILE

```
void CloseFile(void)
{
    callNum = 999;
    strcpy(dept, "END");
    enroll = 0;
```

The above statements mean: Add a trailer record to the end of the master file. The constants *999, END*, and *0*, are assigned to the variables *callNum, dept*, and *enroll*, respectively.

```
    outMF << callNum << " " << dept << " " << enroll << endl;
    outMF.close();
    return;
}
```

The above statements mean: Write the trailer record to the master file. Then close the file and return to the *MAINLINE*.

Sample Program CHAP13B (Creating the Transaction File)

Sample program CHAP13B (Figure 13.9, p. 428) creates a transaction file for the course registration system. Like the master file, the transaction records are written to the disk in ascending order by call number, as shown in Figure 13.10 (p. 430).

The specifications, logic design, and program listing follow.

Input (keyboard):

For each course, prompt for and enter the following data. Field size and type are shown in parentheses.

Call number	(3 int)
Department & number	(15 char)
Student enrollment	(2 int)

Output (course.trn):

The transaction file output is shown in Figure 13.11 (p. 430) .

Processing Requirements:

- Open the transaction file for output.
- Prompt for and enter the transaction data.
- Write the input data to the transaction file.
- After creating the file, write a trailer record at the end of the transaction file to indicate the end of the data.

Pseudocode:

```
START
Clear the screen
Open file
If file opened
   Prompt and enter the call number
   LOOP until call number = –1
      Prompt and enter the rest of the data
      Write the input to the transaction file
      Prompt and enter the call number
   End LOOP
   Write the trailer record to the transaction file
   Close file
END
```

Hierarchy Chart: See Figure 13.7.

Program Flowchart: See Figure 13.8.

Dissection of Sample Program CHAP13B

This program is similar to the one used to create the master file. The only difference is that one creates the transaction file and the other creates the master file.

Updating the Master File—Part I

Sample program CHAP13C does not really update the course master file. Since the update logic is somewhat complex, our goal here is only to construct the top-level control logic and to test it—to see if we can get it to work. We will, for now, ignore the details of how to actually apply the transaction updates to the master file.

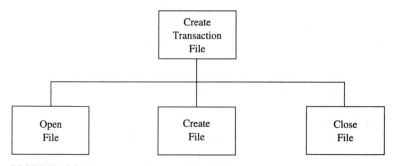

FIGURE 13.7   Hierarchy Chart for CHAP13B

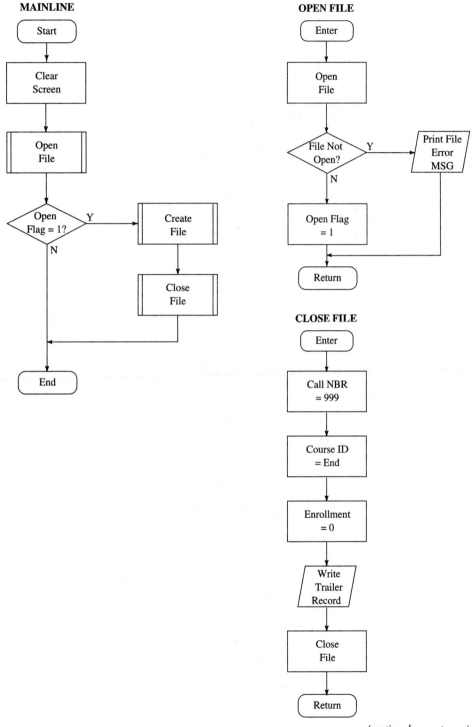

FIGURE 13.8 Program Flowchart for CHAP13B

(continued on next page)

CREATE FILE

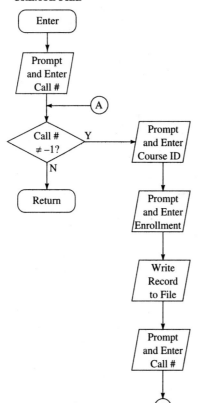

FIGURE 13.8 *Continued*

```
//---------- CREATE TRANSACTION FILE----------------------
//  This program accepts input from the keyboard and creates
//  the course transaction file.
//
//          PROGRAM-ID: CHAP13B
//          PROGRAMMER: David M. Collopy
//          RUN DATE:   mm/dd/yy
//***********************************************************

//---------- PREPROCESSING DIRECTIVES ---------------------
#include<iostream.h>
#include<fstream.h>
#include<conio.h>
#include<string.h>
```

FIGURE 13.9 Sample Program CHAP13B: Creates Course Transaction File from User Input

```
//----------- FUNCTION PROTOTYPES ---------------------------

void OpenFile(void);          // open transaction file
void LoadFile(void);          // load transaction file
void CloseFile(void);         // close transaction file

//----------- PROGRAM SETUP --------------------------------

//**  C O U R S E   T R A N S A C T I O N   R E C O R D

ofstream outTF;          // file object name
int  callNum;            // call number
char dept[15];           // department & number
int  enroll;             // student enrollment

//----------------------------------------------------------
//               MAINLINE CONTROL
//----------------------------------------------------------
main()
{
    clrscr();                    // clear the screen
    OpenFile();                  // open transaction file
    if (!outTF.fail())  {
        LoadFile();              // load transaction file
        CloseFile()              // close transaction file
    }
    return 0;
}
//----------------------------------------------------------
//               OPEN TRANSACTION FILE
//----------------------------------------------------------
void OpenFile(void)
{
    outTF.open("a:course.trn");   // open for output
    if (outTF.fail())  {
        cout << "Transaction file open failed " << endl;
    }
    return;
}
//----------------------------------------------------------
//               LOAD TRANSACTION FILE
//----------------------------------------------------------
void LoadFile(void)
{
    cout << "\nEnter call number or '-1' to quit: ";
    cin >> callNum;
    cin.get();                    // clear keyboard buffer
    while (callNum != -1)  {
        cout << "               Enter department & number: ";
```

(continued on next page)

FIGURE 13.9 *Continued*

```
            cin.get(dept, 15);
            cout << "                Enter student enrollment: ";
            cin >> enroll;
            outTF << callNum << " " << dept << " "
                  << enroll << endl;
            cout << "\nEnter call number or '-1' to quit: ";
            cin >> callNum;
            cin.get();                  // clear keyboard buffer
        }
    return;
}
//-----------------------------------------------------------
//              CLOSE TRANSACTION FILE
//-----------------------------------------------------------
void CloseFile(void)
{
    callNum = 999;
    strcpy(dept, "END");
    enroll = 0;
    outTF << callNum << " " << dept << " " << enroll << endl;
    outTF.close();
    return;
}
```

FIGURE 13.9   *Continued*

```
Enter call number or '-1' to quit: 400
        Enter department & number: ENG200
           Enter student enrollment: 18
Enter call number or '-1' to quit: 500
            :              :
            :              :
```

FIGURE 13.10   Transaction File Data Entry Screen for CHAP13B

```
400  ENG200  18
500  HIST225  37
500  HIST225  42
700  MATH120  20
800  PHYS251  17
850  PSY101  35
999  END  0          ◄─── trailer record
```

FIGURE 13.11   Transaction File Output for CHAP13B

The major processing logic performed by sample program CHAP13C is as follows: compare the transaction keys to the master keys and, based on the results of the comparison, print one of the three messages shown in Table 13.1. In other words, we are printing messages that correspond to the updates, rather than actually performing the updates. It may be helpful to refer to the input files and screen output for sample program CHAP13C (Figures 13.15 and 13.16, p. 439) as we discuss the update messages.

According to Table 13.1, we want the program to print UPDATE MASTER when the keys are equal. This message implies that the data stored in the current transaction is applied to the current master record. The update logic should allow multiple transactions for any given master record as long as the transactions are grouped together.

We want the program to print ADD NEW MASTER when the transaction key is less than the master record key. This message implies that the data stored in the transaction should be used to create a new master record; that is, the transaction data is written to a new record in the master file.

We want the program to print WRITE MASTER when the transaction key is greater than the master record key. This message implies that there is no new data for that record in the transaction file, so either the old master record or the updated master record is written to the new master file.

In the above cases, we are assuming that the records of both files are arranged in ascending order by call number.

Checkpoint 13B

1. What is the major processing logic performed by the sample program in CHAP13C?
2. If the transaction key is equal to the master key, which message would print?
   a. UPDATE MASTER
   b. ADD NEW MASTER
   c. WRITE MASTER
3. If the transaction key is greater than the master key, which message would print?
   a. UPDATE MASTER
   b. ADD NEW MASTER
   c. WRITE MASTER
4. If the transaction key is less than the master key, which message would print?
   a. UPDATE MASTER
   b. ADD NEW MASTER
   c. WRITE MASTER
5. What happens when a new master record is created?
6. What is implied by the UPDATE MASTER message?

TABLE 13.1   Update Messages

Compare Keys	Update Messages
Tkey = Mkey	UPDATE MASTER
Tkey < Mkey	ADD NEW MASTER
Tkey > Mkey	WRITE MASTER

Sample Program CHAP13C

Sample program CHAP13C (Figure 13.14, p. 436) displays update messages on the screen. The record keys are compared to determine which message to print. The input files are shown in Figure 13.15 and the output is shown in Figure 13.16.

The following specifications apply:

Input (disk files):

Transaction file	(*course.trn*)
Master file	(*course.mst*)

Output (screen):

The output is shown in Figure 13.16.

Processing Requirements:

- Open the transaction file and master file for input.
- Read a transaction and a master record.
- Compare the keys to determine the processing and print the message corresponding to the update.
- Close the files.

Pseudocode:

```
START
Clear the screen
Open files
If files opened
   (Read Transaction Record)
   (Read Master Record)
   LOOP until both files out of data
      If Tkey = Mkey
         Print UPDATE MASTER
         (Read Transaction Record)
      else if Tkey < Mkey
         Print ADD NEW MASTER
         (Read Transaction Record)
      else
         Print WRITE MASTER
         (Read Master Record)
   End LOOP
   Close files
END

ENTER (Read Transaction Record)
If not end of file
   Read transaction record
RETURN
```

ENTER (Read Master Record)
If not end of file
   Read master record
RETURN

Hierarchy Chart: See Figure 13.12.

Program Flowchart: See Figure 13.13.

Dissection of Sample Program CHAP13C

After clearing the screen and opening the files, the *MAINLINE* reads the first transaction and the first master record. As long as the transaction key and the master key are not equal to 999 (the end-of-file indicator), the program branches to the update module.

    Note that if one or both files cannot be opened, the program stops the run.

UPDATE PROCESSING

```
void UpdProcess(void)
{
    if (Tkey == Mkey)   {
        cout << endl << UpdMsg << Tkey;
        ReadTran();
    }
```

The above statements mean: If the transaction and master keys are equal, print the UPDATE MASTER message and the transaction key and read the next transaction. Otherwise, skip to the next statement.

```
    else if (Tkey < Mkey)   {
        cout << endl << AddMsg << Tkey;
        ReadTran();
    }
```

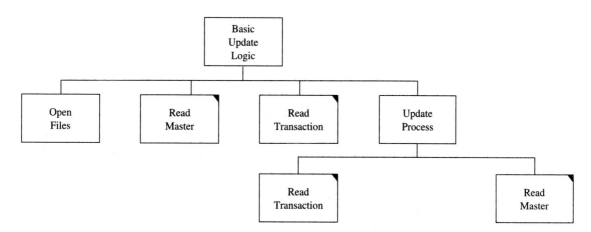

FIGURE 13.12 Hierarchy Chart for CHAP13C

MAINLINE

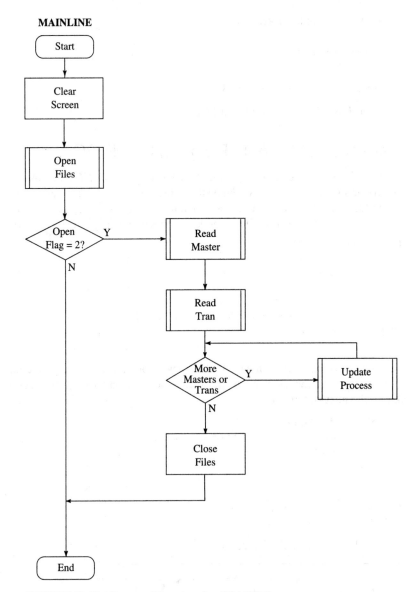

FIGURE 13.13   Program Flowchart for CHAP13C

The preceding statements mean: If the transaction key is less than the master key, print the
ADD NEW MASTER message and the transaction key and read the next transaction. Otherwise, skip to the next statement.

```
    else {
        cout << endl << WrtMsg << Mkey;
        ReadMast();
    }
    return;
}
```

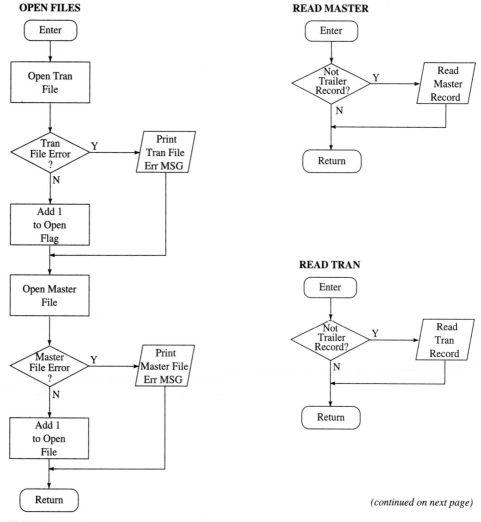

FIGURE 13.13 *Continued*

(continued on next page)

If control reaches this point in the program, then a match was not found for the other two conditions. Then by default, the transaction key is greater than the master key. Hence, the program prints the WRITE MASTER message and the master key and reads the next master record.

The return statement sends control back to the *MAINLINE.*

Updating the Master File—Part II

Now that we have developed and tested the top-level control logic, we are ready to update the master file. Once again, to avoid becoming entangled in unnecessary details, we will focus only on the update logic and, for the time being, assume that there are no errors in either the transaction file or the master file.

UPDATE PROCESS

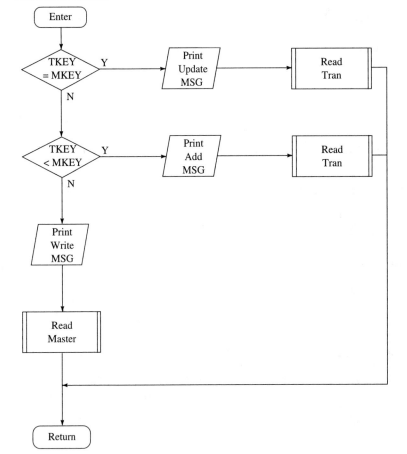

FIGURE 13.13   *Continued*

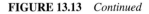

```
//---------- BASIC UPDATE LOGIC ----------------------------
//    This program illustrates the basic update logic. It
//    reads the transaction and master files and prints
//    update messages.
//
//            PROGRAM-ID: CHAP13C
//            PROGRAMMER: David M. Collopy
//            RUN DATE:   mm/dd/yy
//*************************************************************

//---------- PREPROCESSING DIRECTIVES ----------------------
#include<iostream.h>
```

FIGURE 13.14   Sample Program CHAP13C: Performs the Basic Update Logic and Prints Update Messages

```
#include<fstream.h>
#include<conio.h>
//---------- FUNCTION PROTOTYPES --------------------------

void OpenFiles(void);          // open files
void ReadTran(void);           // read transaction record
void ReadMast(void);           // read master record
void UpdProcess(void);         // update processing

//---------- PROGRAM SETUP --------------------------------

//**  T R A N S A C T I O N   R E C O R D

ifstream inTF;          // tran file object name
int  Tkey;              // tran key: call number
char Tdept[15];         // department & number
int  Tenroll;           // student enrollment

//**  M A S T E R   R E C O R D

ifstream inMF;          // mast file object name
int  Mkey;              // mast key: call number
char Mdept[15];         // department & number
int  Menroll;           // student enrollment

//**  P R O G R A M   V A R I A B L E S

char UpdMsg[] = " Update Master: Tran key = ";
char AddMsg[] = "Add New Master: Tran key = ";
char WrtMsg[] = "  Write Master: Mast key = ";

//--------------------------------------------------------
//              MAINLINE CONTROL
//--------------------------------------------------------
main()
{
    clrscr();                       // clear the screen
    OpenFiles();                    // open files
    if (!inTF.fail() && !inMF.fail()) {
        ReadMast();                 // read master record
        ReadTran()                  // read trans record
        while ((Tkey != 999) || (Mkey != 999))
            UpdProcess();
        inTF.close()                // close trans file
        inMF.close()                // close master file
    }
    return 0;
}
//--------------------------------------------------------
//              OPEN FILES
//--------------------------------------------------------
```

(continued on next page)

FIGURE 13.14 *Continued*

```
void OpenFiles(void)
{
    inTF.open("a:course.trn");         // open trans for input
    if (inTF.fail())  {
        cout << "Transaction file open failed " << endl;
    }
    inMF.open("a:course.mst");         // open mast for input
    if (inMF.fail())  {
        cout << "Master file open failed " << endl;
    }
    return;
}
//------------------------------------------------------------
//              READ TRANSACTION RECORD
//------------------------------------------------------------
void ReadTran(void)
{
    if (Tkey != 999)
        inTF >> Tkey >> Tdept >> Tenroll;
    return;
}
//------------------------------------------------------------
//              READ MASTER RECORD
//------------------------------------------------------------
void ReadMast(void)
{
    if (Mkey != 999)
        inMF >> Mkey >> Mdept >> Menroll;
    return;
}
//------------------------------------------------------------
//              UPDATE PROCESSING
//------------------------------------------------------------
void UpdProcess(void)
{
    if (Tkey == Mkey)  {
        cout << endl << UpdMsg << Tkey;
        ReadTran();
    }
    else if (Tkey < Mkey)  {
        cout << endl << AddMsg << Tkey;
        ReadTran();
    }
    else  {
        cout << endl << WrtMsg << Mkey;
        ReadMast();
    }
    return;
}
```

FIGURE 13.14 *Continued*

```
    Transaction File              Master File

       400  ENG200  18           100  ACCT101  24
       500  HIST225  37          200  BIOL101  19
       500  HIST225  42          300  CHEM201  21
       700  MATH120  20          400  ENG200  16
       800  PHYS251  17          500  HIST225  33
       850  PSY101  35           600  MGT330   29
       999  END  0               700  MATH120  14
                                 800  PHYS251  20
                                 900  SPAN111  12
                                 999  END  0
```

FIGURE 13.15   Input Files for CHAP13C

```
    Write Master: Mast key = 100
    Write Master: Mast key = 200
    Write Master: Mast key = 300
   Update Master: Tran key = 400
    Write Master: Mast key = 400
   Update Master: Tran key = 500
   Update Master: Tran key = 500
    Write Master: Mast key = 500
    Write Master: Mast key = 600
   Update Master: Tran key = 700
    Write Master: Mast key = 700
   Update Master: Tran key = 800
    Write Master: Mast key = 800
  Add New Master: Tran key = 850
    Write Master: Mast key = 900
```

FIGURE 13.16   Screen Output for CHAP13C

Let's pause briefly to discuss what to do if the program results in an abnormal end (abend). An **abend** occurs when certain logic errors prevent the program from running to completion. Usually this means that some of the transactions were applied (correctly or incorrectly) to the master file. Once the errors are found and corrected, restart the program. Don't assume that part of the update is correct and that you can continue where the program ended during the last run. It is much safer to correct the errors and rerun the update from the start.

For the next two programs, we will consider six types of updates that will require the use of a special code called a **transaction code** to tell the update logic how to apply the transaction to the master file. These codes are defined as follows:

1. *Add students:* When students register for a course, they must be added to the master record. The transaction enrollment is added to the master record enrollment.

2. *Drop students:* When students drop a course, they must be removed from the master record. The transaction enrollment is subtracted from the master record enrollment.

3. *Change enrollment:* When the student count does not agree with the enrollment shown in the master record, it must be adjusted to reflect the actual count. Hence, the transaction enrollment replaces the enrollment stored in the master record.

4. *Change department:* When the course department or number is incorrect, it must be corrected. The department data coded in the transaction replaces the department data stored in the master record.

5. *Add master record:* When new courses are added to the class schedule, they must be added to the master file. New courses are coded as transactions and are inserted into the master file in call number order.

6. *Delete master record:* When courses are deleted from the class schedule, they must be removed from the master file. Old master records are removed by copying only the active courses to the new master file.

Checkpoint 13C

1. What causes an abend?
2. (True or False) When an abend occurs, fix the errors and continue processing where the program ended.
3. What code is used to tell the update logic how to apply a transaction to the master file?

Sample Program CHAP13D

Sample program CHAP13D (Figure 13.19, p. 446) reads the transaction records and updates the master file. Errors are not considered. The input files are shown in Figure 13.20 (p. 449) and the new master file (output) is shown in Figure 13.21 (p. 449).

The following specifications apply:

Input (disk files):

Transaction file	(*course.trn*)
Old master file	(*course.mst*)

Output (new.mst):

The new master file is shown in Figure 13.21.

Processing Requirements:

- Open the transaction file and old master file for input.
- Open the new master file for output.
- Read a transaction and a master record.
- Compare keys and use the transaction code to update the master file.
- Close the files.

Pseudocode:

```
START
Clear screen
Open files
If files opened
   (Read Transaction Record)
   (Read Master Record)
   LOOP until both file out of data
      If Tkey = Mkey
         If transaction code = delete record
            (Read Master Record)
            (Read Transaction Record)
         else
            (Update Master Record)
      else
         If Tkey < Mkey
            Write transaction record to new master
            (Read Transaction Record)
         else
            Write old master record to new master file
            (Read Master Record)
   End LOOP
   Close files
END

ENTER: Update Master Record
If transaction code = 1
   Add transaction enrollment to master enrollment
If transaction code = 2
   Subtract transaction enrollment from master enrollment
If transaction code = 3
   Move transaction enrollment to master enrollment
else
   Move transaction course ID to master course ID
(Read Transaction Record)
RETURN
```

Hierarchy Chart: See Figure 13.17.

Program Flowchart: See Figure 13.18.

Dissection of Sample Program CHAP13D

Notice that several department fields in the transaction file are shown as dashes (Figure 3.20). This means that these department fields are empty. We could have used the null character to accomplish the same thing. It is, however, important to realize that a field cannot be left blank. Something must be coded in each field to satisfy the file input statement when it reads the transactions. Otherwise, the input will be incorrectly assigned to the transaction variables.

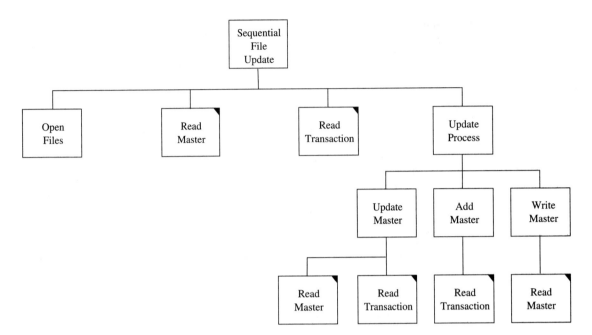

FIGURE 13.17 Hierarchy Chart for CHAP13D

After the first transaction and master records are read, the program proceeds to update the master file.

```
UPDATE PROCESSING

void UpdProcess(void)
{
    if (Tkey == Mkey)
        UpdMast();
```

The above statement means: If the keys are equal, branch to *UpdMast* and perform the processing activities given there. Otherwise, skip to the next statement.

```
    else if (Tkey < Mkey)
        AddMast();
```

The above statement means: If the transaction key is less than the master key, branch to *AddMast* and perform the processing activities given there. Otherwise, skip to the next statement.

```
    else
        WrtMast();
```

If control reaches this point in the program, then a match was not found for the other two conditions. Hence, the transaction key is greater than the master key, and the program branches to *WrtMast* to perform the processing given there.

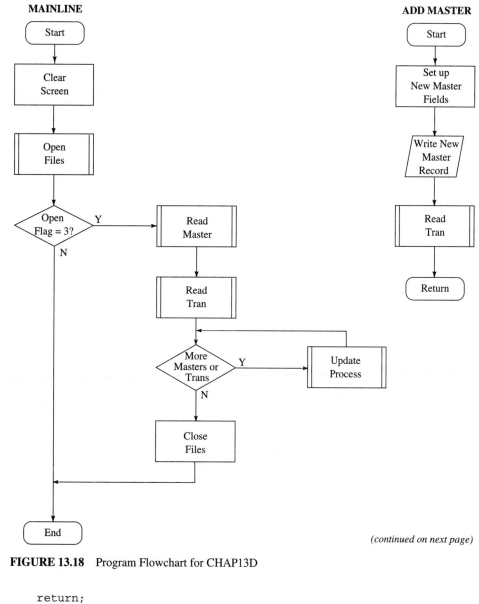

FIGURE 13.18   Program Flowchart for CHAP13D

(continued on next page)

```
    return;
}
```

The above statement means: Return to the *MAINLINE*.

```
UPDATE MASTER RECORD

void UpdMast(void)
{
    if (Tcode == 6)
        ReadMast();
```

OPEN FILE

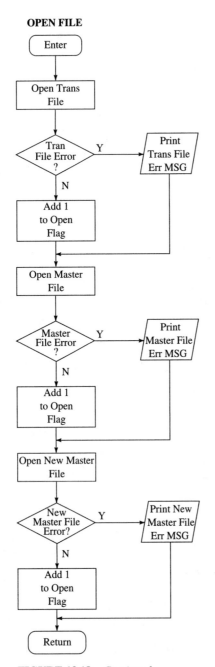

READ MASTER

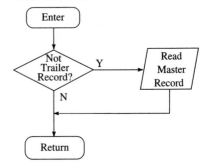

READ TRAN

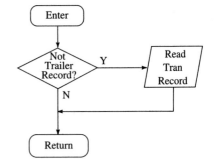

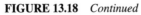

FIGURE 13.18   *Continued*

The preceding statement means: If the transaction code equals 6, then delete the current master record by reading the next master record. By reading the next master record, the current master record is not written to the new master file. Hence, the current master record is deleted.

UPDATE PROCESS

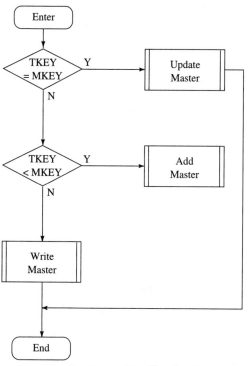

WRITE MASTER

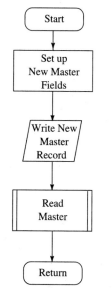

UPDATE MASTER

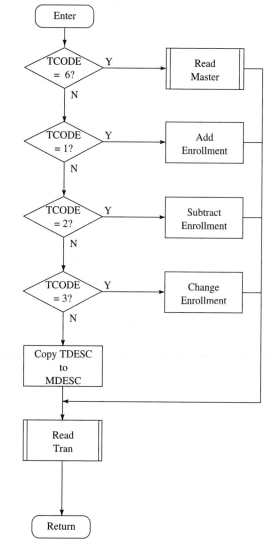

(continued on next page)

FIGURE 13.18 *Continued*

```
//---------- SEQUENTIAL FILE UPDATE ----------------------
//   This program uses transaction codes to update the master
//   file. Errors are not considered.
//
//            PROGRAM-ID: CHAP13D
//            PROGRAMMER: David M. Collopy
//            RUN DATE:   mm/dd/yy
//**************************************************************

//---------- PREPROCESSING DIRECTIVES ----------------------
#include<iostream.h>
#include<fstream.h>
#include<conio.h>
#include<string.h>
//---------- FUNCTION PROTOTYPES ---------------------------

void OpenFiles(void);          // open files
void ReadTran(void);           // read transaction record
void ReadMast(void);           // read master record
void UpdProcess(void);         // update processing
void UpdMast(void);            // update master record
void AddMast(void);            // add master record
void WrtMast(void);            // write master record

//---------- PROGRAM SETUP --------------------------------

//**  T R A N S A C T I O N   R E C O R D

ifstream inTF;                 // tran file object name
int  Tkey;                     // tran key: call number
char Tdept[15];                // department & number
int  Tenroll;                  // student enrollment
int  Tcode;                    // transaction code

//**  M A S T E R   R E C O R D

ifstream inMF;                 // mast file object name
int  Mkey;                     // mast key: call number
char Mdept[15];                // department & number
int  Menroll;                  // student enrollment

//**  N E W   M A S T E R   R E C O R D

ofstream outMF;                // new mast file object name
int  NMkey;                    // new mast key: call number
char NMdept[15];               // department & number
int  NMenroll;                 // student enrollment
```

FIGURE 13.19   Sample Program CHAP13D: Updates the Master File—No Errors

```
//------------------------------------------------------------
//              MAINLINE CONTROL
//------------------------------------------------------------
main()
{
    clrscr();                           // clear the screen
    OpenFiles();                        // open files
    if (!inTF.fail() && !inMF.fail() && !outMF.fail())  {
        ReadMast();                     // read master record
        ReadTran()                      // read trans record
        while ((Tkey != 999) || (Mkey != 999))
            UpdProcess();
        inTF.close()                    // close trans file
        inMF.close()                    // close master file
        outMF.close()                   // close new mast file
    }
    return 0;
}
//------------------------------------------------------------
//              OPEN FILES
//------------------------------------------------------------
void OpenFiles(void)
{
    intTF.open("a:course.trn");      // open for input
    if (inTF.fail())  {
        cout << "Transaction file open failed " << endl;
    }
    inMF.open("a:course.mst");       // open for input
    if (inMF.fail())  {
        cout << "Master file open failed " << endl;
    }
    outMF.open("a:course.mst");      // open for output
    if (outMF.fail())  {
        cout << "New master file open failed " << endl;
    }
    return;
}
//------------------------------------------------------------
//              READ TRANSACTION RECORD
//------------------------------------------------------------
void ReadTran(void)
{
    if (Tkey != 999)
        inTF >> Tkey >> Tdept >> Tenroll >> Tcode;
    return;
}
//------------------------------------------------------------
//              READ MASTER RECORD
//------------------------------------------------------------
```

(continued on next page)

FIGURE 13.19 *Continued*

```cpp
void ReadMast(void)
{
    if (Mkey != 999)
        inMF >> Mkey >> Mdept >> Menroll;
    return;
}
//-------------------------------------------------------------
//              UPDATE PROCESSING
//-------------------------------------------------------------
void UpdProcess(void)
{
    if (Tkey == Mkey)
        UpdMast();                  // update master record
    else if (Tkey < Mkey)
        AddMast();                  // add master record
    else
        WrtMast();                  // write master ecord
    return;
}
//-------------------------------------------------------------
//              UPDATE MASTER RECORD
//-------------------------------------------------------------
void UpdMast(void)
{
    if (Tcode == 6)                 // delete master
        ReadMast();
    else if (Tcode == 1)            // add students
        Menroll = Menroll + Tenroll;
    else if (Tcode == 2)            // drop students
        Menroll = Menroll - Tenroll;
    else if (Tcode == 3)            // change enrollment
        Menroll = Tenroll;
    else
        strcpy(Mdept, Tdept);       // change dept & number
    ReadTran();                     // read transaction
    return;
}
//-------------------------------------------------------------
//              ADD MASTER RECORD
//-------------------------------------------------------------
void AddMast(void)
{
    NMkey = Tkey;
    strcpy(NMdept, Tdept);
    NMenroll = Tenroll;
    outMF << NMkey << " " << NMdept << " " << NMenroll << endl;
    ReadTran();                     // read transaction
    return;
}
```

FIGURE 13.19 *Continued*

```
}
//--------------------------------------------------------------
//                  WRITE MASTER RECORD
//--------------------------------------------------------------
void WrtMast(void)
{
    NMkey = Mkey;
    strcpy(NMdept, Mdept);
    NMenroll = Menroll;
    outMF << NMkey << " " << NMdept << " " << NMenroll << endl;
    ReadMast();                        // read master
    return;
}
```

FIGURE 13.19 *Continued*

```
Transaction File                    Master File

300 ---        0    6           100 ACCT101 24
400 ---       24    1           200 BIOL101 19
500 ---        5    2           300 CHEM201 21
500 ---       23    3           400 ENG200  16
650 MKT310    15    5           500 HIST225 33
700 MATH114    0    4           600 MGT330  29
800 ---       55    3           700 MATH120 14
950 THAR101   17    5           800 PHYS251 20
999 END        0    0           900 SPAN111 12
                                999 END 0
```

FIGURE 13.20 Input Files for CHAP13D

```
Updated Master File

100 ACCT101 24
200 BIOL101 19
400 ENG200  40
500 HIST225 23
600 MGT330  29
650 MKT310  15
700 MATH114 14
800 PHYS251 55
900 SPAN111 12
950 THAR101 17
```

FIGURE 13.21 New Master File for CHAP13D

If the transaction code is not equal to 6, skip to the next statement.

```
else if (Tcode == 1)
    Menroll = Menroll + Tenroll;
```

The above statement means: If the transaction code equals 1, then add the transaction enrollment to the master enrollment and store the result in the current master record. Otherwise, skip to the next statement.

```
else if (Tcode == 2)
    Menroll = Menroll - Tenroll;
```

The above statement means: If the transaction code equals 2, then subtract the transaction enrollment from the master enrollment and store the result in the current master record. Otherwise, skip to the next statement.

```
else if (Tcode == 3)
    Menroll = Tenroll;
```

The above statement means: If the transaction code equals 3, then change the course enrollment. Copy the enrollment stored in the transaction to the master record. Otherwise, skip to the next statement.

```
else
    strcpy(Mdept, Tdept);
```

The above statement means: By default, the transaction code specifies a course department/number change. Therefore, copy the department/number stored in the transaction to the master record.

```
    ReadTran();
    return;
}
```

The above statements mean: Read the next transaction record and return to the *UPDATE PROCESSING* module.

```
ADD MASTER RECORD

void AddMast(void)
{
    NMkey = Tkey;
    strcpy(NMdept, Tdept);
    NMenroll = Tenroll;
    outMF << NMkey << " " << NMdept << " " << NMenroll << endl;
    ReadTran();
    return;
}
```

The above statements mean: Add a new record to the master file. Move the data stored in the transaction to the new master record and write the record to the new master file. Read the next transaction and return to the *UPDATE PROCESSING* module.

```
WRITE MASTER RECORD

void WrtMast(void)
{
    NMkey = Mkey;
    strcpy(NMdept, Mdept);
    NMenroll = Menroll;
    outMF << NMkey << " " << NMdept << " " << NMenroll << endl;
    ReadMast();
    return;
}
```

The above statements mean: Write the old master record to the new master file. The old master record may or may not have been updated previously. In any event, it is written to the new master file.

The return statement sends control back to the *UPDATE PROCESSING* module.

Updating the Master File—Part III

With sample program CHAP13D, we now have a working model of the update logic. Although errors were not considered, we are now ready to include them in the next program. When an error is detected by the update program, the transaction record is written to a special **error log** for future reference.

Sample program CHAP13E checks for three types of transaction errors: adding master records that already exist, processing unmatched transactions, and processing invalid transaction codes.

Adding Master Records That Already Exist: Any transaction that adds a record to the master file cannot be processed if the record is already in the master file. This error implies that the transaction key may have been coded incorrectly.

Processing Unmatched Transactions: Any transaction key that does not match a master record key (the keys are not equal) cannot be processed by the program. In other words, the transaction is attempting to update a master record that does not exist. This error implies that the transaction key may have been coded incorrectly.

Processing Invalid Transaction Codes   Any transaction record with a transaction code other than 1–6 is invalid. This error implies that the transaction code was coded incorrectly.

Checkpoint 13D

1. Code the *UPDATE PROCESSING* module for any sequential file update.

2. Identify three common types of transaction errors.

3. Briefly explain the purpose of an error log report.

Sample Program CHAP13E

Sample program CHAP13E (Figure 13.24, p. 457) reads the transaction file, checks for errors, and updates the master file. The input files are shown in Figure 13.25 (p. 461), the new master file (output) is shown in Figure 13.26 (p. 462), and the course error log is shown in Figure 13.27 (p. 462).

The following specifications apply:

Input (disk files):

  Transaction file
  Old master file

Output (new.mst):

The new master file is shown in Figure 13.26, and the course error log is shown in Figure 13.27.

Processing Requirements:

- Open the transaction file and old master file for input.
- Open the new master file for output.
- Read a transaction and a master record.
- Compare keys and use the transaction code to update the master file. (Check the transaction for errors.)
- Close the files.

Pseudocode:

```
START
Clear screen
Open files
If files opened
   (Read Transaction Record)
   (Read Master Record)
   LOOP until no more data (both files empty)
      If Tkey = Mkey
         If transaction code = delete record
            (Read Master Record)
            (Read Transaction Record)
         else
            If transaction code = add record
               Print error message MASTER EXISTS
               (Read Transaction Record)
            else
               (Update Master Record)
      else
         If Tkey < Mkey
            If transaction code = add record
               Write transaction record to new master file
               (Read Transaction Record)
            else
               Print error message UNMATCHED TRANSACTION
               (Read Transaction Record)
```

```
        else
            Write old master record to new master file
            (Read Master Record)
        End LOOP
        Close files
    END

    ENTER: Update Master Record
    If transaction code = 1
        Add transaction enrollment to master enrollment
    If transaction code = 2
        Subtract transaction enrollment from master enrollment
    If transaction code = 3
        Move transaction enrollment to master enrollment
    If transaction code = 4
        Move transaction course ID to master course ID
    else
        Print error message BAD TRANSACTION CODE
        (Read Transaction Record)
    RETURN
```

Hierarchy Chart: See Figure 13.22.

Program Flowchart: See Figure 13.23.

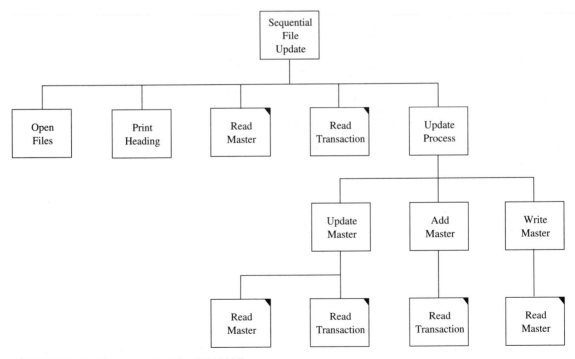

FIGURE 13.22 Hierarchy Chart for CHAP13E

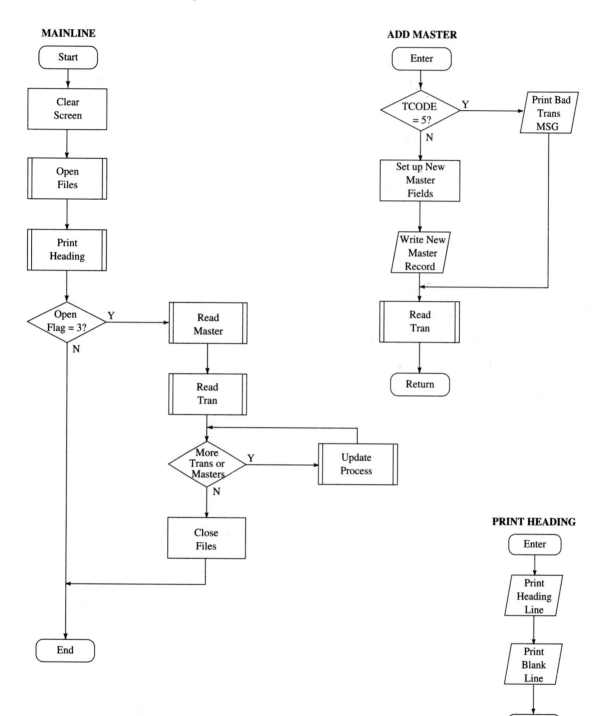

FIGURE 13.23   Program Flowchart for CHAP13E

OPEN FILE

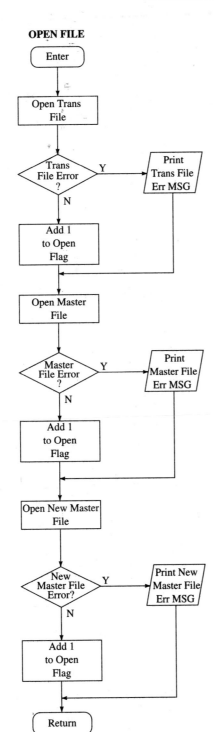

READ MASTER

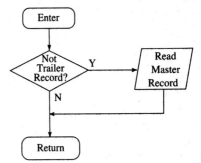

READ TRAN

(continued on next page)

FIGURE 13.23 *Continued*

UPDATE PROCESS

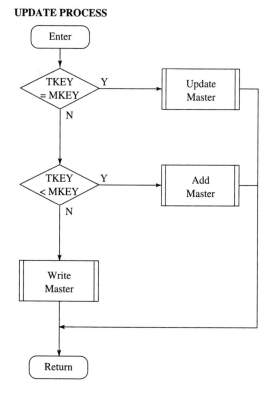

WRITE MASTER

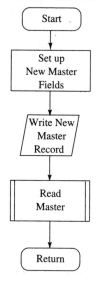

UPDATE MASTER

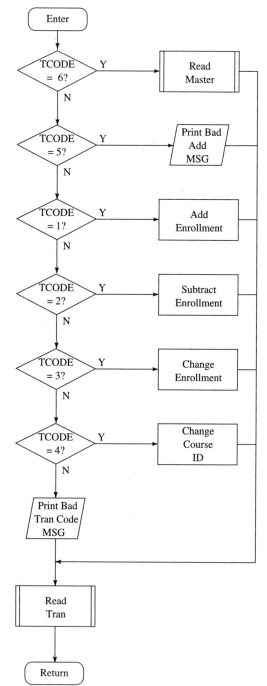

FIGURE 13.23 *Continued*

```
//----------- SEQUENTIAL FILE UPDATE -----------------------
//   This program reads a transaction file, updates the master
//   file, and checks for errors.
//
//            PROGRAM-ID: CHAP13E
//            PROGRAMMER: David M. Collopy
//            RUN DATE:   mm/dd/yy
//-----------------------------------------------------------

//----------- PREPROCESSING DIRECTIVES ---------------------
#include<iostream.h>
#include<fstream.h>
#include<iomanip.h>
#include<conio.h>
#include<string.h>
//----------- FUNCTION PROTOTYPES --------------------------

void OpenFiles(void);          // open files
void PrnHeading(void);         // print heading line
void ReadTran(void);           // read transaction record
void ReadMast(void);           // read master record
void UpdProcess(void);         // update processing
void UpdMast(void);            // update master record
void AddMast(void);            // add master record
void WrtMast(void);            // write master record

//----------- PROGRAM SETUP --------------------------------

//** T R A N S A C T I O N   R E C O R D
ifstream inTF;            // tran file object name
int  Tkey;                // tran key: call number
char Tdept[15];           // department & number
int  Tenroll;             // student enrollment
int  Tcode;               // transaction code

//** M A S T E R   R E C O R D
ifstream inMF;            // mast file object name
int  Mkey;                // mast key: call number
char Mdept[15];           // department & number
int  Menroll;             // student enrollment

//** N E W   M A S T E R   R E C O R D
ofstream outMF;           // new mast file object name
int  NMkey;               // new mast key: call number
char NMdept[15];          // department & number
int  NMenroll;            // student enrollment

//** P R O G R A M   V A R I A B L E S
char PT[] = "         C O U R S E   E R R O R   L O G";
```
(continued on next page)

FIGURE 13.24 Sample Program CHAP13E: Reads Transaction File, Updates Master File, and Checks for Errors

```
char badAdd[22]   = "MASTER EXISTS";
char badTrn[22]   = "UNMATCHED TRANSACTION";
char badTcode[22] = "BAD TRANSACTION CODE";

//**  O P E N    P R I N T E R    F I L E

ofstream prnt("PRN");               // open printer file


//------------------------------------------------------------
//              MAINLINE CONTROL
//------------------------------------------------------------
main()
{
    clrscr();                       // clear the screen
    OpenFiles();                    // open files
    PrnHeading();                   // print heading line
    if (!inTF.fail() && !inMF.fail() && !outMF.fail())  {
        ReadMast();                 // read master record
        ReadTran()                  // read trans record
        while ((Tkey != 999) || (Mkey != 999))
            UpdProcess();
        inTF.close()                // close trans file
        inMF.close()                // close master file
        outMF.close()               // close new mast file
    }
    return 0;
}
//------------------------------------------------------------
//              OPEN FILES
//------------------------------------------------------------
void OpenFiles(void)
{
    intTF.open("a:course.trn");     // open for input
    if (inTF.fail())  {
        cout << "Transaction file open failed " << endl;
    }
    inMF.open("a:course.mst");       // open for input
    if (inMF.fail())  {
        cout << "Master file open failed " << endl;
    }
    outMF.open("a:course.mst");      // open for output
    if (outMF.fail())  {
        cout << "New master file open failed " << endl;
    }
    return;
}
//------------------------------------------------------------
//              PRINT HEADING LINE
//------------------------------------------------------------
```

FIGURE 13.24 *Continued*

```
void PrnHeading(void)
{
    prnt << PT;                  // print heading line
    prnt << endl << endl;        // double space
    return;
}
//-------------------------------------------------------------
//              READ TRANSACTION RECORD
//-------------------------------------------------------------
void ReadTran(void)
{
    if (Tkey != 999)
        inTF >> Tkey >> Tdept >> Tenroll >> Tcode;
    return;
}
//-------------------------------------------------------------
//              READ MASTER RECORD
//-------------------------------------------------------------
void ReadMast(void)
{
    if (Mkey != 999)
        inMF >> Mkey >> Mdept >> Menroll;
    return;
}
//-------------------------------------------------------------
//              UPDATE PROCESSING
//-------------------------------------------------------------
void UpdProcess(void)
                {
    if (Tkey == Mkey)
        UpdMast();                   // update master record
    else if (Tkey < Mkey)
        AddMast();                   // add master record
    else
        WrtMast();                   // write master record
    return;
}
//-------------------------------------------------------------
//              UPDATE MASTER RECORD
//-------------------------------------------------------------
void UpdMast(void)
{
    if (Tcode == 6)                          // delete master
        ReadMast();
    else if (Tcode == 5)  {
```

(continued on next page)

FIGURE 13.24   *Continued*

```
              prnt << endl << setw(3) << Tkey   << " "
                    << setiosflags(ios::left)
                    << setw(15) << Tdept
                    << resetiosflags(ios::left)
                    << setw(2) << Tenroll << " "
                    << setw(1) << Tcode << " "
                    << setiosflags(ios::left)
                    << setw(22) << badAdd;           // master exists
       }
       else if (Tcode == 1)                          // add students
           Menroll = Menroll + Tenroll;
       else if (Tcode == 2)                          // drop students
           Menroll = Menroll - Tenroll;
       else if (Tcode == 3)                          // change enroll
           Menroll = Tenroll;
       else if (Tcode == 4)
           strcpy(Mdept, Tdept);                     // change dept
       else {
           prnt << endl << setw(3) << Tkey   << " "
                    << setiosflags(ios::left)
                    << setw(15) << Tdept
                    << resetiosflags(ios::left)
                    << setw(2) << Tenroll << " "
                    << setw(1) << Tcode << " "
                    << setiosflags(ios::left)
                    << setw(22) << badTcode;         // bad tran code
       }
       ReadTran();                                   // read tran
       return;
   }
   //-----------------------------------------------------------
   //              ADD MASTER RECORD
   //-----------------------------------------------------------
   void AddMast(void)
   {
       if (Tcode != 5)  {
           prnt << endl << setw(3) << Tkey   << " "
                    << setiosflags(ios::left)
                    << setw(15) << Tdept
                    << resetiosflags(ios::left)
                    << setw(2) << Tenroll << " "
                    << setw(1) << Tcode << " "
                    << setiosflags(ios::left)
```

FIGURE 13.24   *Continued*

```
                      << setw(22) << badTrn;          // unmatched tran
        }
        else  {
            NMkey = Tkey;
            strcpy(NMdept, Tdept);
            NMenroll = Tenroll;
            outMF << NMkey << " " << NMdept << " "
                  << NMenroll << endl;
        }
        ReadTran();                                   // read tran
        return;
}
//-----------------------------------------------------------
//                WRITE MASTER RECORD
//-----------------------------------------------------------
void WrtMast(void)
{
    NMkey = Mkey;
    strcpy(NMdept, Mdept);
    NMenroll = Menroll;
    outMF << NMkey << " " << NMdept << " " << NMenroll << endl;
    ReadMast();                                 // read master
    return;
}
```

FIGURE 13.24   *Continued*

Transaction File				Master File		
300	---	0	6	100	ACCT101	24
400	---	24	1	200	BIOL101	19
450	---	0	6	300	CHEM201	21
500	---	5	2	400	ENG200	16
500	---	12	7	500	HIST225	33
500	HIST291	35	5	600	MGT330	29
650	MKT310	15	5	700	MATH120	14
700	MATH114	0	4	800	PHYS251	20
800	---	55	3	900	SPAN111	12
950	THAR101	17	5	999	END	0
970	---	28	3			
999	END	0	0			

FIGURE 13.25   Input Files for CHAP13E

```
Updated Master File

100 ACCT101 24
200 BIOL101 19
400 ENG200  40
500 HIST225 28
600 MGT330  29
650 MKT310  15
700 MATH114 14
800 PHYS251 55
900 SPAN111 12
950 THAR101 17
```

FIGURE 13.26   Output Master File for CHAP13E

```
        C O U R S E   E R R O R   L O G


450                     0  6   UNMATCHED TRANSACTION
500                    12  7   BAD TRANSACTION CODE
500 HIST291            35  5   MASTER EXISTS
970                    28  3   UNMATCHED TRANSACTION
```

FIGURE 13.27   Error Log for CHAP13E

Dissection of Sample Program CHAP13E

With the exception of the error checks and the course error log, the logic for sample program CHAP13E is similar to the logic shown for sample program CHAP13D. The update module remains basically the same.

However, two error checks were added to *UPDATE MASTER RECORD: badAdd* (bad record addition/master exists—we may not add a record to the master file if it already exists) and *badTcode* (bad transaction code—we cannot process transaction codes that fall outside the range of acceptable values).

A third error check was added to *ADD NEW MASTER RECORD: badTrn* (bad transaction record/unmatched transaction—we cannot process transactions, other than new record additions, that do not match an existing master record).

When the program detects an error, the transaction record and its corresponding error message are written to the course error log. The code for the *UPDATE MASTER RECORD* follows:

```
UPDATE MASTER RECORD

void UpdMast(void)
{
```

```
    if (Tcode == 6)
        ReadMast();
    else if (Tcode == 5)  {
        prnt << endl << setw(3) << Tkey  << " "
                << setiosflags(ios::left)
                << setw(15) << Tdept
                << resetiosflags(ios::left)
                << setw(2) << Tenroll << " "
                << setw(1) << Tcode << " "
                << setiosflags(ios::left)
                << setw(22) << badAdd;
    }
    else if (Tcode == 1)
        Menroll = Menroll + Tenroll;
    else if (Tcode == 2)
        Menroll = Menroll - Tenroll;
    else if (Tcode == 3)
        Menroll = Tenroll;
    else if (Tcode == 4)
        strcpy(Mdept, Tdept);
    else {
        prnt << endl << setw(3) << Tkey  << " "
                << setiosflags(ios::left)
                << setw(15) << Tdept
                << resetiosflags(ios::left)
                << setw(2) << Tenroll << " "
                << setw(1) << Tcode << " "
                << setiosflags(ios::left)
                << setw(22) << badTcode;        // bad tran code
    }
    ReadTran();                                 // read tran
    return;
}
```

When the transaction and master keys are equal, control branches to *UPDATE MASTER RECORD* and checks the transaction code to determine what type of update to perform.

If the transaction and the master keys are equal and the transaction code (5) specifies a record addition, the master already exists, so the transaction record and the error message MASTER EXISTS are written to the error log. Control then branches to *ReadTran* and that module reads the next transaction record.

If the transaction code falls outside the range 1–6, then the transaction record and the error message BAD TRANSACTION CODE are written to the error log. Control then branches to *ReadTran* and that module reads the next transaction record.

ADD NEW MASTER RECORD

```
void AddMast(void)
{
    if (Tcode != 5)  {
        prnt << endl << setw(3) << Tkey  << " "
                << setiosflags(ios::left)
                << setw(15) << Tdept
                << resetiosflags(ios::left)
```

```
                        << setw(2) << Tenroll << " "
                        << setw(1) << Tcode << " "
                        << setiosflags(ios::left)
                        << setw(22) << badTrn;
        }
        else {
            NMkey = Tkey;
            strcpy(NMdept, Tdept);
            NMenroll = Tenroll;
            outMF << NMkey << " " << NMdept << " "
                    << NMenroll << endl;
        }
        ReadTran();
        return;
}
```

When the transaction key is less than the master key and the transaction code specifies processing other than a new record addition, then we have an unmatched transaction. The transaction record and the error message UNMATCHED TRANSACTION are written to the error log, and the next transaction is read from the transaction file.

Summary

1. Files are created and maintained to reflect the current business and financial conditions of a company.

2. In business, there are two major types of files: master files and transaction files. A master file contains permanent information about a specific application, whereas a transaction file contains temporary information that is used to update the master file.

3. File maintenance is the process of keeping the master file up to date. It consists of creating the files, updating the master file, and processing the data stored in the master file.

4. Once a need has been identified, a master file is created. Data is collected and organized into records. In turn, the records are organized into a file and stored on disk or tape for future use.

5. File updating refers to the process of updating the master file. New records are added, old records are deleted, and changes are made to the existing records.

6. Transactions are arranged in record key order and are applied to the master file one at a time.

7. Updates to the master file are scheduled on a regular basis. When the file is updated, various reports are produced by the program. Information from the reports is used to monitor the operations of the business.

8. The update logic compares the master key to the transaction key and uses the transaction code to apply the data to the master record.

9. When the master key equals the transaction key, either the data stored in the transaction is used to update the master record or the master record is deleted.

10. When the transaction key is less than the master key, the data stored in the transaction is used to create a new master record.

11. When the transaction key is greater than the master key, the current master record is written to the new master file.

12. An abnormal end (abend) occurs when certain logic errors prevent the program from running to completion. Once the errors have been corrected, the program is executed again.

13. A special code called a transaction code is used to tell the program how to apply the transaction to the master record.

14. Errors detected during the update run are written to an error log. Information provided by the log is used to correct the transactions.

15. Sequential file update programs should be designed to catch the following errors: adding master records that already exist, processing unmatched transactions, and processing invalid transaction codes.

Programming Projects

For each project, design the logic and write the modular structured program to produce the output. Model your program after the sample programs presented in the chapter. Verify your output.

Project 13–1 Course Schedule

Sample program CHAP13E updates the master file and checks for errors. It does not, however, check for input sequence errors. Include an error check in the read modules to ensure that the record keys are in ascending order. Make up four or five additional transaction records and master records, and add them to the input files in out-of-sequence order. When a sequence error is detected, print the record and an error message TRAN OUT OF SEQUENCE or MAST OUT OF SEQUENCE and continue processing.

Project 13–2 Overdue Accounts-1

Update the sequential master file created in Project 12–1. This three-part project creates the transaction file, updates the master file, and prints the overdue accounts report.

Part I: Write a program to create the transaction file for the overdue accounts. For each transaction record, prompt for and enter the data given below. Write the input data to the transaction file.

File Data (overdue.trn):

Enter the transaction data in the order shown.

Account Number	Customer Name	Days Overdue	Balance Due	Trans Code
1000	Sarah Brooks	60	220.00	4
1010	Ryan Davis			1
2450			700.00	3
2730		30		2

3100				5
4890	Amy Clark			1
4900	Marla Stevens	90	594.00	4
6350		60		2
8540				5
9200			300.00	3
9700	Adam Norris	60	475.00	4

The transaction codes (defined below) specify the type of updates to apply to the master file.

1—change customer name
2—change days overdue
3—change balance due
4—add master record
5—delete master record

Part II: Write a second program to update the master file. Open the transaction file and the master file for input. Open the new master file for output. Read a transaction and a master record and compare keys. Use the transaction code to determine the type of update to apply to the master file.

Part III: Upon completing the update, write a third program to read the new master file and print the overdue accounts report shown below. Accumulate a total for amount due and print the total at the end of the report.

```
Author               OVERDUE ACCOUNTS              Page 01
                        mm/dd/yy


Acct Number      Customer Name      Days Overdue      Amount Due

   9999          X-----------X          99             999.99
     :               :                   :                :
     :               :                   :                :
   9999          X-----------X          99             999.99

                                      Total:          9999.99
```

Project 13–3   Overdue Accounts-2

Modify the program in Project 13–2 to include error checks for illegal transaction codes, unmatched transactions, and illegal record additions. Write the errors to an error log. Insert the following transactions into the transaction file. Be sure to insert them in key field (account number) order.

Account Number	Customer Name	Days Overdue	Balance Due	Trans Code
2740		60		2
4080	Corey Adkins	30	233.00	4
5260			652.00	6
5310				5
5700			375.00	3
9630	Pat Rankin	60	342.00	4

Project 13–4   Overdue Accounts-3

Modify the program in Project 13–3 to check for input sequence errors. Test your program by making up four or five additional transaction records and master records. Insert them in the files in out-of-sequence order. Write the sequence errors to the error log.

Project 13–5   Sales Profit-1

Update the sequential master file created in Project 12–3. This three-part project creates the transaction file, updates the master file, and prints the sales profit report.

Part I: Write a program to create the transaction file for the sales department. For each transaction record, prompt for and enter the data given below. Write the input data to the sales transaction file.

File Data (sales.trn):

Enter the transaction data in the order shown.

Number	Salesperson	Total Sales	Cost of Sales	Trans Code
200	Allison Dunn	6518.02	4131.78	4
300	Roy Henderson			1
400				5
700			3191.22	3
940	Sean Zorich	7465.92	5641.39	4

The transaction codes (defined below) specify the type of updates to apply to the master file.

    1—change salesperson name
    2—change total sales
    3—change cost of sales
    4—add master record
    5—delete master record

Part II: Write a second program to update the master file. Open the transaction file and the master file for input. Open the new master file for output. Read a transaction and a master record and compare keys. Use the transaction code to determine the type of update to apply to the master file.

Part III: Upon completing the update, write a third program to read the new master file and print the sales profit report shown below. Compute net profit (sales – cost) and print the result on the detail line. Accumulate the total net profit and print the total at the end of the report.

```
Author                 SALES PROFIT REPORT              Page 01
                           mm/dd/yy


                       Total         Cost of      Net
Num     Salesperson    Sales         Sales        Profit
-------------------------------------------------------------
999     X---------X    99999.99      99999.99     99999.99
 :          :             :             :            :
 :          :             :             :            :
999     X---------X    99999.99      99999.99     99999.99

                                     Total:       999999.99
```

Project 13–6 Sales Profit-2

Modify the program in Project 13–5 to include error checks for illegal transaction codes, unmatched transactions, and illegal record additions. Write the errors to an error log. Insert the following transactions into the transaction file. Be sure to insert them in key field (salesperson number) order.

Number	Salesperson	Total Sales	Cost of Sales	Trans Code
100				7
250		3974.63		2
340	David Kock			1
490			5591.15	3
900	Ann Zimmerman	5793.59	4204.45	4
960				5

Project 13–7 Sales Profit-3

Modify the program in Project 13–6 to check for input sequence errors. Test your program by making up four or five additional transaction records and master records. Insert them in the files in out-of-sequence order. Write the sequence errors to the error log.

Project 13–8 Inventory-1

Update the sequential master file created in Project 12–4. This three-part project creates the transaction file, updates the master file, and prints the inventory status report.

Part I: Write a program to create the transaction file for the inventory system. For each transaction record, prompt for and enter the data given below. Write the data to the inventory transaction file.

File Data (invent.trn):

Enter the transaction data in the order shown.

Item Number	Description	Quantity on Hand	Unit Cost	Trans Code
1000		20		2
1600	Shovels	12	6.29	4
3000				5
4000			2.37	3
4500	Wrenches	18	3.95	4

The transaction codes (defined below) specify the type of update to apply to the master file.

1—change item description
2—change quantity on hand
3—change unit cost
4—add master record
5—delete master record

Part II: Write a second program to update the master file. Open the transaction file and the master file for input. Open the new master file for output. Read a transaction and a master record and compare keys. Use the transaction code to determine the type of update to apply to the master file.

Part III: Upon completing the update, write a third program to read the new master file and print the inventory status report shown below. Accumulate a total for item cost and print the total at the end of the report.

```
Author            INVENTORY STATUS REPORT        Page 01
                        mm/dd/yy


   Item                           Quantity         Item
   Number      Description         on Hand         Cost

   9999        X----------X           99          999.99
     :             :                   :             :
     :             :                   :             :
   9999        X----------X           99          999.99

                          Total Cost:             9999.99
```

Project 13–9 Inventory-2

Change the program in Project 13–8 to include error checks for illegal transaction codes, unmatched transactions, and illegal record additions. Write the errors to an error log. Insert the following transactions into the transaction file. Be sure to insert them in key field (item number) order.

Item Number	Description	Quantity on Hand	Unit Cost	Trans Code
1100				5
2000	Saws	08	7.50	4
2400		24		2
3500			3.49	6
4100	Hatchets			1
5000	Pliers	12	2.65	4
5200			4.17	3

Project 13–10 Inventory-3

Modify the program in Project 13–9 to check for input sequence errors. Test your program by making up four or five additional transaction records and master records. Insert them in the files in out-of-sequence order. Write the sequence errors to the error log.

14 Structures and Random Files

Overview

Learning Objectives

After you have read this chapter and completed the exercises, you should be able to:

- declare data structures and structure variables
- discuss the advantages of random file organization
- create a random file
- use the seekp() and seekg() member functions to move around in a random file
- print data stored in a random file
- update data stored in a random file

Defining a Structure

Until now, we have been using individual data types int, char, and float to describe our programming applications. However, some applications can be processed more efficiently if the individual data types are grouped to form a single unit.

For example, consider an inventory application that consists of the following variables: item number (int), description (char), quantity (int), cost (float), and selling price (float). What we would like to do is access all of the variables as a group (record) or any single item (field) in the group.

C++ uses structures to group data types. A **structure** is a group item that may hold two or more data types, called **members**. A structure may be processed as a single unit, or the members may be processed individually. In simpler terms, a structure is a **record**, and a member of the structure is a **field**.

It may help to think of a structure as a **template** that describes the format of the data. By itself, the template does not reserve storage for the structure. It isn't until a structure variable is declared that storage is allocated to the members of the structure. In other words, a structure merely tells the program what the data looks like.

A structure must be declared before it can be used by the program. The keyword *struct* is used to define a structure or record template.

Format:

```
struct tag  {
    type member 1;
    type member 2;
      :   :
    type member n;
};
```

Example:

```
struct inventory  {
    int    number;
    char   desc[20];
    int    quantity;
    float cost;
    float price;
};
```

In the example, *struct* describes the format of the inventory structure and *tag* gives a name to it. The member declarations describe the fields and their data types. Hence, both the structure and its members have names. For processing purposes, we may reference the entire structure or any member of it.

Defining a Structure Variable

Once a structure has been declared, we may use it to define one or more structure variables. A **structure variable** is a variable that consists of the members described by the data structure. Defining a structure variable reserves storage space for each member of the template.

For example, assume the inventory structure has been defined as shown below. The second *struct* statement defines the structure variable *item* and allocates storage space for the following members—*number* (int), *desc* (char), *quantity* (int), *cost* (float), and *price* (float).

. . . . .

```
struct inventory  {
     int    number;
     char   desc[20];
     int    quantity;
     float  cost;
     float  price;
};


struct inventory item;
```

. . . . .

Essentially, a data structure describes what the data looks like, and a structure variable assigns a memory location to the members of the data structure.

Assigning Data to a Structure Variable

Data may be assigned to a structure variable either at the time it is declared or by the program during the run.

Initializing Data: A structure variable may be initialized when it is declared. For example, the following statements define the template and initialize the structure variable. The first *struct* statement describes the template, whereas the second *struct* defines the structure variable *item* and initializes the members to the values listed.

```
//*****  DEFINE THE INVENTORY TEMPLATE  *******

   struct itemData  {
       int    number;
       char   desc[20];
```

```
        int    quantity;
        float cost;
        float price;
    };
```

```
//*****  DEFINE THE STRUCTURE VARIABLE  *******
```

```
    struct itemData item = {0, "", 0, 0.0, 0.0};
```

The values enclosed within braces and separated by commas are assigned on a positional basis to the variables described in the record template; the first value is assigned the first member, the second value is assigned the second member, and so forth. Consequently, 0 is assigned to *number*, null is assigned to *desc*, 0 is assigned to *quantity*, 0.0 is assigned to *cost*, and 0.0 is assigned to *price*.

Interactive Input: Data may be assigned to a structure variable by prompting the user to enter the data at the keyboard. The example shown below prompts for the data one field at a time and assigns it to the members as it is entered by the user.

```
   .  .  .  .  .
```

```
struct inventory  {
    int    number;
    char   desc[20];
    int    quantity;
    float cost;
    float price;
};
```

```
struct inventory item;
```

```
   .  .  .  .  .
```

```
    cout << "       Enter item number: ";
    cin >> item.number;
    cout << " Enter item description: ";
    cin >> item.desc;
    cout << " Enter quantity on hand: ";
    cin >> item.quantity;
    cout << "         Enter item cost: ";
    cin >> item.cost;
    cout << "    Enter selling price: ";
    cin  >> item.price;
```

```
   .  .  .  .  .
```

Notice that a dot (.), called a dot operator, appears in the input (*cin*) statements. The **dot operator** links the structure variable to the members of the data template. For example, the first *cin* assigns the input to the *number* member of the *item* variable. The structure variable is coded on the left side of the dot operator and the member is coded on the right.

Checkpoint 14A

1. Define the term *structure*.

2. (True or False) A structure may be processed as a single unit or the members may be processed individually.

3. (True or False) The following statements assign a memory location to the members of the data structure.

```
struct payroll  {
    char  employee[20];
    float payRate;
    int   hoursWorked;
};
```

4. What is a structure variable?

5. Code the statements to define a structure variable called *grossPay* using the *payroll* template from Exercise 3. Then code the statements to assign data to the members by prompting the user to enter data at the keyboard.

6. Explain the purpose and use of a dot operator.

Random File Organization

Random file organization stores data on disk in random order. The word *random* implies that the data may be read or written in any order. Thus the user may skip around in the file, rather than passing through the records sequentially one by one. Unlike sequential files, random files do not require that the records be arranged in key field order.

Random file processing (**direct access**) offers the advantage of fast data retrieval; any record can be accessed in a matter of seconds. For example, if the user wants to view a specific record in the file, the program can go directly to that record and retrieve the data stored there.

Random access can be compared to selecting a song recorded on a CD. When you make a selection, the CD player automatically locates and plays the song for you.

For applications that require access to a small number of records at any given time, random file organization provides fast and efficient retrieval. However, it can be rather cumbersome and slow for applications that require access to all or most of the records in a large file, particularly if the records must be processed in sequential order.

Opening a Random File

A file must be opened before the program can do anything with it. According to the following statement, the course file is opened for input and/or output:

```
file.open("a:course.fil", ios::in | ios::out);
```

The manipulator *ios::out* tells the compiler that data is written to the random file. The manipulator *ios::in* indicates that once data is written to the course file it may also be read.

When the course file is successfully opened, the open() member function passes the address of the file to the file object identifier *randfile*. The open() function always sets the file pointer to the beginning of the file. Once the file is opened, the position of the file pointer is maintained by the program.

Writing a Record to a Random File

Format:

```
file.write((char *) &structVar, size);
```

Header File: *fstream.h*

Purpose: To write a record to a random file. The write() member function includes arguments that specify the address of the beginning of the file, the address pointer to the structure variable (record), and the size of the structure (record template).

The *char * operator* specifies the address of the beginning of the file where the data will be put. The *&structVar* specifies the address from which to get the data. The *size* parameter returns the number of bytes or characters (length) associated with the record template.

Example:

```
file.write((char *) &course, sizeof(courseData));
```

At run time, the output statement writes one record to the output file stream. Notice that the second argument uses the *sizeof* operator to determine the length of the record. This special operator computes the number of bytes associated with the *courseData* structure. For example, if `sizeof(struct courseData)` equals 17, then the size argument specifies that 17 bytes of data will be written to the file.

Creating a Random File

Let's continue with the course scheduling application introduced in Chapter 12. In order to create a random file, we need to describe the data structure, declare the record variable, and reserve space for the file records. Essentially, we will initialize the structure variable and write empty records to the file. The idea is to prepare the file for storing future data.

Creating a random file involves the following tasks:

1. Declare the file name and assign it to the output file stream.
2. Define the data structure.
3. Define and initialize the empty record.
4. Open the file for output.
5. Write empty records to the file.
6. Close the file.

This process is illustrated in sample program CHAP14A. The course file is created from the initial values assigned to the empty record variable.

Checkpoint 14B

1. Briefly explain random file organization.
2. (True or False) Random files require the records to be arranged in key field order.

3. What is the advantage of random file processing? When is random file processing used?

4. What statement writes a record to a random file?

5. Identify the arguments specified in a write() statement. Briefly explain each.

6. The special operator used to compute the number of bytes associated with a structure is the _____ operator.

7. List the six steps involved in creating a random file.

Sample Program CHAP14A

Sample program CHAP14A (Figure 14.3, p. 480) creates a random access file for the courses offered at the branch campus of Central State College. Each record is initialized and written to the file. In the interest of brevity, the file has been set up for 20 records.

The following specifications apply:

Input (internal):

Define the course data structure and the members given below. Field size and type are shown in parentheses.

Call number	(3 int)
Department & number	(15 char)
Student enrollment	(2 int)

Output (course.fil):

The random access file is shown in Figure 14.4 (p. 481).

Processing Requirements:

- Define and initialize the empty record.
- Open the file for output.
- Write empty records to the file.
- Close the file.

Pseudocode:

```
START
Clear the screen
Open file
If file opened
   Define the empty record
   LOOP for record number <= 20
      Write the empty record to the file
   End LOOP
   Close file
END
```

Hierarchy Chart: See Figure 14.1.

Program Flowchart: See Figure 14.2.

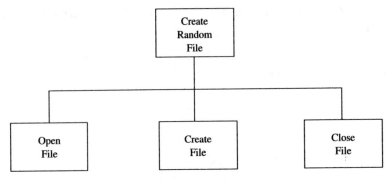

FIGURE 14.1 Hierarchy Chart for CHAP14A

Dissection of Sample Program CHAP14A

COURSE RECORD

```
ofstream file;
```

The above statement defines the output file stream. The file object name *file* is assigned to the output file stream (*ofstream*). The identifier *file* will be used to hold the address of the course file.

```
struct courseData   {
    int   callNum;
    char dept[15];
    int   enroll;
};
```

The above statements mean: Declare the record data structure and give it the name *course-Data.* The structure describes the members—*callNum* (int), *dept* (char), and *enroll* (int).

This *struct* statement only describes the format of the structure, it does not reserve storage space for it.

```
struct courseData empty = {0, "", 0};
```

The above statement defines the empty record, reserves storage space for it, and initializes the member fields: *callNum* to 0, *dept* to Null string, and *enroll* to 0.

PROGRAM VARIABLES

```
int   recNum;
```

The above statement defines the record number. Record number is used as the control variable in the *for* loop that writes the empty records to the course file.

OPEN RANDOM FILE

```
void OpenFile(void)
{
    file.open("a:rcourse.fil");
```

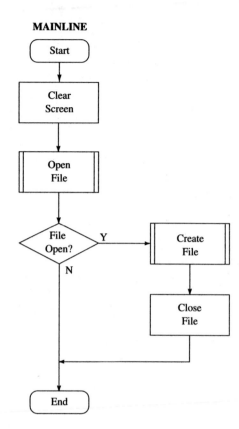

MAINLINE

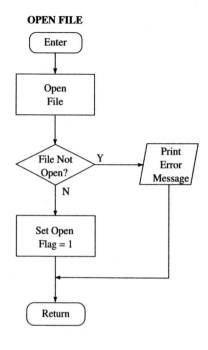

OPEN FILE

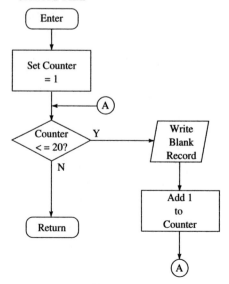

CREATE FILE

FIGURE 14.2 Program Flowchart for CHAP14A

```
//---------- CREATE RANDOM FILE---------------------------
//    This program creates a random file of 20 empty
//    records.
//
//          PROGRAM-ID: CHAP14A
//          PROGRAMMER: David M. Collopy
//          RUN DATE:   mm/dd/yy
//*********************************************************

//---------- PREPROCESSING DIRECTIVES ---------------------
#include<iostream.h>
#include<fstream.h>
#include<conio.h>
//---------- FUNCTION PROTOTYPES --------------------------

void OpenFile(void);            // open random file
void LoadFile(void);            // load empty records


//---------- PROGRAM SETUP --------------------------------

//** C O U R S E   R E C O R D

ofstream file;                  // output file object
struct courseData  {            // course data structure
    int  callNum;               // call number
    char dept[15];              // department & number
    int  enroll;                // student enrollment
};
struct courseData empty = {0, "", 0};      // record values

//** P R O G R A M   V A R I A B L E S

int recNum;                     // record number
//---------------------------------------------------------
//              MAINLINE CONTROL
//---------------------------------------------------------
main()
{
    clrscr();                   // clear the screen
    OpenFile();                 // open random file
```

FIGURE 14.3 Sample Program CHAP14A: Creates a Random File of 20 Empty Records

```
    if (!file.fail())  {
        LoadFile();                 // load empty records
        file.close();               // close random file
    }
    return 0;
}
//-----------------------------------------------------------
//              OPEN RANDOM FILE
//-----------------------------------------------------------
void OpenFile(void)
{
    file.open("a:rcourse.fil");                 // open for output
    if (file.fail())  {
        cout << "Random file open failed " << endl;
    }
    return;
}
//-----------------------------------------------------------
//              LOAD EMPTY RECORDS
//-----------------------------------------------------------
void LoadFile(void)
{
    for (recNum = 1; recNum <= 20; recNum++)
        file.write((char *) &empty, sizeof(courseData));
    return;
}
```

FIGURE 14.3 *Continued*

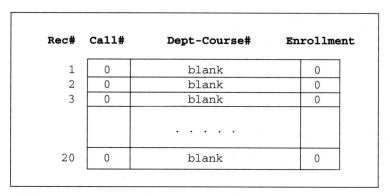

Rec#	Call#	Dept-Course#	Enrollment
1	0	blank	0
2	0	blank	0
3	0	blank	0
		. . . . .	
20	0	blank	0

FIGURE 14.4   File Output for CHAP14A

```
        if (file.fail())  {
            cout << "Random file open failed " << endl;
        }
        return;
}
```

The preceding statements mean: Open the course file for output. If the file is opened, the address of the file is assigned to the file identifier name and the open() function returns the value 1. But if the file cannot be opened, null is assigned to file identifier name and the error message is displayed on the screen.

LOAD EMPTY RECORDS

```
void LoadFile(void)
{
    for (recNum = 1; recNum <= 20; recNum++)
        file.write((char *) &empty, sizeof(courseData));
    return;
}
```

The above statements mean: As long as the value of *recNum* is less than or equal to 20, write an empty record to the file. The record size is determined by the *sizeof* operator, which returns the number of characters associated with the empty record.

Moving the File Pointer

Formats:

```
        seekp(offset, origin);
        seekg(offset, origin);
```

Header File: *fstream.h*

Purpose: To move the file position pointer. The seek function is used to position the file pointer to a specific location in a random file. The suffix *p* indicates a *seek put* operation; it is used to set the file pointer prior to executing a file write statement. The suffix *g* indicates a *seek get* operation; it is used to set the file pointer prior to executing a file read. The statement consists of two arguments that specify the file position offset and the origin or starting point.

The file position offset may be a constant, a variable, or an expression that specifies the number of bytes from the starting point. By specifying a plus or minus offset, we may move the file position pointer forward or backward in the file. The origin is the starting point in the file. The origin values are shown in Table 14.1.

TABLE 14.1   Origin Values

Origin	Meaning
ios::beg	Seek from the beginning of the file.
ios::cur	Seek from the current position.
ios::end	Seek from the end of the file.

Examples:

1. `file.seekg(0, ios::beg);`
2. `file.seekp(17, ios::cur);`
3. `file.seekp(-17, ios::cur);`
4. `file.seekg(0, ios::end);`
5. `file.seekp((recNum-1)*sizeof(courseData), ios::beg);`

The first example sets the file pointer to the beginning of the file. Examples 2 and 3 set the file pointer forward 17 bytes and backward 17 bytes, respectively, from the current position in the file. Example 4 sets the file pointer to the end of the file.

The last example sets the file pointer to a position that is offset from the beginning of the file. For example, if *recNum* = 2 and the *sizeof* operator returns a 17, then, according to the calculation given below, the offset is 17 bytes:

`(recNum-1)*sizeof(courseData) = (2 - 1) * 17 = 17`

Writing Data to a Random File

Sample program CHAP14A created a random file of 20 empty records. Now we are ready to load the file with live data. Since we are using random file organization, we may load the data in any order we wish.

Loading a random file involves the following tasks:

1. Declare the file name and assign it to the file stream.
2. Define the data structure and the structure variable.
3. Open the file for input/output.
4. Prompt and enter the data.
5. Assign the input to the structure variable.
6. Set the file pointer and write the data to the file.
7. Close the file.

The load process is illustrated in sample program CHAP14B. Pay close attention to how seekp() and write() are used to set the file pointer and write the input data to the file.

Checkpoint 14C

1. Explain the purpose of the seek statement.
2. Identify the arguments that appear in the seek statement. Briefly explain each.
3. (True or False) It is possible to move the file pointer forward in a file but not backward.
4. Identify the meaning of each origin.
   a. ios::beg
   b. ios::cur
   c. ios::end
5. List seven tasks involved in writing data to a random access file.

Sample Program CHAP14B

Sample program CHAP14B (Figure 14.7, p. 487) prompts the user to enter the data at the keyboard and loads the course file. The data entry screen is shown in Figure 14.8 (p. 488)

The following specifications apply:

Input (disk file and keyboard):

Disk file: Random access file (*course.fil*)
Keyboard: For each course record, prompt for and enter the following data. Field size and type are shown in parentheses.

Call number	(3 int)
Department & number	(15 char)
Student enrollment	(2 int)

Output (course.fil):

The random access file is shown in Figure 14.9 (p. 489).

Processing Requirements:

- Open the file for input/output.
- Prompt for and enter the data.
- Assign the input to the structure variable.
- Write the structure variable (record) to the file.
- Close the file.

Pseudocode:

```
START
Clear the screen
Open file
If file opened
   Prompt and enter call number
   LOOP until call number = –1
      Prompt and enter the rest of the data
      Write the record to file
      Clear the screen
      Prompt and enter call number
   End LOOP
   Close file
END
```

Hierarchy Chart: See Figure 14.5.

Program Flowchart: See Figure 14.6.

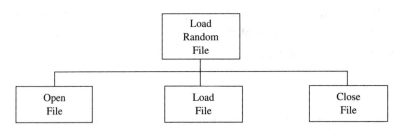

FIGURE 14.5   Hierarchy Chart for CHAP14B

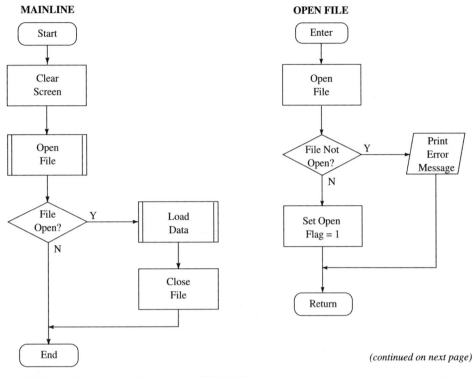

MAINLINE

OPEN FILE

FIGURE 14.6   Program Flowchart for CHAP14B

(continued on next page)

Dissection of Sample Program CHAP14B

First, the file pointer, the course data structure, and the structure variable are defined. The record number is also defined as before.

Second, the *MAINLINE* sends control to the module that opens the random file. If the file is opened, the program proceeds to load the input data to the file. But if the file cannot be opened, the program prints an error message and stops the run.

```
LOAD COURSE FILE

void LoadFile(void)
{
    clrscr();
    cout << "\nEnter record# 1 - 20 or '-1' to quit: ";
    cin >> recNum;
```

The above statements mean: Clear the screen and prompt the user to enter a record number 1 through 20, or –1 to quit. Read the record number, convert it to an integer, and assign the result to *recNum*.

```
    while (recNum != -1)  {
```

The above statement means: As long as the value of *recNum* is not equal to –1, execute the statements in the body of the loop. Otherwise, return to the *MAINLINE*.

LOAD DATA

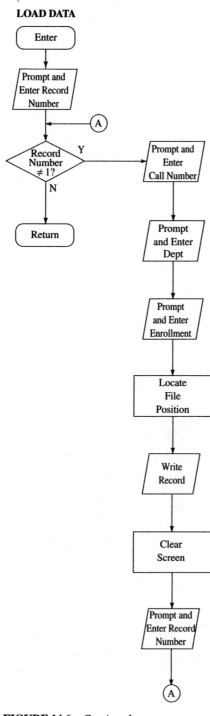

FIGURE 14.6 *Continued*

```
//---------- LOAD RANDOM FILE--------------------------------
//  This program loads data randomly into the course file.
//
//              PROGRAM-ID: CHAP14B
//              PROGRAMMER: David M. Collopy
//              RUN DATE:   mm/dd/yy
//***********************************************************

//---------- PREPROCESSING DIRECTIVES ----------------------
#include<iostream.h>
#include<fstream.h>
#include<conio.h>

//---------- FUNCTION PROTOTYPES ---------------------------

void OpenFile(void);            // open course file
void LoadFile(void);            // load course file

//---------- PROGRAM SETUP ---------------------------------

//**  C O U R S E   R E C O R D

fstream file;                   // I/O file object
struct courseData  {            // course data structure
    int  callNum;               // call number
    char dept[15];              // department & number
    int  enroll;                // student enrollment
};

struct courseData course;       // course record

//**  P R O G R A M    V A R I A B L E S

int recNum;                     // record number
//---------------------------------------------------------
//                MAINLINE CONTROL
//---------------------------------------------------------
main()
{
    OpenFile();                 // open course file
    if (!file.fail())  {
        LoadFile();             // load course file
        file.close();           // close course file
    }
    return 0;
}
```

FIGURE 14.7   Sample Program CHAP14B: Loads Data Randomly into the Course File

```
//------------------------------------------------------------
//              OPEN COURSE FILE
//------------------------------------------------------------
void OpenFile(void)
{
    file.open("a:rcourse.fil", ios::in | ios::out);
    if (file.fail())  {
        cout << "Course file open failed " << endl;
    }
    return;
}
//------------------------------------------------------------
//              LOAD COURSE FILE
//------------------------------------------------------------
void LoadFile(void)
{
    clrscr();
    cout << "\nEnter record# 1 - 20 or '-1' to quit: ";
    cin >> recNum;
    while (recNum != -1)  {
        cout << "          Enter course call number: ";
        cin >> course.callNum;
        cout << "          Enter course description: ";
        cin >> course.dept;
        cout << "          Enter student enrollment: ";
        cin >> course.enroll;
        file.seekp((recNum-1)*sizeof(courseData), ios::beg);
        file.write((char *) &course, sizeof(courseData));
        clrscr();
        cout << "\nEnter record# 1 - 20 or '-1' to quit: ";
        cin >> recNum;
    }
    return
}
```

FIGURE 14.7   *Continued*

```
Enter Record# 1 - 20 or '-1' to quit:___
            Enter course call number:___
            Enter course description:___
             Enter course enrollment:___
```

FIGURE 14.8   Data Entry Screen for CHAP14B

Rec#	Call#	Dept-Course#	Enrollment
1	400	ENG200	16
2	300	CHEM201	21
3	600	MGT330	29
4	200	BIOL101	19
5	0		
6	500	HIST225	33
7	900	SPAN111	12
8	700	MATH120	14
9	800	PHYS251	20
10	100	ACCT101	24
		. . . . .	
20	0		0

FIGURE 14.9   File Output for CHAP14B

```
cout << "           Enter course call number: ";
cin >> course.callNum;
cout << "           Enter course description: ";
cin >> course.dept;
cout << "           Enter student enrollment: ";
cin >> course.enroll;
```

The above statements mean: Prompt the user to enter the course data and assign the input to the member variables. The *cout* statements prompt for the input, and the *cin* statements assign the data to the course record.

```
file.seekp((recNum-1)*sizeof(courseData), ios::beg);
```

The above statement means: Move the file position pointer to the position that is offset from the beginning of the file. For example, if the user enters 2 for *recNum* and the *sizeof* operator returns a 17, then, according to the calculation given below, the offset is 17 bytes.

```
(recNum-1)*sizeof(struct courseData) = (2 - 1) * 17 = 17
```

In other words, the *seek* operation moves the file position pointer forward 17 bytes from the beginning of the file. This location represents the address to the second record position in the file.

Notice that 1 was subtracted from *recNum*. This causes the file position pointer to move to the beginning of the second record.

```
file.write((char *) &course, sizeof(courseData));
```

The above statement means: Write the record stored in the *course* structure variable to the file. The record size is determined by the *sizeof* operator.

```
        clrscr();
        cout << "\nEnter record# 1 - 20 or '-1' to quit: ";
        cin >> recNum;
    }
    return;
}
```

The previous statements mean: Clear the screen and prompt the user to enter a record number 1 through 20 to continue or –1 to quit. Read the input, convert it to an integer, and assign the result to *recNum*.

Reading a Record from a Random File

Format:

```
file.read((char *) &structVar, size);
```

Header File: *fstream.h*

Purpose: To read a record from a random file. The read() member function includes arguments that specify the address of the beginning of the input file, the address pointer to the structure variable (record), and the size of the structure (record template).

The *char* * operator specifies the address of the beginning of the file from which to get the data. The *&structVar* specifies the address where the incoming data should be put. The *size* parameter returns the number of bytes (the length) associated with the record template.

Example:

```
file.read((char *) &course, sizeof(courseData));
```

At run time, the input statement reads one record from the input file stream, the size of which is determined by the *sizeof* operator, and stores the data in the structure variable *course*.

Reading and Printing a Random File

The random course file created in sample program CHAP14B was stored on disk. Since the data was written directly to the disk, we have no way of knowing for sure what was actually placed in the file. Hence, it would be wise to look at the file and verify that the data was correctly written to the disk.

Reading and printing a random access file involve the following tasks:

1. Declare the file name and assign it to the file stream.
2. Define the data structure and the structure variable.
3. Open the file for input/output.
4. Read a record and assign the data to the structure variable.
5. Display the record on the screen.
6. Close the file.

This process is illustrated in sample program CHAP14C. The program uses the fread() to read the course file and prints a copy of the records to a report.

Checkpoint 14D

1. Explain the purpose of the read() statement.

2. Identify the arguments used in the read() statement and explain each.

3. In your own words, explain how this statement works:

```
file.read((char *) &course, sizeof(courseData));
```

4. Define the account data structure and the members given below. Field size and type are shown in parentheses.

Account number	(4 int)
Customer name	(15 char)
Days overdue	(2 int
Balance due	(6.2 float)

5. Using the statements coded in Exercise 4, code the module to read and print the contents of the overdue account file. Assume the file contains a maximum of 20 records and the file object identifier was defined as *filein;*.

Sample Program CHAP14C

Sample program CHAP14C reads and prints a copy of the course file created in sample program CHAP14B. (Figure 14.12, p. 494). Each record is read from the disk and written to the output report. Figure 14.13 (p. 495) shows the output. The following specifications apply:

Input (course.fil):

For each course record, read the following data from the random file. Field size and type are shown in parentheses.

Call number	(3 int)
Department & number	(15 char)
Student enrollment	(2 int)

Output (screen):

The output is shown in Figure 14.13.

Processing Requirements:

- Open the file for input/output.
- Read a record into the structure variable.
- Write the nonempty records to the report.
- Close the file.

Pseudocode:

```
START
Clear the screen
Open file
If file opened
```

```
Print the heading line
LOOP for record number <= 20
    Read a record
    If call number not = 0
        Print the record
End LOOP
Close file
END
```

Hierarchy Chart: See Figure 14.10.

Program Flowchart: See Figure 14.11.

Dissection of Sample Program CHAP14C

Since the *PROGRAM SETUP, MAINLINE,* and *OPEN COURSE FILE* modules are similar to those shown for sample program CHAP14B, we will skip them and begin the dissection with the *READ AND PRINT COURSE FILE* module.

```
READ AND PRINT COURSE FILE

void ReadFile(void)
{
    cout << "\nRec# Call#  Dept-Course#  Enrollment";
    cout << "\n-----------------------------------";
```

The above statements print the report heading lines.

```
    for (recNum = 1; recNum <= 20; recNum++)  {
```

The above statement means: As long as the current value of *recNum* is less than or equal to 20, execute the statement body of the *for* loop.

```
        file.seekg((recNum-1)*sizeof(courseData), ios::beg);
        file.read((char *) &course, sizeof(courseData));
```

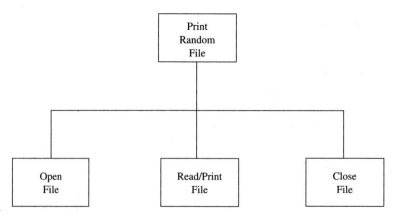

FIGURE 14.10   Hierarchy Chart for CHAP14C

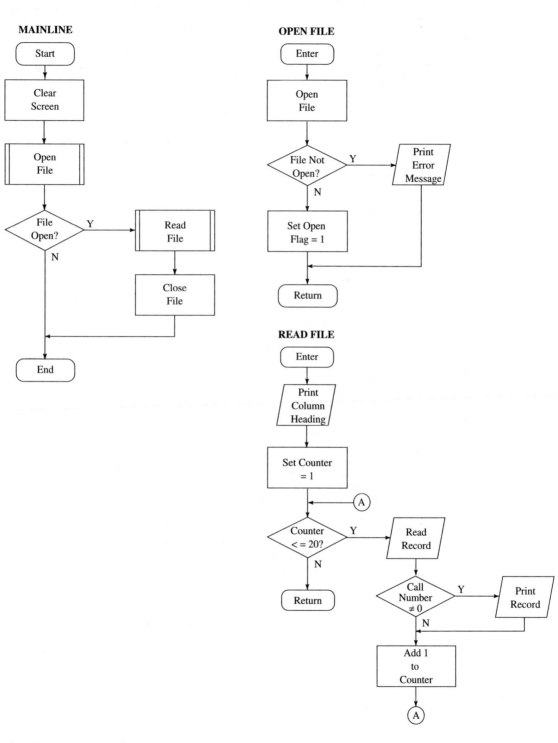

FIGURE 14.11   Program Flowchart for CHAP14C

```
//---------- PRINT RANDOM FILE-------------------------------
//   This program reads and prints the data stored in the
//   course file.
//
//          PROGRAM-ID: CHAP14C
//          PROGRAMMER: David M. Collopy
//          RUN DATE:   mm/dd/yy
//***********************************************************

//---------- PREPROCESSING DIRECTIVES ----------------------
#include<iostream.h>
#include<fstream.h>
#include<iomanip.h>
#include<conio.h>

//---------- FUNCTION PROTOTYPES ---------------------------

void OpenFile(void);              // open course file
void ReadFile(void);              // read & print course file

//---------- PROGRAM SETUP ---------------------------------

//**  C O U R S E   R E C O R D

fstream file;                     // I/O file object
struct courseData  {              // course data structure
    int  callNum;                 // call number
    char dept[15];                // department & number
    int  enroll;                  // student enrollment
};

struct courseData course;         // course record

//**  P R O G R A M   V A R I A B L E S

int recNum;                       // record number
//-----------------------------------------------------------
//              MAINLINE CONTROL
//-----------------------------------------------------------
main()
{
    clrscr();                     // clear the screen
    OpenFile();                   // open course file
    if (!file.fail())  {
        ReadFile();               // read & print course file
        file.close();             // close course file
    }
    return 0;
}
//-----------------------------------------------------------
```

FIGURE 14.12 Sample Program CHAP14C: Reads and Prints the Course Records to the Screen

```
//               OPEN COURSE FILE
//------------------------------------------------------------
void OpenFile(void)
{
    file.open("a:rcourse.fil", ios::in | ios::out);
    if (file.fail())  {
        cout << "Course file open failed " << endl;
    }
    return;
}
//------------------------------------------------------------
//             READ AND PRINT COURSE FILE
//------------------------------------------------------------
void ReadFile(void)
{
    cout << "\nRec# Call#  Dept-Course#  Enrollment";
    cout << "\n------------------------------------";
    for (recnum = 1; recNum <= 20; recNum++)  {
        file.seekg((recNum-1)*sizeof(courseData), ios::beg);
        file.read((char *) &course, sizeof(courseData));
        if (course.callNum != 0)  {
            cout << setw(2) << recNum
                 << setw(7) << course.callNum
                 << "   " << setiosflags(ios::left)
                 << setw(14) << course.dept
                 << resetiosflags(ios::left)
                 << setw(6) << course.enroll << endl;
        }
    }
    return
}
```

FIGURE 14.12   *Continued*

```
Rec# Call#  Dept-Course#  Enrollment
------------------------------------
  1   400   ENG200           16
  2   300   CHEM201          21
  3   600   MGT330           29
  4   200   BIOL101          19
  6   500   HIST225          33
  7   900   SPAN111          12
  8   700   MATH120          14
  9   800   PHYS251          20
 10   100   ACCT101          24
```

FIGURE 14.13   File Output for CHAP14C (Notice that record numbers 5 and 11–20 are not on the report.)

The preceding statements mean: Locate the record position specified by the seek get, read one record from the file stream, and put the input data in the *course* structure variable. The record size is determined by the *sizeof* operator.

```
if (course.callNum != 0)  {
    cout << setw(2) << recNum
            << setw(7) << course.callNum
            << "    " << setiosflags(ios::left)
            << setw(14) << course.dept
            << resetiosflags(ios::left)
            << setw(6) << course.enroll << endl;
}
```

The above statements mean: If the value of the call number is not equal to 0, then print the record on the screen. Any value other than 0 indicates that live data is stored in the record.

```
    }
    return;
}
```

The above statement means: After processing the *for* loop, return to the *MAINLINE*.

Updating a Random File

As the enrollment changes, so must the data stored in the course file. From Chapter 13, we know that file updating refers to the process of changing the data stored in a file. From time to time, new courses are added, old courses are deleted, and changes are made to the current courses. The following sample program allows the user to the modify the contents of the course file and to maintain the integrity of the data stored there.

Updating a random access file involves the following tasks:

1. Declare the file name and assign it to the file stream.
2. Define the data structure and the structure variable.
3. Open the file for input/output.
4. Prompt the user to select the update option (menu).
5. Enter the data and update the file.
6. Close the file.

The update process is illustrated in sample program CHAP14D. The menu-driven program instructs the user to select from a series of available file updating options.

Sample Program CHAP14D

Sample program CHAP14D is menu driven (Figure 14.16, p. 504). It accepts data from the keyboard, checks for errors, and updates the course file. The selection menu is shown in Figure 14.17 (p. 509); the data entry screens are shown in Figures 14.18 through 14.20 (p. 509–510).

The following specifications apply:

Menu Choices:

1. Update enrollment
2. Add courses
3. Delete courses
4. Display all courses
5. Quit

Input (disk file and keyboard):

Disk file: Random access file (*course.fil*)
Keyboard: For options 1–3, prompt for and enter the following data:

Option	Input Data
1	Record number and enrollment count
2	Record number, call number, department and number, and student enrollment
3	Record number

Output (course.fil):

The updated random file is shown in Figure 14.21 (p. 510).

Processing Requirements:

- Open the file for input/output.
- Display the menu options and prompt for a selection.
- Perform the processing specified by the option selected. Enter the data transaction and update the file as needed.
- Close the file.

Pseudocode:

```
START
Set choice = 0
Open file
If file opened
   LOOP until choice = 5 (quit)
      Clear screen
      Display menu and enter choice
      Based on choice, perform the processing
         choice 1—(Update enrollment)
         choice 2—(Add courses)
         choice 3—(Delete courses)
         choice 4—(Display all courses)
   End LOOP
   Close the file
END

ENTER: Update Enrollment
```

Clear screen
Prompt and enter record number
LOOP while record number not = −1
   Read record
   If call number = 0
     Print error message RECORD DOES NOT EXIST
   else
     Display record
     Prompt and enter enrollment change
     Update enrollment
     Write record
   Prompt and enter record number
RETURN

ENTER: Add Courses
Clear screen
Prompt and enter record number
LOOP while record number not = −1
   Read record
   If call number not = 0
     Print error message RECORD ALREADY EXISTS
   else
     Prompt and enter new record
     Write record
   Prompt and enter record number
RETURN

ENTER: Delete Courses
Clear screen
Prompt and enter record number
LOOP while record number not = −1
   Read record
   If call number = 0
     Print error message RECORD DOES NOT EXIST
   else
     Write empty record
   Prompt and enter record number
RETURN

ENTER: Display All Courses
Clear screen
Reset file pointer to start of file
Print report heading lines
LOOP for record number <= 20
   Read record
   If call number not = 0
     Print record
RETURN

Hierarchy Chart: See Figure 14.14.

Program Flowchart: See Figure 14.15.

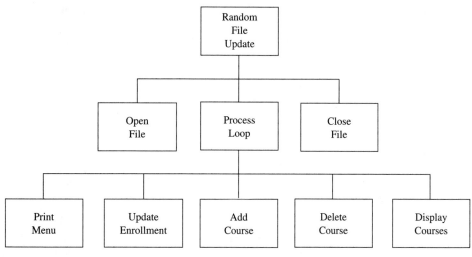

FIGURE 14.14   Hierarchy Chart for CHAP14D

Dissection of Sample Program CHAP14D

PROCESSING LOOP

```
void ProcessLoop(void)
{
    while (choice < 5)  {
        PrintMenu();
        switch (choice)  {
        case 1:
            UpdEnroll();
            break;
        case 2:
            AddCourses();
            break;
        case 3:
            DletCourses();
            break;
        case 4:
            DisplayAll();
            break;
        default:
            break;
        }
    }
    return;
}
```

The above module compares *choice* to the case labels. If a match is found, control branches to the module associated with the matching label. If a match is not found, control skips to the *default* case and returns to the *while* statement.

MAINLINE

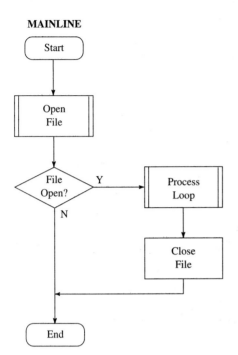

OPEN FILE

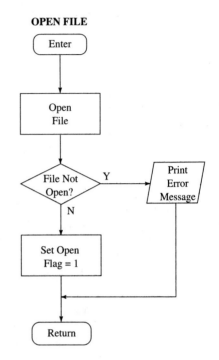

PROCESS LOOP

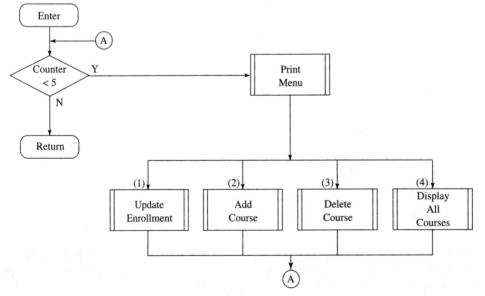

FIGURE 14.15   Program Flowchart for CHAP14D

PRINT MENU

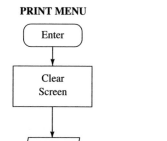

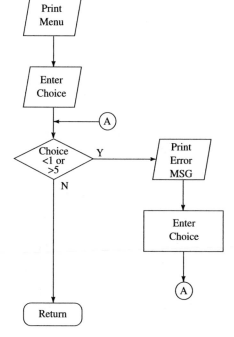

UPDATE ENROLLMENT

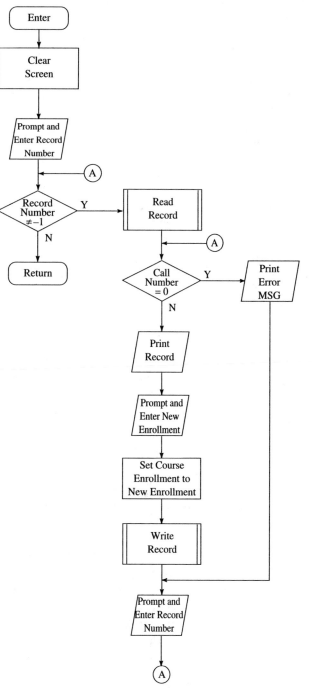

(continued on next page)

FIGURE 14.15   *Continued*

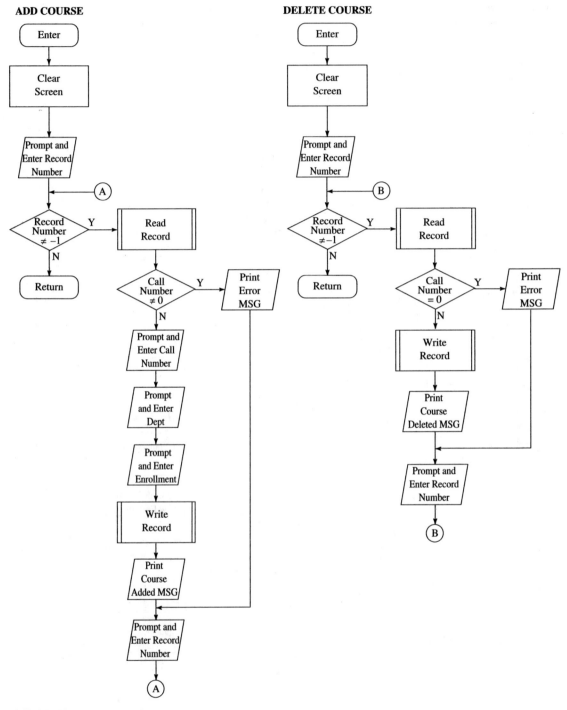

FIGURE 14.15   *Continued*

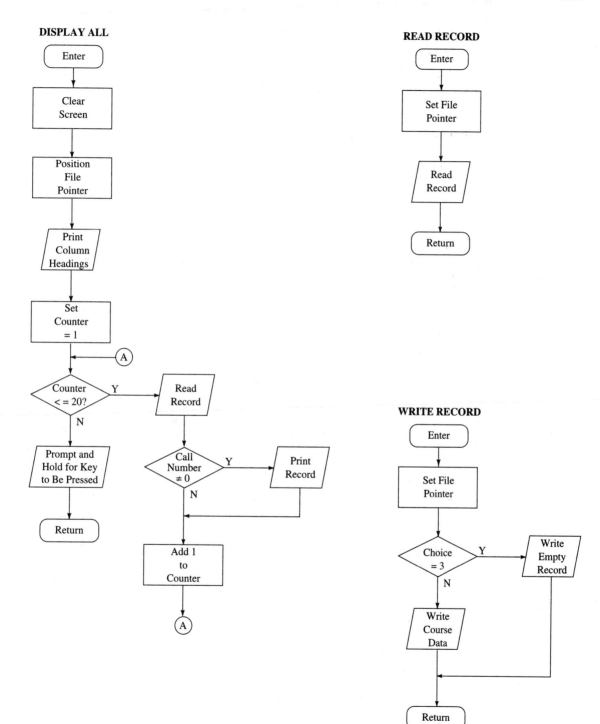

FIGURE 14.15 *Continued*

```
//---------- RANDOM FILE UPDATE --------------------------
//   This program randomly updates the course file.
//
//          PROGRAM-ID: CHAP14D
//          PROGRAMMER: David M. Collopy
//          RUN DATE:   mm/dd/yy
//*********************************************************

//---------- PREPROCESSING DIRECTIVES ----------------------

#include<iostream.h>
#include<fstream.h>
#include<iomanip.h>
#include<conio.h>

//---------- FUNCTION PROTOTYPES ---------------------------

void OpenFile(void);            // open course file
void ProcessLoop(void);         // processing loop
void UpdEnroll(void);           // update enrollment
void AddCourses(void);          // add courses
void DletCourses(void);         // delete courses
void DisplayAll(void);          // display all courses
void ReadRecord(void);          // read a record
void WriteRecord(void);         // write a record
void PrintMenu(void);           // print menu

//---------- PROGRAM SETUP ---------------------------------

//**  C O U R S E   R E C O R D

fstream file;                   // I/O file object
struct courseData  {            // course data structure
    int  callNum;               // call number
    char dept[15];              // department & number
    int  enroll;                // student enrollment
};
struct courseData course;               // course record
struct courseData empty = {0, "", 0};   // initial values

//**  P R O G R A M    V A R I A B L E S

int recNum;                     // record number
int choice = 0;                 // set menu choice to 0
int newEnroll;                  // new enollment count
char wait;                      // wait for key to be pressed
//-----------------------------------------------------------
//              MAINLINE CONTROL
//-----------------------------------------------------------
main()
{
```

FIGURE 14.16 Sample Program CHAP14D: Randomly Updates the Course File

```
        OpenFile();                      // open course file
        if (!file.fail())  {
            ProcessLoop();               // processing loop
            file.close();                // close course file
        }
        return 0;
}
//-------------------------------------------------------------
//                OPEN COURSE FILE
//-------------------------------------------------------------
void OpenFile(void)
{
    file.open("a:rcourse.fil", ios::in | ios::out);
    if (file.fail())  {
        cout << "Course file open failed " << endl;
    }
    return;
}
//-------------------------------------------------------------
//                PROCESSING LOOP
//-------------------------------------------------------------
void ProcessLoop(void)
{
    while (choice < 5)  {
        PrintMenu();                     // print menu
        switch (choice)  {
        case 1:
            UpdEnroll();                 // update enrollment
            break;
        case 2:
            AddCourses();                // add courses
            break;
        case 3:
            DletCourses();               // delete courses
            break;
        case 4:
            DisplayAll();                // display all courses
            break;
        default:
            break;                       //quit
        }
    }
    return;
}
//-------------------------------------------------------------
//                PRINT MENU
//-------------------------------------------------------------
void PrintMenu(void)
```

(continued on next page)

FIGURE 14.16 *Continued*

```
{
    clrscr();
    cout << "\nCourse Maintenance System\n";
    cout << "\nSelect one:\n\n"
         << "    1.   Update enrollment\n"
         << "    2.   Add courses\n"
         << "    3.   Delete courses\n"
         << "    4.   Display all courses\n"
         << "    5.   Quit\n"
         << "\nEnter choice (1 - 5) ===> ";
    cin >> choice;
    while (choice < 1 || choice > 5)   {
        cout << "\nError: Re-enter choice (1 - 5) ===> ";
        cin choice;
    }
    return;
}
//-----------------------------------------------------------
//              UPDATE ENROLLMENT
//-----------------------------------------------------------
void UpdEnroll(void)
{
    clrscr();
    cout << "\nUPDATE ENROLLMENT: Enter Rec# 1 - 20"
         << " or '-1' to quit: ";
    cin >> recNum;
    while (recNum != -1)   {
        ReadRecord();
        if (course.callNum == 0)
            cout << "\nError: Record does not exist";
        else   {
            cout << endl << recNum << "    "
                 << course.callNum << "    "
                 << course.dept
                 << setw(14) << course.enroll << endl;
            cout << "\Enter change in enrollment: ";
            cin >> newEnroll;
            course.enroll = newEnroll;
            WriteRecord();
        }
        cout << "\nUPDATE ENROLLMENT: Enter Rec# 1 - 20"
             << " or '-1' to quit: ";
        cin >> recNum;
    }
    return;
}
//-----------------------------------------------------------
//              ADD COURSES
```

FIGURE 14.16 *Continued*

```
//------------------------------------------------------------
void AddCourses(void)
{
    clrscr();
    cout << "\nADD COURSE: Enter Rec# 1 - 20"
        << " or '-1' to quit: ";
    cin >> recNum;
    while (recNum != -1)  {
        ReadRecord();
        if (course.callNum == 0)
            cout << "\nError: Record already exists ";
        else  {
            cout << "            Enter call number: ";
            cin >> course.callNum;
            cout << "             Enter department: ";
            cin >> course.dept;
            cout << "              Enter enrollment: ";
            cin >> course.enroll;
            WriteRecord();
            cout << "\nRecord# " << recNum << " added to "
                << "the course file ";
        }
        cout << "\nADD COURSE: Enter Rec# 1 - 20"
            << " or '-1' to quit: ";
        cin >> recNum;
    }
    return;
}
//------------------------------------------------------------
//              DELETE COURSES
//------------------------------------------------------------
void DletCourses(void)
{
    clrscr();
    cout << "\nDELETE COURSE: Enter Rec# 1 - 20"
        << " or '-1' to quit: ";
    cin >> recNum;
    while (recNum != -1)  {
        ReadRecord();
        if (course.callNum == 0)
            cout << "\nError: Record does not exist ";
        else  {
            WriteRecord();
            cout << "\nRecord# " << recNum << " deleted from "
                << "the course file ";
        }
        cout << "\nDELETE COURSE: Enter Rec# 1 - 20"
            << " or '-1' to quit: ";
```

(continued on next page)

FIGURE 14.16   *Continued*

```
            cin >> recNum;
        }
    return;
}
//-------------------------------------------------------------
//              DISPLAY ALL COURSES
//-------------------------------------------------------------
void DisplayAll(void)
{
    cout << "\nRec# Call#  Dept-Course#  Enrollment";
    cout << "\n-----------------------------------";
    for (recnum = 1; recNum <= 20; recNum++)  {
        file.seekg((recNum-1)*sizeof(courseData), ios::beg);
        file.read((char *) &course, sizeof(courseData));
        if (course.callNum != 0)  {
            cout << setw(2) << recNum
                 << setw(7) << course.callNum
                 << "   " << setiosflags(ios::left)
                 << setw(14) << course.dept
                 << resetiosflags(ios::left)
                 << setw(6) << course.enroll << endl;
        }
    }
    cout << "\n\nPress RETURN to continue";
    wait = getch();              // wait for key to be pressed
    return
}
//-------------------------------------------------------------
//              READ A RECORD
//-------------------------------------------------------------
void ReadRecord(void)
{
    file.seekg((recNum-1)*sizeof(courseData), ios::beg);
    file.read((char *) &course, sizeof(courseData));
    return;
}
//-------------------------------------------------------------
//              WRITE A RECORD
//-------------------------------------------------------------
void WriteRecord(void)
{
    file.seekp((recNum-1)*sizeof(courseData), ios::beg);
    if (choice == 3)
        file.write((char *) &empty, sizeof(courseData));
    else
        file.write((char *) &course, sizeof(courseData));
    return;
}
```

FIGURE 14.16 *Continued*

```
Course Maintenance System

Select one:

    1.  Update enrollment
    2.  Add courses
    3.  Delete courses
    4.  Display all courses
    5.  Quit


Enter choice (1 - 5) ===>____
```

FIGURE 14.17   Menu Options for CHAP14D

```
UPDATE ENROLLMENT: Enter Rec# 1 - 20 or '-1' to quit: 12

Error: Record does not exit

UPDATE ENROLLMENT: Enter Rec# 1 - 20 or '-1' to quit: 8

8    700    MATH120                14

Enter change in enrollment: 10

UPDATE ENROLLMENT: Enter Rec# 1 - 20 or '-1' to quit: -1
```

FIGURE 14.18   Choice 1: Update Enrollment

```
ADD COURSE: Enter Rec# 1 - 20 or '-1' to quit: 3

Error: Record already exists

ADD COURSE: Enter Rec# 1 - 20 or '-1' to quit: 5
            Enter call number: 650
              Enter department: MKT310
              Enter enrollment: 15

Record# 5 added to the course file

ADD COURSE: Enter Rec# 1 - 20 or '-1' to quit: -1
```

FIGURE 14.19   Choice 2: Add Courses

```
DELETE COURSE: Enter Rec# 1 - 20 or '-1' to quit: 14

Error: Record does not exist

DELETE COURSE: Enter Rec# 1 - 20 or '-1' to quit: 7

Record# 7 deleted from the course file

DELETE COURSE: Enter Rec# 1 - 20 or '-1' to quit: -1
```

FIGURE 14.20   Choice 3: Delete Courses

```
Rec# Call#   Dept-Course#   Enrollment
------------------------------------
 1    400    ENG200            16
 2    300    CHEM201           21
 3    600    MGT330            29
 4    200    BIOL101           19
 5    650    MKT310            15
 6    500    HIST225           33
 8    700    MATH120           10
 9    800    PHYS251           20
10    100    ACCT101           24
```

FIGURE 14.21   Choice 4: Display All Courses

PRINT MENU

```
void PrintMenu(void)
{
    clrscr();
    cout << "\nCourse Maintenance System\n";
    cout << "\nSelect one:\n\n"
         << "   1.  Update enrollment\n"
         << "   2.  Add courses\n"
         << "   3.  Delete courses\n"
         << "   4.  Display all courses\n"
         << "   5.  Quit\n"
         << "\nEnter choice (1 - 5) ===> ";
    cin >> choice;
```

The above statements display the course maintenance menu on the screen. The menu prompts the user to either select a processing option (1–4) or 5 to quit. The input statement assigns the selection to *choice*.

```
    while (choice < 1 || choice > 5)  {
        cout << "\nError: Re-enter choice (1 - 5) ===> ";
        cin choice;
    }
    return;
}
```

The *while* loop performs a range check to ensure that *choice* is valid. If *choice* is valid, control returns to the *PROCESSING LOOP*. Otherwise, the user is instructed to re-enter a valid selection.

UPDATE ENROLLMENT

```
void UpdEnroll(void)
{
    clrscr();
    cout << "\nUPDATE ENROLLMENT: Enter Rec# 1 - 20"
         << " or '-1' to quit: ";
    cin >> recNum;
    while (recNum != -1)   {
        ReadRecord();
        if (course.callNum == 0)
            cout << "\nError: Record does not exist";
        else  {
            cout << endl << recNum << "    "
                 << course.callNum << "    "
                 << course.dept
                 << setw(14) << course.enroll << endl;
            cout << "\Enter change in enrollment: ";
            cin >> newEnroll;
            course.enroll = newEnroll;
            WriteRecord();
        }
        cout << "\nUPDATE ENROLLMENT: Enter Rec# 1 - 20"
             << " or '-1' to quit: ";
        cin >> recNum;
    }
    return;
}
```

When *choice* is 1, control branches to *UpdEnroll* and prompts the user to enter the number of the record that requires an update. If *recNum* is not –1, the program reads the record into the structure variable. If *course.callNum* is 0, then the record does not exist and the error message is displayed on the screen. Control then prompts the user to enter the next record number or –1 to quit.

If *course.callNum* is not 0, the program displays the record on the screen and prompts the user to enter the new enrollment. The new enrollment is placed in the record, and the record is written back to the file.

```
ADD COURSES

void AddCourses(void)
{
    clrscr();
    cout << "\nADD COURSE: Enter Rec# 1 - 20"
         << " or '-1' to quit: ";
    cin >> recNum;
    while (recNum != -1)  {
        ReadRecord();
        if (course.callNum == 0)
            cout << "\nError: Record already exists ";
        else  {
            cout << "              Enter call number: ";
            cin >> course.callNum;
            cout << "              Enter department: ";
            cin >> course.dept;
            cout << "              Enter enrollment: ";
            cin >> course.enroll;
            WriteRecord();
            cout << "\nRecord# " << recNum << " added to "
                 << "the course file ";
        }
        cout << "\nADD COURSE: Enter Rec# 1 - 20"
             << " or '-1' to quit: ";
        cin >> recNum;
    }
    return;
}
```

When *choice* is 2, control branches to *AddCourses* and prompts the user to enter the record number of the record being added to the file. If *recNum* is not –1, the program reads the record into the structure variable. If *course.callNum* is not 0, then the record already exists and the error message is displayed on the screen. Control then prompts the user to enter the next record number or –1 to quit.

If the call number is 0, the program prompts the user to enter the new data. The new data is placed in the record, and the record is written back to the file.

```
DELETE COURSES

void DletCourses(void)
{
    clrscr();
    cout << "\nDELETE COURSE: Enter Rec# 1 - 20"
         << " or '-1' to quit: ";
    cin >> recNum;
    while (recNum != -1)  {
        ReadRecord();
        if (course.callNum == 0)
            cout << "\nError: Record does not exist ";
```

```
        else  {
            WriteRecord();
            cout << "\nRecord# " << recNum << " deleted from "
                << "the course file ";
        }
        cout << "\nDELETE COURSE: Enter Rec# 1 - 20"
            << " or '-1' to quit: ";
        cin >> recNum;
    }
    return;
}
```

When *choice* is 3, control branches to *DletCourses* and prompts the user to enter the record number of the record being deleted from the file. If *recNum* is not –1, the program reads the record into the structure variable. If *course.callNum* is 0, then the record does not exist and the error message is displayed on the screen. Control then prompts the user to enter the next record number or –1 to quit.

If the call number is not 0, the program writes an empty record back to the file. Hence, a record is deleted from the file by writing an empty record in its place.

DISPLAY ALL COURSES

```
void DisplayAll(void)
{
    cout << "\nRec# Call#  Dept-Course#  Enrollment";
    cout << "\n----------------------------------";
    for (recnum = 1; recNum <= 20; recNum++)  {
        file.seekg((recNum-1)*sizeof(courseData), ios::beg);
        file.read((char *) &course, sizeof(courseData));
        if (course.callNum != 0)  {
            cout << setw(2) << recNum
                << setw(7) << course.callNum
                << "   " << setiosflags(ios::left)
                << setw(14) << course.dept
                << resetiosflags(ios::left)
                << setw(6) << course.enroll << endl;
        }
    }
    cout << "\n\nPress RETURN to continue";
    wait = getch();                 // wait for key to be pressed
    return
}
```

When *choice* is 4, control defaults to *DisplayAll* and prints a report of all the records stored in the file. If *course.callNum* does not equal 0, the program prints the record on the report. Any value other than 0 indicates that live data is stored in the record.

After reading and printing the file, control returns to the *MAINLINE*.

READ A RECORD

```
void ReadRecord(void)
{
```

```
    file.seekg((recNum-1)*sizeof(courseData), ios::beg);
    file.read((char *) &course, sizeof(courseData));
    return;
}
```

The seek get sets the file pointer to the address location specified by the offset. The read() retrieves the record and stores the data in the *course* structure variable.

```
WRITE A RECORD

void WriteRecord(void)
{
    file.seekp((recNum-1)*sizeof(courseData), ios::beg);
    if (choice == 3)
        file.write((char *) &empty, sizeof(courseData));
    else
        file.write((char *) &course, sizeof(courseData));
    return;
}
```

The seek put sets the file pointer to the address location specified by the offset. According to the value of *choice*, one of two structure variables is written to the file. If *choice* is 3, the empty record is written to the file. Otherwise, the data stored in the *course* record is written to the file.

Summary

1. Structures are used to group multiple data types. A structure is a group item that is made up of two or more related data types.

2. A structure defines a record and its members; a member defines a field.

3. A structure may be processed as a single unit, or the members may be processed individually.

4. The keyword *struct* defines the format of the data, and *tag* assigns a name to the structure. Member definitions define the names of the members and their data types.

5. A structure variable assigns a memory location to the members of the data structure.

6. Data may be assigned to a structure either at the time the structure is declared or by the program during the run.

7. A structure may be initialized by assigning values to the structure variable. The values are assigned to the member variables on a positional basis—the first value is assigned the first member, the second value is assigned the second member, and so forth.

8. Data may be assigned to a structure variable by prompting the user to enter it at the keyboard.

9. The dot operator links the structure variable to the member of the structure. The structure variable is coded on left of the dot operator and the member name is coded on the right.

10. Random file organization stores data on disk in random order. Random file access allows the user to skip around in the file.

11. Random file processing offers the advantage of fast data retrieval. For example, if the user wants a specific record from the random file, the program can go directly to the record and retrieve the data.

12. Random access can be rather cumbersome and slow for applications that require access to all or most of the records in a large file, particularly if the records must be processed in sequential order.

13. Use the open() member function to open a random file. Random access files may be opened for input or output or for both input and output.

14. The write() member function writes data to a random file. The statement consists of arguments that specify the beginning of the file, the address to the structure variable, and the record length.

15. The *sizeof* operator may be used to determine the number of bytes associated with the structure variable.

16. Creating a random file involves the following steps: (1) declare the file object variable; (2) define the data structure; (3) define and initialize the empty record; (4) open the file for output; (5) write empty records to the file; and (6) close the file.

17. The seek function is used to move the file pointer to a specific location in a random file prior to executing a read or write operation. The statement consists of two arguments that specify the file pointer offset and the origin.

18. Loading a random file involves the following steps: (1) declare the file object variable; (2) define the data structure and the structure variable; (3) open the file for input and output; (4) prompt and enter the data; (5) assign the input to the structure variable; (6) set the file pointer and write the data to the file; and (7) close the file.

19. The read() member function reads data from a random file. The statement consists of arguments that specify the beginning of the file, the address to the structure variable, and the record length.

20. Reading and printing the contents of a random file involves the following tasks: (1) declare the file object pointer; (2) define the data structure and the structure variable; (3) open the file for input and output; (4) read a record and assign the data to the structure variable; (5) print the record; and (6) close the file.

21. Updating a random access file involves the following tasks: (1) declare the file object variable; (2) define the data structure and the structure variable; (3) open the file for input and output; (4) determine the update type; (5) enter the transaction and update the record; and (6) close the file.

Programming Projects

For each project, design the logic and write the modular structured program to produce the output. Model your program after the sample programs presented in the chapter. Verify your output.

Project 14–1 Overdue Accounts-1

Write a program to create a random access file for the overdue accounts. Write a total of 30 empty records to the file.

Input (internal):

Define the account data structure and the members given below. Field size and type are shown in parentheses.

Account number	(4 int)
Customer nam	(15 char)
Days overdue	(2 int)
Balance due	(6.2 float)

Output (overdue.fil):

Initialized random access file

Processing Requirements:

- Define and initialize the empty record.
- Open the file for output.
- Write empty records to the file.
- Close the file.

Project 14–2 Overdue Accounts-2

Write a program to prompt the user to enter the data at the keyboard and load the overdue accounts file created in Project 14–1.

Input (disk file and keyboard):

Disk file: Random access file (*overdue.fil*)

Keyboard: For each customer record, prompt for and enter the following data. Field size and type are shown in parentheses.

1. Account number (4 int)
2. Customer name   (15 char)
3. Days overdue   (2 int)
4. Balance due   (6.2 float)

File Data (keyboard):

Use the data given below to load the overdue accounts file. The numbers shown above the columns correspond to the fields described for the input. The record numbers are shown on the left.

Rec#	1	2	3	4
20	6350	Susan Cope	90	600.00
11	2730	Rita Fox	90	740.00

5	3100	Alvin Porter	90	550.00
27	4080	Corey Adkins	30	233.00
9	5260	Brian Knox	30	625.00
21	7720	Lisa Wilson	60	417.00
26	9200	Tori Landis	90	235.00
17	4890	Amy Wyatt	30	700.00
14	1010	David Ryan	90	400.00
15	9630	Pat Rankin	60	342.00
28	2450	Marie Hill	30	754.00
3	8540	Matt Hart	90	900.00

Output (overdue.fil):

Random access file

Processing Requirements:

- Open the file for input and output.
- Prompt for and enter the data.
- Assign the input to the structure variable.
- Write the structure variable (record) to the file.
- Close the file.

Project 14–3 Overdue Accounts-3

Write a menu program that allows the user to select from several file updating options. Prompt and enter the data, check for errors, and update the overdue accounts file from Project 14–2. Write the input errors to an error log.

Menu Choices:

1. Update accounts
2. Add accounts
3. Delete accounts
4. Display all accounts
5. Quit

Input(disk file and keyboard):

Disk file: Random access file (*overdue.file*)

Keyboard: For options 1–3, prompt for and enter the following data:

Option	Input Data
1	Record number, account number, customer name, days overdue, and amount due
2	Record number, account number, customer name, days overdue, and amount due
3	Record number

File Data (keyboard):

Enter the updates in the random order shown. For each, use the menu option to apply the data to the record specified by the record number.

Menu Option	Record Number	Account Number	Customer Name	Days Overdue	Balance Due
delete	2				
update	17	4890	Amy Clark	30	700.00
add	23	1000	Sarah Brooks	60	220.00
delete	3				
update	14	1010	Ryan Davis	90	400.00
add	11	9630	Pat Rankin	60	342.00
add	7	9700	Adam Norris	60	475.00
update	22	6350	Susan Cope	60	600.00
update	28	2450	Marie Hill	30	700.00
delete	5				
add	9	4080	Corey Adkins	30	233.00
update	11	2730	Rita Fox	30	740.00
update	26	9200	Tori Landis	90	300.00
add	18	4900	Marla Stevens	90	594.00
update	25	2740	Tia Marlowe	30	135.00

Output (overdue.fil):

Updated random access file

Processing Requirements:

- Open the file for input and output.
- Display the menu options and prompt for a selection.
- Enter the data and update the file.
- Close the file.

Project 14–4   Overdue Accounts-4

Write a program to read the updated overdue accounts file in Project 14–3 and print the overdue accounts report shown below. Accumulate a total for amount due and print the total at the end of the report.

```
Author                  OVERDUE ACCOUNTS                 Page 01
                          mm/dd/yy


Acct Number     Customer Name     Days Overdue     Amount Due

   9999         X----------X           99            999.99
     :               :                  :               :
     :               :                  :               :
   9999         X----------X           99            999.99

                                      Total:         9999.99
```

Processing Requirements:

- Open the file for input and output.
- Read the overdue accounts file.
- Print a report of the overdue accounts.
- Accumulate a total for amount due and print it at the end of the report.
- Close the file.

Project 14–5 Sales Profit-1

Write a program to create a random access file for the sales department. Write a total of 20 empty records to the file.

Input (internal):

Define the sales data structure and the members given below. Field size and type are shown in parentheses.

Salesperson number	(3 int)
Salesperson name	(15 char)
Total sales	(8.2 float)
Cost of sales	(8.2 float)

Output (sales.fil):

Initialized random access file

Processing Requirements:

- Define and initialize the empty record.
- Open the file for output.
- Write empty records to the file.
- Close the file.

Project 14–6 Sales Profit-2

Write a program to prompt the user to enter the data at the keyboard and load the sales file created in Project 14–5.

Input (disk file and keyboard):

Disk file: Random access file (*sales.file*)

Keyboard: For each sales record, prompt for and enter the following data. Field size and type are shown in parentheses.

1. Salesperson number   (3 int)

2. Salesperson name   (15 char)

3. Total sales   (8.2 float)

4. Cost of sales   (8.2 float)

File Data (keyboard):

Use the data given below to create the sales file. The numbers shown above the columns correspond to the fields described for the input. The record numbers are shown on the left.

Rec#	1	2	3	4
19	400	Tara Perkins	12710.14	9735.38
11	700	Dennis Tian	4567.51	3119.22
5	300	Roy Hickle	2245.78	1072.49
12	100	Lisa Conrad	8120.52	6450.71
7	900	Ann Zimmerman	5793.59	4204.45

Output (sales.fil):

Random access file

Processing Requirements:

- Open the file for input and output.
- Prompt for and enter the data.
- Assign the input to the structure variable.
- Write the structure variable (record) to the file.
- Close the file.

Project 14–7   Sales Profit-3

Write a menu program that allows the user to select from several file processing options. Prompt and enter the data, check for errors, and update the sales file from Project 14–6. Write the input errors to an error log.

Menu Choices:

1. Update sales records

2. Add sales records

3. Delete sales records

4. Display all sales records

5. Quit

Input (disk file and keyboard):

Disk file: Random access file (*sales.fil*)
Keyboard: For options 1–3, prompt for and enter the following data:

Option	Input Data
1	Record number, salesperson number, salesperson name, total sales, and cost of sales
2	Record number, salesperson number, salesperson name, total sales, and cost of sales
3	Record number

File Data (keyboard):

Enter the updates in the random order shown. For each, use the menu option to apply the data to the record specified by the record number.

Menu Option	Record Number	Salesperson Number	Salesperson Name	Total Sales	Cost of Sales
add	7	900	Ann Zimmerman	5793.59	4204.45
update	4	340	David Kock	4339.16	2124.83
update	5	300	Roy Henderson	2245.78	1072.49
update	16	490	Michael Torres	9634.28	5593.15
add	14	940	Sean Zorich	7465.92	5641.39
update	11	700	Dennis Tian	4567.51	3191.22
update	9	250	Robert Minelli	3974.63	2016.24
delete	19				
add	2	200	Allison Dunn	6518.02	4131.78

Output (sales.fil):

Updated random access file

Processing Requirements:
- Open the file for input and output.
- Display the menu options and prompt for a selection.
- Enter the data and update the file.
- Close the file.

Project 14–8 Sales Profit-4

Write a program to read the updated sales file (see Project 14–7) and print the sales profit report shown below. Accumulate a total for net profit and print the total at the end of the report.

```
Author                   SALES PROFIT REPORT           Page 01
                             mm/dd/yy
                         Total           Cost of        Net
Num    Salesperson       Sales           Sales          Profit
-----------------------------------------------------------------
999    X---------X       99999.99        99999.99       99999.99
 :         :                :               :              :
 :         :                :               :              :
999    X---------X       99999.99        99999.99       99999.99

                                         Total:         999999.99
```

Processing Requirements:
- Open the file for input and output.
- Read the sales file.
- Print a report of the sales profit.
- Accumulate a total for net profit and print it at the end of the report.
- Close the file.

15 Indexed Files

Learning Objectives

After you have read this chapter and completed the exercises, you should be able to:

- explain the purpose and use of indexed files
- create and load an indexed file
- read and print data stored in an indexed file
- update data stored in an indexed file

Indexed File Organization

Sequential files store data in key field order. Whether the number of change transactions is large or small, a sequential file update always creates and writes a new file to the disk. To update the 100th record, the program copies the first 99 records to the disk, updates the 100th record, and copies the remainder of the file to the disk. Certainly, this process is slow and time consuming.

Although random files store data in random order, they, too, have limitations. For example, random files can waste disk space because empty record positions go unfilled. Additionally, random files store and retrieve data by record number. For many applications, this simply will not work. For example, social security numbers, serial numbers, ZIP codes, and customer names do not easily equate to a series of record numbers that fall in the range 1 to n.

Indexed files, however, do not impose these restrictions on us. Although they are more complicated to use, indexed files use a key field to access the data and save disk space. By definition, an **indexed file** is a pseudofile organization method that consists of an array and a random access file. The array holds the record keys and the random file holds the data. Since the record keys are stored directly in memory and not in a file, they can be read quickly by the program. After the file has been processed, the keys stored in the array are copied to a sequential file for future reference.

Because of the way C++ accesses files, the process of locating a key stored in an array takes far less time than searching for it in a file. C++ accesses files through special input/output (I/O) control routines that are part of the computer's operating system access method. Each time a record is read from a file, the program executes the I/O routines to access the data. Overall, the time associated with performing these routines is significantly longer than the time required to locate the key stored in an array.

Once again, consider the course registration system for Central State College. The key array and random access data file are shown in Figure 15.1. Assume the user enters the call number 200. To access the record, the program searches the array and compares the 200—the search key—to each call number stored in the array until a match is found or the end of the array is encountered. For a match, the subscript of the array is used to access the data stored in the random file. Notice that a match is found where subscript equals 3. Hence, the course data is stored in the random access file at record number 4 (subscript + 1).

	Key Array		DATA FILE		
			Call#	Dept-Course	Enrollment
Sub 0	400	Rec# 1	400	ENG200	16
1	300	2	300	CHEM201	21
2	600	3	600	MGT330	29
>3	200	4	200	BIOL101	19
4	500	5	500	HIST225	33
5	900	6	900	SPAN111	12
6	700	7	700	MATH120	14
7	800	8	800	PHYS251	20
8	100	9	100	ACCT101	24
				. . . .	
19	0	20	0	blank	0

FIGURE 15.1   Indexed File

Creating an Indexed File

In the section that follows, we will create an indexed file for the course scheduling application for Central State College. To create the indexed file, we must define a key array and a random data file. Later, we will copy the array to a sequential file for future reference. Our objective is to reserve disk space for the course records and to set up an array to track the record keys.

Creating an indexed file involves the following tasks:

1. Set up indexed file—define sequential key file, random data file, and key array.
2. Open sequential and random files.
3. Set the key array to 0.
4. Write empty records to the random file.
5. Copy the key array to the sequential file.
6. Close the files.

This process is illustrated in sample program CHAP15A. Both the sequential key file and the random data file are initialized by the program.

Checkpoint 15A

1. (True or False) A sequential file update always creates and writes a new file to the disk.
2. (True or False) A disadvantage of random files is that they can waste disk space.
3. Briefly define and explain an indexed file.
4. List six steps involved in creating an indexed file.
5. Briefly explain how a record is located using indexed-file organization.

Sample Program CHAP15A

Sample program CHAP15A (Figure 15.4, p. 528) creates and initializes an indexed file for the courses offered at the branch campus of Central State College. As before, the size of the file has been limited to 20 records.

The following specifications apply:

Input (internal):

Define the course data structure and the members given below. Field size and type are shown in parentheses.

Call number	(3 int)
Department & number	(15 char)
Student enrollment	(2 int)

Output (disk files):

Sequential key file	(*course.key*)
Random data file	(*course.dat*)

The files are shown in Figure 15.5 (p. 530).

Processing Requirements:

- Define and initialize the empty record.
- Define a sequential key file, a random data file, and a key array.
- Open the sequential file and random file for output.
- Set the elements of the array to 0.
- Write empty records to the random file.
- After creating the indexed file, copy the array to the sequential file.
- Close the files.

Pseudocode:

```
START
Create array
Clear screen
Open files
If files opened
   Define the empty record
   LOOP for record number <= 20
      Set array element to 0
      Write the empty record to the data file
   End LOOP
   LOOP for record number <= 20
      Save array elements in the key file
   End LOOP
   Close files
END
```

Hierarchy Chart: See Figure 15.2.

Program Flowchart: See Figure 15.3.

Dissection of Sample Program CHAP15A

```
KEY RECORD
ofstream keyFile;
```

The above statement defines the output file stream for the sequential key file. The file object name *keyFile* is assigned to the output file stream (*ofstream*). The identifier *keyFile* will be used to hold the address of the key file.

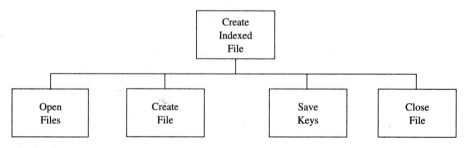

FIGURE 15.2   Hierarchy Chart for CHAP15A

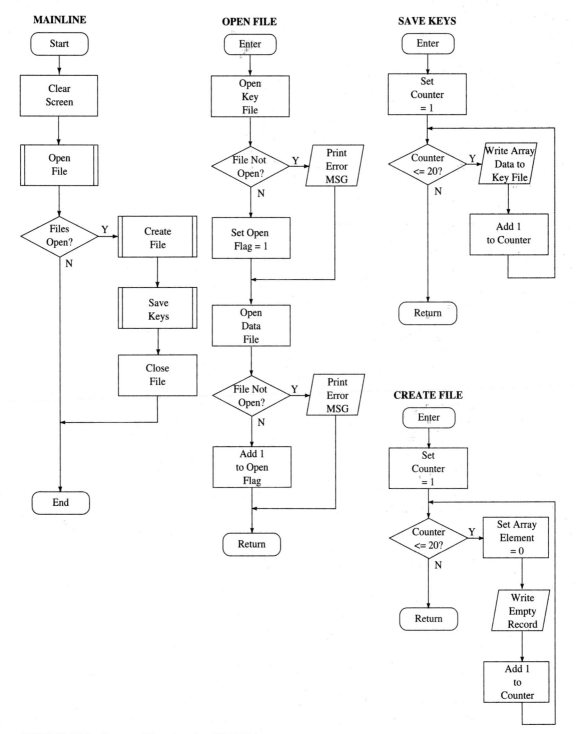

FIGURE 15.3   Program Flowchart for CHAP15A

```
//----------- CREATE INDEXED FILE--------------------------
//  This program uses an array and a random access file to
//  create an indexed file of 20 empty records.
//
//           PROGRAM-ID: CHAP15A
//           PROGRAMMER: David M. Collopy
//           RUN DATE:   mm/dd/yy
//**********************************************************

//----------- PREPROCESSING DIRECTIVES ---------------------
#include<iostream.h>
#include<fstream.h>
#include<conio.h>
//----------- FUNCTION PROTOTYPES ---------------------------

void OpenFiles(void);          // open program files
void CreateFile(void);         // create indexed file
void SaveKeys(void);           // save record keys

//----------- PROGRAM SETUP --------------------------------
//** K E Y   R E C O R D

ofstream keyFile;              // sequential file object

//** D A T A   R E C O R D

ofstream file;                 // random file object
struct courseData  {           // course data structure
    int  callNum;              // call number
    char dept[15];             // department & number
    int  enroll;               // student enrollment
};

struct courseData empty = {0, "", 0};       // record values

//** P R O G R A M   V A R I A B L E S
int key[20];                   // 20 element key array
int recNum;                    // record number

//----------------------------------------------------------
//              MAINLINE CONTROL
//----------------------------------------------------------
main()
{
    clrscr();                  // clear the screen
    OpenFiles();               // open program files
```

FIGURE 15.4   Sample Program CHAP15A: Creates an Indexed File of 20 Empty Records

```cpp
    if (!keyFile.fail() && !dataFile.fail())  {
        CreateFile();            // create indexed file
        SaveKeys();              // save record keys
        keyFile.close();         // close key file
        dataFile.close();        // close data file
    }
    return 0;
}
//------------------------------------------------------------
//              OPEN PROGRAM FILES
//------------------------------------------------------------
void OpenFiles(void)
{
    keyFile.open("a:course.key");            // open for output
    if (keyFile.fail())
        cout << "Key file open failed " << endl;

    dataFile.open("a:course.dat");           // open for output
    if (dataFile.fail())
        cout << "Data file open failed " << endl;

    return;
}
//------------------------------------------------------------
//              CREATE INDEXED FILE
//------------------------------------------------------------
void CreateFile(void)
{
    for (recNum = 1; recNum <= 20; recNum++)  {
        key[recNum - 1] = 0;
        dataFile.write((char *) &empty, sizeof(courseData));
    }
    return;
}
//------------------------------------------------------------
//              SAVE RECORD KEYS
//------------------------------------------------------------
void SaveKeys(void)
{
    for (recNum = 1; recNum <= 20; recNum++)  {
        keyFile << key[recNum - 1] << endl;
    }
    return;
}
```

FIGURE 15.4 *Continued*

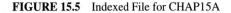

	Key File		Call#	**D A T A F I L E** Dept-Course #	Enrollment
Sub 0	0	Rec# 1	0	blank	0
1	0	2	0	blank	0
2	0	3	0	blank	0
			. . . . .		
19	0	20	0	blank	0

FIGURE 15.5   Indexed File for CHAP15A

DATA RECORD

```
ofstream dataFile;
struct courseData  {
    int   callNum;
    char dept[15];
    int   enroll;
};
```

The above statements mean: Define the output file stream for the random data file and the format of the course data structure. The structure describes the members—*callNum* (int), *dept* (char), and *enroll* (int).

```
struct courseData empty = {0,"", 0};
```

The above statement defines the empty record, reserves storage space for it, and initializes the data fields: *callNum* to 0, *dept* to Null string, and *enroll* to 0.

PROGAM VARIABLES

```
int   key[20];
int   recNum;
```

The above statements define the file open flag, the key array, and the record number. The flag is set to 0, and the array reserves storage for 20 call numbers.

MAINLINE CONTROL

```
main()
{
    clrscr();
    OpenFiles();
    if (!keyFile.fail() && !dataFile.fail())  {
        CreateFile();
        SaveKeys();
        keyFile.close();
        dataFile.close();
    }
    return 0;
}
```

The *MAINLINE* clears the screen and executes the modules in the order listed. The *if* statement determines whether to perform the statements enclosed within the braces. If the sequential and random files were opened, processing continues. Otherwise, the program returns a 0 to the operating system and terminates the run.

OPEN PROGRAM FILES

```
void OpenFiles(void)
{
    keyFile.open("a:course.key");
    if (keyFile.fail())
        cout << "Key file open failed " << endl;
```

The above statements mean: Open the sequential key file for output. If the file is opened, the address of the key file is passed to the file object and the open() member function returns the value 1. But if the file cannot be opened, null is passed to the file object and the error message is displayed on the screen.

```
    dataFile.open("a:course.dat");
    if (dataFile.fail())
        cout << "Data file open failed " << endl;

    return;
}
```

The above statements mean: Open the random data file for output. If the file is opened, the address of the data file is passed to the file object and the open() member function returns the value 1. If the file cannot be opened, null is passed to the file object and the error message is displayed on the screen.

CREATE INDEXED FILE

```
void CreateFile(void)
{
    for (recNum = 1; recNum <= 20; recNum++)  {
        key[recNum - 1] = 0;
        dataFile.write((char *) &empty, sizeof(courseData));
    }
    return;
}
```

The above statements mean: As long as *recNum* is less than or equal to 20, store a 0 in the array and write the empty record to the random file. The expression `recNum - 1` specifies the subscript of the corresponding element in the array. The record number is adjusted to produce the subscript. Remember, subscripts are numbered starting with 0.

SAVE RECORD KEYS

```
void SaveKeys(void)
{
    for (recNum = 1; recNum <= 20; recNum++)  {
        keyFile << key[recNum - 1] << endl;
    }
    return;
}
```

The preceding statements mean: As long as *recNum* is less than or equal to 20, copy the call number stored in the array to the sequential key file. This module saves the course call numbers on disk.

Writing Data to an Indexed File

Now that the indexed file has been created, we are ready to load the file with live data. Since we are using an indexed file, we may enter the data in any order we wish.

Loading an indexed file involves the following tasks:

1. Set up the indexed file—define sequential key file, random data file, and key array.
2. Load the key array.
3. Open sequential and random files.
4. Prompt and enter the data.
5. Store the keys in the array and write the data to the random file.
6. Copy the array to the sequential file.
7. Close the files.

The load process is illustrated in sample program CHAP15B. Notice how the key array and the sequential file work together to maintain the record keys.

Sample Program CHAP15B

Sample program CHAP15B (Figure 15.8, p. 536) prompts the user to enter the data at the keyboard and loads the indexed file. The record keys are copied to the sequential file, and the data is written to the random file.

The following specifications apply:

Input (disk files and keyboard):

Disk files: Sequential key file   *(course.key)*
            random data file   *(course.dat)*

Keyboard: For each course record, prompt for and enter the following data. Field size and type are shown in parentheses.

Call number	(3 int)
Department & number	(15 char)
Student enrollment	(2 int)

Output (disk files):

Sequential key file   *(course.key)*
Random data file   *(course.dat)*

The files are shown in Figure 15.9 (p. 538).

Processing Requirements:

• Define a sequential key file, a random data file, and a key array.
• Open the sequential file for input, load the array, and close the file.

- Open the sequential file for output and the random file for input/output.
- Prompt for and enter the data.
- Store the record keys in the array and write the data to the random file.
- After loading the file, copy the array to the sequential file.
- Close the files.

Pseudocode:

```
START
Create array
Clear screen
Open sequential file
If file opened
   Load the array
   Close the key file
Open files
If files opened
   Prompt and enter the record number
   LOOP until record number = –1
       Prompt and enter the data
       Store the key in array
       Write the record to the random file
       Prompt and enter the record number
   End LOOP
   LOOP for record number <= 20
       Copy array to the sequential file
   End LOOP
   Close files
END
```

Hierarchy Chart: See Figure 15.6.

Program Flowchart: See Figure 15.7.

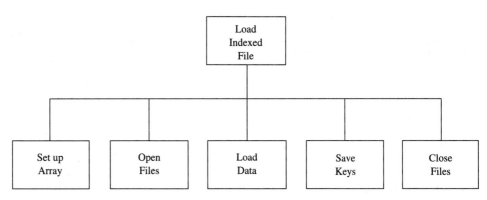

FIGURE 15.6   Hierarchy Chart for CHAP15B

MAINLINE

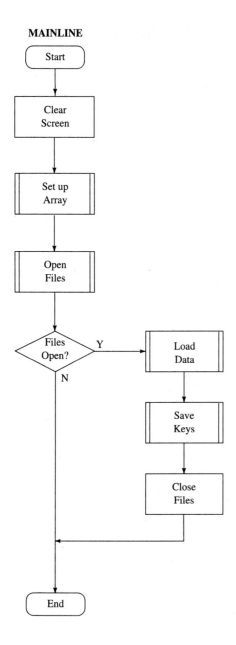

SET UP ARRAY

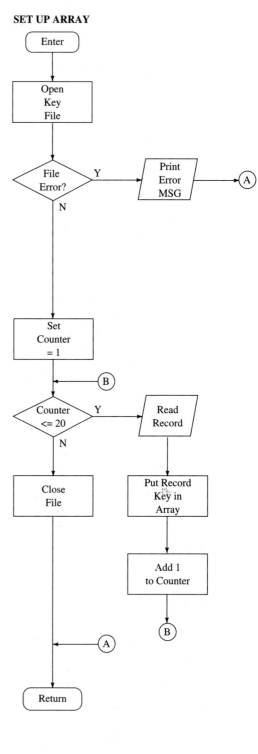

FIGURE 15.7   Program Flowchart for CHAP15B

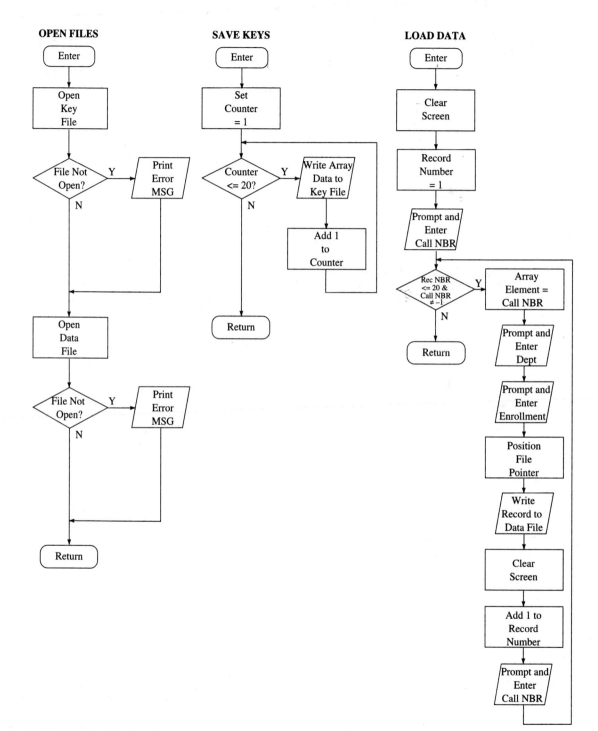

FIGURE 15.7 *Continued*

```
//---------- LOAD INDEXED FILE----------------------------
//  This program loads data randomly into an indexed file.
//
//            PROGRAM-ID: CHAP15B
//            PROGRAMMER: David M. Collopy
//            RUN DATE:   mm/dd/yy
//*********************************************************

//---------- PREPROCESSING DIRECTIVES --------------------
#include<iostream.h>
#include<fstream.h>
#include<conio.h>

//---------- FUNCTION PROTOTYPES -------------------------

void SetupArray(void);          // set up key array
void OpenFiles(void);           // open program files
void LoadData(void);            // load array and data file
void SaveKeys(void);            // save record keys

//---------- PROGRAM SETUP -------------------------------

//**  K E Y   R E C O R D

fstream keyFile;                // sequential file object

//**  D A T A   R E C O R D

fstream file;                   // random file object
struct courseData  {            // course data structure
    int  callNum;               // call number
    char dept[15];              // department & number
    int  enroll;                // student enrollment
};
struct courseData course;       // course record

//**  P R O G R A M   V A R I A B L E S

int key[20];                    // 20 element key array
int recNum;                     // record number
//--------------------------------------------------------
//               MAINLINE CONTROL
//--------------------------------------------------------
main()
{
    clrscr();                   // clear the screen
    SetupArray();               // set up key array
    OpenFiles();                // open program files
    if (!keyFile.fail() && !dataFile.fail())  {
        LoadData();             // load array and data file
```

FIGURE 15.8   Sample Program CHAP15B: Writes Data Randomly to an Indexed File

```
            SaveKeys();              // save record keys
            keyFile.close();         // close key file
            dataFile.close();        // close data file
        }
        return 0;
}
//------------------------------------------------------------
//               SET UP ARRAY
//------------------------------------------------------------
void SetupArray(void)
{
    keyFile.open("a:course.key", ios::in));
    if (keyFile.fail())
        cout << "Key file open failed " << endl;
    else {
        for (recNum = 1; recNum <= 20; recNum++)  {
            keyFile >> key[recnum - 1];
        }
        keyFile.close();
    }
    return;
}
//------------------------------------------------------------
//               OPEN PROGRAM FILES
//------------------------------------------------------------
void OpenFiles(void)
{
    keyFile.open("a:course.key", ios::out);
    if (keyFile.fail())
        cout << "Key file open failed " << endl;

    dataFile.open("a:course.dat", ios::in | ios::out);
    if (dataFile.fail())
        cout << "Data file open failed " << endl;

    return;
}
//------------------------------------------------------------
//               LOAD ARRAY AND DATA FILE
//------------------------------------------------------------
void LoadData(void)
{
    clrscr();
    recNum = 1;
    cout << "     Enter call number or '-1' to quit: ";
    cin >> course.callNum;
    while (recNum <= 20 && course.callNum != -1)  {
```

(continued on next page)

FIGURE 15.8 *Continued*

```
            key[recNum - 1] =  course.callNum;
            cout << "              Enter department & number: ";
            cin >> course.dept;
            cout << "              Enter student enrollment: ";
            cin >> course.enroll;
            dataFile.seekp((recNum-1)*sizeof(courseData), ios::beg);
            dataFile.write((char *) &course, sizeof(courseData));
            clrscr();
            recNum = recNum + 1;
            cout << "      Enter call number or '-1' to quit: ";
            cin >> course.callNum;
        }
        return;
    }
    //-----------------------------------------------------------
    //              SAVE RECORD KEYS
    //-----------------------------------------------------------
    void SaveKeys(void)
    {
        for (recNum = 1; recNum <= 20; recNum++)  {
            keyFile << key[recNum - 1] << endl;
        }
        return;
    }
```

FIGURE 15.8   *Continued*

	Key File		Call#	DATA FILE Dept-Course#	Enrollment
Sub 0	400	Rec# 1	400	ENG200	16
1	300	2	300	CHEM201	21
2	600	3	600	MGT330	29
3	200	4	200	BIOL101	19
4	500	5	500	HIST225	33
5	900	6	900	SPAN111	12
6	700	7	700	MATH120	14
7	800	8	800	PHYS251	20
8	100	9	100	ACCT101	24
				. . . . .	
19	0	20	0	blank	0

FIGURE 15.9   Indexed File for CHAP15B

Dissection of Sample Program CHAP15B

For the most part, the front end of the program remains the same. Like sample program CHAP15A, the file pointers, the course data structure, the key array, and the record number are defined in the *PROGRAM SETUP*.

This time, however, the structure variable defines the course record:

```
struct courseData course;
```

The input data entered by the user is assigned to the course record and is written to the random data file.

Essentially, the *MAINLINE* clears the screen, loads the key array, opens the random file, and prompts the user to enter the input. Afterwards, the program copies the contents of the array to the sequential file and closes the files.

```
SET UP ARRAY

void SetupArray(void)
{
    keyFile.open("a:course.key", ios::in));
    if (keyFile.fail())
        cout << "Key file open failed " << endl;
    else {
        for (recNum = 1; recNum <= 20; recNum++) {
            keyFile >> key[recnum - 1];
        }
        keyFile.close();
    }
    return;
}
```

The above statements mean: Open the sequential key file for input and pass the address of the file to the file object. If the file was not opened, then display the error message on the screen. But if the file was opened, then load the keys (zeros) into the array. As long as *recNum* is less than or equal to 20, read a key from the file and store it in the array. After loading the array, close the file.

```
LOAD ARRAY AND DATA FILE

void LoadData(void)
{
    clrscr();
    recNum = 1;
```

The above statements mean: Clear the screen and set *recNum* to 1.

```
    cout <<"    Enter call number or '-1' to quit: ";
    cin >> course.callNum;
```

The above statements mean: Prompt the user to enter the call number or –1 to quit. Get the call number, convert it to an integer, and assign the result to the *course.callNum* field of the course record.

```
      while (recNum <= 20 && course.callNum != -1)   {
```

The above statement means: As long as *recNum* is less than or equal to 20 and the *course.callNum* is not equal to –1, execute the statements in the body of the loop.

```
      key[recNum - 1] = course.callNum;
```

This statement copies the course call number to the key array. The expression `recNum -` 1 specifies the subscript and tells the program where to store the call number in the array.

```
        cout << "              Enter department & number: ";
        cin >> course.dept;
        cout << "              Enter student enrollment: ";
        cin >> course.enroll;
```

The above statements mean: Prompt the user to enter the course data (department and enrollment), and assign the input to the fields in the course record.

```
        dataFile.seekp((recNum-1)*sizeof(courseData), ios::beg);
        dataFile.write((char *) &course, sizeof(courseData));
```

The seekp() sets the file pointer to the address location specified by the offset expression. The write() writes the data stored in the course record to the random data file.

```
        clrscr();
        recNum = recNum + 1;
        cout << "     Enter call number or '-1' to quit:   ";
        cin >> course.callNum;
    }
    return;
}
```

The above statements mean: Clear the screen, increment *recNum*, and prompt the user to enter the call number of the next course. The *while* loop continues until the user enters a –1 to quit. Afterwards, the program returns to the *MAINLINE*.

Reading and Printing an Indexed File

The sequential and random files created in sample program CHAP15B were stored on disk. Since the record keys and course data were written directly to the disk, we have no way of knowing for sure what was actually stored in the files. Therefore, it would be a good idea to look at the files and verify that the contents are correct.

Reading and printing an indexed file involves the following tasks:

1. Set up the indexed file—define sequential key file, random data file, and key array.

2. Load the key array.

3. Open sequential and random files.

4. Read the record keys and course data.

5. Write the nonempty records to the report.

6. Close the files.

This process is illustrated in sample program CHAP15C.

Sample Program CHAP15C

Sample program CHAP15C (Figure 15.12, p. 545) reads and prints a copy of the indexed file created in sample program CHAP15B. The record keys and their corresponding data records are read from the disk and written to the output report. Figure 15.13 (p. 547) shows output.

The following specifications apply:

Input (disk files):

Sequential key file   (*course.key*)
Random data file   (*course.fil*)

Output (screen):

The output report is shown in Figure 15.13.

Processing Requirements:

- Define a sequential key file, a random data file, and a key array.
- Open the sequential file for input, load the array, and close the file.
- Open the random file for input.
- Write the nonempty course records to the report.
- Close the random file.

Pseudocode:

```
START
Create array
Clear screen
Open sequential file
If file opened
   Load the array
   Close sequential file
Open random file
If file opened
   Print the heading line
   LOOP for record number <= 20
      Read the key from the array
      If the key is not = 0
         Read the corresponding course data
         Write the key and course data to the report
   End LOOP
   Close random file
END
```

Hierarchy Chart: See Figure 15.10.

Program Flowchart: See Figure 15.11.

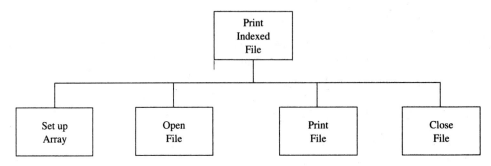

FIGURE 15.10   Hierarchy Chart for CHAP15C

Dissection of Sample Program CHAP15C

MAINLINE CONTROL

```
main()
{
    clrscr();
    SetupArray();
    OpenFile();
    if (!keyFile.fail() && !dataFile.fail())  {
        PrintFile();
        keyFile.close();
        dataFile.close();
    }
    return 0;
}
```

The above statements mean: Clear the screen and execute the modules in the order given—*SetupArray, OpenFile*, and *PrintFile*. After printing the report, the *MAINLINE* closes the random file.

SetupArray opens the sequential file, loads the call numbers into the key array, and closes the file; *OpenFile* opens the random file. If both files were opened, control branches to the *PrintFile* module, reads the records, and displays them on the screen. But if the files were not opened, control prints the error message and terminates the program.

PRINT KEY AND COURSE DATA

```
void PrintFile(void)
{
    cout << "\nRec# Key  Call#  Dept-Course#    Enrollment";
    cout << "\n---------------------------------------------";
```

The above statements display the report heading lines on the screen.

```
    for (recNum = 1; recNum <= 20; recNum++)  {
```

The above statement means: As long as *recNum* is less than or equal to 20, execute the statements in the body of the loop.

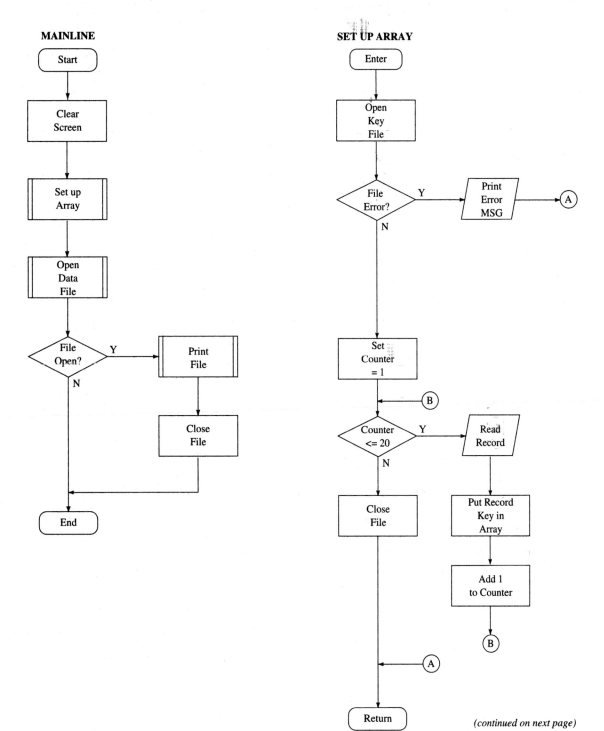

FIGURE 15.11   Program Flowchart for CHAP15C

(continued on next page)

OPEN FILE

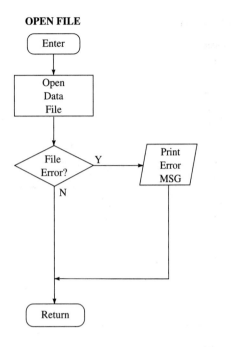

PRINT FILE

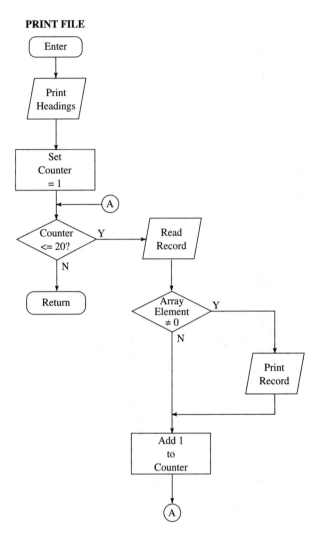

FIGURE 15.11   *Continued*

```
dataFile.seekg((recNum-1)*sizeof(courseData), ios::beg);
dataFile.read((char *) &course, sizeof(courseData));
```

The preceding statements mean: Locate the current record position and read a record from the random file and store the data in the course record.

```
if (key[recNum - 1] != 0)  {
    cout << setw(2) << recNum
        << setw(7) << key[recNum - 1]
        << setw(6) << course.callNum << "    "
        << setiosflags(ios::left)
        << setw(14) << course.dept
        << resetiosflags(ios::left)
        << setw(6) << course.enroll << enroll;
```

```
//---------- PRINT INDEXED FILE----------------------------
//   This program reads and prints the data stored in the
//   course file.
//
//              PROGRAM-ID: CHAP15C
//              PROGRAMMER: David M. Collopy
//              RUN DATE:   mm/dd/yy
//*********************************************************

//---------- PREPROCESSING DIRECTIVES ----------------------
#include<iostream.h>
#include<fstream.h>
#include<iomanip.h>
#include<conio.h>

//---------- FUNCTION PROTOTYPES ---------------------------

void SetupArray(void);          // set up key array
void OpenFile(void);            // open data file
void PrintFile(void);           // print key and course data

//---------- PROGRAM SETUP ---------------------------------

//** K E Y    R E C O R D

fstream keyFile;                // sequential file object

//** D A T A    R E C O R D

fstream file;                   // random file object
struct courseData  {            // course data structure
    int  callNum;               // call number
    char dept[15];              // department & number
    int  enroll;                // student enrollment
};
struct courseData course;       // course record

//** P R O G R A M    V A R I A B L E S

int key[20];                    // 20 element key array
int recNum;                     // record number
//----------------------------------------------------------
//            MAINLINE CONTROL
//----------------------------------------------------------
main()
{
    clrscr();                   // clear the screen
    SetupArray();               // set up key array
```
(continued on next page)

FIGURE 15.12   Sample Program CHAP15C: Reads an Indexed File and Copies the Record Data to the Output Report

```
    OpenFile();                    // open data file
    if (!keyFile.fail() && !dataFile.fail())  {
        PrintFile();               // print key and data file
        keyFile.close();           // close key file
        dataFile.close();          // close data file
    }
    return 0;
}
//-------------------------------------------------------------
//              SET UP ARRAY
//-------------------------------------------------------------
void SetupArray(void)
{
    keyFile.open("a:course.key", ios::in));
    if (keyFile.fail())
        cout << "Key file open failed " << endl;
    else  {
        for (recNum = 1; recNum <= 20; recNum++)  {
            keyFile >> key[recnum - 1];
        }
        keyFile.close();
    }
    return;
}
//-------------------------------------------------------------
//              OPEN DATA FILE
//-------------------------------------------------------------
void OpenFile(void)
{
    dataFile.open("a:course.dat", ios::in);
    if (dataFile.fail())
        cout << "Data file open failed " << endl;

    return;
}
//-------------------------------------------------------------
//              PRINT KEY AND COURSE DATA
//-------------------------------------------------------------
void PrintFile(void)
{
    cout << "\nRec#  Key  Call#  Dept-Course#  Enrollment";
    cout << "\n----------------------------------------\n";
    for (recNum = 1; recNum <= 20; recNum++)  {
        dataFile.seekg((recNum-1)*sizeof(courseData), ios::beg);
```

FIGURE 15.12 *Continued*

```
        dataFile.read((char *) &course, sizeof(courseData));
        if (key[recNum - 1] != 0)  {
            cout << setw(2) << recNum
                 << setw(7) << key[recNum - 1]
                 << setw(6) << course.callNum << "    "
                 << setiosflags(ios::left)
                 << setw(14) << course.dept
                 << resetiosflags(ios::left)
                 << setw(6) << course.enroll << enroll;
        }
    }
    return;
}
```

FIGURE 15.12 *Continued*

```
Rec#  Key  Call#  Dept-Course#    Enrollment
-----------------------------------------------
 1    400   400   ENG200             16
 2    300   300   CHEM201            21
 3    600   600   MGT330             29
 4    200   200   BIOL101            19
 5    500   500   HIST225            33
 6    900   900   SPAN111            12
 7    700   700   MATH120            14
 8    800   800   PHYS251            20
 9    100   100   ACCT101            24
```

FIGURE 15.13   File Output for CHAP15C

```
        }
    }
    return;
}
```

The preceding statements (p. 544) mean: If the call number stored in the array is not equal to 0, then print the record number, array key, and course data on the report. Otherwise, skip the record and go back to the *for* statement.

Control returns to the *MAINLINE* after the file has been processed.

Updating an Indexed File

From time to time, it may be necessary to update the contents of an indexed file in order to keep it current. For our course scheduling system, we would like to delete courses that are no longer offered, add new courses, and change the data for existing courses.

Deleting a Course: A delete is made by locating the call number of the deleted course in the array and changing it to 0. A deleted course is not actually removed from the random file until a new record is written over the old one.

Adding a Course: An add is made by locating the first empty element in the array—call number 0. The new call number is stored in the array, and the course data is written to the corresponding record position in the random file.

Changing an Existing Course: A change is made to an existing course by locating the call number in the array, retrieving the record from the random file, updating the record, and writing it back to the file.

Updating an indexed file involves the following tasks:

1. Set up the indexed file—define sequential key file, random data file, and key array.
2. Load the key array.
3. Open sequential and random files.
4. Prompt the user to select the update option (menu).
5. Enter the data and update the array and the random file.
6. Copy the array to the sequential file.
7. Close the files.

The update process is illustrated in sample program CHAP15D. The menu program instructs the user to select from a series of available updating options.

Checkpoint 15B

1. Explain how a record is deleted from an indexed file.
2. How is a record added to an indexed file?
3. What is the process for changing a record in an indexed file?

Sample Program CHAP15D

Sample program CHAP15D (Figure 15.16, p. 557) is menu driven. It accepts data from the keyboard, checks for errors, and updates the course file. The selection menu is shown in Figure 15.17 (p. 563). Screens corresponding to the various menu choices are shown in Figures 15.18 through 15.22 (pp. 563–564).

The following specifications apply:

Menu Choices:
1. Update enrollment
2. Add courses
3. Delete courses
4. Display all courses
5. Quit

Input (disk files and keyboard):

Disk files: Sequential key file   (*course.key*)
                 Random data file   (*course.dat*)

Keyboard: For menu options 1–3, prompt for and enter the following data:

Option	InputData
1	Call number and enrollment count
2	Call number, department and number, and student enrollment
3	Call number

Output (disk files):

Sequential key file   (*course.key*)
Random data file   (*course.dat*)

Processing Requirements:

- Define a sequential key file, a random data file, and a key array.
- Open the sequential file for input, load the array, and close the file.
- Open the sequential file for output and the random file for input/output.
- Display the menu options and prompt for a selection.
- Enter the data and update the array and the random file.
- After updating the file, copy the array to the sequential file.
- Close the files.

Pseudocode:

```
START
Create array
Set choice = 0
Open sequential file
If file opened
   LOOP until record number <= 20
      Load record into the array
   End LOOP
   Close sequential file
Open files
If files opened
   LOOP until choice = 5 (quit)
      Clear screen
      Display menu and enter choice
      Based on choice, perform the processing
         choice 1—(Update Enrollment)
         choice 2—(Add a Course)
         choice 3—(Delete a Course)
         choice 4—(Display All Courses)
   End LOOP
   LOOP for record number <= 20
      Copy the array to the sequential file
   End LOOP
   Close the files
END
```

ENTER: Update Enrollment
Clear screen
Prompt and enter the call number
Look up call number in array
If call number not found
   Print error message RECORD DOES NOT EXIST
   Wait for Enter key to be pressed to continue
else
   Read and display record
   Prompt and enter enrollment change
   Update enrollment
   Write record to random file
RETURN

ENTER: Add a Record
Clear screen
Prompt and enter the call number
Look up call number in array
If call number found
   Print error message RECORD ALREADY EXISTS
   Wait for Enter key to be pressed to continue
else
   Find first empty element in array
   Prompt and enter new record
   Store call number in array and write record to random file
RETURN

ENTER: Delete a Course
Clear screen
Prompt and enter the call number
Look up call number in array
If call number not found
   Print error message RECORD DOES NOT EXIST
   Wait for Enter key to be pressed to continue
else
   Set array element to 0
   Print message RECORD DELETED
   Wait for Enter key to be pressed to continue
RETURN

ENTER: Display All Courses
Clear screen
Reset file pointer to start of file
Print report heading lines
LOOP for record number <= 20
   Read call number from array
   If call number not = 0
     Read record
     Print record
RETURN

Hierarchy Chart: See Figure 15.14.

Program Flowchart: See Figure 15.15.

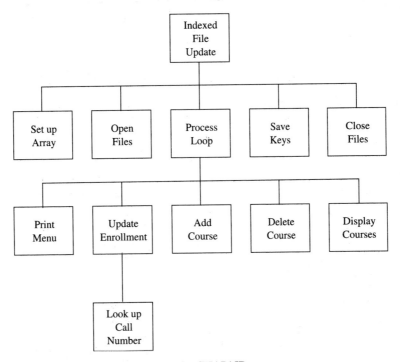

FIGURE 15.14   Hierarchy Chart for CHAP15D

Dissection of Sample Program CHAP15D

```
UPDATE ENROLLMENT
void UpdEnroll(void)
{
    clrscr();
    cout << "\nUPDATE ENROLLMENT:";
    LookUpCallNum();
```

The above statements mean: Clear the screen, print the title line, and branch to look up the call number.

```
    if (loc == -1)  {
        cout << "\nError: Record does not exist";
        cout << " - press 'Enter' to continue ";
        wait = getch();
    }
    else  {
        dataFile.seekg((loc-1)*sizeof(courseData), ios::beg);
        dataFile.read((char *) &course, sizeof(courseData));
```

The above statements mean: If the lookup call number was not found in the array, then print the error message and wait for the user to continue. If the call number was found, then move the file pointer to the position in the data file that corresponds to the offset. The read() member function gets the data from the random file and stores it in the course record.

MAINLINE

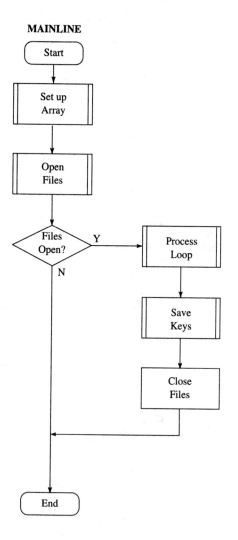

SET UP ARRAY

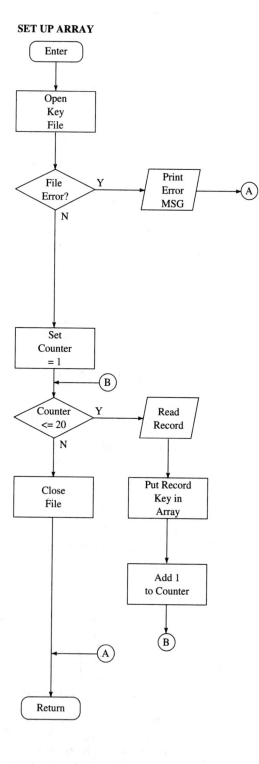

FIGURE 15.15   Program Flowchart for CHAP15D

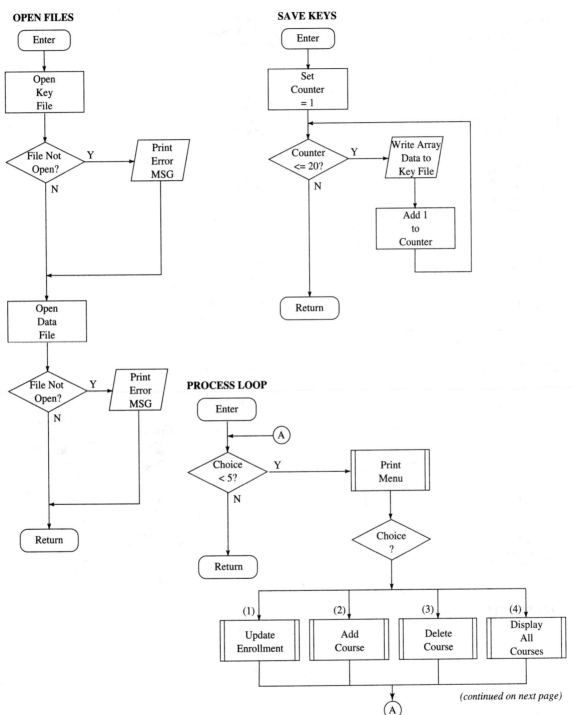

OPEN FILES

Enter

Open
Key
File

File Not
Open? → Y → Print
Error
MSG

N

Open
Data
File

File Not
Open? → Y → Print
Error
MSG

N

Return

SAVE KEYS

Enter

Set
Counter
= 1

Counter
<= 20? → Y → Write Array
Data to
Key File

N

Add 1
to
Counter

Return

PROCESS LOOP

Enter

A

Choice
< 5? → Y → Print
Menu

N

Choice
?

Return

(1) Update
Enrollment

(2) Add
Course

(3) Delete
Course

(4) Display
All
Courses

A

(continued on next page)

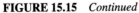

FIGURE 15.15   *Continued*

PRINT MENU

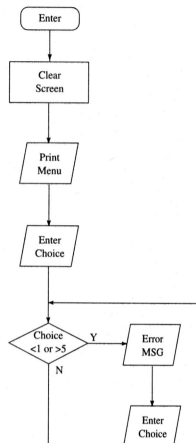

**LOOK UP
CALL NUMBER**

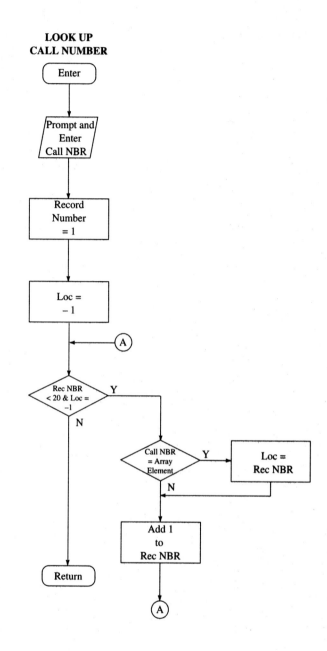

FIGURE 15.15   *Continued*

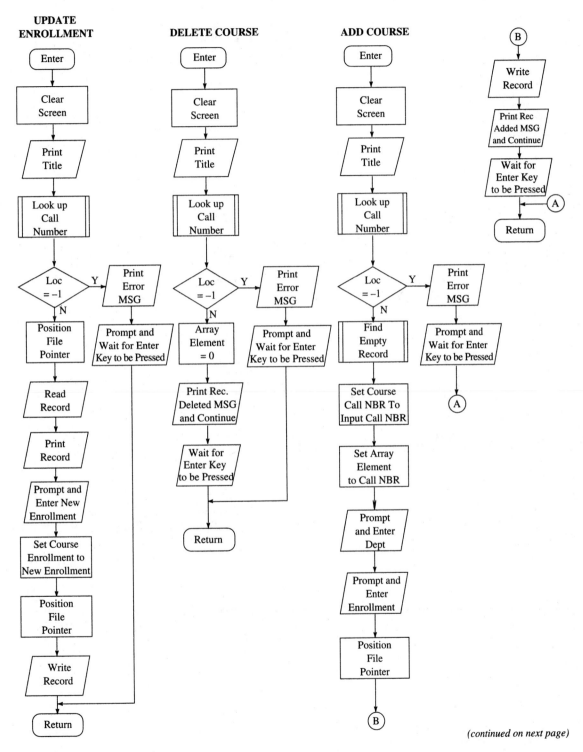

FIGURE 15.15   *Continued*

(continued on next page)

**FIND EMPTY
RECORD**

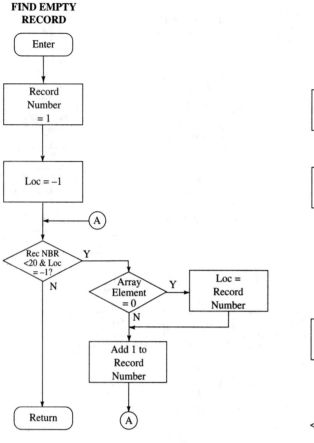

**DISPLAY
ALL COURSES**

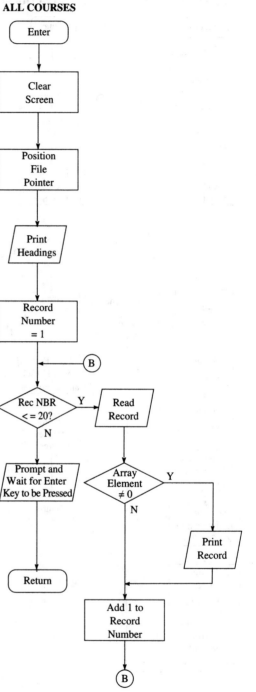

FIGURE 15.15   *Continued*

```
//----------- INDEXED FILE UPDATE --------------------------
// This program randomly access and updates the course file.
//
//              PROGRAM-ID: CHAP15D
//              PROGRAMMER: David M. Collopy
//              RUN DATE:   mm/dd/yy
//*************************************************************

//----------- PREPROCESSING DIRECTIVES ---------------------
#include<iostream.h>
#include<fstream.h>
#include<iomanip.h>
#include<conio.h>

//----------- FUNCTION PROTOTYPES --------------------------

void SetupArray(void);          // set up key array
void OpenFiles(void);           // open program files
void ProcessLoop(void);         // processing loop
void PrintMenu(void);           // print menu
void UpdEnroll(void);           // update enrollment
void LookUpCallNum(void);       // look up call number
void FindEmptyRec(void);        // find empty record
void AddCourse(void);           // add course
void DletCourse(void);          // delete course
void DisplayAll(void);          // display all courses
void SaveKeys(void);            // save record keys

//----------- PROGRAM SETUP --------------------------------

//** K E Y   R E C O R D

fstream keyFile;                // sequential file object

//** D A T A   R E C O R D

fstream file;                   // random file object
struct courseData  {            // course data structure
   int  callNum;                // call number
   char dept[15];               // department & number
   int  enroll;                 // student enrollment
};
struct courseData course;       // course record

//** P R O G R A M   V A R I A B L E S

int key[20];                    // 20 element key array
int recNum;                     // record number
int choice = 0;                 // menu choice
int iCallNum;                   // input call number
```

(continued on next page)

FIGURE 15.16   Sample Program CHAP15D: Randomly Updates the Indexed File

```
    int iEnroll;                    // input enrollment
    int loc;                        // location of call number
    char wait;                      // wait for Enter key to be pressed
    //------------------------------------------------------------
    //              MAINLINE CONTROL
    //------------------------------------------------------------
    main()
    {
        SetupArray();                   // set up key array
        OpenFiles();                    // open program files
        if (!keyFile.fail() && !dataFile.fail())  {
            ProcessLoop();              // processing loop
            SaveKeys();                 // save record keys
            keyFile.close();            // close key file
            dataFile.close();           // close data file
        }
        return 0;
    }
    //------------------------------------------------------------
    //              SET UP ARRAY
    //------------------------------------------------------------
    void SetupArray(void)
    {
        keyFile.open("a:course.key", ios::in));
        if (keyFile.fail())
            cout << "Key file open failed " << endl;
        else  {
            for (recNum = 1; recNum <= 20; recNum++)  {
                keyFile >> key[recnum - 1];
            }
            keyFile.close();
        }
        return;
    }
    //------------------------------------------------------------
    //              OPEN PROGRAM FILES
    //------------------------------------------------------------
    void OpenFiles(void)
    {
        keyFile.open("a:course.key", ios::out));
        if (keyFile.fail())
            cout << "Key file open failed " << endl;
        dataFile.open("a:course.dat", ios::in | ios::out);
        if (dataFile.fail())
            cout << "Data file open failed " << endl;

        return;
    }
```

FIGURE 15.16 *Continued*

```
//-----------------------------------------------------------
//                PROCESSING LOOP
//-----------------------------------------------------------
void ProcessLoop(void)
{
    while (choice < 5)  {
        PrintMenu();                    // print menu
        switch (choice)  {
        case 1:
            UpdEnroll();                // update enrollment
            break;
        case 2:
            AddCourse();                // add course
            break;
        case 3:
            DletCourse();               // delete course
            break;
        case 4:
            DisplayAll();               // display all courses
            break;
        default:
            break;
        }
    }
    return;
}
//-----------------------------------------------------------
//                PRINT MENU
//-----------------------------------------------------------
void PrintMenu(void)
{
    clrscr();
    cout << "\nCourse Maintenance System\n ";
    cout << "\nSelect one:\n\n";
    cout << "  1)   Update enrollment\n";
    cout << "  2)   Add a course\n";
    cout << "  3)   Delete a course\n";
    cout << "  4)   Display all courses\n";
    cout << "  5)   Quit\n";
    cout << "\nEnter choice (1 - 5) ===> ";
    cin >> choice;
    cin.get();                          // clear Enter keycode
    while (choice < 1 || choice > 5)  {
        cout << "\nError: Re-enter choice (1 - 5) ===> ";
        cin >> choice;
        cin.get();                      // clear Enter keycode
    }
    return;
}
```

(continued on next page)

FIGURE 15.16   *Continued*

```
//------------------------------------------------------------
//                  UPDATE ENROLLMENT
//------------------------------------------------------------
void UpdEnroll(void)
{
    clrscr();
    cout << "\nUPDATE ENROLLMENT: ";
    LookUpCallNum();
    if (loc == -1)  {
        cout << "\nError: Record does not exist";
        cout << " - press 'Enter' to continue ";
        wait = getch();      // wait for Enter key to be pressed
    }
    else  {
        dataFile.seekg((loc-1)*sizeof(courseData), ios::beg);
        dataFile.read((char *) &course, sizeof(courseData));
        cout << endl << course.callNum << "    "
            << course.dept << setw(14)
            << course.enroll << endl;
        cout << "\nEnter new enrollment: ";
        cin >> iEnroll;
        course.enroll = iEnroll;
        dataFile.seekp((loc-1)*sizeof(courseData), ios::beg);
        dataFile.write((char *) &course, sizeof(courseData));
    }
    return;
}
//------------------------------------------------------------
//                  LOOK UP CALL NUMBER
//------------------------------------------------------------
void LookUpCallNum(void)
{
    cout << " Enter call number: ";
    cin >> iCallNum;
    recNum = 1:
    loc = -1;
    while (recNum <= 20 && loc == -1)  {
        if (iCallNum == key[recNum-1])
            loc = recNum;        // location found
        recNum = recNum + 1;;
    }
    return;
}
//------------------------------------------------------------
//                  DELETE COURSE
//------------------------------------------------------------
void DletCourse(void)
{
    clrscr();
```

FIGURE 15.16   *Continued*

```
        cout << "\nDELETE COURSE: ";
        LookUpCallNum();
        if (loc == -1)  {
            cout << "\nError: Record does not exist";
            cout << " - press 'Enter' to continue ";
            wait = getch();      // wait for Enter key to be pressed
            }
        else  {
            key[loc-1] = 0;
            cout << "\nRecord deleted";
            cout << " - press 'Enter' to continue ";
            wait = getch();      // wait for Enter key to be pressed
        }
        return;
}
//------------------------------------------------------------
//              ADD COURSE
//------------------------------------------------------------
void AddCourse(void)
{
    clrscr();
    cout << "\nADD COURSE: ";
    LookUpCallNum();
    if (loc != -1)  {
        cout << "\nError: Record already exists";
        cout << " - press 'Enter' to continue ";
        wait = getch();      // wait for Enter key to be pressed
    }
    else  {
        FindEmptyRec();
        key[loc-1] = iCallNum;
        course.callNum = iCallNum;
        cout << "            Enter department & number: ";
        cin >> course.dept;
        cout << "            Enter student enrollment: ";
        cin >> course.enroll;
        dataFile.seekp((loc-1)*sizeof(courseData), ios::beg);
        dataFile.write((char *) &course, sizeof(courseData));
        cout << "\nCall# " << iCallNum << " added"
            << " - press 'Enter' to continue ";
        wait = getch();    // wait for Enter key to be pressed
    }
    return;
}
//------------------------------------------------------------
//              FIND EMPTY RECORD
//------------------------------------------------------------
void FindEmptyRec(void)
```

(continued on next page)

FIGURE 15.16   *Continued*

```
{
    recNum = 1:
    loc = -1;
    while (recNum <= 20 && loc == -1)  {
        if (key[recNum-1] == 0)
            loc = recNum;          // location found
        recNum = recNum + 1;;
    }
    return;
}
//------------------------------------------------------------
//               DISPLAY ALL COURSES
//------------------------------------------------------------
void DisplayAll(void)
{
    clrscr();
    cout << "\nRec#  Key  Call#  Dept-Course#  Enrollment";
    cout << "\n-------------------------------------------\n";
    for (recNum = 1; recNum <= 20; recNum++)  {
        dataFile.seekg((recNum-1)*sizeof(courseData), ios::beg);
        dataFile.read((char *) &course, sizeof(courseData));
        if (key[recNum - 1] != 0)  {
            cout << setw(2) << recNum
                << setw(7) << key[recNum-1]
                << setw(6) << course.callNum << "    "
                << setiosflags(ios::left)
                << setw(14) << course.dept
                << resetiosflags(ios::left)
                << setw(6) << course.enroll << enroll;
        }
    }
    cout << "\nPress 'Enter' to continue";
    wait = getch();          // wait for Enter key to be pressed
    return;
}
//------------------------------------------------------------
//               SAVE RECORD KEYS
//------------------------------------------------------------
void SaveKeys(void)
{
    for (recNum = 1; recNum <= 20; recNum++)  {
        keyFile << key[recNum-1] << endl;
    }
    return;
}
```

FIGURE 15.16 *Continued*

```
Course Maintenance System
Select one:

    1)  Update enrollment
    2)  Add a course
    3)  Delete a course
    4)  Display all courses
    5)  Quit

Enter choice (1 - 5) ===>__
```

FIGURE 15.17   Menu Options for CHAP15D

```
UPDATE ENROLLMENT: Enter call number: 450
Error: Record does not exist - press 'Enter' to continue

UPDATE ENROLLMENT: Enter call number: 700
700    MATH120                14
Enter new enrollment: 23
```

FIGURE 15.18   Choice 1: Update Enrollment

```
DELETE COURSE: Enter call number: 630

Error: Record does not exist - press 'Enter' to continue

DELETE COURSE: Enter call number: 900

Record deleted - press 'Enter' to continue
```

FIGURE 15.19   Choice 3: Delete Course

```
Rec#  Key  Call#  Dept-Course#  Enrollment
-------------------------------------------
  1   400   400   ENG200            16
  2   300   300   CHEM201           21
  3   600   600   MGT330            29
  4   200   200   BIOL101           19
  5   500   500   HIST225           33
  7   700   700   MATH120           23
  8   800   800   PHYS251           20
  9   100   100   ACCT101           24
```

FIGURE 15.20   Choice 4: Display All Courses (Note that the sixth record has been deleted.)

```
ADD COURSE: Enter call number: 600

Error: Record already exists - Press 'Enter'
to continue

ADD COURSE: Enter call number: 310
          Enter department & number: CIS252
          Enter student enrollment: 17

Call #310 added - press 'Enter' to continue
```

FIGURE 15.21   Choice 2: Add Course

```
Rec#  Key   Call#  Dept-Course#  Enrollment
--------------------------------------------
 1    400   400    ENG200          16
 2    300   300    CHEM201         21
 3    600   600    MGT330          29
 4    200   200    BIOL101         19
 5    500   500    HIST225         33
 6    310   310    CIS252          17
 7    700   700    MATH120         23
 8    800   800    PHYS251         20
 9    100   100    ACCT101         24
```

FIGURE 15.22   Choice 4: Display All Courses (Note that the sixth record now holds the new course.)

```
cout << endl << course.callNum << "    "
     << course.dept << setw(14)
     << course.enroll << endl;
```

The above statements mean: Display the record retrieved from the file on the screen. This is done to verify that the correct record has been retrieved by the program.

```
cout << "\nEnter new enrollment: ";
cin >> iEnroll;
course.enroll = iEnroll;
```

The above statements mean: Prompt the user to enter the new student enrollment, and assign the input to the *course.enroll* field of the course record.

```
      dataFile.seekp((loc-1)*sizeof(courseData), ios::beg);
      dataFile.write((char *) &course, sizeof(courseData));
   }
   return;
}
```

The preceding statements mean: Reset the file pointer to the previous record position in the random file and write the data stored in the course record back to the file. Control then returns to the *PROCESSING LOOP* and displays the menu.

LOOK UP CALL NUMBER

```
void LookUpCallNum(void)
{
    cout << " Enter call number: ";
    cin >> iCallNum;
```

The above statements mean: Prompt the user to enter the call number, and assign the input to *iCallNum*.

```
    recNum = 1;
    loc = -1;
```

The above statements mean: Initialize record number and location. This is done in preparation for the call number lookup.

```
    while (recNum <= 20 && loc == -1)  {
        if (iCallNum == key[recNum - 1])
            loc = recNum;
        recNum = recNum + 1;
        }
    return;
}
```

The above statement means: As long as *recNum* is less than or equal to 20 and *loc* equals −1, search the array for the input call number and increment *recNum*. If the input call number is found, then set *loc* to *recNum*. Control exits the loop when a match is found or the end of the array is encountered.

DELETE COURSE

```
void DletCourse(void)
{
    clrscr();
    cout << "\nDELETE COURSE: ";
    LookUpCallNum();
    if (loc == -1)  {
        cout << "\nError: Record does not exist";
        cout << " - press 'Enter' to continue ";
        wait = getch();
        }
    else  {
        key[loc-1] = 0;
        cout << "\nRecord deleted";
        cout << " - press 'Enter' to continue ";
        wait = getch();
        }
    return;
}
```

The preceding statements mean: Clear the screen, print the title line, and branch to look up the call number. If the call number is not found in the key array, print the error message and wait for the user to continue. If the call number is found, replace it with 0, print the delete message, and wait for the user to continue.

ADD COURSE

```
void AddCourse(void)
{
    clrscr();
    cout << "\nADD COURSE: ";
    LookUpCallNum();
    if (loc != -1)  {
        cout << "\nError: Record already exists";
        cout << " - press 'Enter' to continue ";
        wait = getch();
    }
```

The above statements mean: Clear the screen, print the title line, and branch to look up the call number. If the lookup call number is found in the array, then print the error message and wait for the user to continue.

```
    else  {
        FindEmptyRec();
        key[loc - 1] = iCallNum;
        course.callNum = iCallNum;
```

The above statements mean: Branch and find the first empty element in the array. Store the input call number in the array and assign the input call number to the *course.callNum* field of the course record.

```
        cout << "              Enter department & number: ";
        cin >> course.dept;
        cout << "              Enter student enrollment: ";
        cin >> course.enroll;
```

The above statements mean: Prompt for and enter the department and student enrollment and assign them to the *course.dept* and *course.enroll* fields, respectively.

```
        dataFile.seekp((loc-1)*sizeof(courseData), ios::beg);
        dataFile.write((char *) &course, sizeof(courseData));
        cout << "\nCall# " << iCallNum << " added"
             << " - press 'Enter' to continue ";
        wait = getch();
    }
    return;
}
```

The above statements mean: Set the file pointer to the record location that corresponds to the array subscript and write the course record to the random file. Print the add message and wait for the user to continue.

```
FIND EMPTY RECORD

void FindEmptyRec(void)
{
    recNum = 1;
    loc = -1;
    while (recNum <= 20 && loc == -1)  {
        if (key[recNum-1] == 0)
            loc = recNum;
        recNum = recNum + 1;
    }
    return;
}
```

The above statements mean: Initialize record number and location. As long as *recNum* is less than or equal to 20 and *loc* equals –1, search the array for the first empty element. If the value stored in the element is 0, then set *loc* to *recNum* and exit the loop.

```
DISPLAY ALL COURSES

void DisplayAll(void)
{
    clrscr();
    cout << "\nRec#  Key  Call#  Dept-Course#  Enrollment";
    cout << "\n---------------------------------------------\n";
    for (recNum = 1; recNum <= 20; recNum++)  {
        dataFile.seekg((recNum-1)*sizeof(courseData), ios::beg);
        dataFile.read((char *) &course, sizeof(courseData));
        if (key[recNum - 1] != 0)  {
            cout << setw(2) << recNum
                 << setw(7) << key[recNum-1]
                 << setw(6) << course.callNum << "    "
                 << setiosflags(ios::left)
                 << setw(14) << course.dept
                 << resetiosflags(ios::left)
                 << setw(6) << course.enroll << enroll;
        }
    }
    cout << "\nPress 'Enter' to continue";
    wait = getch();
    return;
}
```

The above statements mean: Clear the screen, set the file pointer to the beginning of the random file, and print the report title lines. As long as *recNum* is less than or equal to 20, execute the statements in the body of the loop.

If the call number stored in the array is not equal to 0, print the record number, array key, and course data on the report. Otherwise, skip the print statement and go back to the *for* loop.

Summary

1. Indexed files store data on disk in random order. Although more complicated to work with, indexed files provide relatively fast access to the information stored on disk.

2. Indexed files use record keys to access the data and save disk space.

3. An indexed file is a pseudofile organization method that consists of a key array and a random access file. The array holds the record keys, and the random file holds the corresponding data.

4. To locate a given record, the program searches the array and compares the search key to the record keys stored in the array. On a match, the program uses the array subscript to access the data stored in the random file.

5. To create an indexed file, the programmer defines a key array and a random data file. The objective is to reserve disk space for the data and to set up an array to track the record keys.

6. Once disk space has been reserved for the records, the data is loaded into the file—the keys are stored in the array and the records are written to the random file. Later the array is copied to a sequential file for future reference.

7. After the file has been loaded, the records are read one by one and copied to an output report to verify that the data was correctly loaded into the file.

8. A delete is made by locating the key of the deleted record in the array and changing it to 0. A deleted record is not removed from the random file until a new record is written over the old one.

9. An add is made by locating the first empty element in the array. The new record key is stored in the array, and the data is written to the corresponding record position in the random file.

10. A change is made to an existing record by locating the key in the array, retrieving the record, updating the data, and writing the record back to the file.

Programming Projects

For each project, design the logic and write the modular structured program to produce the output. Model your program after the sample programs presented in the chapter. Verify your output.

Project 15–1 Overdue Accounts-1

Write a program to create an indexed file for the overdue accounts. Write a total of 30 empty records to the file.

Input (internal):

Define the account data structure and the members given below. Field size and type are shown in parentheses.

Account number	(4 int)
Customer name	(15 char)
Days overdue	(2 int)
Balance due	(6.2 float)

Output (disk files):

Sequential key file   (*overdue.key*)
Random data file   (*overdue.dat*)

Processing Requirements:

- Define and initialize the empty record.
- Define a sequential file, a random file, and a key array .
- Open the sequential file and the random file for output.
- Set the elements of the array to 0.
- Write empty records to the random file.
- After creating the file, copy the array to the sequential file.
- Close the files.

Project 15–2 Overdue Accounts-2

Write a program to prompt the user to enter the data at the keyboard, and load the indexed file created in Project 15–1.

Input (disk files and keyboard):

Disk files: Sequential key file   (*overdue.key*)
                 Random data file   (*overdue.dat*)

Keyboard: For each customer record, prompt for and enter the following data. Field size and type are shown in parentheses.

1. Account number   (4 int)
2. Customer name   (15 char)
3. Days overdue   (2 int)
4. Balance due   (6.2 float)

File Data (keyboard):

Use the data given below to load the indexed file. The numbers shown above the columns correspond to the fields described for the input.

1	2	3	4
6350	Susan Cope	90	600.00
2730	Rita Fox	90	740.00
3100	Alvin Porter	90	550.00
4080	Corey Adkins	30	233.00
5260	Brian Knox	30	625.00
7720	Lisa Wilson	60	417.00
9200	Tori Landis	90	235.00
4890	Amy Wyatt	30	700.00
1010	David Ryan	90	400.00
9630	Pat Rankin	60	342.00
2450	Marie Hill	30	754.00
8540	Matt Hart	90	900.00

Output (disk files):

Sequential key file   (*overdue.key*)
Random data file   (*overdue.dat*)

Processing Requirements:

- Define a sequential file, a random file, and an array.
- Open the sequential file for input, load the array, and close the file.
- Open the sequential file and the random file for output.
- Prompt for and enter the data.
- Store the record keys in the array and write the records to the random file.
- After loading the file, copy the array to the sequential file.
- Close the files.

Project 15–3 Overdue Accounts-3

Write a menu program that allows the user to select from several file updating options. Prompt and enter the data, check for errors, and update the indexed file from Project 15–2. Write the input errors to an error log.

Menu Choices:

1. Update accounts
2. Add accounts
3. Delete accounts
4. Display all accounts
5. Quit

Input (disk files and keyboard):

Disk files: Sequential key file   (*overdue.key*)
            Random data file   (*overdue.dat*)

Keyboard: For options 1–3, prompt for and enter the following data:

Option	Input Data
1	Account number, customer name, days overdue, and amount due
2	Account number, customer name, days overdue, and amount due
3	Account number

File Data (keyboard):
Enter the updates in the random order shown. For each, use the menu option to apply the data to the record specified by the account number.

Menu Option	Account Number	Customer Name	Days Overdue	Balance Due
delete	1450			
update	4890	Amy Clark	30	700.00
add	1000	Sarah Brooks	60	220.00
delete	8540			
update	1010	Ryan Davis	90	400.00
add	9630	Pat Rankin	60	342.00

add	9700	Adam Norris	60	475.00
update	6350	Susan Cope	60	600.00
update	2450	Marie Hill	30	700.00
delete	3100			
add	4080	Corey Adkins	30	233.00
update	2730	Rita Fox	30	740.00
update	9200	Tori Landis	90	300.00
add	4900	Marla Stevens	90	594.00
update	2740	Tia Marlowe	30	135.00

Output (disk files):

Sequential key file   (*overdue.key*)
Random data file   (*overdue.dat*)

Processing Requirements:

- Define a sequential file, a random file, and an array.
- Open the sequential file for input, load the array, and close the file.
- Open the sequential file for output and the random file for input/output.
- Display the menu options and prompt for a selection.
- Enter the data and update the array and the random file.
- After updating the file, copy the array to the sequential file.
- Close the files.

Project 15–4 Overdue Accounts-4

Write a program to read the updated indexed file in Project 15–3 and print the overdue accounts report shown below. Accumulate a total for amount due, and print the total at the end of the report.

```
Author                OVERDUE ACCOUNTS              Page 01
                         mm/dd/yy

Acct Number      Customer Name     Days Overdue      Amount Due

   9999          X----------X          99            999.99
    :                :                  :               :
    :                :                  :               :
   9999          X----------X          99            999.99

                                    Total:          9999.99
```

Processing Requirements:

- Define a sequential key file, a random data file, and an array.
- Open the sequential file for input, load the array, and close the file.
- Open the random file for input.
- Write the nonempty account records to the report.
- Accumulate a total for amount due and print it at the end of the report.
- Close the random file.

Project 15–5 Sales Profit-1

Write a program to create an indexed file for the sales department. Write a total of 20 empty records to the file.

Input (internal):

Define the sales data structure and the members given below. Field size and type are shown in parentheses.

Salesperson number	(3 int)
Salesperson name	(15 char)
Total sales	(8.2 float)
Cost of sales	(8.2 float)

Output (disk files):

Sequential key file	(*sales.key*)
Random data file	(*sales.dat*)

Processing Requirements:

- Define and initialize the empty record.
- Define a sequential key file, a random data file, and a key array.
- Open the sequential file and the random file for output.
- Set the elements in the array to 0.
- Write empty records to the random file.
- After creating the file, copy the array to the sequential file.
- Close the files.

Project 15–6   Sales Profit-2

Write a program to prompt the user to enter the data at the keyboard and load the indexed file created in Project 15–5.

Input (disk files and keyboard):

Disk files:	Sequential key file	(*sales.key*)
	Random data file	(*sales.dat*)

Keyboard: For each sales record, prompt for and enter the following data. Field size and type are shown in parentheses.

1. Salesperson number	(3 int)
2. Salesperson name	(15 char)
3. Total sales	(8.2 float)
4. Cost of sales	(8.2 float)

File Data (keyboard):

Use the data given below to load the indexed file. The numbers shown above the columns correspond to the fields described for the input.

1	2	3	4
400	Tara Perkins	12710.14	9735.38
700	Dennis Tian	4567.51	3119.22
300	Roy Hickle	2245.78	1072.49
100	Lisa Conrad	8120.52	6450.71
900	Ann Zimmerman	5793.59	4204.45

Output (disk files):

Sequential key file	(*sales.key*)
Random data file	(*sales.dat*)

Processing Requirements:

- Define a sequential key file, a random data file, and an array.
- Open the sequential file for input, load the array, and close the file.
- Open the sequential file and the random file for input.
- Prompt for and enter the data .
- Store the record keys in the array, and write the sales data to the random file.
- After loading the file, copy the array to the sequential file.
- Close the files.

Project 15–7   Sales Profit-3

Write a menu program that allows the user to select from several file processing options. Prompt and enter the data, check for errors, and update the sales file from Project 15–6. Write the input errors to an error log.

Menu Choices:

1. Update sales records

2. Add sales records

3. Delete sales records

4. Display all sales records

5. Quit

Input (disk files and keyboard):

Disk files: Sequential key file	(*sales.key*)
Random data file	(*sales.dat*)

Keyboard: For options 1–3, prompt for and enter the following data:

Option	Input Data
1	Salesperson number, salesperson name, total sales, and cost of sales
2	Salesperson number, salesperson name, total sales, and cost of sales
3	Salesperson number

File Data (keyboard):

Enter the updates in the random order shown. For each, use the menu option to apply the data to the record specified by the salesperson number.

Menu Option	Salesperson Number	Name	Total Sales	Cost of Sales
add	900	Ann Zimmerman	5793.59	4204.45
update	340	David Kock	4339.16	2124.83
update	300	Roy Henderson	2245.78	1072.49
update	490	Michael Torres	9634.28	5593.15
add	940	Sean Zorich	7465.92	5641.39

update	700	Dennis Tian	4567.51	3191.22
update	250	Robert Minelli	3974.63	2016.24
delete	400			
add	200	Allison Dunn	6518.02	4131.78

Output (disk files):

Sequential key file   (*sales.key*)
Random data file   (*sales.dat*)

Processing Requirements:

- Define a sequential key file, a random data file, and a key array.
- Open the sequential file for input, load the array, and close the file.
- Open the sequential file for output and the random file for input/output.
- Display the menu options and prompt for a selection.
- Enter the data and update the indexed file.
- After updating the file, copy the array to the sequential file.
- Close the files.

Project 15–8 Sales Profit-4

Write a program to read the updated indexed file in Project 15–7 and print the sales profit report shown below. Accumulate a total for net profit and print the total at the end of the report.

```
Author                SALES PROFIT REPORT           Page 01
                          mm/dd/yy


                      Total           Cost of        Net
Num    Salesperson    Sales           Sales          Profit
------------------------------------------------------------
999    X---------X    99999.99        99999.99       99999.99
  :         :             :               :              :
  :         :             :               :              :
999    X---------X    99999.99        99999.99       99999.99

                                      Total:         999999.99
```

Processing Requirements:

- Define a sequential key file, a random data file, and an array.
- Open the sequential file for input, load the array, and close the file.
- Open the random file for input mode.
- Write the nonempty sales records to the output report.
- Accumulate a total for net profit and print it at the end of the report.
- Close the random file.

Appendix A
ASCII Table

Dec	Char		Dec	Char	
0	NUL	(null)	22	SYN	control char
1	SOH	control char	23	ETB	control char
2	STX	control char	24	CAN	control char
3	ETX	control char	25	EM	control char
4	EOT	control char	26	SUB	control char
5	ENQ	control char	27	ESC	(escape)
6	ACK	control char	28	FS	(cursor right)
7	BEL	(bell)	29	GS	(cursor left)
8	BS	control char	30	RS	(cursor up)
9	HT	(tab)	31	US	(cursor down)
10	LF	(line feed)	32	SP	(space)
11	VT	(home)	33	!	
12	FF	(form feed)	34	"	
13	CR	(return)	35	#	
14	SO	control char	36	$	
15	SI	control char	37	%	
16	DLE	control char	38	&	
17	DC1	control char	39	'	
18	DC2	control char	40	(	
19	DC3	control char	41	)	
20	DC4	control char	42	*	
21	NAK	control char	43	+	

Dec	Char	Dec	Char
44	,	86	V
45	-	87	W
46	.	88	X
47	/	89	Y
48	0	90	Z
49	1	91	[
50	2	92	\
51	3	93	]
52	4	94	^
53	5	95	—
54	6	96	`
55	7	97	a
56	8	98	b
57	9	99	c
58	:	00	d
59	;	01	e
60	<	02	f
61	=	03	g
62	>	04	h
63	?	05	i
64	@	106	j
65	A	107	k
66	B	108	l
67	C	109	m
68	D	110	n
69	E	111	o
70	F	112	p
71	G	113	q
72	H	114	r
73	I	115	s
74	J	116	t
75	K	117	u
76	L	118	v
77	M	119	w
78	N	120	x
79	O	121	y
80	P	122	z
81	Q	123	{
82	R	124		
83	S	125	}
84	T	126	~
85	U	127	DEL (delete)

Appendix B
Programming Standards

Standards provide uniform guidelines for planning, coding, and testing programs. Programming standards are established by management to improve the quality of their information systems and to increase the productivity of the programmers. The standards below were used to construct the sample programs in this textbook.

General

Plan and design the logic first. Use the hierarchy chart to identify the modules and the relationships among them. Use the logic design to write the program code. Keep the code simple. Write as if you were coding the program for someone else to read and maintain.

Variables

One-word identifier names are written in lowercase letters. If two or more words are used to create a name, capitalize the first letter in each word except the first. Each name should be self-documenting. Examples of variable names are *sales, profit, topSales, firstName, costOfSales*, and *quantOnHand*.

Statements

Code one statement (or function) per line. If the statement is too long for one line, break the statement, indent four positions, and continue on the next line. See the example shown below.

```
prnt << TL << setw(4) << hours << setw(5) << payRate
    << stew(7) << grossPay << endl;
```

Modules

Names: Capitalize the first letter in each word used to create the module name. Each name should be self-documenting. Examples of module names are *PrnHeadings()*, *ProcessLoop()*, *InputNum()*, *CalcCommis()*, *PrnDetail()*, and *PrnTopSales()*.

Order: The *main()* is always first. After *main()*, the modules are arranged in processing order, that is, in the order that they are called and executed by the program.

Braces and Indentation: The statement body of each module is enclosed within braces and indented (aligned) four positions. Follow the example shown below.

```
//------------------------------------------------------------
//              PRINT DETAIL LINE
//------------------------------------------------------------
void PrnDetail(void)
{
    prnt << TL << setw(4) << hours << setw(6) << payRate
         << stew(7) << grossPay << endl;
    return;
}
```

Programmer-Defined Functions

Names: One-word function names are written in lowercase letters. If two or more words are used to create a function name, then capitalize the first letter in each word except the first. In either case, add *fn* to the end of the name. The suffix *fn* indicates that the identifier represents a programmer-defined function. Each name should be self-documenting. Examples of programmer-defined function names are *averagefn()*, *sumfn()*, *leftMarginfn()*, *areafn()*, and *variancefn()*.

Order: Group the programmer-defined functions and place them at the end of the program.

Braces and Indentation: The statement body of each function is enclosed within braces and indented (aligned) four positions.
Follow the example shown below.

```
//----------- fn: compute average ----------------
float averagefn(float x, float y)
{
    float result;

    result = (x + y) / 2;
    return result;
}
```

Program Documentation

Program documentation appears at the top of the program and includes the name of the program, the purpose of the program, the program file name, the programmer, and the run date. Follow the example shown next.

```
//----------- COMMISSION ------------------------------------
//     Compute and print a monthly sales commission report
//     for the Beale-Ross Corporation.
//
//            PROGRAM-ID: COMMISS
//            PROGRAMMER: David M. Collopy
//            RUN DATE:   mm/dd/yy
//
//*************************************************************
```

Preprocessing Directives

Group the preprocessing directives together. Follow the example shown below.

```
//----------- PREPROCESSING DIRECTIVES ----------------------

#include<iostream.h>
#include<fstream.h>
#include<iomanip.h>
#include<conio.h>
#include<string.h>
```

Function Prototypes

Group the function prototypes together. Write a brief comment to describe each. Follow the example shown below.

```
//----------- FUNCTION PROTOTYPES ---------------------------

void PrnHeadings(void);       // print headings
void ProcessLoop(void);       // processing loop
void InputNum(void);          // input salesperson number
void InputData(void);         // input sales data
void CalcCommis(void);        // calculate commission
void FindTopPerson(void);     // find top salesperson
void PrnDetail(void);         // print detail line
void PrnTopPerson(void);      // print top salesperson
```

Program Setup

This section defines the titles and column headings, record formats, and constants and variables required by the program.

Report Titles and Headings: As a standard, the variables (written in capital letters) *PT, HL, DL, TL,* and *SL* are used to define the Page Titles, Heading Lines, Detail Lines, Total Lines, and Summary Lines, respectively. Follow the example shown below.

```
//----------- PROGRAM SETUP ---------------------------------

//** H E A D I N G   L I N E S

char PT1[] = " B E A L E - R O S S   C O R P O R A T I O N";
char PT2[] = "           Monthly Sales Report";
```

```
char HL1[] = "S a l e s p e r s o n      Monthly      Earned";
char HL2[] = "Num      Name                 Sales   Commission";
char HL3[] = "------------------------------------------------";
char SL1[] = "Top Salesperson: ";
char SL2[] = "    Total Sales: ";
```

Records: Record formats are defined after the report titles and column headings. Write a brief comment to describe each. Follow the example shown below.

```
//** S A L E S    R E C O R D

int    salesNum:               // salesperson number
char   name[21];               // salesperson name
float  sales;                  // monthly sales
```

Constants and Variables: The program constants and variables are defined after the record formats. Write a brief comment to describe each. Follow the example shown below.

```
//** P R O G R A M   V A R I A B L E S

float commission;              // sales commission
char  topName[21];             // top salesperson
float topSales = 0.0;          // top sales amount
```

Loops and Decisions

As a rule, enclose the statement body in braces and indent each statement four positions. Although C++ does not require braces for a one-statement body, we will continue to use them for clarity. Follow these examples.

while:
```
           InputData();
           while (credits < 45)   {
               Calculations();
               Prnline();
               InputData();
           }
```

nested while:
```
           outer = 1;
           while (outer <= 3)   {
               cout << "\n Outside " << outer;
               inner = 1;
               while (inner <= 2)   {
                   cout << "\n   Inside " << inner;
                   inner++;
               }
               outer++;
           }
```

do/while:
```
           InputID();
           do   {
               InputData();
               Calculations();
```

```
                PrnLine();
                InputID();
            } while (studentID != 0);
```

nested
do/while:
```
            outer = 1;
            do  {
                cout << "\n Outside " << outer;
                inner = 1;
                do  {
                    cout << "\n  Inside " <<  inner;
                    inner++;
                } while (inner <= 2);
                outer++;
            } while (outer <= 3);
```

for:
```
            for (num = 1; num <= 5; num++)  {
                CalcSquare();
                CalcSum();
                PrnLine();
            }
```

nested
for:
```
            for (outer = 1; outer <= 3; outer++)  {
                cout << "\n Outside " << outer;
                for (inner = 1; inner <= 2; inner++)  {
                    cout << "\n  Inside " << inner;
                }
            }
```

if:
```
            if (credits < 45)  {
                printf("Welcome freshman");
            }
```

nested
if:
```
            if (credits < 45)  {
                if (female == 1)  {
                    femaleFresh++;
                    cout << "Welcome lady freshman";
                }
            }
```

if/else:
```
            if (credits < 45)  {
                cout << "Welcome freshman";
            }
            else  {
                cout << "Welcome upperclassman";
            }
```

nested
if/else:
```
            if (credits < 45)  {
                cout << "Welcome freshman";
            }
            else if (credits < 90)  {
                cout << "Welcome sophomore";
            }
            else if (credits < 135)  {
```

```
                        cout << "Welcome junior";
                   }
                   else  {
                        cout << "Welcome senior";
                   }

switch:     switch (choice)  {
               case 1:
                   cout << "Action movie\n";
                   break;
               case 2:
                   cout << "Comedy movie\n";
                   break;
               case 3:
                   cout << "Drama movie\n";
                   break;
               case 4:
                   cout << "Scifi movie\n";
                   break;
               default:
                   cout << "Invalid choice\n";
                   break;
               }
```

Appendix C
Other C/C++ Input/Output Functions

Even though the input/output functions shown below apply primarily to C programs, they are part of the standard input/output library and may be used with C++ programs. *Note:* These functions require the *stdio.h* header file.

Input Functions

Standard Input

getchar():   The getchar() function reads a character from the keyboard.

> Example:
> ```
> char inchar;
> inchar = getchar();
> ```

The first character entered at the keyboard is assigned to *inchar*. The getchar() function waits for the Enter key to be pressed before assigning the character to the variable.

gets():   The gets() function reads a string from the keyboard.

> Example:
> ```
> char instring[21];
> instring = gets();
> ```

The input stream, up to 20 characters, is assigned to *instring*. The gets() function waits for the Enter key to be pressed before assigning the data to the variable.

scanf():   The scanf() function formats data read from the keyboard.

> Example:
> ```
> float score;
> scanf("%f", &score);
> ```

If a decimal number is entered at the keyboard, scanf() reads the input stream and converts it to a floating-point value *(%f)* and assigns the result to *score*.

File Input

fgetc():   The fgetc() function reads a character from a specific file.

Example:
```
FILE *inFile;
char inchar;
inchar = fgetc(inFile);
```

The fgetc() function reads a character from the file specified by the file pointer argument *inFile* and assigns it to the variable called *inchar*.

fgets():   The fgets() function reads a string from a specific file.

Example:
```
FILE *inFile;
char instring[21];
fgets(instring, 20, inFile);
```

The fgets() function reads up to 20 characters of data from the file specified by the file pointer argument *inFile* and assigns the input to *instring*.

fscanf():   The fscanf() function uses a format specifier to read data from a specific file.

Example:
```
FILE *inFile;
int  inNum;
char instring[21];
fscanf(inFile, "%d %s", &inNum, instring);
```

The fscanf() function reads two items from the file, converts the first one to a decimal integer *(%d)* and the second to a string *(%s)*, and assigns the results to *inNum* and *instring*, respectively.

Output Functions

Standard Output

putchar():   The putchar() function prints a character on the screen.

Example:
```
char outchar = 'A';
putchar(outchar);
putchar('B');
```

The first putchar() prints the letter A on the screen, whereas the second prints the letter B. The output is AB.

puts():   The puts() function prints a string on the screen.

Example:
```
char name[] = "Daniel";
puts(name);
puts(" Webster");
```

The first puts() prints Daniel on the screen and the second prints Webster. The output is Daniel Webster.

printf():   The printf() function formats data printed on the screen.

Example: `float score = 87.4;`
           `printf("Your test score is: %f", score);`

The printf() function prints the message enclosed within double quotation marks and the score on the screen: `Your test score is: 87.4`.

File Output

fputc():   The fputc() function writes a character to a specific file.

Example: `FILE *outFile;`
           `char outchar = 'A';`
           `fputc(outchar, outFile);`

The fputc() function writes the letter `A` to the file specified by the file pointer argument *outFile*.

fputs():   The fputs() function writes a string to a specific file.

Example: `FILE *outFile;`
           `char outstring[] = "Hammers  24");`
           `fputc(outstring, outFile);`

The fputc() function writes the string data to the file specified by the file argument *outFile*.

fprintf():   The fprintf() function formats data written to a specific file.

Example: `FILE *outFile;`
           `char desc[] = "Hammers";`
           `int quant = 24;`
           `fprintf(outFile, "%s %d\n", desc, quant);`

The fprintf() function writes the item description and item quantity to the file specified by the file pointer argument *outFile*.

Appendix D
Math and Related
Functions

The basic math, trigonometric, and logarithmic functions require the *math.h* header file, whereas the random number functions require the *stdio.h* header file.

Basic Math Functions

abs(x):   The abs(x) function returns the absolute value of the integer x. The argument and return value are type *integer*.

  Examples: abs(4) returns 4
              abs(–4) returns 4

fabs(x):   The fabs(x) function returns the absolute value of x. The argument and return value are type *double*.

  Examples: fabs(5.63) returns 5.0
              fabs(–5.63) returns 5.0

ceil(x):   The ceil(x) function returns x raised to the nearest whole number. The argument and return value are type *double*.

  Examples: ceil(7.15) returns 8.0
              ceil(–7.15) returns –7.0

floor(x):   The floor(x) function returns x lowered to the nearest whole number. The argument and the return value are type *double*.

  Examples: floor(7.15) returns 7.0
              floor(–7.15) returns –8.0

pow(x, y):   The pow(x, y) function returns the floating-point value x^y. The arguments x and y are type *double*.

   Example: pow(7.0, 2.0) returns 49.0

sqrt(x):   The sqrt(x) function returns the square root of x. The argument and return value are type *double*.

   Example: sqrt(81.0) returns 9.0

Trigonometric Functions

sin(x):   The sin(x) function returns the sine of angle x. The argument is expressed in radians, and the return value is type *double*.

   Example: sin(45.0) returns 0.8509

cos(x):   The cos(x) function returns the cosine of angle x. The argument is expressed in radians, and the return value is type *double*.

   Example: cos(10.0) returns –0.8390

tan(x):   The tan(x) function returns the tangent of angle x. The argument is expressed in radians, and the return value is type *double*.

   Example: tan(25.0) returns –0.1335

Logarithmic Functions

exp(x):   The exp(x) function returns the natural logarithm e^x. The argument x is type *double*.

   Example: exp(.637) returns 2.8907

log(x):   The log(x) function returns the natural logarithm of the positive argument x.

   Example: log(7.14) returns 4.4874

log10(x):   The log10(x) function returns the base 10 logarithm of the positive argument x.

   Example: log10(14.3) returns 2.2505

Random Number Functions

rand(x):   The rand(x) function returns a random number in the range 0 to 32767. It returns the same set of random numbers each time the function is executed.

srand(x):   The srand(x) function seeds the random number generator and changes the set of values returned by rand() each time it is executed.

Appendix E
Answers to Checkpoint Exercises

Chapter 1

Checkpoint 1A

1. A computer is an electronic device that accepts input, processes it according to a given set of instructions, and provides the results of the processing.
2. Applications software, written for end users, is designed to perform a specific task. Systems software, normally supplied by the manufacturer of the computer, consists of utility programs and operating aids. It includes the computer's operating system and related software that manages the system's resources and controls the operations of the hardware.
3. Input devices translate data from a language people understand, such as English, into a language that the computer understands. Examples of input devices are the keyboard and the mouse. Output devices translate data from a form that the computer understands into a form that people understand. Examples of output devices are printers and monitors.
4. The central processing unit is considered to be the heart of the computer. It consists of the control unit, the arithmetic/logic unit, and the storage unit. The control unit supervises and monitors the computer's activities. The arithmetic/logic unit performs computations and evaluates relationships. The storage unit, also known as main memory, holds data to be processed by the computer.
5. Primary storage, or main memory, is temporary storage. When the computer's power is disrupted, the contents of primary storage are lost. Secondary storage is permanent storage. If the computer's power is turned off, data will still remain on secondary storage media.
6. Data is organized by characters, fields, records, files, and databases.

Checkpoint 1B

1. A properly used program development process will help to produce a more reliable program in less time—one that can be maintained more easily throughout its use.

2. The seven steps in the Program Development Process are:
   a. Define the problem: Write a brief statement describing the purpose of the program.
   b. Analyze the problem: Analyze the input, output, and processing. Organize the processing tasks.
   c. Design the program logic: Develop the instructions for the computer to follow by using hierarchy charts, pseudocode, or flowcharts.
   d. Code the program: Translate the logic into program statements. Write out the statements on paper.
   e. Key in the program: Enter the program statements into the computer.
   f. Test and debug the program: Run the program. Fix any errors.
   g. Gather the program documentation: Assemble the documentation for the program.

3. The purpose of the guidelines is to provide a set of standards or procedures that help produce reports that are easy to read and understand.

4. A syntax error is a violation of the rules of a programming language. A logic error is an error in the design or the implementation of the design.

5. Source programs, created by the programmer, exist in people-readable form. Object programs, created by the computer from the source programs, are the machine code equivalent of the source programs. Object programs exist in computer-readable form.

Checkpoint 1C

1. Two methods for designing program logic are:
   a. Pseudocode: English-like statements that outline or describe the processing tasks required by the program
   b. Flowcharts: pictorial diagrams showing individual functions, detailed processing steps, and the sequence of operations required by the program

2. a. valid
   b. invalid
   c. invalid
   d. valid
   e. invalid
   f. invalid
   g. invalid
   h. valid
   i. invalid
   j. valid

3. Identifiers are names assigned to program variables by the programmer. Keywords are reserved words that have special meaning to the compiler.

4. C++ interprets *namein, NameIn,* and *NAMEIN* as three different identifier names. It is important to keep case sensitivity in mind when coding statements in C++.

Chapter 2

Checkpoint 2A

1. A C++ program consists of a collection of logically related functions. These functions interact with one another to perform the required processing. A module is a self-contained, logical unit of a program that performs a major processing task. A function is a procedure that returns a value.

2. The *#define* directive tells the preprocessor to substitute all occurrences of the *IDENTI-FIER* with the constant. For example, in the direction *#define PAYRATE 19.50*, the preprocessor would substitute all occurrences of *PAYRATE* in the program with the constant value *19.50*. The defined constant retains its value during the program run. Symbolic constants are coded in uppercase letters to make them stand out.

3. The input/output stream header file enables the program to perform basic input and output operations such as accepting data from the keyboard and displaying data on the screen.

4. The main() function is the controlling function of a C++ program. This function signals the start of the executable statements. Each program must have a main() function.

5. a. The / at the beginning of the line should be //. The / at the end of the line should be deleted.
   b. OK
   c. There should not be a semicolon after `main()`.
   d. There should be a semicolon after `total_amount`.
   e. OK
   f. The colon after `wages` should be a semicolon.
   g. OK
   h. There should not be an ampersand (&) before `result`.
   i. OK
   j. The three variables (`num1, num2,` and `num3`) should be separated by the extraction operator (>>).

6. The logic error in this program is the placement of the arithmetic expression to calculate result. This statement should be placed before the `cout` since you can't print the result until you have calculated it.

7. a. 2.7
   b. 16.0
   c. 9.0
   d. 16.8
   e. error
   f. 125.0

8. A global variable is declared outside of main() and is available to the whole program. A local variable is declared inside a specific function and is available only to that function.

Checkpoint 2B

1. An array is a collection of related items. A character array is a collection of characters that make up a string.

2. The *return* statement is used to transfer control from one function back to another function.

3. a. valid
   b. valid
   c. invalid: should be type long or a decimal value
   d. valid
   e. invalid: [7] should be [8]
   f. invalid: should be type *float*
   g. invalid: semicolon missing at end of statement
   h. invalid: I should be enclosed in single quotation marks
   i. invalid: length should be omitted or value should be enclosed in double quotation marks
   j. invalid: should be type *int*

4. a. invalid: equal sign should be omitted
   b. invalid: identifier should be in all caps
   c. invalid: # sign missing from *define*
   d. valid
   e. invalid: # sign missing from *define* and semicolon should be omitted

5. a. `cost = 61`
   b. `amountDue = 2`
   c. `outcome = 139.00`
   d. `result = 757.00`

6. `#define DISCOUNT   7.85`

7. `char title[21];`

8. `cout << setw(5) << average;`

9. `cin >> iNum1 >> iNum2 >> lNum >> fNum >> dNum;`

Chapter 3

Checkpoint 3A

1. Modular structured programming provides a way to manage the programming task by dividing a large task into smaller pieces.

2. a. sequence: executing program statements one after another in the order that they appear in the program
   b. selection: deciding between two different processing paths by making a comparison between items
   c. iteration: repeating a series of statements a specific number of times

3. `float function1(int);`

4. `void function2(char);`

5. `void Output(void);`

Checkpoint 3B

1. Top-down design is a programming technique that develops the high-level control logic first and then proceeds downward, level by level, to develop the detailed processing steps that the program must accomplish. Modular programming is a design strategy that breaks up a program into a series of self-contained modules that are designed, programmed, and tested independently.

2. Each module should have one entry point and one exit point. Each module should perform exactly one task. Each program should include meaningful variable names, remarks, line comments, simple coding structures, and no more than 24 statements per module.

3. Programs are easier to maintain, easier to design and code, more reliable, easier to read and understand, easier to test and debug, and documentation is easier to write and maintain.

Chapter 4

Checkpoint 4A

1. a. `strcat(firstName, lastName);`
   b. `strcat(lastName, firstName);`
   c. `strcat(message, firstName);`

2. `strcpy(message, lastName);`

3. a. nonzero
   b. 0
   c. nonzero

4. a. 11
   b. 6
   c. 3
   d. 24

5. a. invalid: *company* isn't large enough to hold the combined string
   b. invalid: *company* isn't large enough to hold *extension*
   c. valid
   d. invalid: *company* isn't large enough to hold the combined string

Checkpoint 4B

1. Iteration and loop processing is the process of repeating a series of statements a specific number of times or until a specified condition is met.

2. a. (1) true
   b. (1) true
   c. (0) false
   d. (0) false
   e. (0) false

3. a. (0) false
    b. (1) true
    c. (1) true
    d. (1) true
    e. (1) true
    f. (0) false

Checkpoint 4C

1. a. `sold = sold - 1;`
    b. `amount = amount - 1;`
    c. `addOne = addOne + 1;`
    d. `page = page + 1;`

2. a. `numberStudents++;`   or   `++numberStudents;`
    b. `employees--;`   or   `--employees;`
    c. `row++;`   or   `++row;`
    d. `qtyOnHand--;`   or   `--qtyOnHand;`

3. Initialize the control variable, test the condition, perform the statements inside the loop when the condition is true, modify the control variable, and branch back to the *while* statement.

4. a. 10   20   30   40   50
    b. 0   1   2   3   4   5   6   7   8
    c. 10   9   8   7   6   5   4   3   2   1
    d. Nothing; the loop is never executed.

Checkpoint 4D

1. A *while* loop tests the condition before entry into the loop. Therefore, it is possible that the body of the loop may not be executed. A *do/while* loop tests the condition after entry into the loop. Therefore, the body of a *do/while* loop will always be executed at least once.

2.  ```
    for(count = 2; count <= 11; count = count + 2)   {
         cout << count;
    }
    ```

    Note: Since the *for* loop contains only one statement, the braces may be omitted. However, it is a good habit to always include the braces.

3. 1   2   3   2   4   6

Checkpoint 4E

1. The *cout* statement displays the output on the screen, whereas printer output displays the output on the printer. To use the printer, we must include the *fstream.h* header file and define the printer file object. The printer file is opened and closed.

2. The statement will print the following line on the printer:

    ```
    Welcome to C++.
    ```
    ```

3. a. invalid: *cout* displays output on the screen
   b. invalid: must use the insertion operator (<<)
   c. invalid: must use the insertion operator (<<)

Chapter 5

Checkpoint 5A

1. Unconditional branching sends control directly to a specific location in the program. Conditional branching takes place only if a certain condition is met.

2. a. conditional
   b. unconditional
   c. conditional

3. a. `Thank you.`
   b. `Tax = 0.60`
   c. `Tax = 2.50`
   d. `Color is Red.`
   e. Nothing prints.

Checkpoint 5B

1. Using the *goto* statement is considered poor programming. *Goto* statements result in messy code and unreliable programs.

2. `Fish, Poultry, Beef, Pork`

3. `Invalid choice`

4. `Bean, Broccoli, Chili, Potato`
   `Fish, Poultry, Beef, Pork`
   `Cake, Pie, Ice Cream, Cookie`

   By omitting the *break* statements, control falls through each case rather than branching to the end of the *switch* statement. Be careful to include *break* statements as needed.

Chapter 6

Checkpoint 6A

1. range checks, code checks, and cross-reference checks

2. Make the menu easy to read, center the menu on the screen, keep it simple, and make the choices clear.

3. True

4. The getch() function reads a single character from the keyboard. This function neither displays the character typed on the screen nor waits for the user to press the Enter key.

Chapter 7

Checkpoint 7A

1. A file is a collection of related records that pertain to a specific application. A record is a collection of related data fields. A field is a set of character positions grouped together to form a single unit of information.

2. A file that consists of data that the programmer can read and modify. A text editor is used to create and save the data.

3. No. As long as the data fields are separated by at least one blank space, the data does not have to be aligned into columns. Doing so, however, makes the data in the text file easier to read and modify.

4. `#include<fstream.h>`
   `ifstream fileIn;`

5. The declaration *ifstream fileIn;* associates the file object name, *fileIn*, with the input file stream. In other words, it associates a name with the input file stream.

Checkpoint 7B

1. a. Checks the disk directory for the file name.
   b. Establishes an input file buffer.
   c. Sets the file pointer to the beginning of the file.

2. `employFile.open("b:employ.dat");`

3. `employFile >> employNum;`
   `employFile.get(lastName, 20) >> payrate >> hrsWorked;`

4. `if (!employFile.eof())`

5. `employFile.close();`

Checkpoint 7C

1. a. Create the file: Using a text editor, key in one record per line. Save the file on disk.
   b. Setup the input file stream: The file object identifier associates a name to the input file stream.
   c. Define the record format: The file data fields must be defined in the program.
   d. Open the file: A file must be opened before data can be accessed from it.
   e. Read a record: The file stream identifier reads the data from the disk and assigns the various fields to the program variables.
   f. Close the file: Closing a file releases the input buffer.

2. A trailer record is a special record that is placed at the end of the file (trails the data) by the programmer. The trailer record provides an additional method of detecting the end of the file.

3. `while (employNum != 0)`

Chapter 8

Checkpoint 8A

1. A page break occurs when the number of lines printed equals the limit established for the page.
2. The purpose of a page counter is to keep track of the number of pages printed. The purpose of a line counter is to keep track of the number of detail lines printed per page.
3. If line count > maximum lines per page
   Set line count to 0
   Add 1 to page number
   Advance to the next page
   Print titles, page number, and column headings

Checkpoint 8B

1. A control field is a data item in the input record that is used to sequence the records in ascending order. The purpose of a control field is to determine when to perform a control break.
2. Control break processing involves grouping related records and then processing them together as a group. The control field is used to determine when there is a change in the group so a subtotal can be printed.
3. Records arranged in control field order can be processed together to produce a subtotal.
4. If previous control field not = current control field
   Print control field subtotal
   Add 3 to line count
   Set previous control field = current control field
   Set control field subtotal to 0

Chapter 9

Checkpoint 9A

1. Management uses multilevel control break reports to analyze various areas within the organization. For example, management may want to compare the profitability among regional offices within the company. Or management may want to analyze the performance of each department within a particular region. This information helps management to identify the strengths and weaknesses of an organization. The ability to develop control break programs is essential to providing management with the needed reports.
2. a. Design the output on a printer spacing chart.
   b. Arrange the data in sequential order.
   c. Develop the logic to perform a control break when a control field changes value.
3. 3, 4, 5, 11

4. MAJOR CONTROL BREAK
   a. Do minor control break.
   b. Print major subtotal.
   c. Increment line count.
   d. Set major subtotal to 0.

   MINOR CONTROL BREAK
   a. Print minor subtotal.
   b. Increment line count.
   c. Save the input.
   d. Set minor subtotal to 0.

Checkpoint 9B

1. A major control field is the most inclusive of subtotals. An intermediate control field is the next most inclusive subtotal. A minor control field is the least inclusive subtotal. For example, the program for CHAP9B treats location as the major control field because it includes as part of its subtotal the subtotals for agency, manager, and building. The agency and manager fields are treated as intermediate control fields because they include the building subtotal. Building is treated as the minor control field. Note that none of the program subtotals for location, agency, or manager are included in the building subtotal.

2. Since a control break may occur at any level, the logic must be designed so the inner levels print first. Hence, if a control break occurs at the major level, the minor subtotal is printed first, then the intermediate level subtotal(s) are printed, and finally, the major subtotal is printed. If a control break occurs at the intermediate level, the minor subtotal is printed first, followed by the intermediate subtotal. When a break occurs at the intermediate level, the major subtotal is not printed. If a control break occurs at the minor level, only the minor level subtotal is printed.

3. MAJOR CONTROL BREAK
   a. Do intermediate control break.
   b. Print major subtotal.
   c. Increment line count.
   d. Set major subtotal to 0.

   INTERMEDIATE CONTROL BREAK
   a. Do minor control break.
   b. Print intermediate subtotal.
   c. Increment line count.
   d. Set intermediate subtotal to 0.

   MINOR CONTROL BREAK
   a. Print minor subtotal.
   b. Increment line count.
   c. Save the input.
   d. Set minor subtotal to 0.

Chapter 10

Checkpoint 10A

1. An array is a set of variables that is given one name. An element is one item of data in an array. Elements in an array have the same data type. Together, the elements in an array resemble a list of related objects.

2. Character arrays hold nonnumeric or string data, such as employee name or product description. Numeric arrays hold integer or floating-point values. Integer and floating-point values are stored in separate arrays.

3. Since arrays store data in memory, data can be entered into the computer once and processed repeatedly. Without arrays, the same data would have to be repeatedly entered into the computer before it could be processed.

4. To create or define an array, you must specify a data type, an array name, and the size of the array. Data type specifies whether the array will hold numeric or character data. An array name specifies how the program will reference the array—its identifier. The size specifies how many elements are in the array.

5. a. `float amount[48];`
   b. `int   qtyOnHand[450];`
   c. `float price[25];`

6. The size of each element must also be specified when defining a character array.

7. a. `char employeeName[268][20];`
   b. `char address[100][30];`
   c. `char socSecNbr[50][11];`

Checkpoint 10B

1. A subscript is an integer value that is used to reference a specific element in an array.

2. True

3. 0 (zero)

4. False. Subscripts may never be negative, and they must not exceed the size of the array minus one.

5. Using a variable as a subscript allows the program to change the value of the subscript. For example, a variable subscript may be incremented in a *for* loop. You don't have this flexibility when using an integer constant.

Checkpoint 10C

1. a. Initialize the elements when the array is declared.
   b. Prompt the user to enter data at the keyboard.
   c. Load data into the array from a file.

2. The second statement will cause an error. The only time string data may be directly assigned to an array element is when the array is declared (as in the first statement).

3. Since the array data is stored in memory, you can't see the data. Hence, you can't be sure the array was loaded correctly. To verify that the array was loaded correctly, it is good practice to print the array immediately after you finish loading it.

4. The only difference is that array variables are subscripted to identify the specific elements being referenced.

5. Parallel arrays consist of two or more single arrays that are related in some way. In other words, the elements in one array correspond to the elements in the other array. Parallel arrays have the same number of elements defined for each array in the parallel set.

6.
```
//----------- LOAD ARRAYS ----------------------------------
for (i = 0; i < 5; i++)  {
    cout << "Enter employee name: ";
    cin.get(employee[i], 20);
    cin.get();
    cout << "Enter hourly pay rate: ";
    cin >> hourlyRate[i];
}


//----------- PRINT ARRAYS ---------------------------------
for (i = 0; i < 5; i++)  {
    cout << setiosflags(ios::left)
        << setw(20) << employee[i]
        << resetiosflags(ios::left)
            << setiosflags(ios::fixed)
                << setiosflags(ios::showpoint)
            << setw(5) << setprecision(2)
        << hourlyRate[i] << endl;
}
```

Checkpoint 10D

1. Array lookup is the process of locating data stored in an array. The ability to search an array for a particular element allows us to display that element or to update the data in that element.

2. a. direct reference: uses subscripts to directly access a specific element. For example, *sales[5]* would be a direct reference to the *6th* element in the sales array.

   b. sequential search: searches the array one element at a time, beginning with the *0th* element, until a match is found.

3.
```
//----------- INPUT DATA ----------------------------------
cout << "Enter the description to search for: ";
cin.get(inputDesc, 20);
cin.get();
cout << "Enter the new quantity: ";
cin >> newQty;
cin.get();
```

```
//----------- SEQUENTIAL SEARCH --------------------------
i = 0;
sub = -1;
while (i < 5 && sub == -1)  {
    if (strcmp(inputDesc, description[i]) == 0)  {
        sub = i;
    }
    i = i + 1;
}


//---------- UPDATE QUANTITY ----------------------------
if (sub == -1)  {
    cout << "Description not found";
}
else  {
    qtyOnHand[sub] = qtyOnHand[sub] + newQty;
}
```

Checkpoint 10E

1. Sorting is the process of arranging data in a given order. Character data may be sorted in alphabetical order. Numeric data may be sorted in ascending or descending order.

2. a. Bubble sort: Useful for short lists, the bubble sort works by repeatedly comparing and exchanging adjacent elements until they are arranged in the specified order.
   b. Shell sort: A more efficient sort, the Shell sort works by repeatedly comparing and exchanging elements over a series of gaps until the array is arranged in the specified order.

3. a. For the first pass, the gap is calculated as the size of the array divided by 2.
   b. For subsequent passes, the gap is calculated as the value of the previous gap divided by 2, until the length of the gap equals 1.

4.
```
size = 10;
gap = size / 2;
while (gap > 0)  {
    swap = 1;
    while (swap == 1)  {
        swap = 0;
        for (i = 0; i < size - gap; i++)  {
            if (list[i] > list[i + gap])  {
                temp = list[i];
                list[i] = list[i + gap];
                list[i + gap] = temp;
                swap = 1;
            }
        }
    }
    gap = gap / 2;
}
```

Chapter 11

Checkpoint 11A

1. row, column
2. `nbr[2][3];`
3. No. A two-dimension array must be referenced with two subscripts. The first subscript always represents the row; the second subscript always represents the column.
4. a. invalid: Row subscript exceeds row range of the table.
   b. invalid: Column subscript is negative. Subscripts may not be negative.
   c. valid

Checkpoint 11B

1. a data type, an array name, and the size of the row and column subscripts
2.

3.
```
int students[6][2] = { 8,  6,
                      15, 12,
                      20, 19,
                       7,  4,
                      10,  9,
                       3,  1};
```
4. a. interactive input: The data is entered by the user when the program runs.
   b. file input: The data is input from a file when the program runs.
5.
```
for (row = 0; row < 6; row++)   {
    for (col = 0; col < 2; col++)   {
        cout << endl << student[row][col]);
    }
}
```

Checkpoint 11C

1. Direct reference assumes that there is a direct relationship between the user's input and the subscripts. An element is accessed by explicitly specifying the row and column values.

   Sequential search is used when there is no direct relationship between the user's input and the array subscript(s). The program compares the user's input to elements in the array until a match is found.

2.
```
// --------- DIRECT REFERENCE LOOKUP --------------------
cout << "\nEnter the item number or '-1' to Quit: ";
cin >>item;
```

```
    while (item != -1)  {
        cout << "\nEnter the model number: ";
        cin >> model;
        cout << "Price = " << price[item][model];
        cout << "\nEnter the item number or '-1' to Quit: ";
        cin >> item;
    }
```

3. 44.78

4.
```
//--------- SEQUENTIAL SEARCH LOOKUP ----------------
r = 0;
row = -1;
cout << "Enter the appliance name: ";
cin >> appliance;
cin.get();
cout << "Enter the model number: ";
cin >> model;
cin.get();
while (r < 3 && row == -1)  {
    if (strcmp(appliance, item[r]) == 0)  {
        row = r;
    }
    r = r + 1;
}

//--------- CHECK FOR ITEM MATCH --------------------
if (row == -1)  {
    cout << "\nAppliance not found";
}
else  {
    cout << "Price = " << price[row][model - 1];
}
```

Checkpoint 11D

1. `int table[3][4][5];`

2. three

3. three

4. four

Chapter 12

Checkpoint 12A

1. a. field: a collection of characters that describes a single unit of data
   b. record: a collection of related data items or fields that contains information about a single unit in the file
   c. file: a collection of related records that pertains to a specific data processing application

2. A record key or key field is a special field that uniquely identifies each record in a file. A key field is used to access records and to arrange records in a specific order.

3. Sequential file organization stores records on disk or tape in key field order. Although ascending order (from the lowest value to the highest) is normally used, it is perfectly acceptable to organize the key fields in descending (high to low) order.

4. Sequential file organization offers efficient use of storage since the records are stored one after the other (in a specific order). Sequential file organization also provides fast and efficient processing when all or most of the records in the file are to be processed.

5. a. Declare the file object variable as the output file stream.
   b. Define the record format—the fields of the record.
   c. Open the file.
   d. Prompt for and enter the file data.
   e. Write the data to the file.
   f. Close the file.

Checkpoint 12B

1. a. Declare the file object name as the input file stream.
   b. Define the record fields.
   c. Open the file.
   d. Read the records from the file.
   e. Display the records on the screen.
   f. Close the file.

2.
```
void ReadFile(void)
{
    inFile >> name >> hourlyPay >> hoursWorked;
    inFile.get();
    while (!inFile.eof())  {
        prnt << endl << setiosflags(ios::left)
             << setw(15) << name
             << resetiosflags(ios::left)
             << setiosflags(ios::fixed)
             << setiosflags(ios::showpoint)
             << setprecision(2) << setw(5) << hourlyPay
             << setw(2) << hoursWorked;
        inFile >> name >> hourlyPay >> hoursWorked;
        inFile.get();
    }
    return;
}
```

Checkpoint 12C

1. Records are added to the end of a sequential file by specifying *append* in the open statement.

2. `outFile.open("a:test.dat", ios::app);`

3. a. Declare the file object name as the output stream.
    b. Define the record fields.
    c. Open the file in *append* mode.
    d. Prompt for and enter the file data.
    e. Write the data to the end of the file.
    f. Close the file.

Chapter 13

Checkpoint 13A

1. a. master file: contains permanent information about a particular data processing application that changes over time
   b. transaction file: contains temporary information that is used to update the master file
2. Sequential file maintenance is the process of keeping the master file current. It consists of creating the transaction and master files, updating the master file, and processing the data stored in the master file.
3. File updating refers to the process of changing the master file over time to include new information. Even though the master file is a permanent repository of information, things change, and the file must be maintained to reflect those changes. Periodically, new records are added, old records are deleted, and current records are changed.
4.

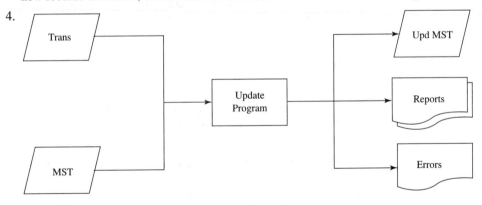

Checkpoint 13B
1. Compare the master key to the transaction key and print one of three messages.
2. a
3. c
4. b
5. The transaction data is written to the master file.
6. This message implies that the transaction data is applied to the current master record.

Checkpoint 13C

1. An abend occurs when certain logic errors prevent the program from running to completion.
2. False. When an abend occurs, you should fix the errors, then restart the program.
3. transaction code

Checkpoint 13D

1.
```
void UpdProcess(void)
{
    if (Tkey == Mkey)
        UpdMast();
    else
        if (Tkey < Mkey)
            AddMast();
        else
            WrtMast();
    return;
}
```

2. a. adding master records that already exist
   b. processing unmatched transactions
   c. processing invalid transaction codes
3. When an error is detected by the update program, the transaction record is written to an error log report. This information is used to correct the transactions.

Chapter 14

Checkpoint 14A

1. A structure is a group item that may hold two or more related data types called *members*. In simpler terms, a structure is a record, and a member is a field.
2. True
3. False. The above statements define or declare the structure only. They do not assign memory location.
4. A structure variable is a variable that consists of the members described by the data structure. Defining a structure variable reserves storage space for each member of the template.
5.
```
struct payroll grossPay;
cout << "Enter the employee name: ";
cin >> grossPay.employee;
cout << "Enter the hourly pay rate: ";
cin >> grossPay.payRate;
cout << "Enter the hours worked: ";
cin >> grossPay.hoursWorked;
```
6. The dot operator links the structure variable to the members of the data template. The structure variable is coded on the left side of the dot operator and the member is coded on the right.

Checkpoint 14B

1. Random file organization stores data on disk in random order. Since data may be read or written in any order, the user may skip around in the file rather than pass through the records sequentially.
2. False. Unlike sequential files, random files do not require the records to be arranged in key field order.
3. Random file processing offers the advantage of fast data retrieval. It is used when an application requires access to a small number of records.
4. the write() member function
5. a. *char *:* Specifies the address of the beginning of the file where the data will be put.
   b. *&structVar:* Specifies the address from which to get the data.
   c. *size:* Indicates the length of the record template.
6. sizeof
7. a. Declare the file object variable as the output file stream.
   b. Define the data structure.
   c. Define and initialize the empty record.
   d. Open the file for output.
   e. Write empty records to the file.
   f. Close the file.

Checkpoint 14C

1. The seek statement is used to position the file pointer to a specific location in a random file prior to executing a read or write operation.
2. a. *offset:* Specifies the number of bytes from the starting point.
   b. *origin:* Specifies the starting point.
3. False. By specifying a plus or minus offset, the file pointer may be moved forward (plus) or backward (minus).
4. a. seek from the beginning of the file
   b. seek from the current position in the file
   c. seek from the end of the file
5. a. Declare the file object variable as the input file stream.
   b. Define the data structure and structure variable.
   c. Open the file for input.
   d. Prompt and enter the data.
   e. Assign the input to the structure variable.
   f. Set the file pointer and write the data to the file.
   g. Close the file.

Checkpoint 14D

1. The read() statement is used to read data from a random file.
2. a. *char *:* Specifies the address of the beginning of the file from which to get the data.
   b. *&structVar:* Specifies the address where the incoming data should be put.
   c. *size:* Indicates the length of the record template.

3. The statement reads a record from the beginning of the *file* and stores the incoming data in the *course* structure variable. The length of the record is determined by the size of *courseData*.

4.
```
struct accounts   {
      int    acctNbr;
      char   name[15];
      int    days;
      float  balDue;
};

struct accounts overdue;
```

5.
```
void ReadFile(void)
{
    for (recNum = 1; recNum <= 20; recNum++)   {
        file.seekg((recNum-1)*sizeof(accounts), ios::beg);
        file.read((char *) &overdue, sizeof(accounts);
        if (overdue.acctNbr != 0)   {
            cout << setw(4) << overdue.acctNbr
                 << "  " << setiosflags(ios::left)
                 << setw(15) << overdue.name
                 << resetiosflags(ios::left)
                 << setw(2) << overdue.days
                 << setiosflags(ios::fixed)
                 << setiosflags(ios::showpoint)
                 << setprecision(2) << setw(6) << overdue.balDue;
        }
    }
    return;
}
```

Chapter 15

Checkpoint 15A

1. True

2. True

3. An indexed file is a pseudofile organization method that consists of an array and a random access file. The array holds the record keys, and the random file holds the data. After the file has been processed, the keys stored in the array are copied to a sequential file for future use.

4. a. Set up the indexed file: declare key array, random data file, and sequential key file.
   b. Open the files.
   c. Set the key array to 0.
   d. Write empty records to the random data file.
   e. Copy the key array to the sequential key file.
   f. Close the files.

5. The user enters the value for the key field. The program searches the array for a match. When a match is found, the array element number is used as the record number for the random access file which contains the data.

Checkpoint 15B

1. The key field is located in the array and its value is replaced by a zero. The random file itself still contains the data for the record; however, the record can no longer be referenced since its key field is no longer located in the array. Therefore, a deleted record is not actually removed from the random file until a new record overwrites it.

2. The first empty element (value of 0) in the array is located. The new key field value is stored in this element, and the data is written to the corresponding position in the random file.

3. The key of the record to be changed is located in the array. Then the corresponding record is retrieved from the random file. The appropriate fields are modified. Finally, the record is rewritten to the random file.

Index